by
soaporsalad

Rocketship Entertainment, LLC
rocketshipent.com

Tom Akel, CEO & Publisher • Rob Feldman, CTO • Jeanmarie McNeely, CFO
Brandon Freeberg, Dir. of Campaign Mgmt. • Phil Smith, Art Director • Jed Keith, Social Media

BAD LOVE volume 1 | Softcover Edition ISBN: 978-1-952126-88-8 | Hardcover Edition ISBN: 978-1-952126-89-5
First printing. May 2023. Copyright © Sabrina Yang. All rights reserved. Published by Rocketship Entertainment, LLC. 136 Westbury Ct.
Doylestown, PA 18901. Contains material orginally published online as "Bad Love". "Bad Love", the Bad Love logo, and the likenesses of
all characters herein are trademarks of Sabrina Yang. "Rocketship" and the Rocketship logo are trademarks of Rocketship Entertainment,
LLC. No part of this publication may be reproduced or transmitted, in any form or by any means, without the express written consent of
Sabrina Yang or Rocketship Entertainment, LLC. All names, characters, events, and locales in this publication are entirely fictional. Any
resemblance to actual persons (living or dead), events, or places, without satiric intent, is coincidental. Printed in China.

for this edition, production by **Jimmy Deoquino** and **Phil Smith**

BAD LOVE

@soaporsalad

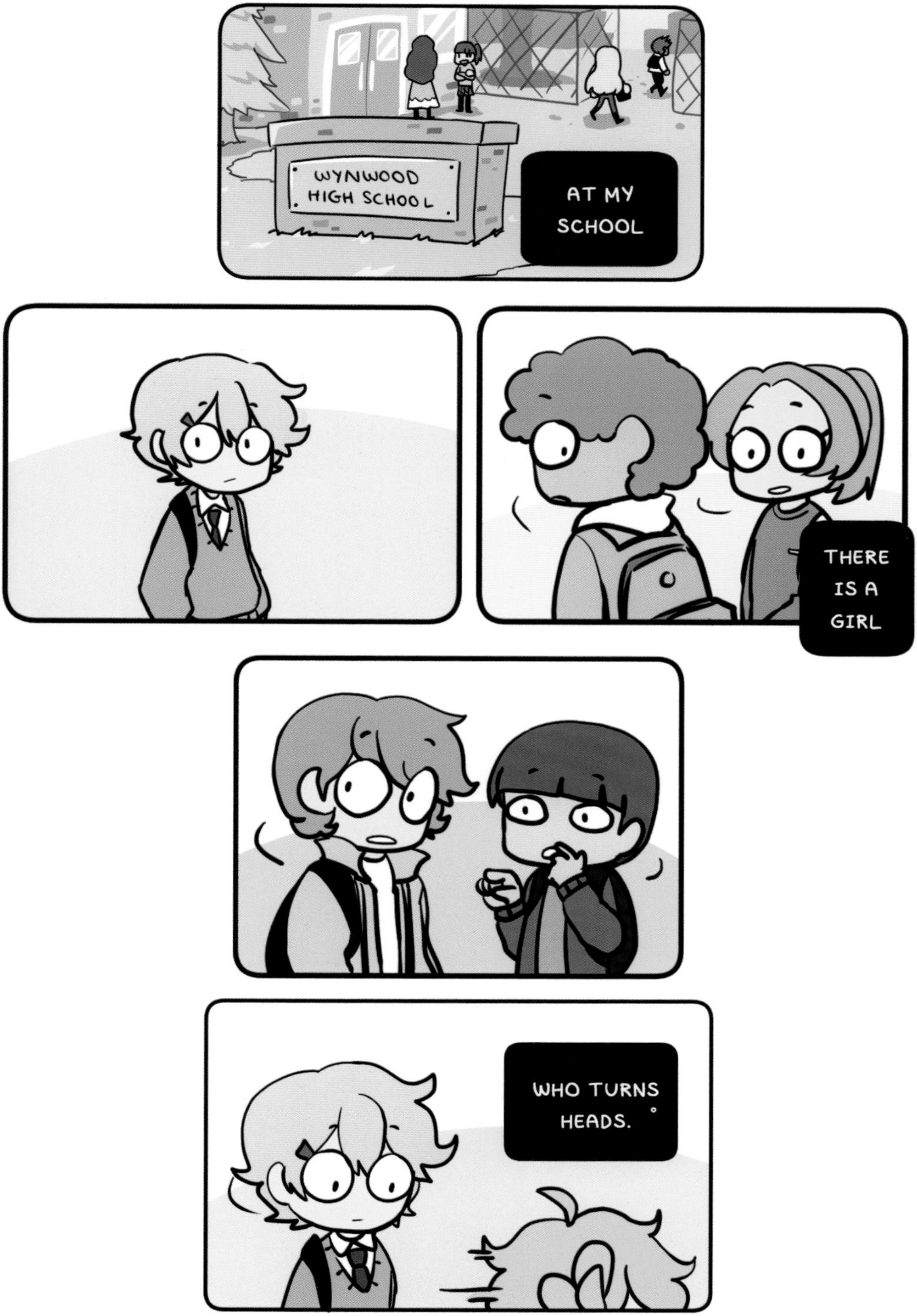
WYNWOOD HIGH SCHOOL
AT MY SCHOOL
THERE IS A GIRL
WHO TURNS HEADS.

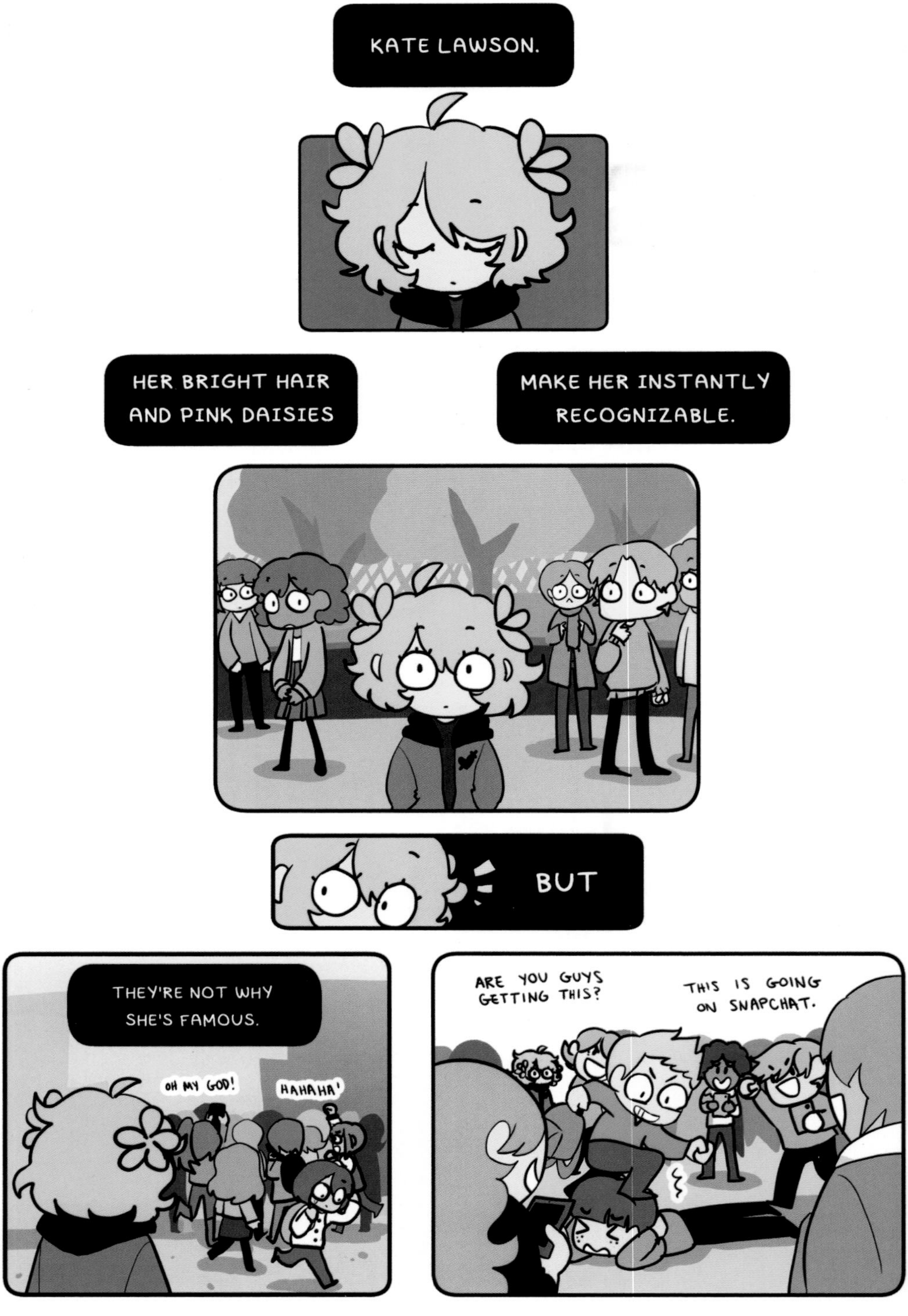
KATE LAWSON.
HER BRIGHT HAIR AND PINK DAISIES
MAKE HER INSTANTLY RECOGNIZABLE.
BUT
THEY'RE NOT WHY SHE'S FAMOUS.
OH MY GOD!
HAHAHA!
ARE YOU GUYS GETTING THIS?
THIS IS GOING ON SNAPCHAT.

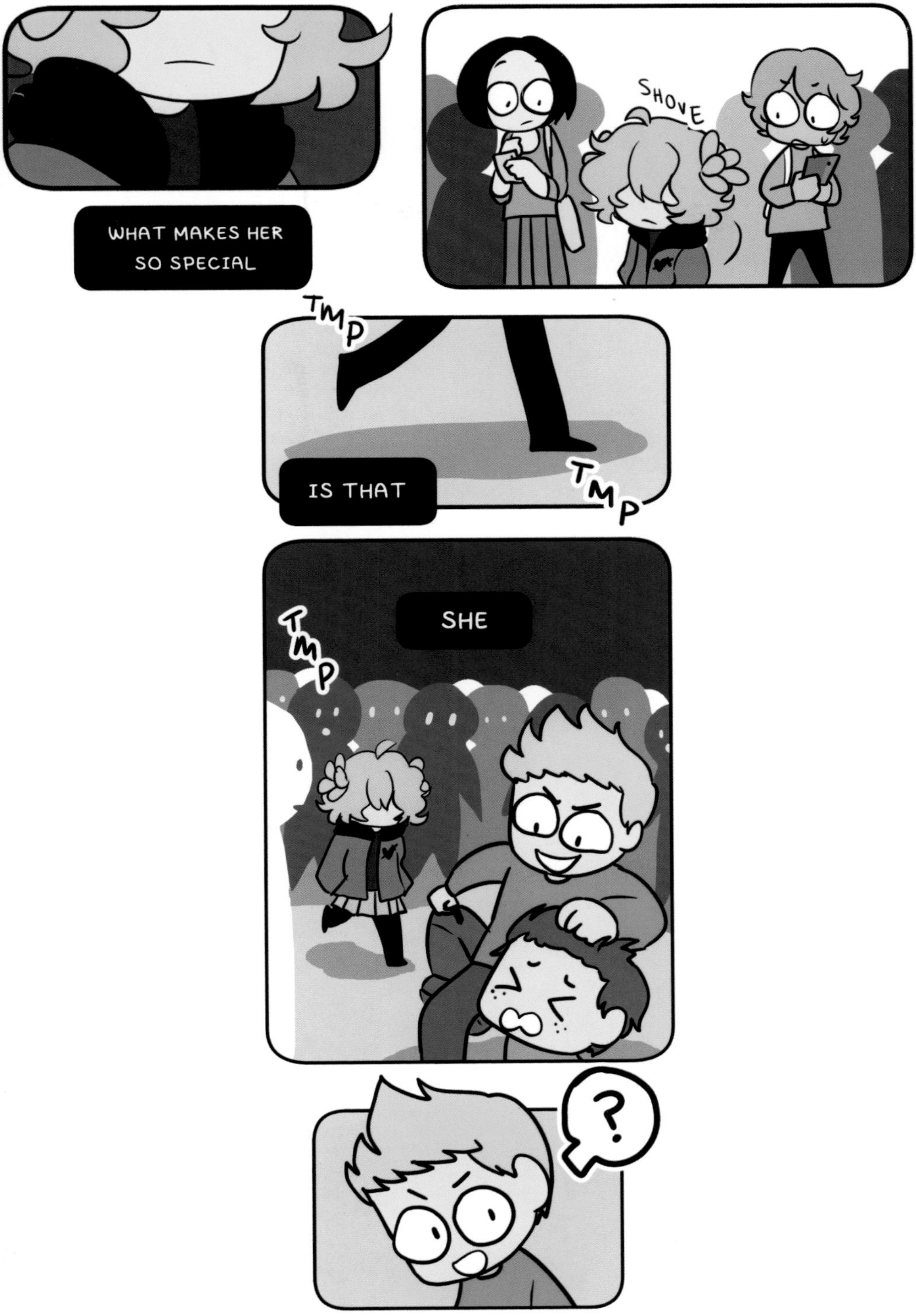

WHAT MAKES HER SO SPECIAL
SHOVE
TMP
IS THAT
TMP
SHE
TMP
?

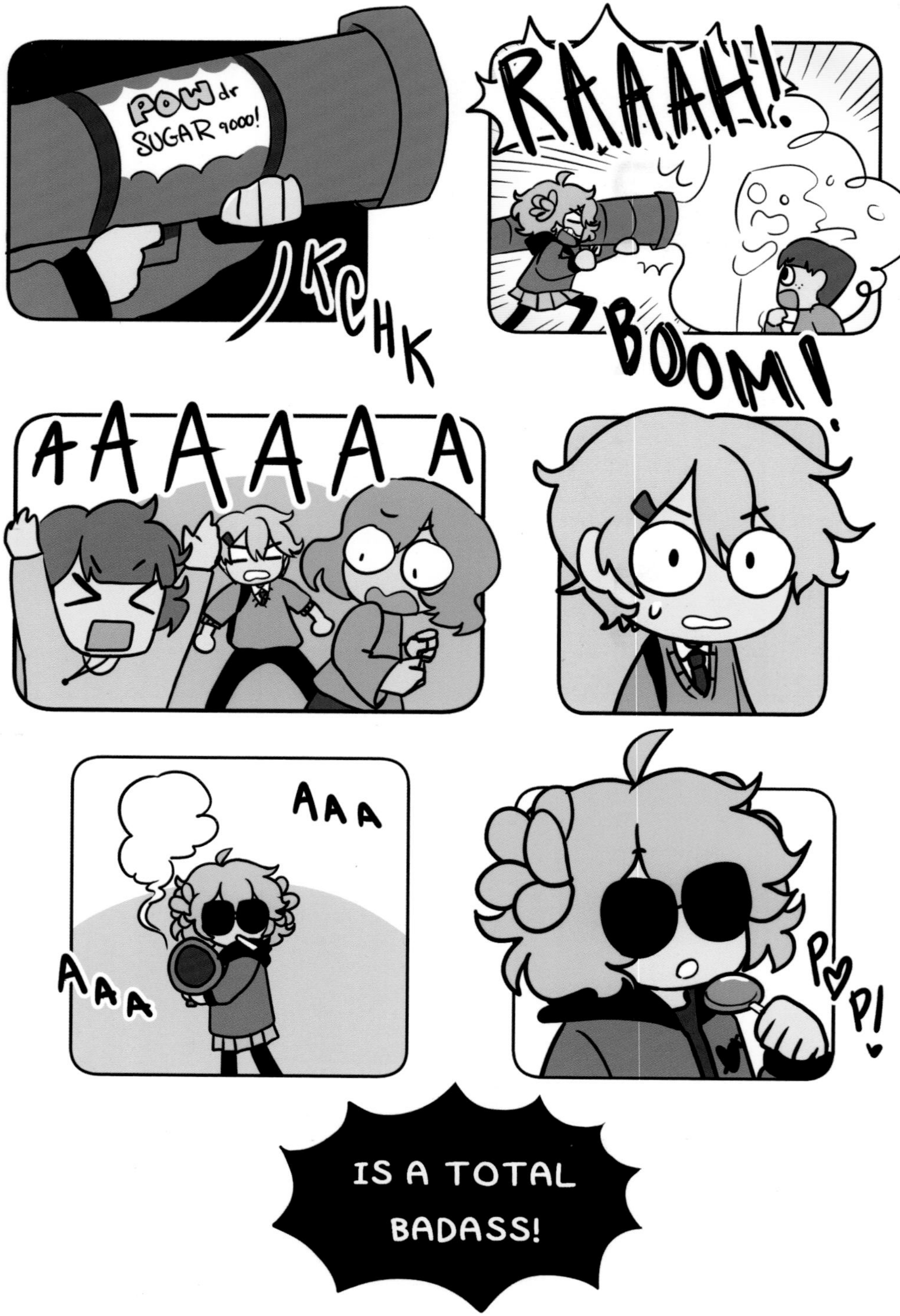
POW dr SUGAR 9000!
KCHK
RAAAH!
BOOM!
AAAAAA
AAA
AAA
POP!
IS A TOTAL BADASS!

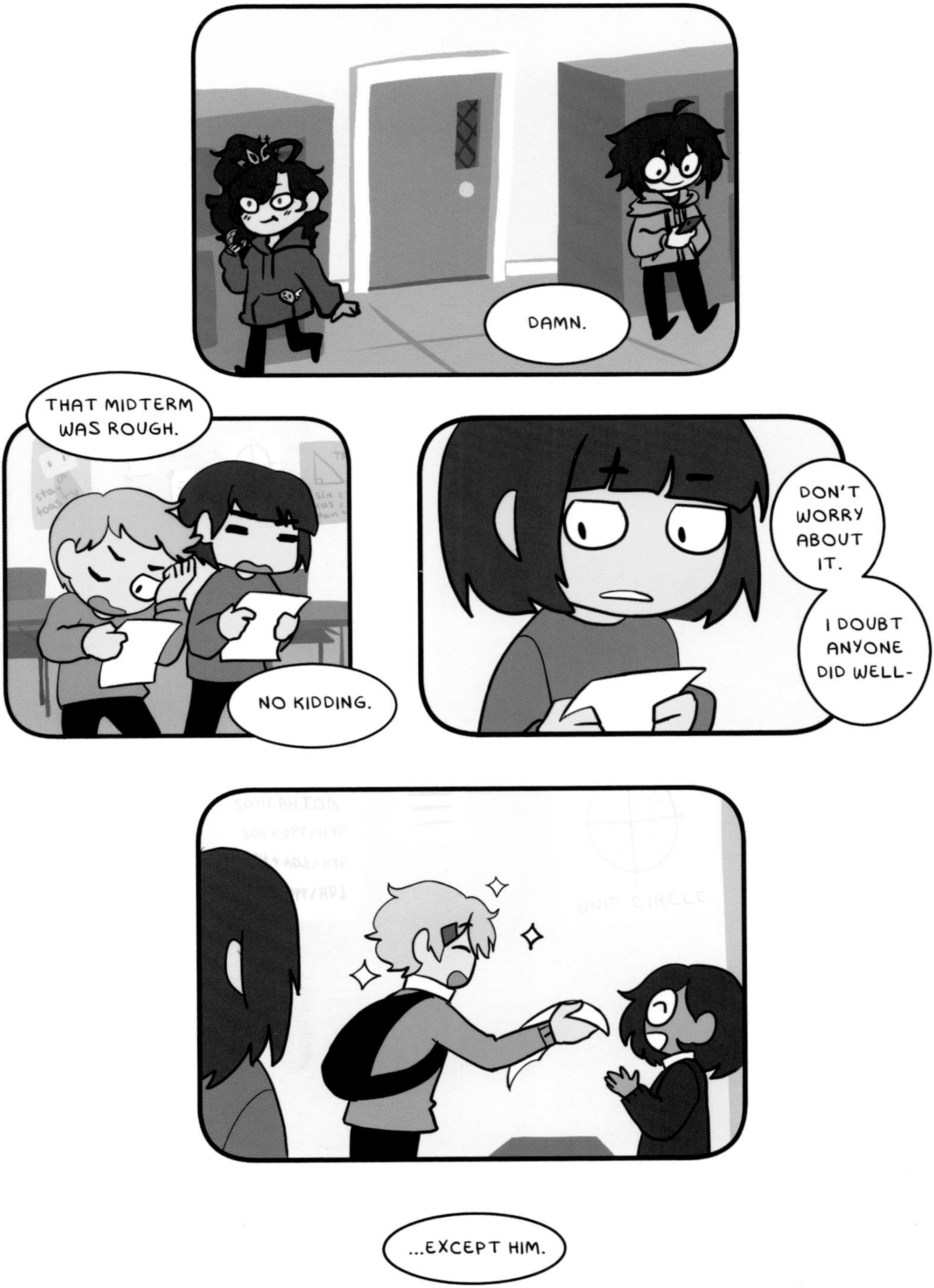
DAMN.
THAT MIDTERM WAS ROUGH.
NO KIDDING.
DON'T WORRY ABOUT IT.
I DOUBT ANYONE DID WELL-
...EXCEPT HIM.

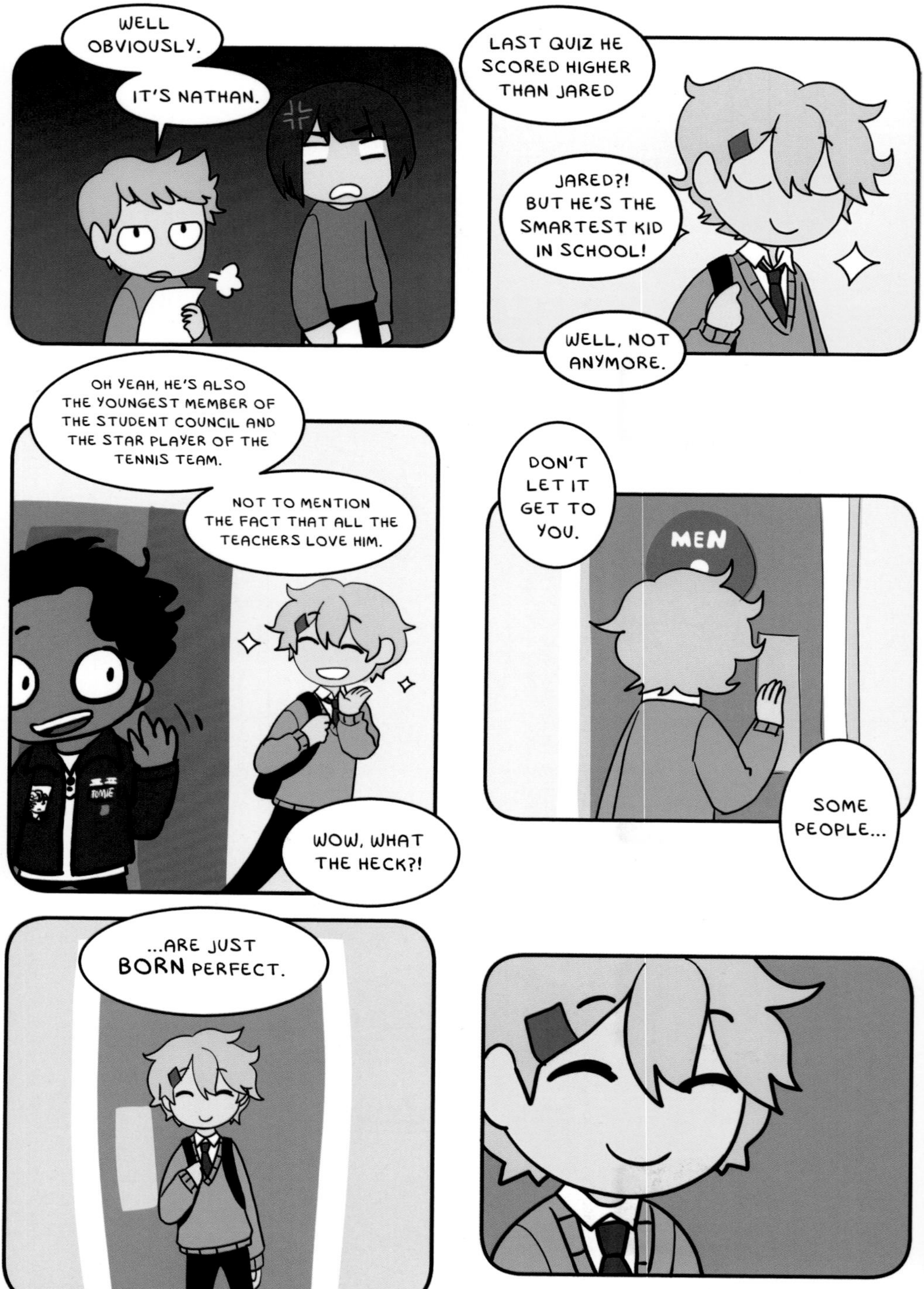
WELL OBVIOUSLY.
IT'S NATHAN.
LAST QUIZ HE SCORED HIGHER THAN JARED
JARED?! BUT HE'S THE SMARTEST KID IN SCHOOL!
WELL, NOT ANYMORE.
OH YEAH, HE'S ALSO THE YOUNGEST MEMBER OF THE STUDENT COUNCIL AND THE STAR PLAYER OF THE TENNIS TEAM.
NOT TO MENTION THE FACT THAT ALL THE TEACHERS LOVE HIM.
WOW, WHAT THE HECK?!
DON'T LET IT GET TO YOU.
MEN
SOME PEOPLE...
...ARE JUST BORN PERFECT.

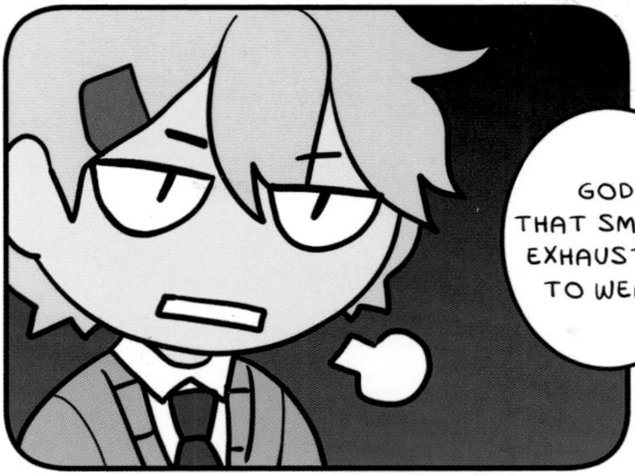
GOD, THAT SMILE'S EXHAUSTING TO WEAR.
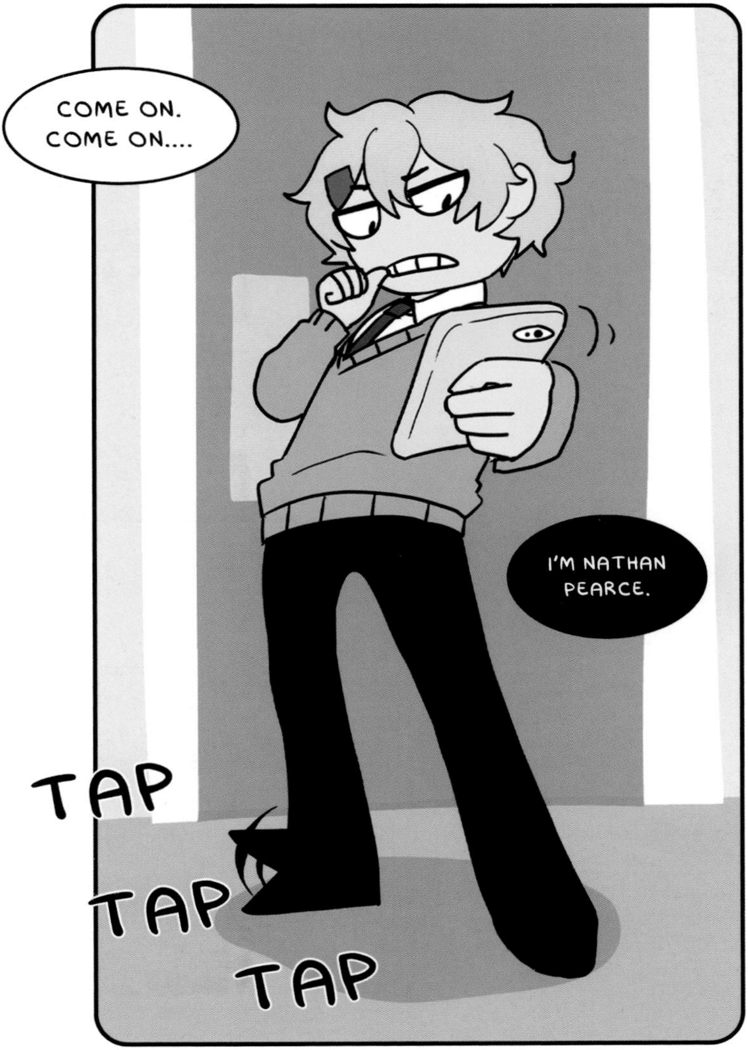
COME ON. COME ON....
I'M NATHAN PEARCE.
TAP
TAP
TAP

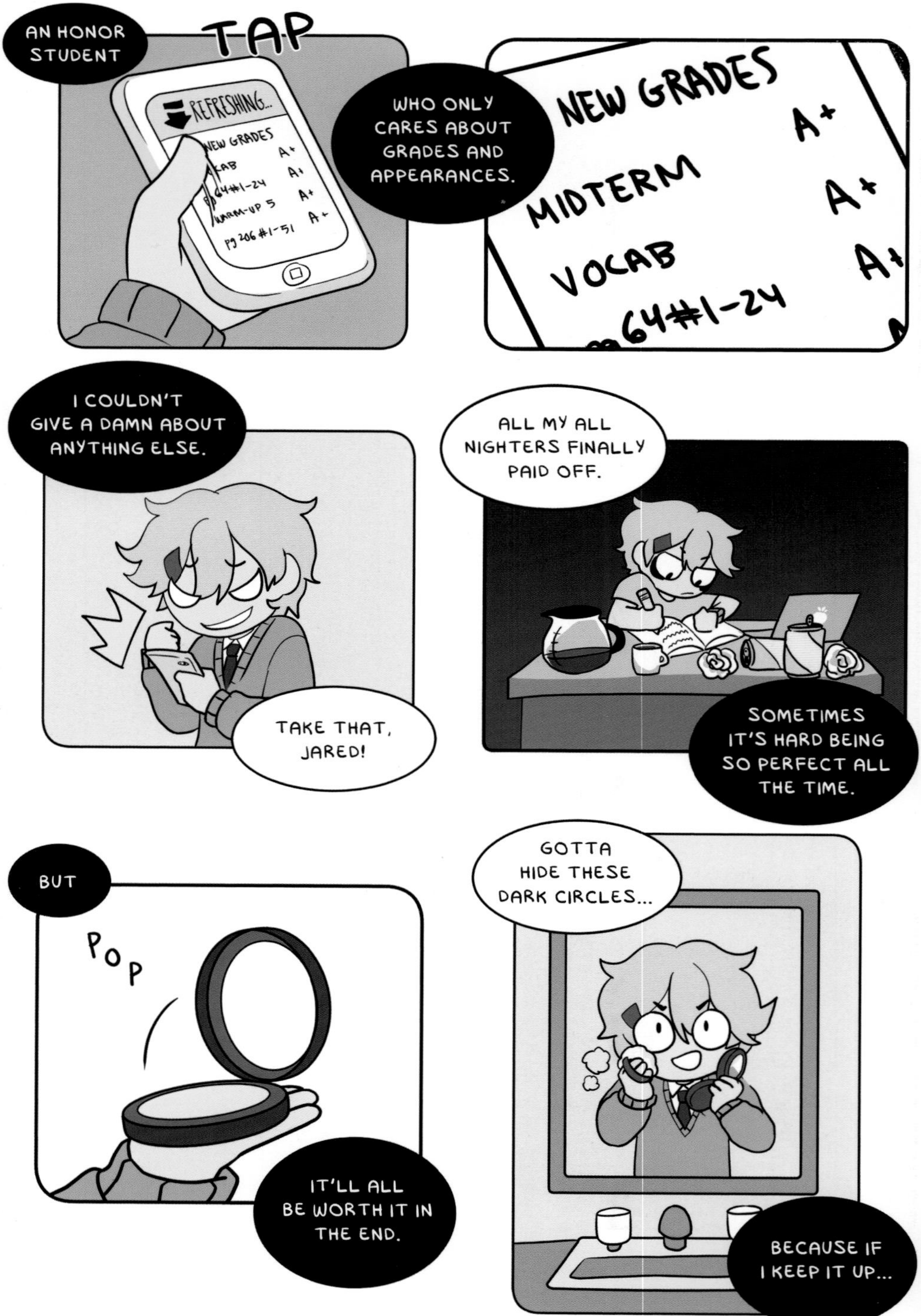
AN HONOR STUDENT
TAP
REFRESHING...
NEW GRADES
WHO ONLY CARES ABOUT GRADES AND APPEARANCES.
NEW GRADES
MIDTERM A+
VOCAB A+
64#1-24
I COULDN'T GIVE A DAMN ABOUT ANYTHING ELSE.
TAKE THAT, JARED!
ALL MY ALL NIGHTERS FINALLY PAID OFF.
SOMETIMES IT'S HARD BEING SO PERFECT ALL THE TIME.
BUT
POP
IT'LL ALL BE WORTH IT IN THE END.
GOTTA HIDE THESE DARK CIRCLES...
BECAUSE IF I KEEP IT UP...

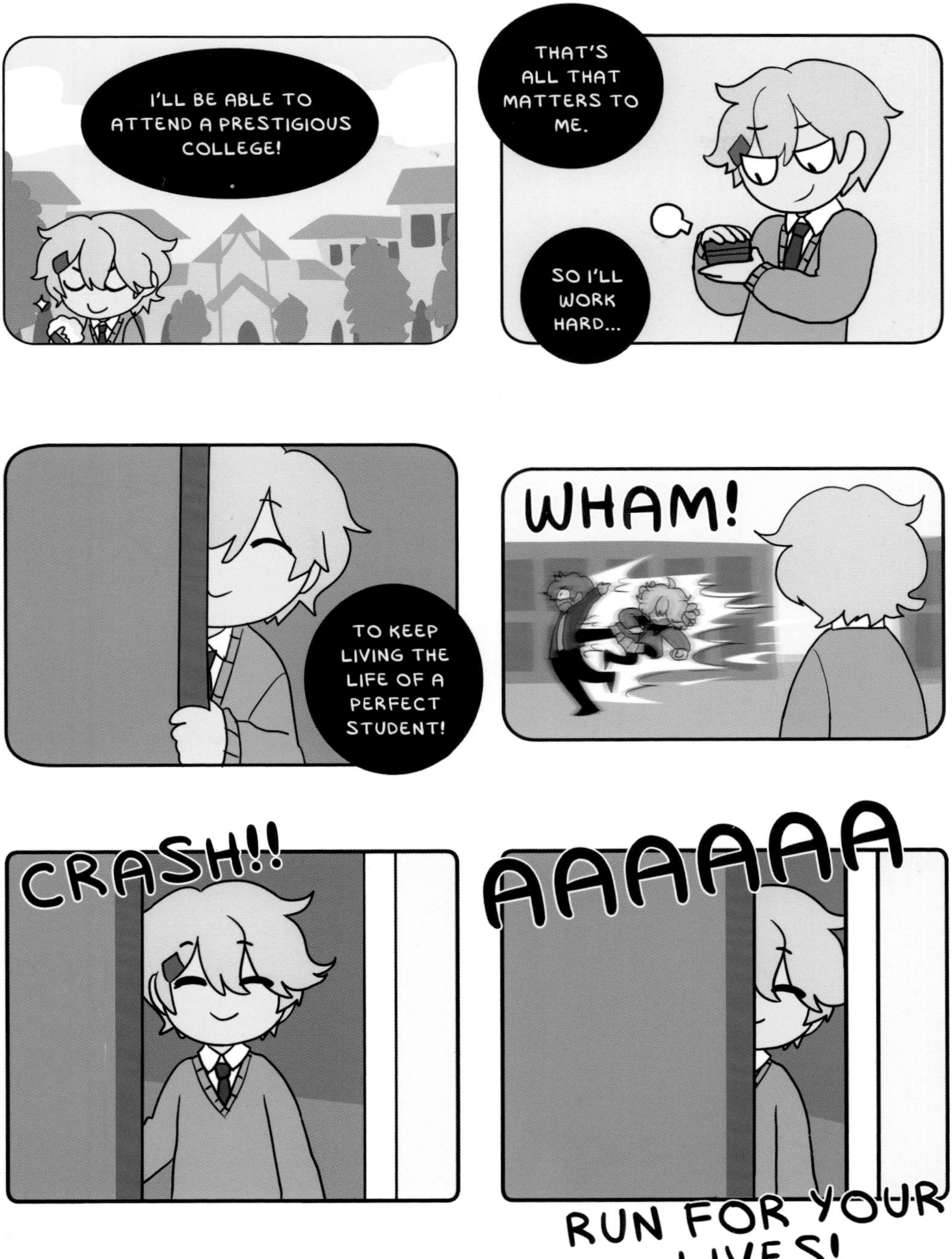

I'LL BE ABLE TO ATTEND A PRESTIGIOUS COLLEGE!
THAT'S ALL THAT MATTERS TO ME.
SO I'LL WORK HARD...
TO KEEP LIVING THE LIFE OF A PERFECT STUDENT!
WHAM!
CRASH!!
AAAAAA
RUN FOR YOUR LIVES!

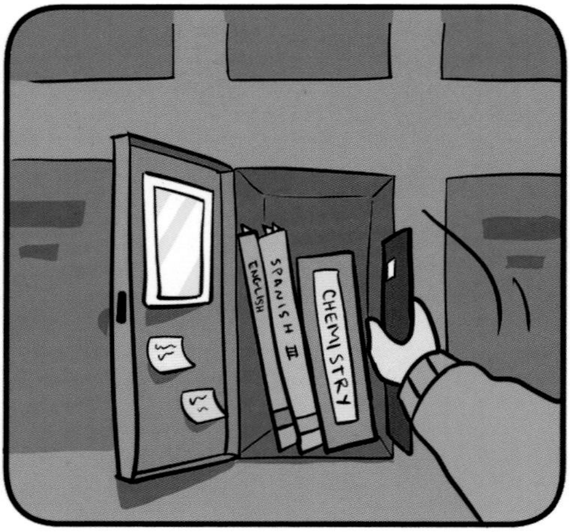
ENGLISH
SPANISH III
CHEMISTRY

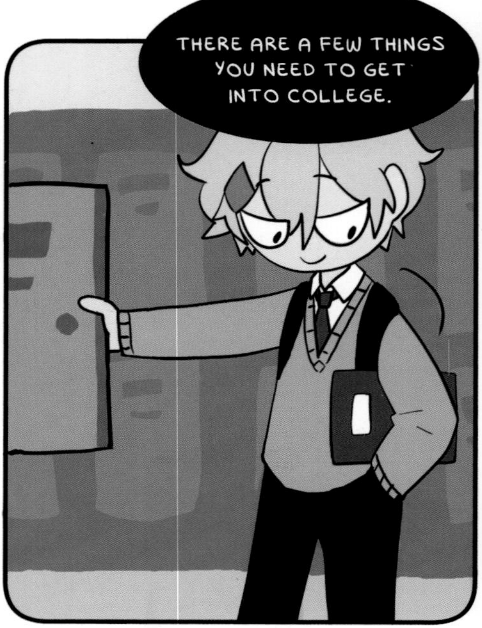
THERE ARE A FEW THINGS YOU NEED TO GET INTO COLLEGE.

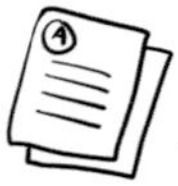

TOP NOTCH GRADES AND TEST SCORES.

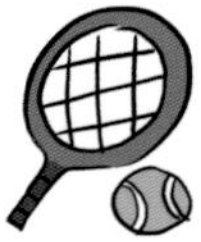

AN ABUNDANCE OF EXTRACURRICULAR ACTIVITIES

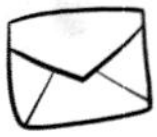

SHINING LETTERS OF RECOMMENDATION

AND FINALLY...

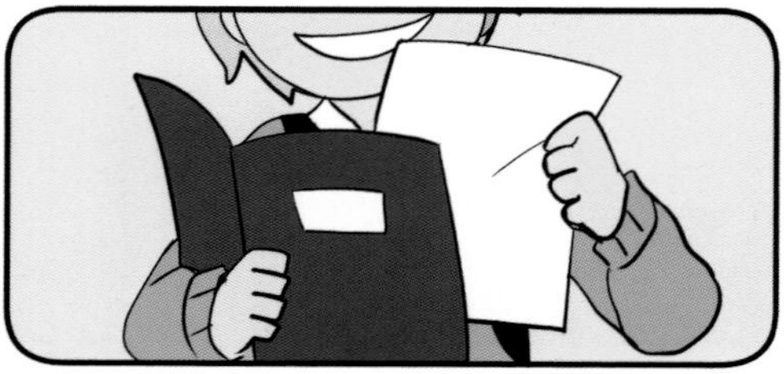

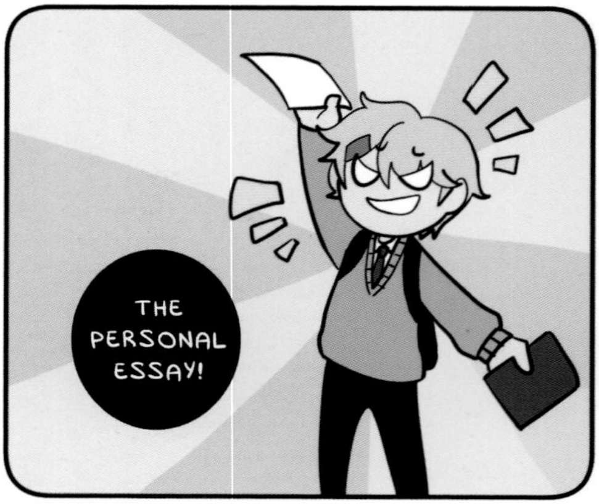
THE PERSONAL ESSAY!

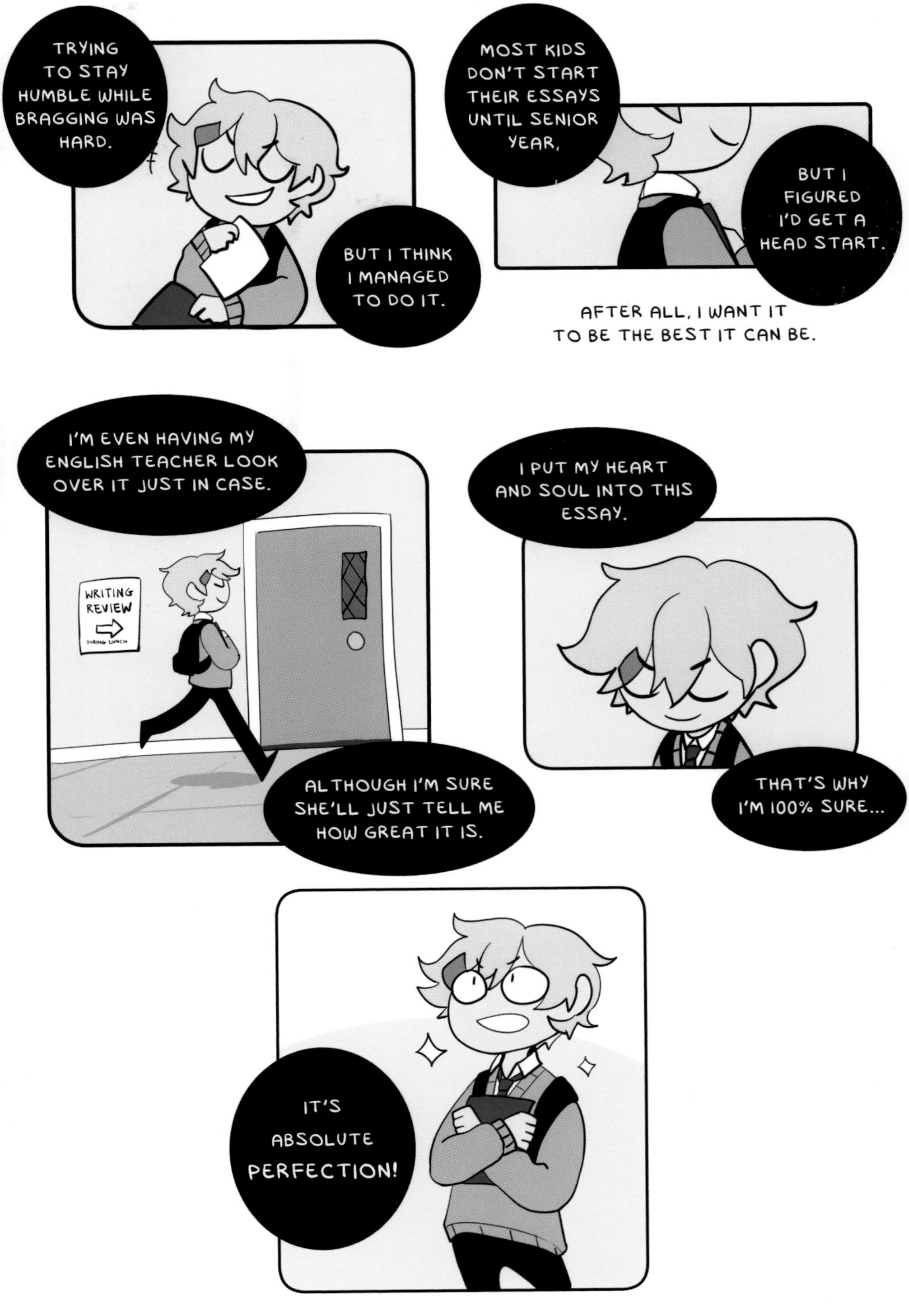
TRYING TO STAY HUMBLE WHILE BRAGGING WAS HARD.
BUT I THINK I MANAGED TO DO IT.
MOST KIDS DON'T START THEIR ESSAYS UNTIL SENIOR YEAR,
BUT I FIGURED I'D GET A HEAD START.
AFTER ALL, I WANT IT TO BE THE BEST IT CAN BE.
I'M EVEN HAVING MY ENGLISH TEACHER LOOK OVER IT JUST IN CASE.
WRITING REVIEW
DURING LUNCH
ALTHOUGH I'M SURE SHE'LL JUST TELL ME HOW GREAT IT IS.
I PUT MY HEART AND SOUL INTO THIS ESSAY.
THAT'S WHY I'M 100% SURE...
IT'S ABSOLUTE PERFECTION!

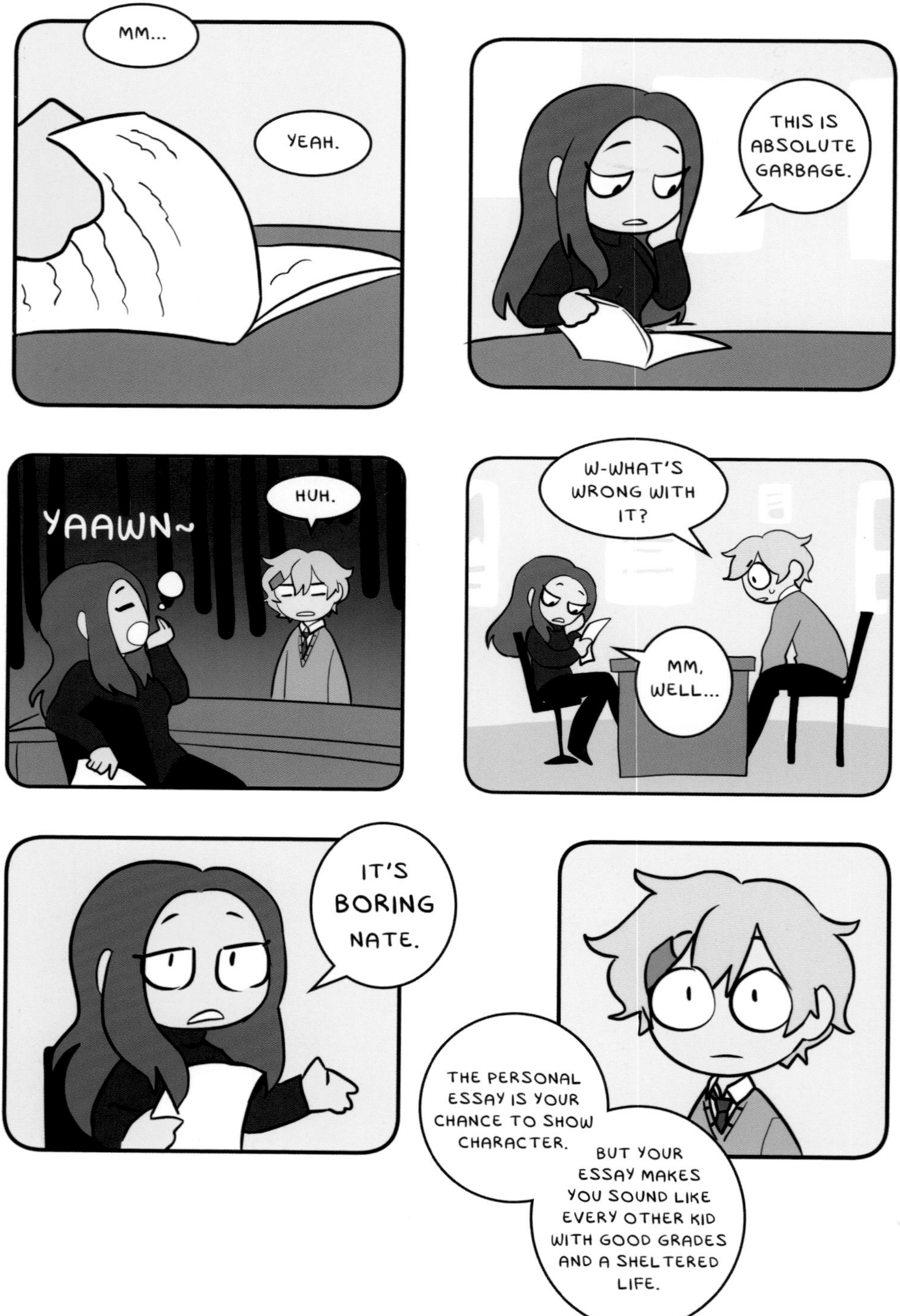
MM...
YEAH.
THIS IS ABSOLUTE GARBAGE.
YAAWN~
HUH.
W-WHAT'S WRONG WITH IT?
MM, WELL...
IT'S BORING NATE.
THE PERSONAL ESSAY IS YOUR CHANCE TO SHOW CHARACTER.
BUT YOUR ESSAY MAKES YOU SOUND LIKE EVERY OTHER KID WITH GOOD GRADES AND A SHELTERED LIFE.

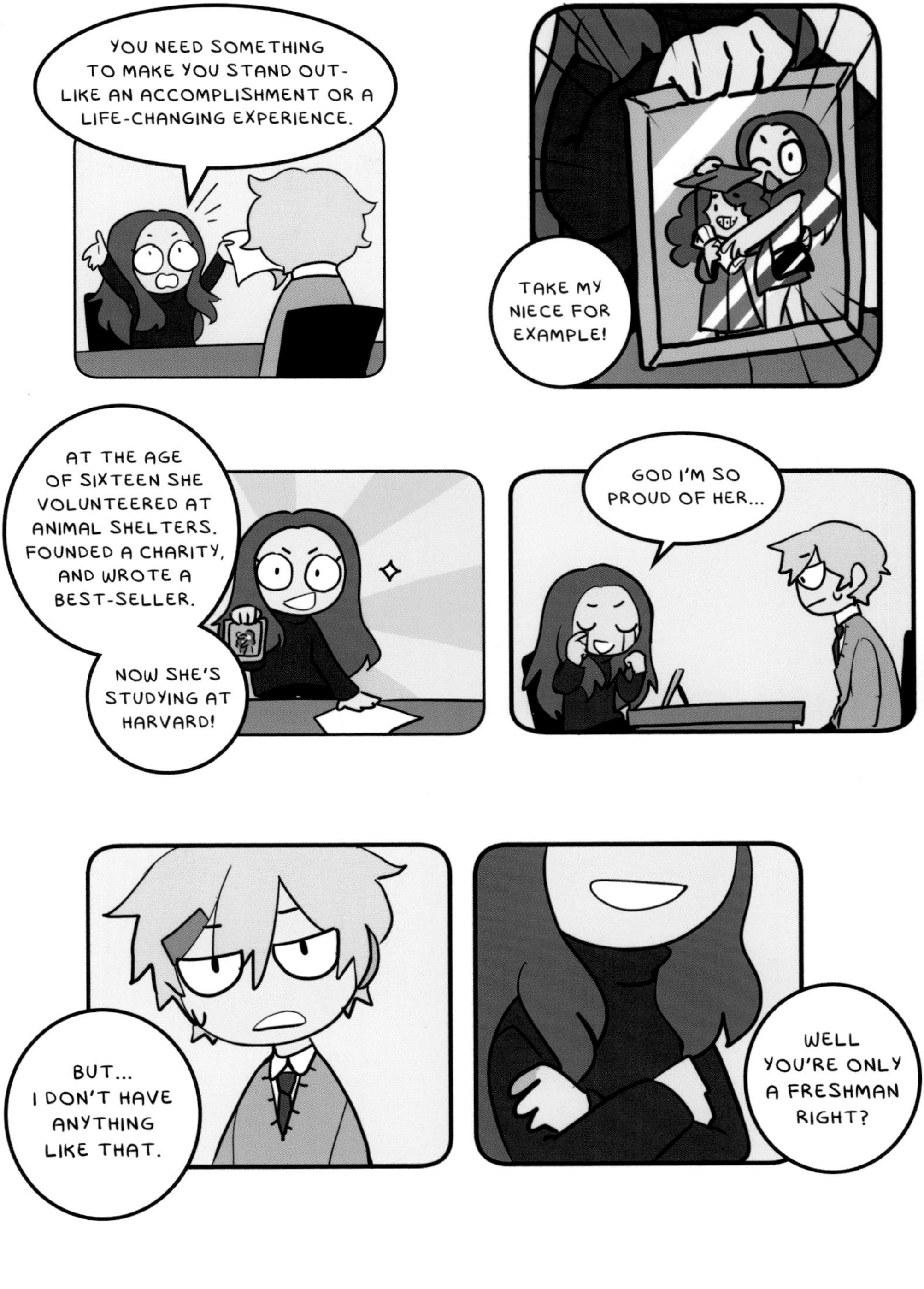
YOU NEED SOMETHING TO MAKE YOU STAND OUT- LIKE AN ACCOMPLISHMENT OR A LIFE-CHANGING EXPERIENCE.
TAKE MY NIECE FOR EXAMPLE!
AT THE AGE OF SIXTEEN SHE VOLUNTEERED AT ANIMAL SHELTERS. FOUNDED A CHARITY, AND WROTE A BEST-SELLER.
NOW SHE'S STUDYING AT HARVARD!
GOD I'M SO PROUD OF HER...
BUT... I DON'T HAVE ANYTHING LIKE THAT.
WELL YOU'RE ONLY A FRESHMAN RIGHT?

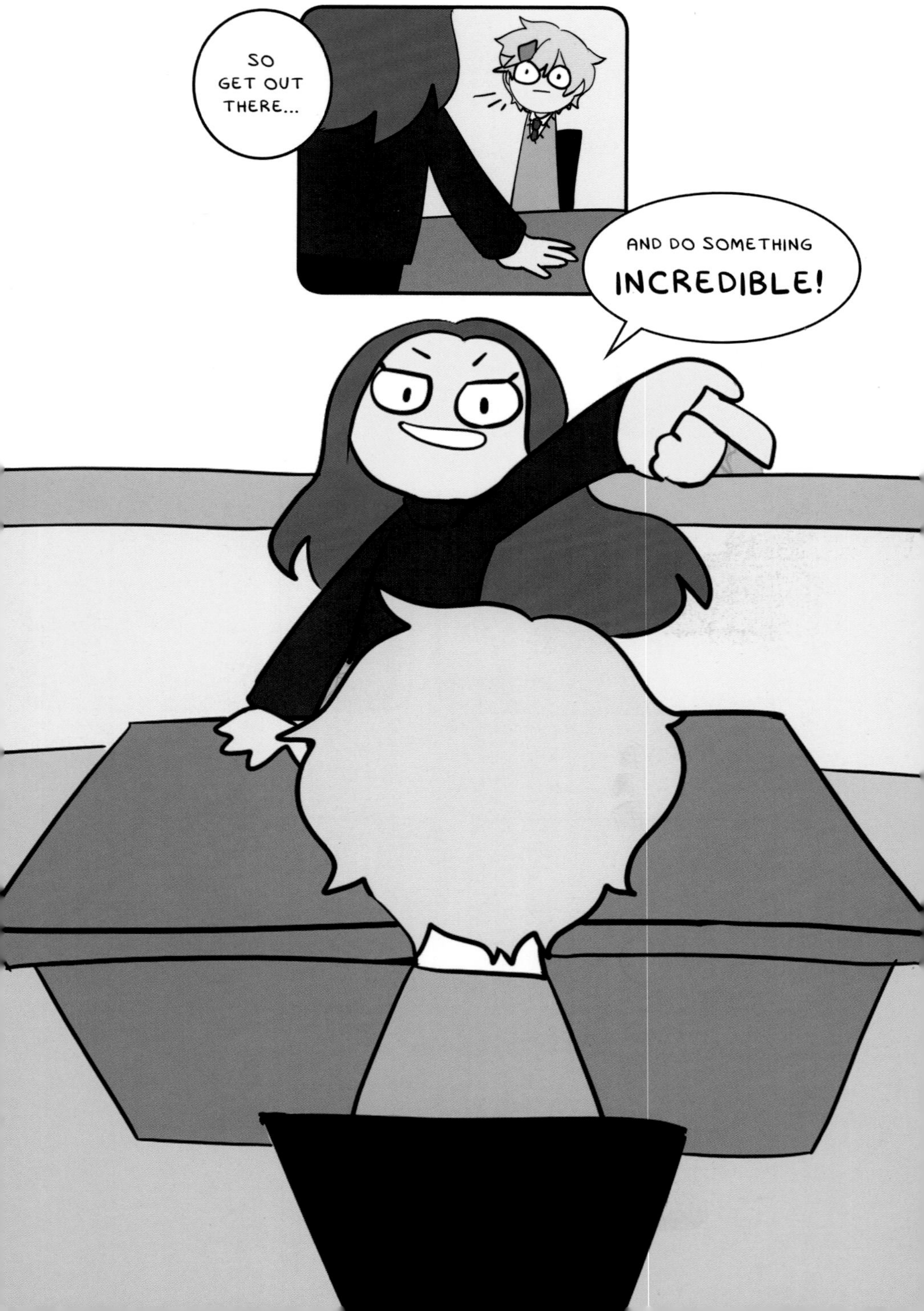
SO GET OUT THERE...
AND DO SOMETHING INCREDIBLE!

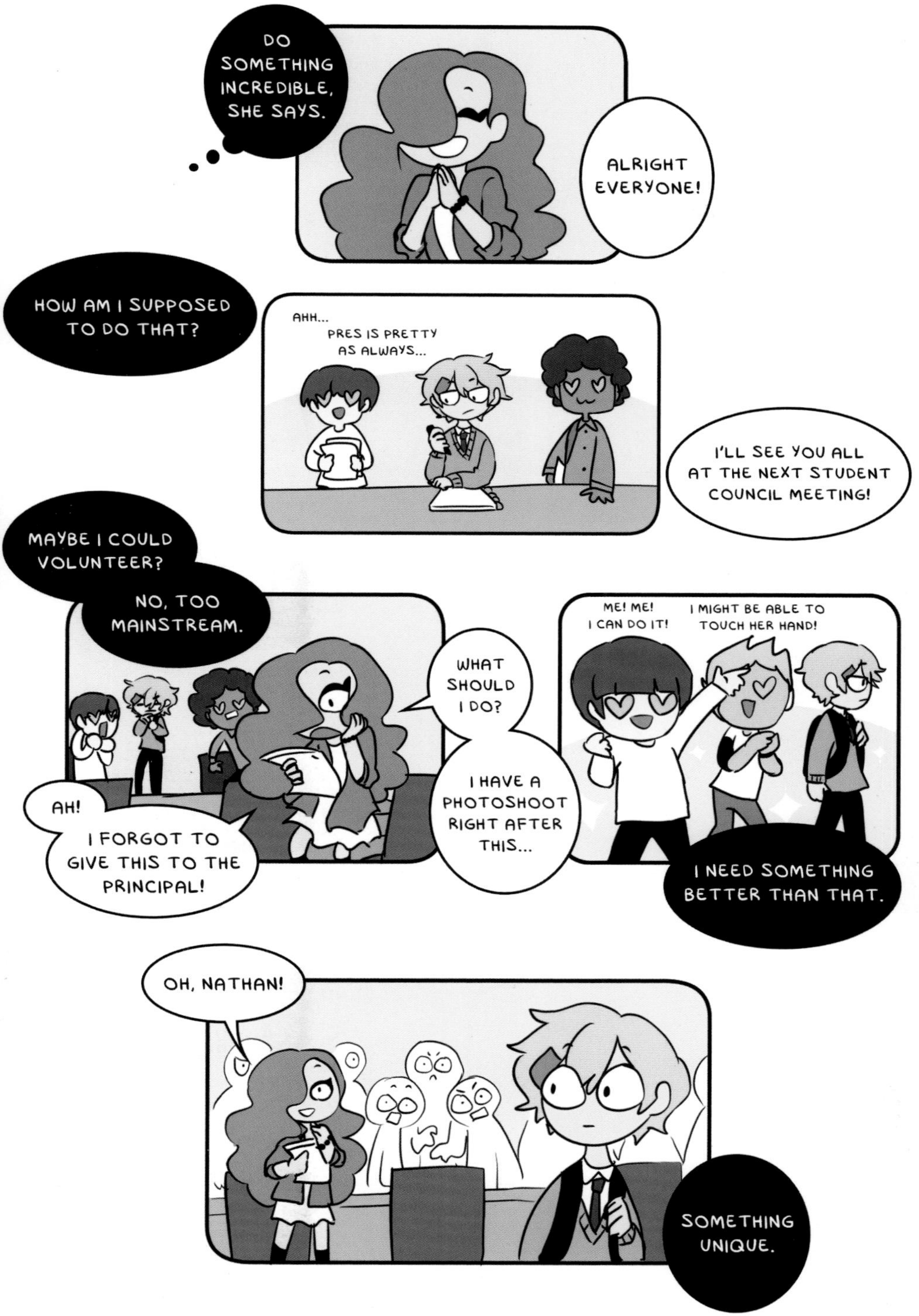
DO SOMETHING INCREDIBLE, SHE SAYS.
ALRIGHT EVERYONE!
HOW AM I SUPPOSED TO DO THAT?
AHH...
PRES IS PRETTY AS ALWAYS...
I'LL SEE YOU ALL AT THE NEXT STUDENT COUNCIL MEETING!
MAYBE I COULD VOLUNTEER?
NO, TOO MAINSTREAM.
WHAT SHOULD I DO?
AH!
I FORGOT TO GIVE THIS TO THE PRINCIPAL!
I HAVE A PHOTOSHOOT RIGHT AFTER THIS...
ME! ME! I CAN DO IT!
I MIGHT BE ABLE TO TOUCH HER HAND!
I NEED SOMETHING BETTER THAN THAT.
OH, NATHAN!
SOMETHING UNIQUE.

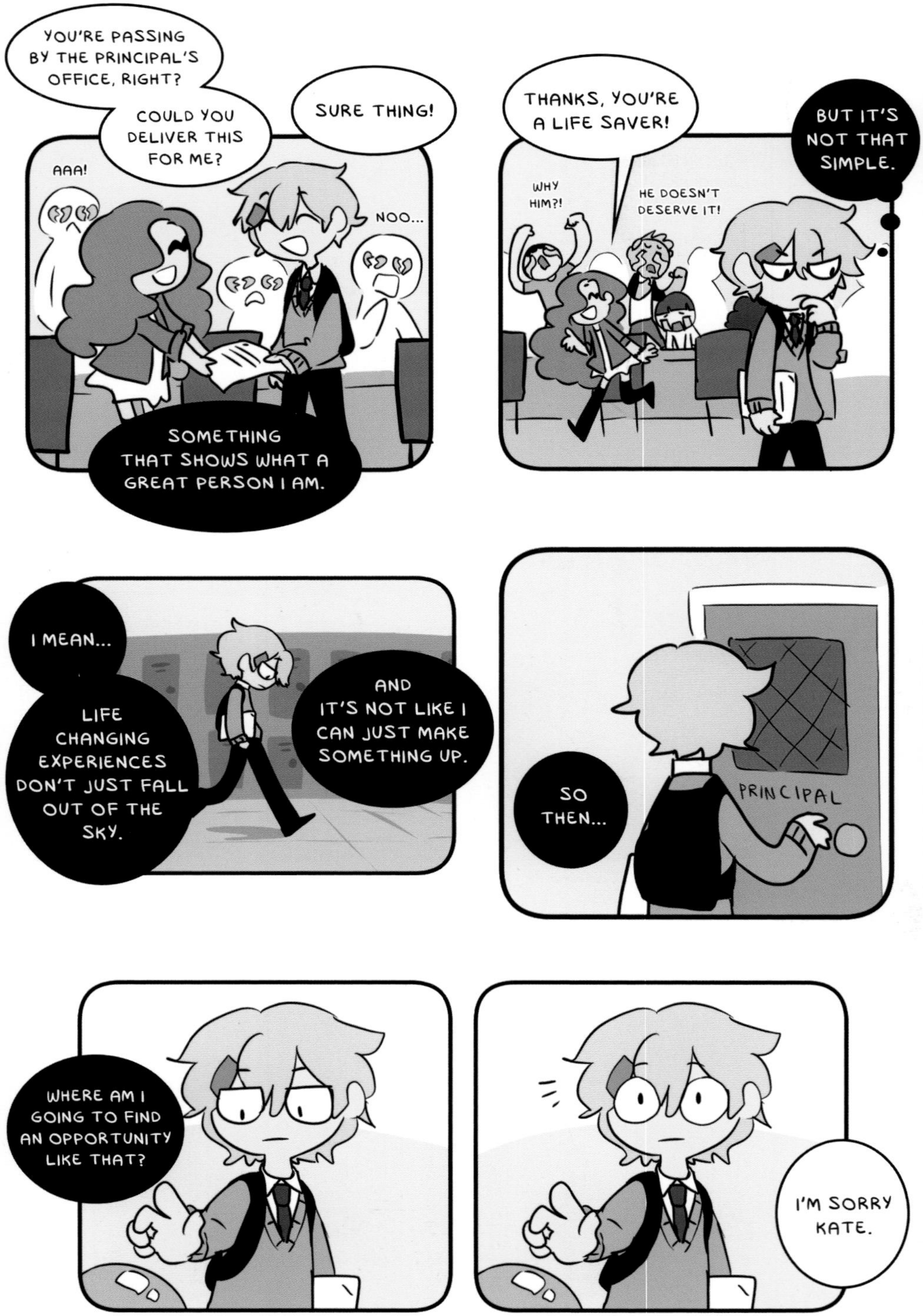
YOU'RE PASSING BY THE PRINCIPAL'S OFFICE, RIGHT?
COULD YOU DELIVER THIS FOR ME?
SURE THING!
AAA!
NOO...
SOMETHING THAT SHOWS WHAT A GREAT PERSON I AM.
THANKS, YOU'RE A LIFE SAVER!
BUT IT'S NOT THAT SIMPLE.
WHY HIM?!
HE DOESN'T DESERVE IT!
I MEAN...
LIFE CHANGING EXPERIENCES DON'T JUST FALL OUT OF THE SKY.
AND IT'S NOT LIKE I CAN JUST MAKE SOMETHING UP.
SO THEN...
PRINCIPAL
WHERE AM I GOING TO FIND AN OPPORTUNITY LIKE THAT?
I'M SORRY KATE.

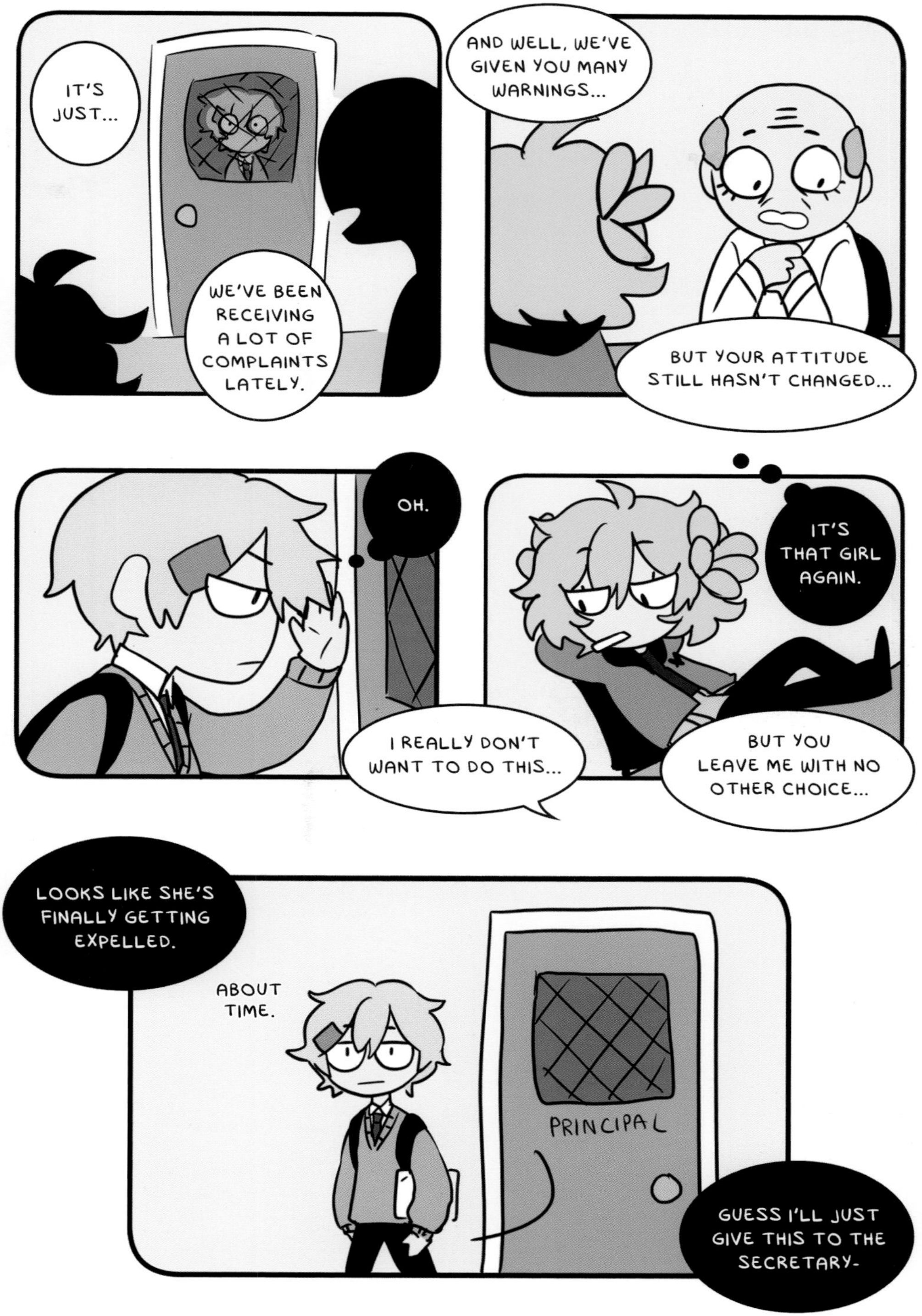
IT'S JUST...
WE'VE BEEN RECEIVING A LOT OF COMPLAINTS LATELY.
AND WELL, WE'VE GIVEN YOU MANY WARNINGS...
BUT YOUR ATTITUDE STILL HASN'T CHANGED...
OH.
I REALLY DON'T WANT TO DO THIS...
IT'S THAT GIRL AGAIN.
BUT YOU LEAVE ME WITH NO OTHER CHOICE...
LOOKS LIKE SHE'S FINALLY GETTING EXPELLED.
ABOUT TIME.
PRINCIPAL
GUESS I'LL JUST GIVE THIS TO THE SECRETARY.

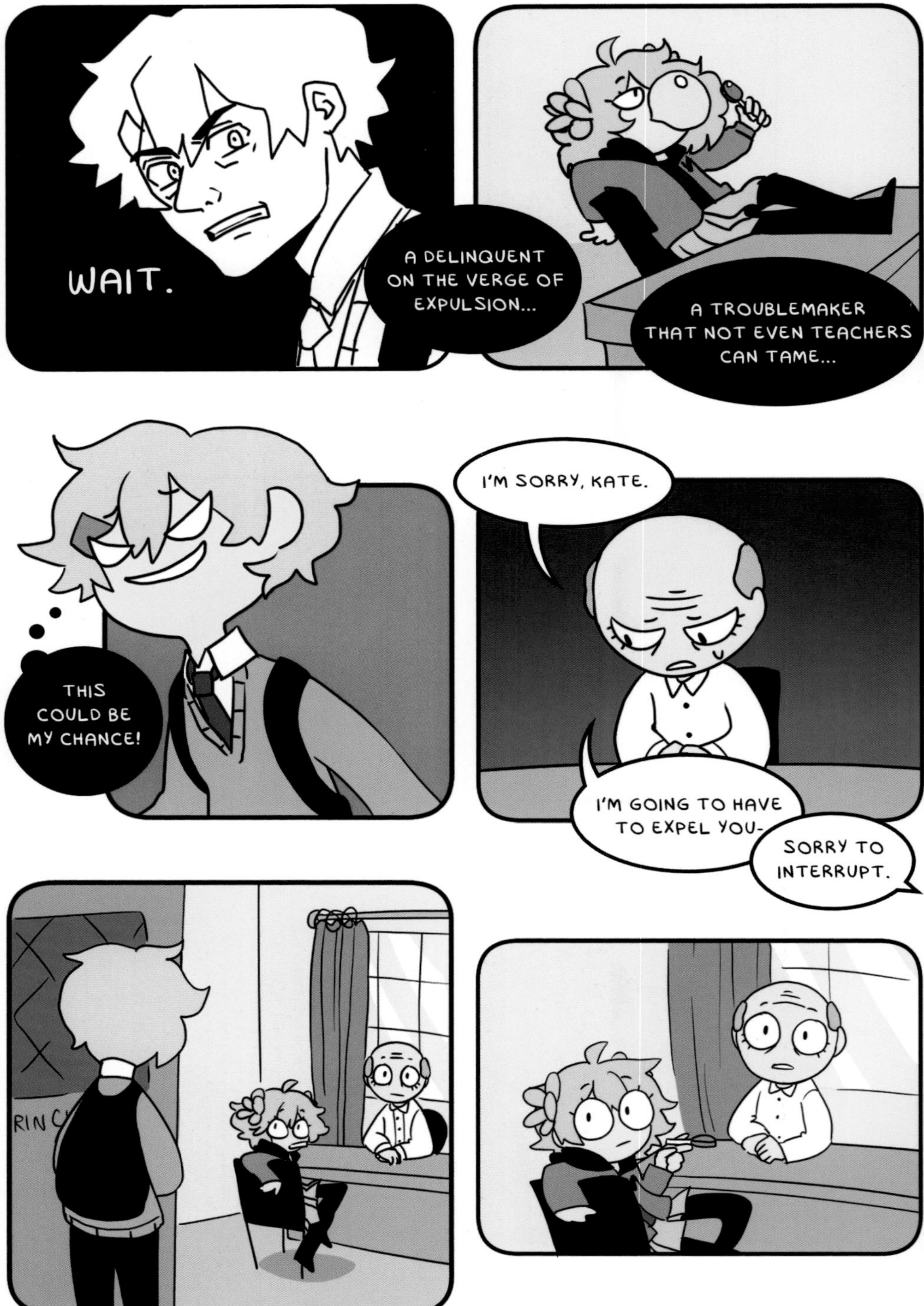
WAIT.
A DELINQUENT ON THE VERGE OF EXPULSION...
A TROUBLEMAKER THAT NOT EVEN TEACHERS CAN TAME...
THIS COULD BE MY CHANCE!
I'M SORRY, KATE.
I'M GOING TO HAVE TO EXPEL YOU-
SORRY TO INTERRUPT.

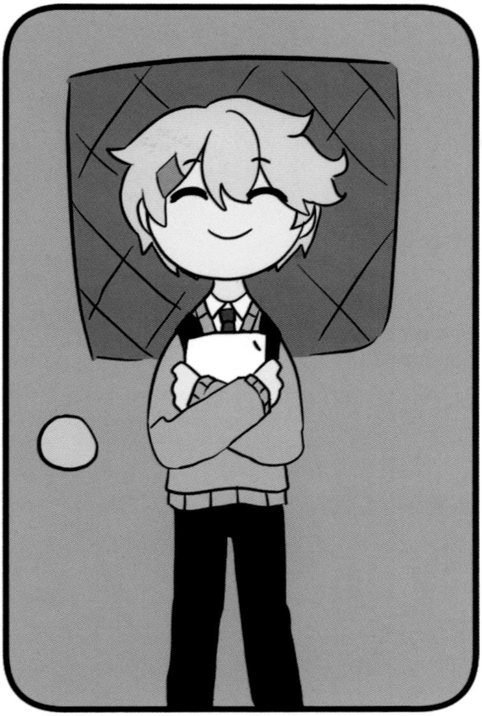

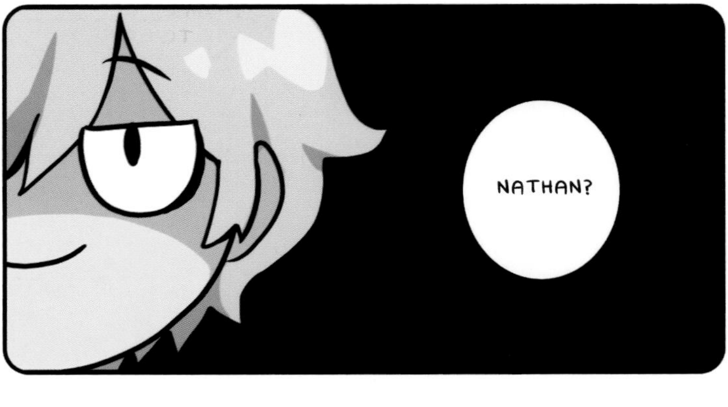
NATHAN?

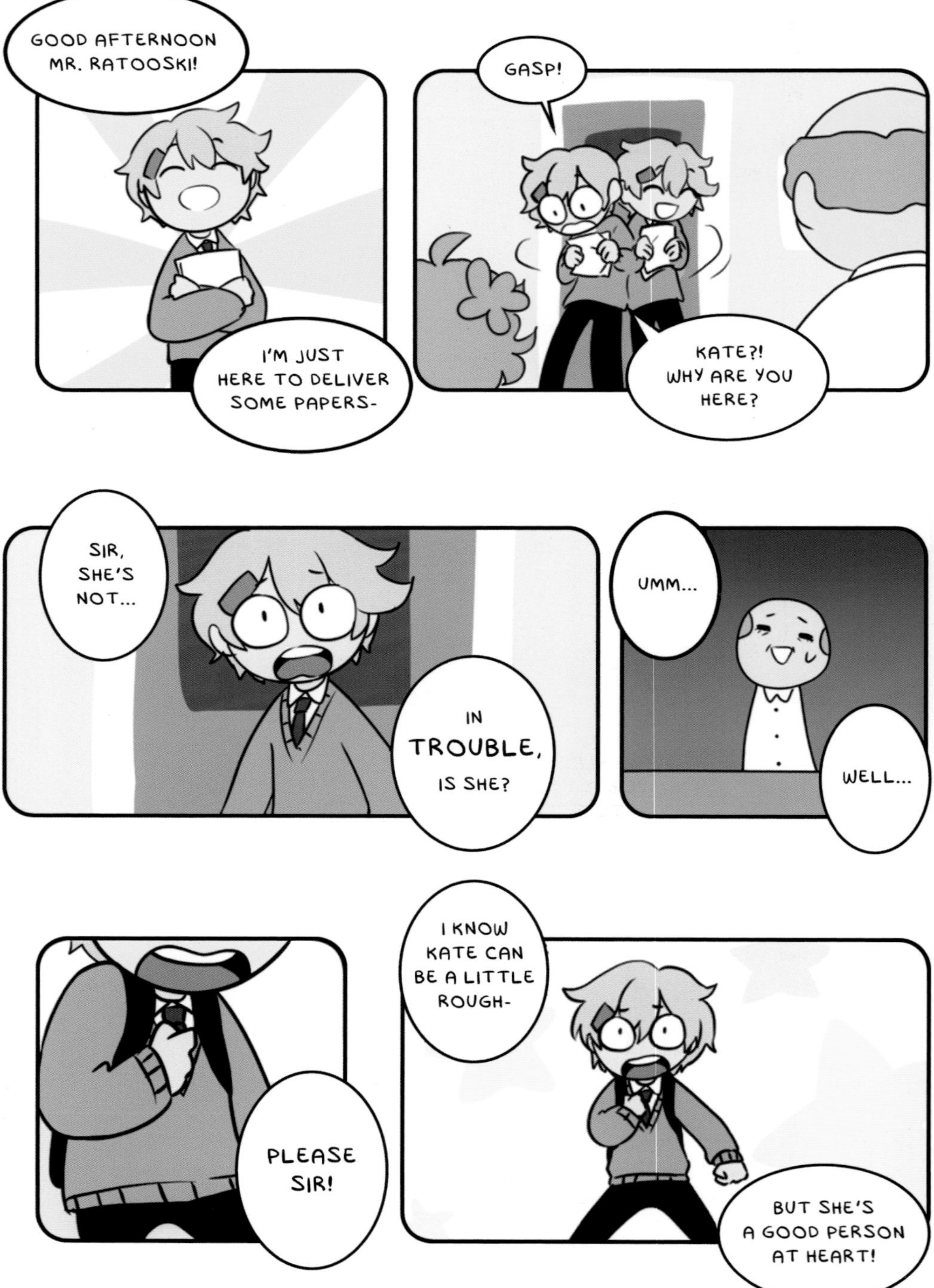
GOOD AFTERNOON MR. RATOOSKI!
I'M JUST HERE TO DELIVER SOME PAPERS-
GASP!
KATE?! WHY ARE YOU HERE?
SIR, SHE'S NOT...
IN TROUBLE, IS SHE?
UMM...
WELL...
PLEASE SIR!
I KNOW KATE CAN BE A LITTLE ROUGH-
BUT SHE'S A GOOD PERSON AT HEART!

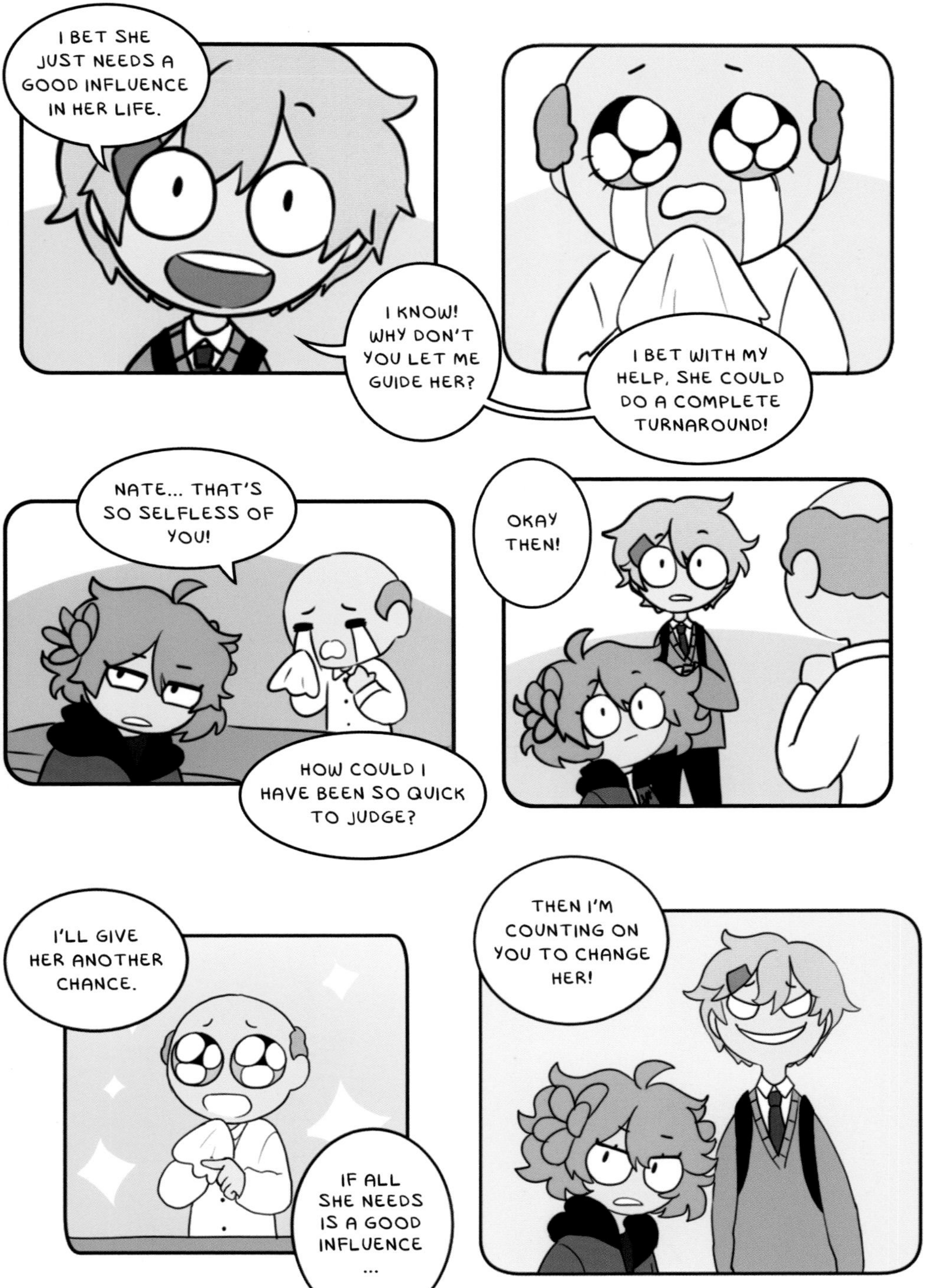
I BET SHE JUST NEEDS A GOOD INFLUENCE IN HER LIFE.
I KNOW! WHY DON'T YOU LET ME GUIDE HER?
I BET WITH MY HELP, SHE COULD DO A COMPLETE TURNAROUND!
NATE... THAT'S SO SELFLESS OF YOU!
HOW COULD I HAVE BEEN SO QUICK TO JUDGE?
OKAY THEN!
I'LL GIVE HER ANOTHER CHANCE.
IF ALL SHE NEEDS IS A GOOD INFLUENCE ...
THEN I'M COUNTING ON YOU TO CHANGE HER!

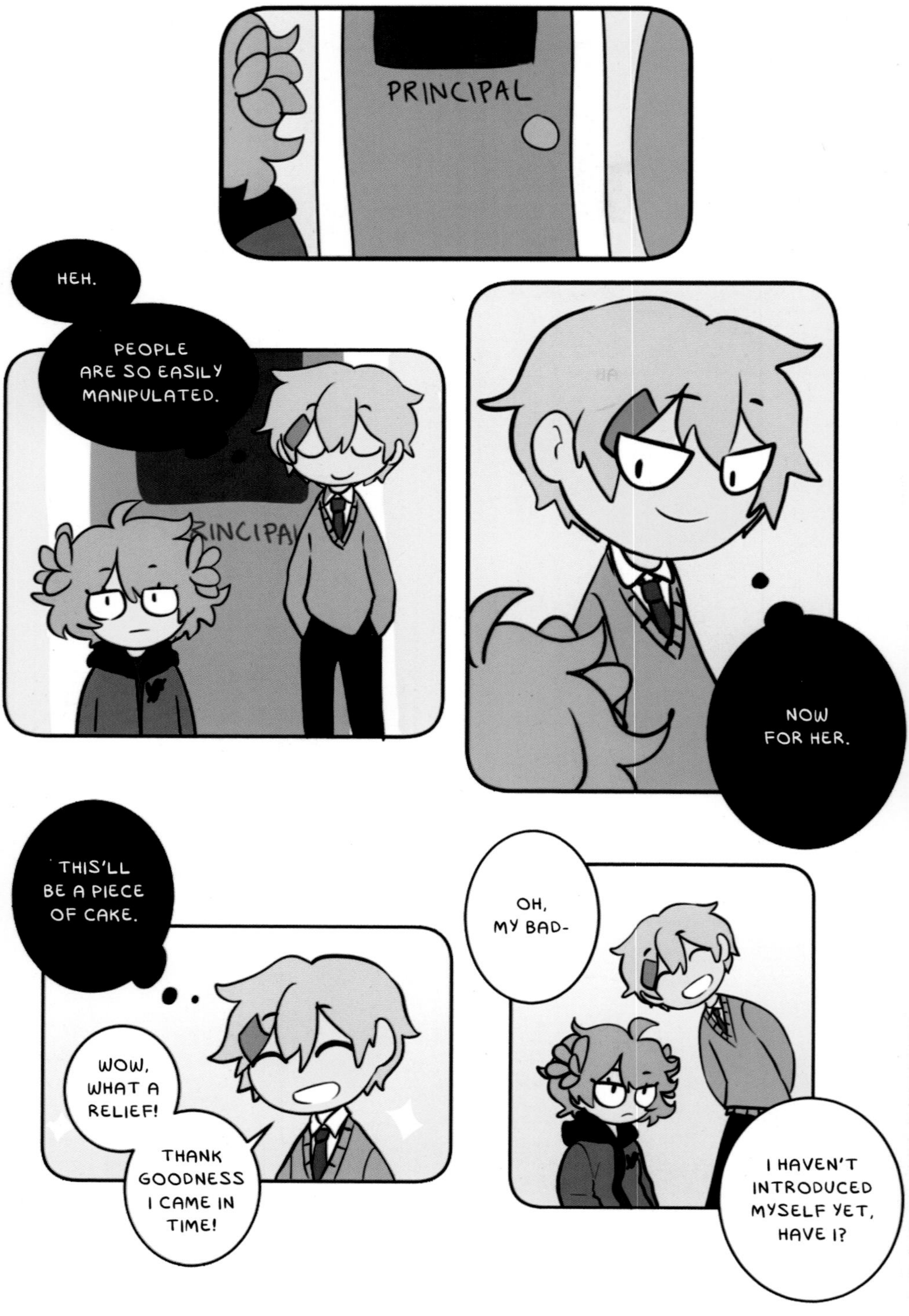
PRINCIPAL
HEH.
PEOPLE ARE SO EASILY MANIPULATED.
PRINCIPAL
HA
NOW FOR HER.
THIS'LL BE A PIECE OF CAKE.
WOW, WHAT A RELIEF!
THANK GOODNESS I CAME IN TIME!
OH, MY BAD-
I HAVEN'T INTRODUCED MYSELF YET, HAVE I?

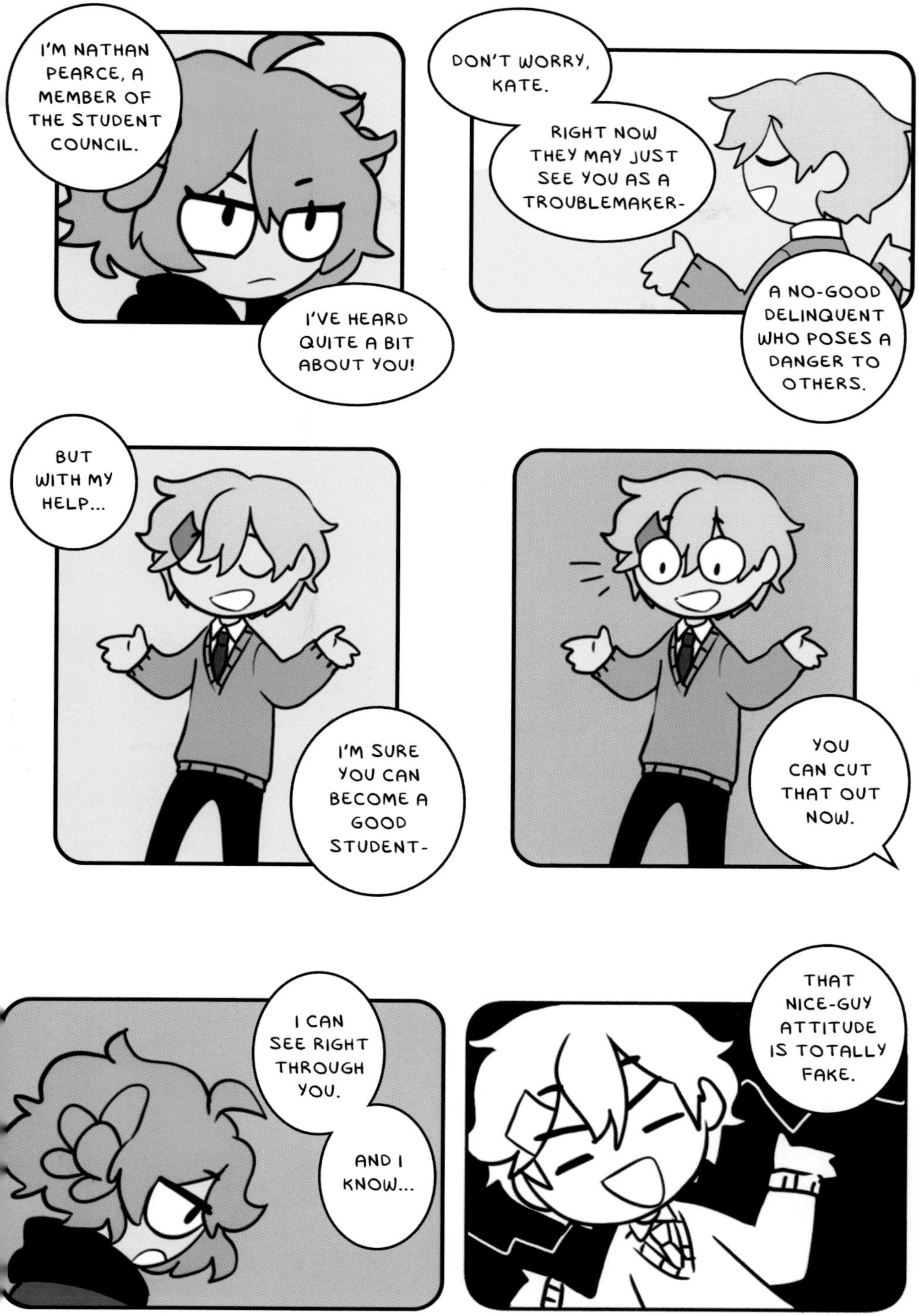
I'M NATHAN PEARCE, A MEMBER OF THE STUDENT COUNCIL.
I'VE HEARD QUITE A BIT ABOUT YOU!
DON'T WORRY, KATE.
RIGHT NOW THEY MAY JUST SEE YOU AS A TROUBLEMAKER-
A NO-GOOD DELINQUENT WHO POSES A DANGER TO OTHERS.
BUT WITH MY HELP...
I'M SURE YOU CAN BECOME A GOOD STUDENT-
YOU CAN CUT THAT OUT NOW.
I CAN SEE RIGHT THROUGH YOU.
AND I KNOW...
THAT NICE-GUY ATTITUDE IS TOTALLY FAKE.

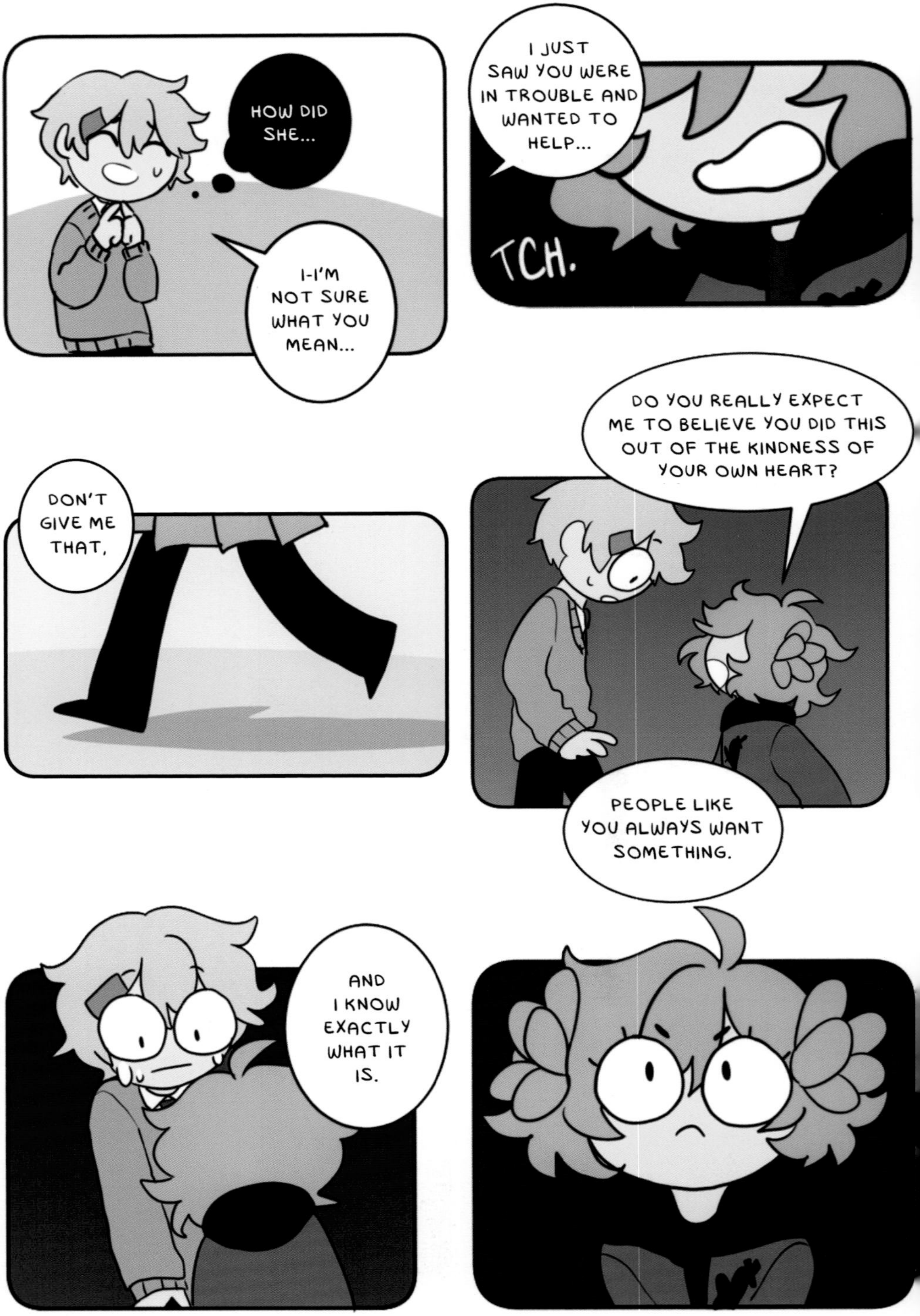
HOW DID SHE...
I-I'M NOT SURE WHAT YOU MEAN...
I JUST SAW YOU WERE IN TROUBLE AND WANTED TO HELP...
TCH.
DON'T GIVE ME THAT,
DO YOU REALLY EXPECT ME TO BELIEVE YOU DID THIS OUT OF THE KINDNESS OF YOUR OWN HEART?
PEOPLE LIKE YOU ALWAYS WANT SOMETHING.
AND I KNOW EXACTLY WHAT IT IS.

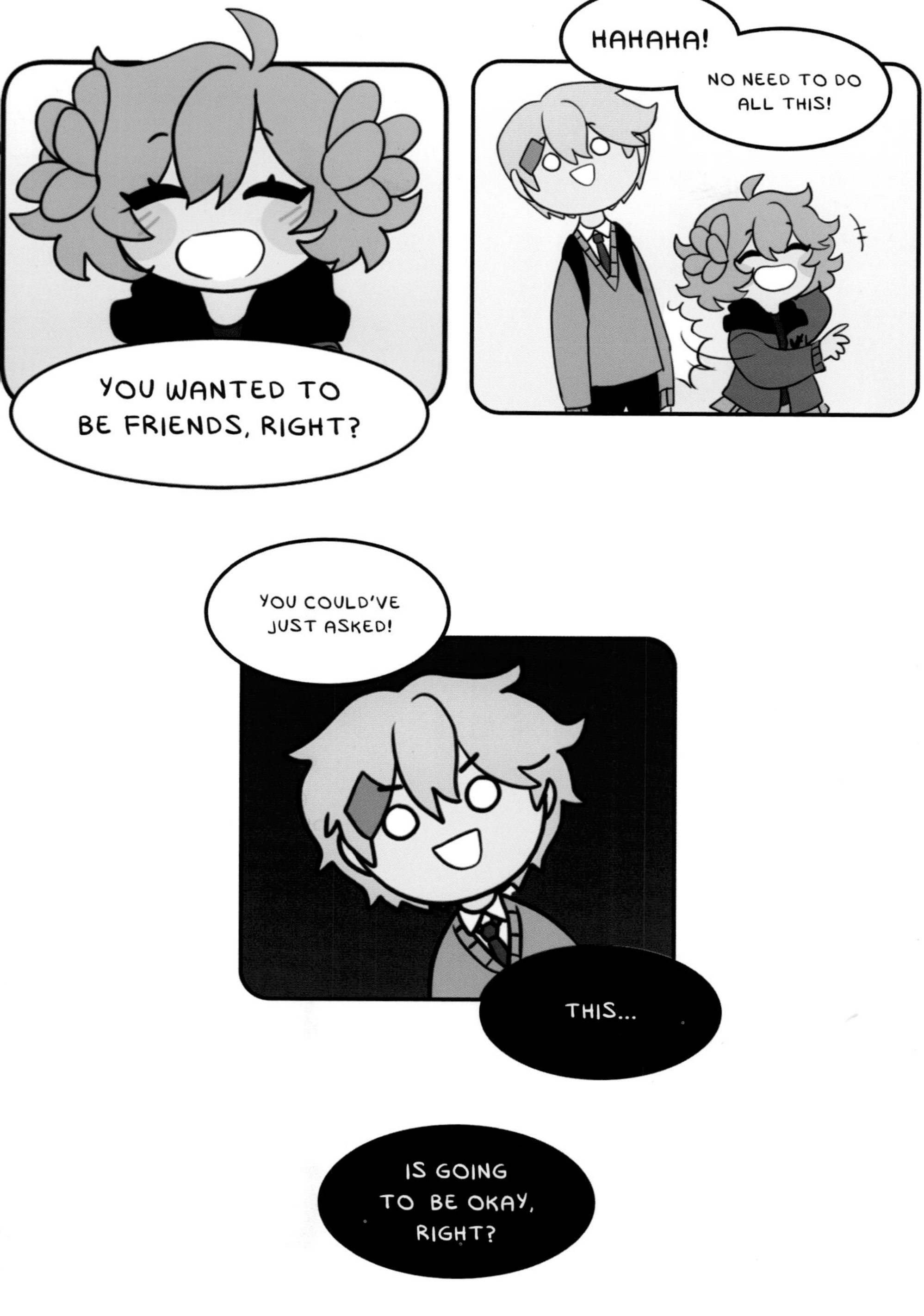
YOU WANTED TO BE FRIENDS, RIGHT?
HAHAHA!
NO NEED TO DO ALL THIS!
YOU COULD'VE JUST ASKED!
THIS...
IS GOING TO BE OKAY, RIGHT?

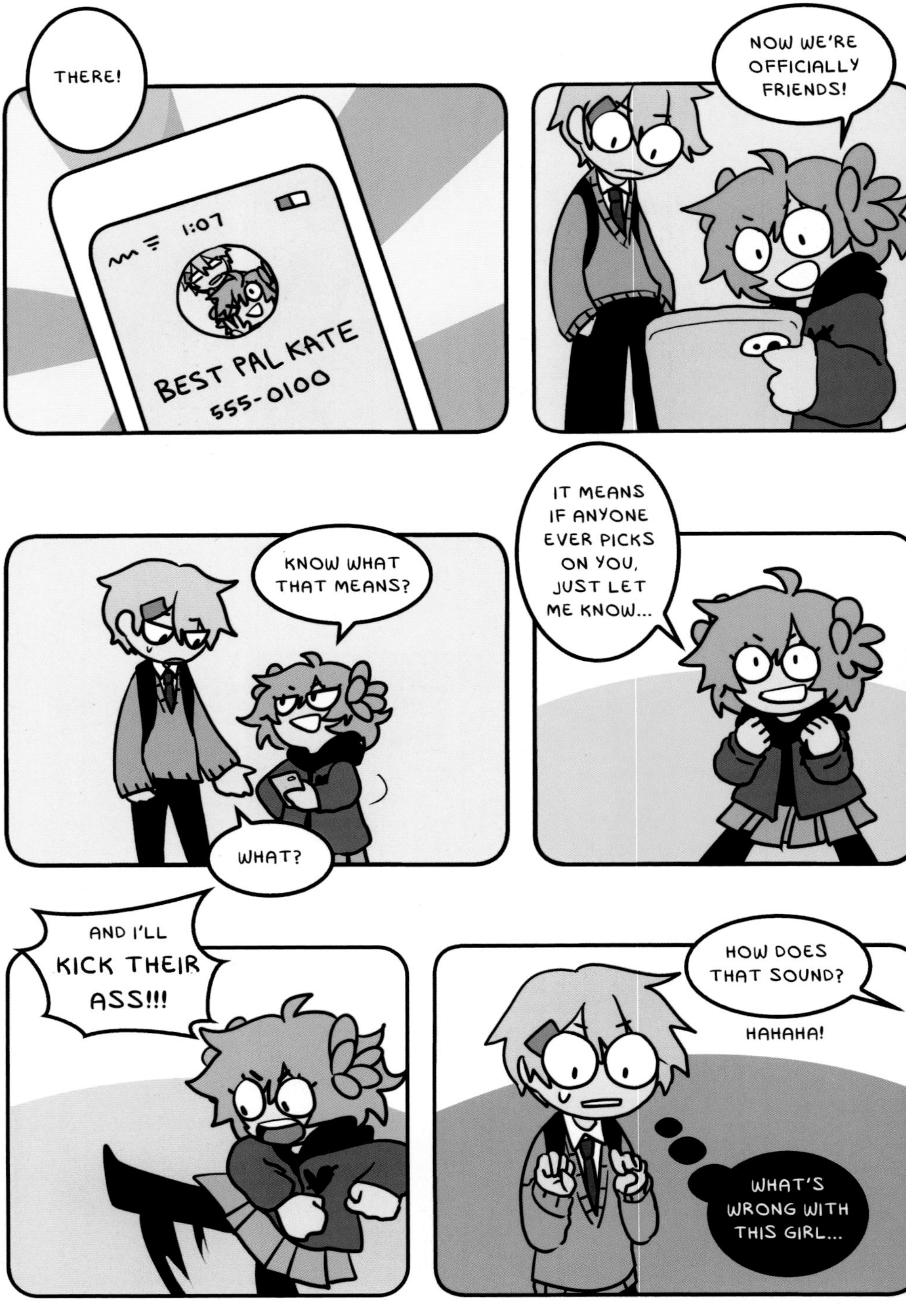
THERE!
1:07
BEST PAL KATE
555-0100
NOW WE'RE OFFICIALLY FRIENDS!
KNOW WHAT THAT MEANS?
WHAT?
IT MEANS IF ANYONE EVER PICKS ON YOU, JUST LET ME KNOW...
AND I'LL KICK THEIR ASS!!!
HOW DOES THAT SOUND?
HAHAHA!
WHAT'S WRONG WITH THIS GIRL...

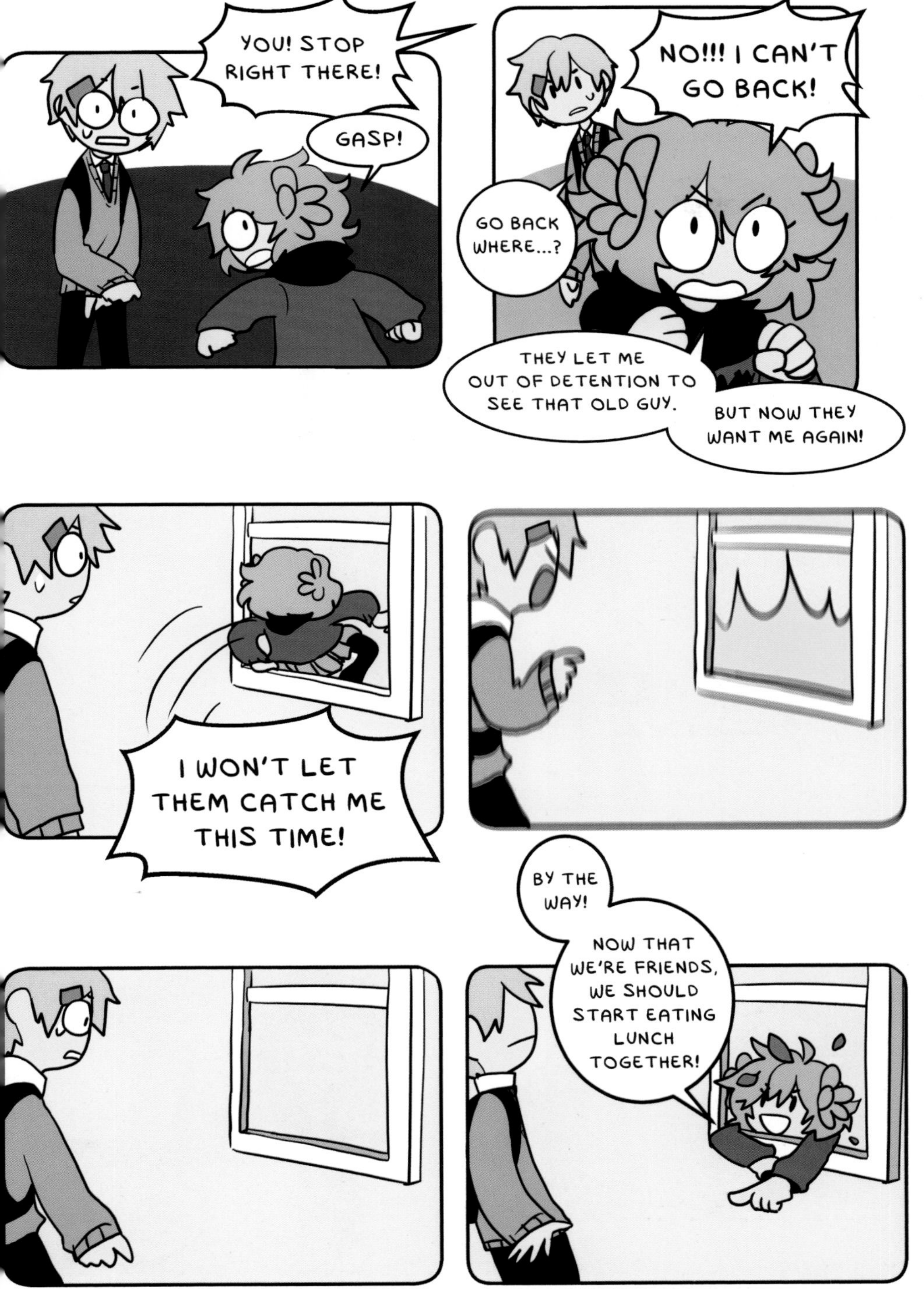
YOU! STOP RIGHT THERE!
GASP!
NO!!! I CAN'T GO BACK!
GO BACK WHERE...?
THEY LET ME OUT OF DETENTION TO SEE THAT OLD GUY.
BUT NOW THEY WANT ME AGAIN!
I WON'T LET THEM CATCH ME THIS TIME!
BY THE WAY!
NOW THAT WE'RE FRIENDS, WE SHOULD START EATING LUNCH TOGETHER!

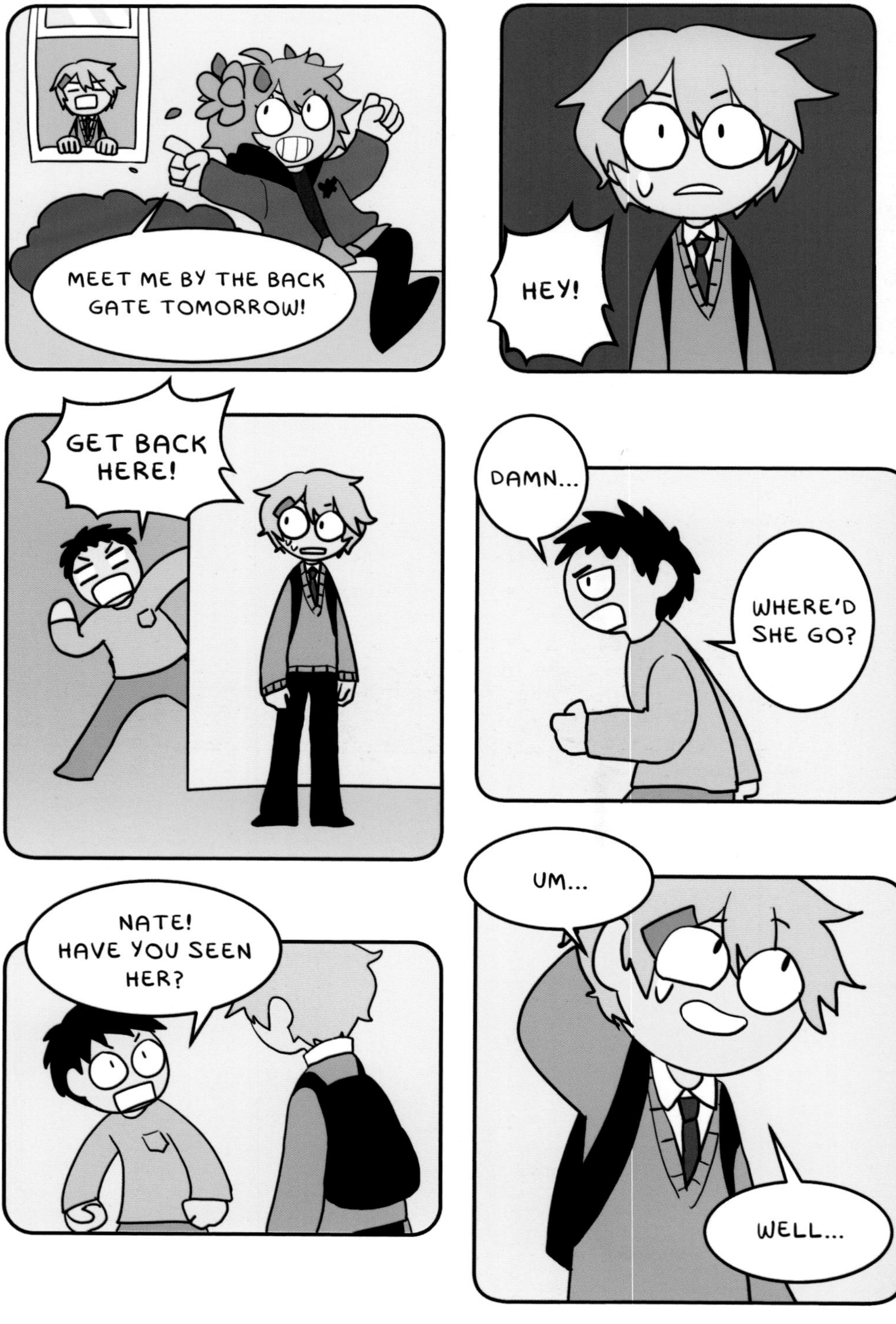
MEET ME BY THE BACK GATE TOMORROW!
HEY!
GET BACK HERE!
DAMN...
WHERE'D SHE GO?
NATE! HAVE YOU SEEN HER?
UM...
WELL...

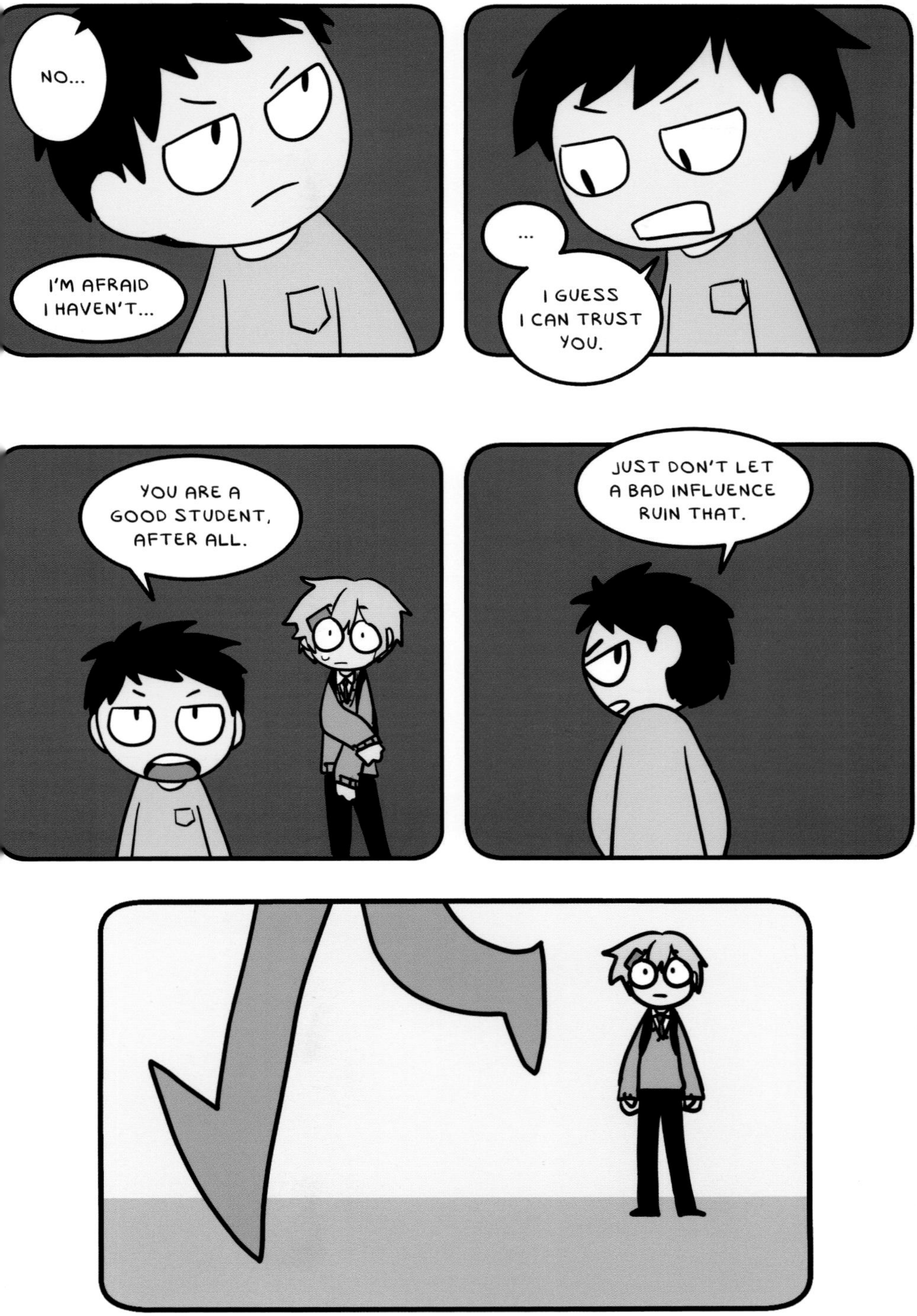
NO...
I'M AFRAID I HAVEN'T...
...
I GUESS I CAN TRUST YOU.
YOU ARE A GOOD STUDENT, AFTER ALL.
JUST DON'T LET A BAD INFLUENCE RUIN THAT.

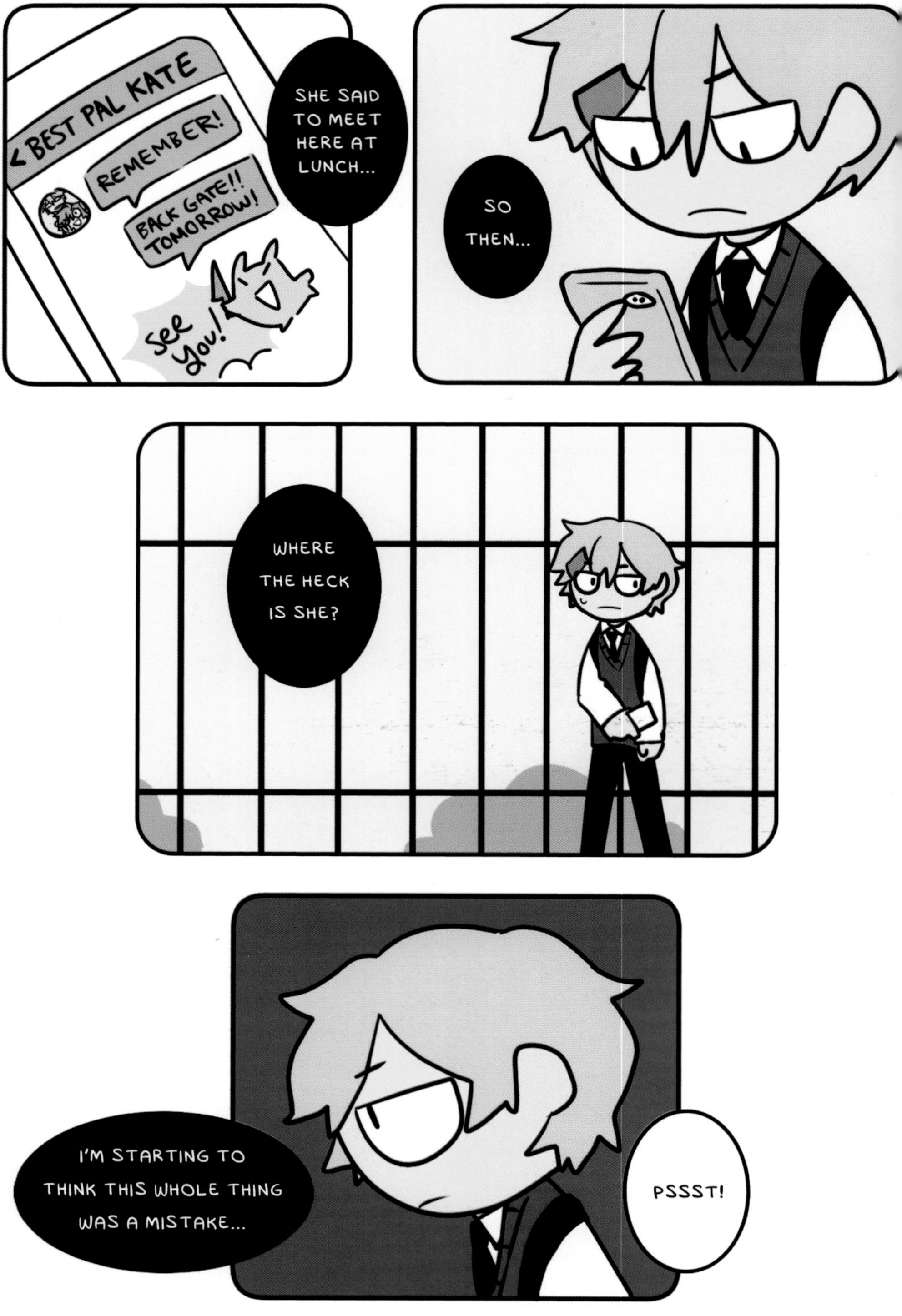
< BEST PAL KATE
REMEMBER!
BACK GATE!! TOMORROW!
See You!
SHE SAID TO MEET HERE AT LUNCH...
SO THEN...
WHERE THE HECK IS SHE?
I'M STARTING TO THINK THIS WHOLE THING WAS A MISTAKE...
PSSST!

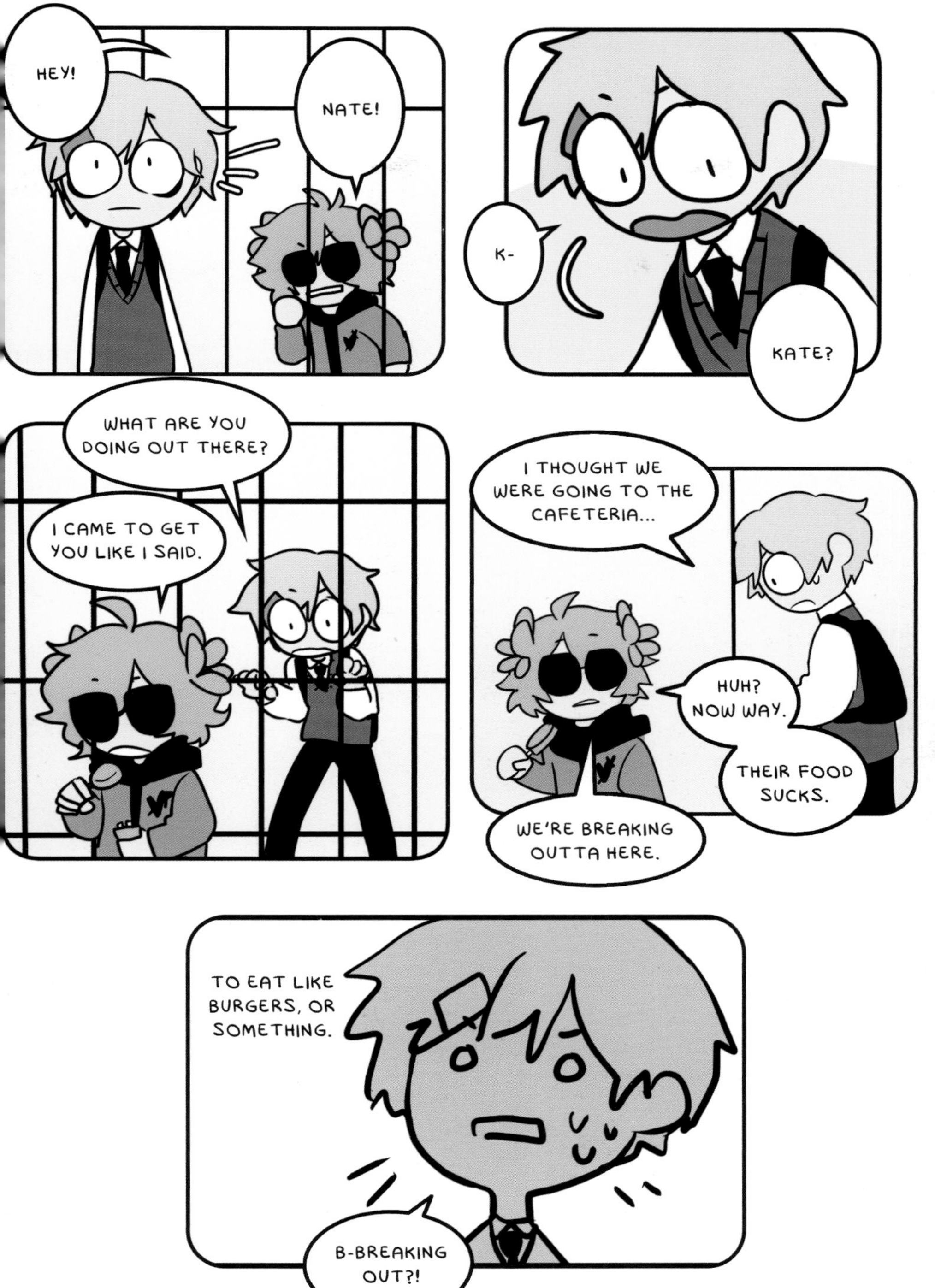
HEY!
NATE!
K-
KATE?
WHAT ARE YOU DOING OUT THERE?
I CAME TO GET YOU LIKE I SAID.
I THOUGHT WE WERE GOING TO THE CAFETERIA...
HUH? NOW WAY.
THEIR FOOD SUCKS.
WE'RE BREAKING OUTTA HERE.
TO EAT LIKE BURGERS, OR SOMETHING.
B-BREAKING OUT?!

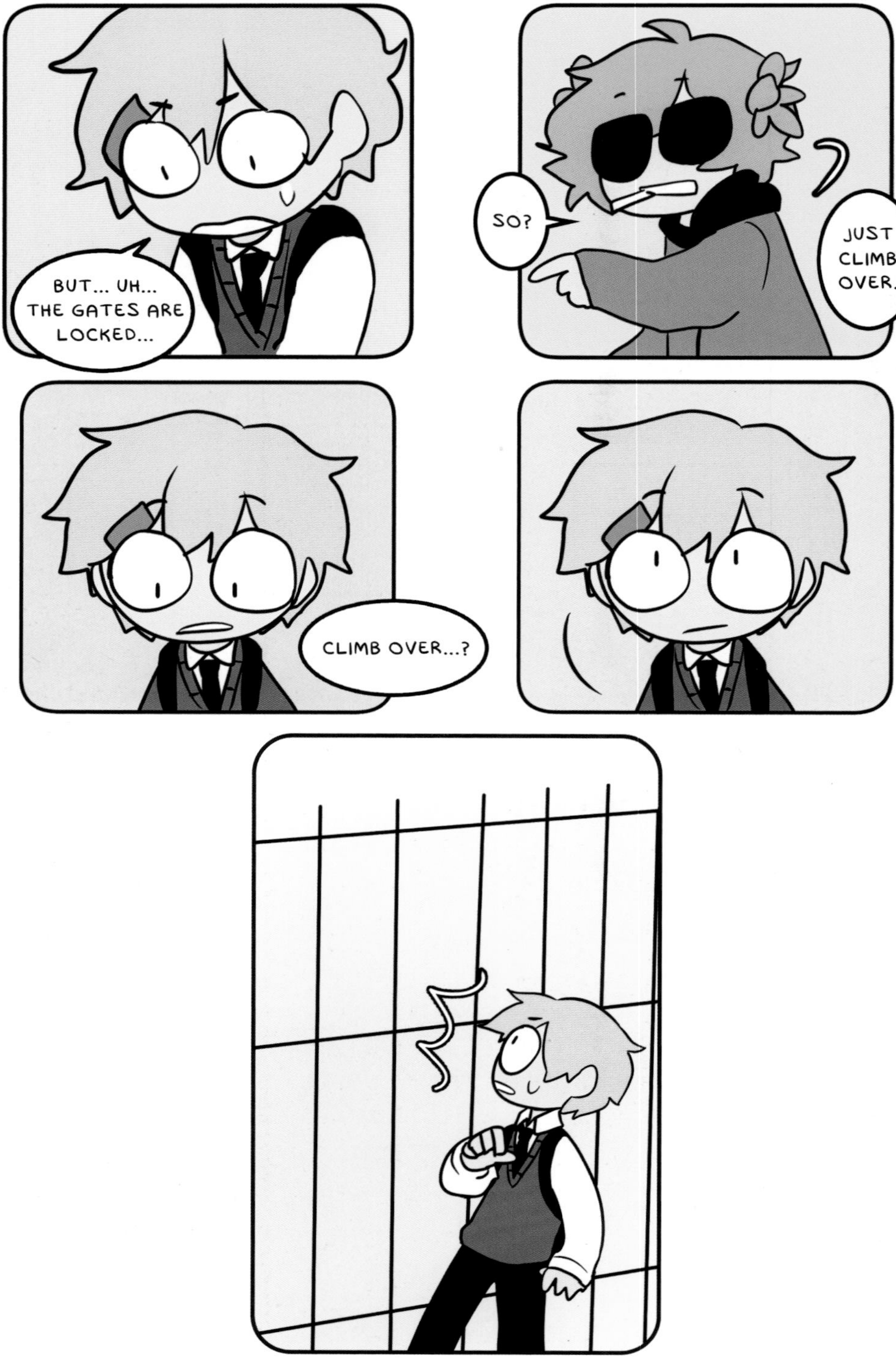
BUT... UH... THE GATES ARE LOCKED...
SO?
JUST CLIMB OVER.
CLIMB OVER...?

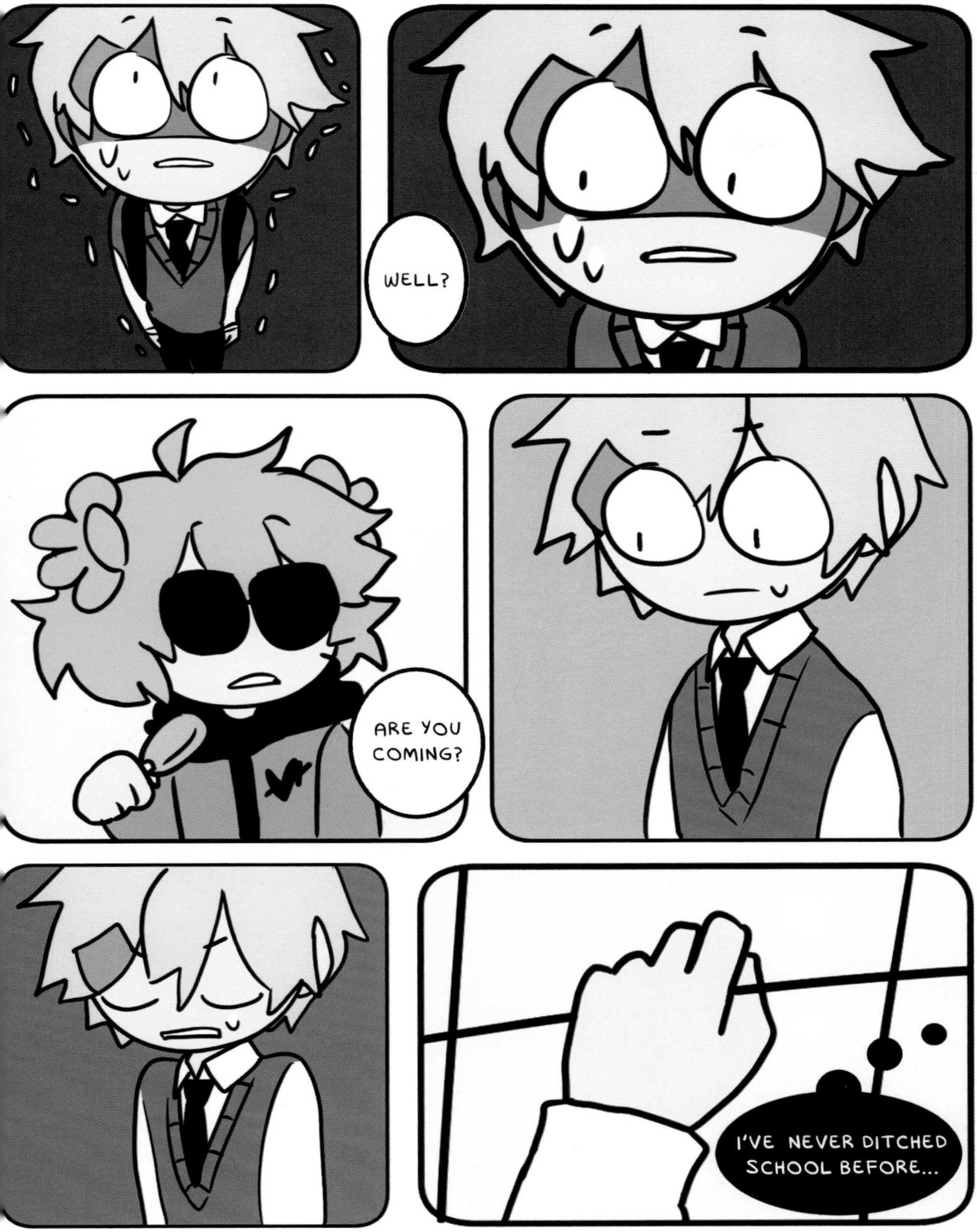
WELL?
ARE YOU COMING?
I'VE NEVER DITCHED SCHOOL BEFORE...

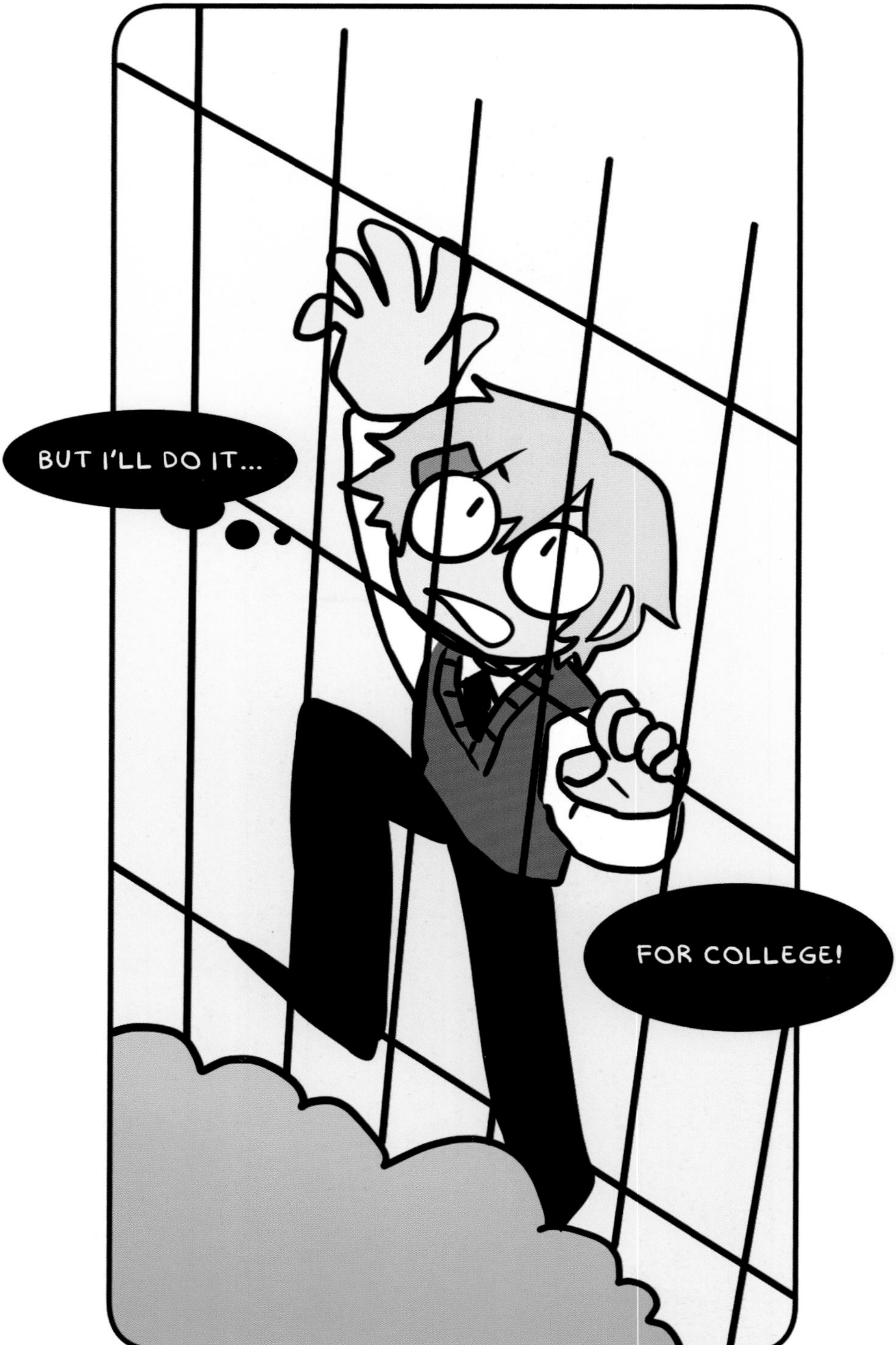
BUT I'LL DO IT...
FOR COLLEGE!

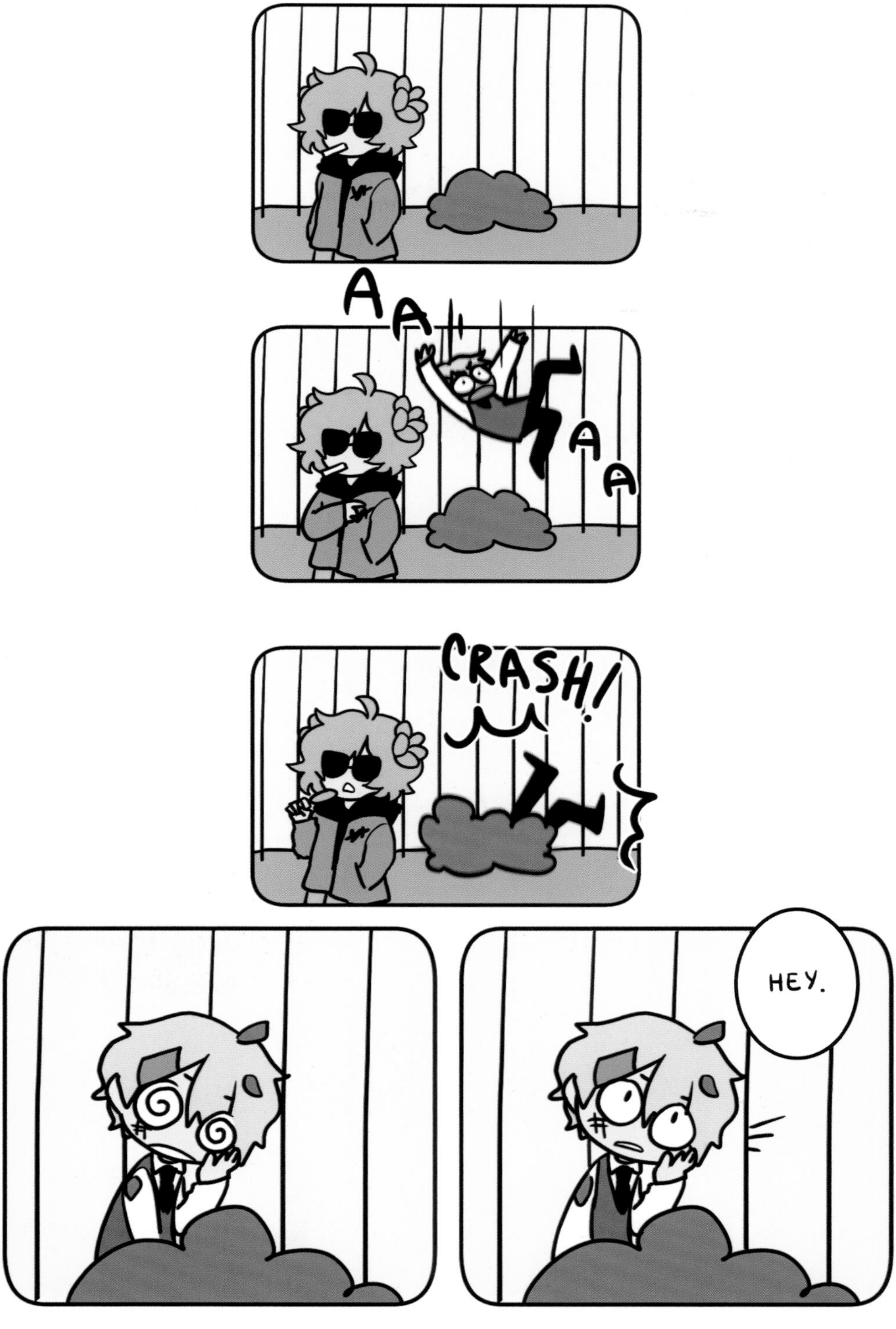
AA
AA
CRASH!
HEY.

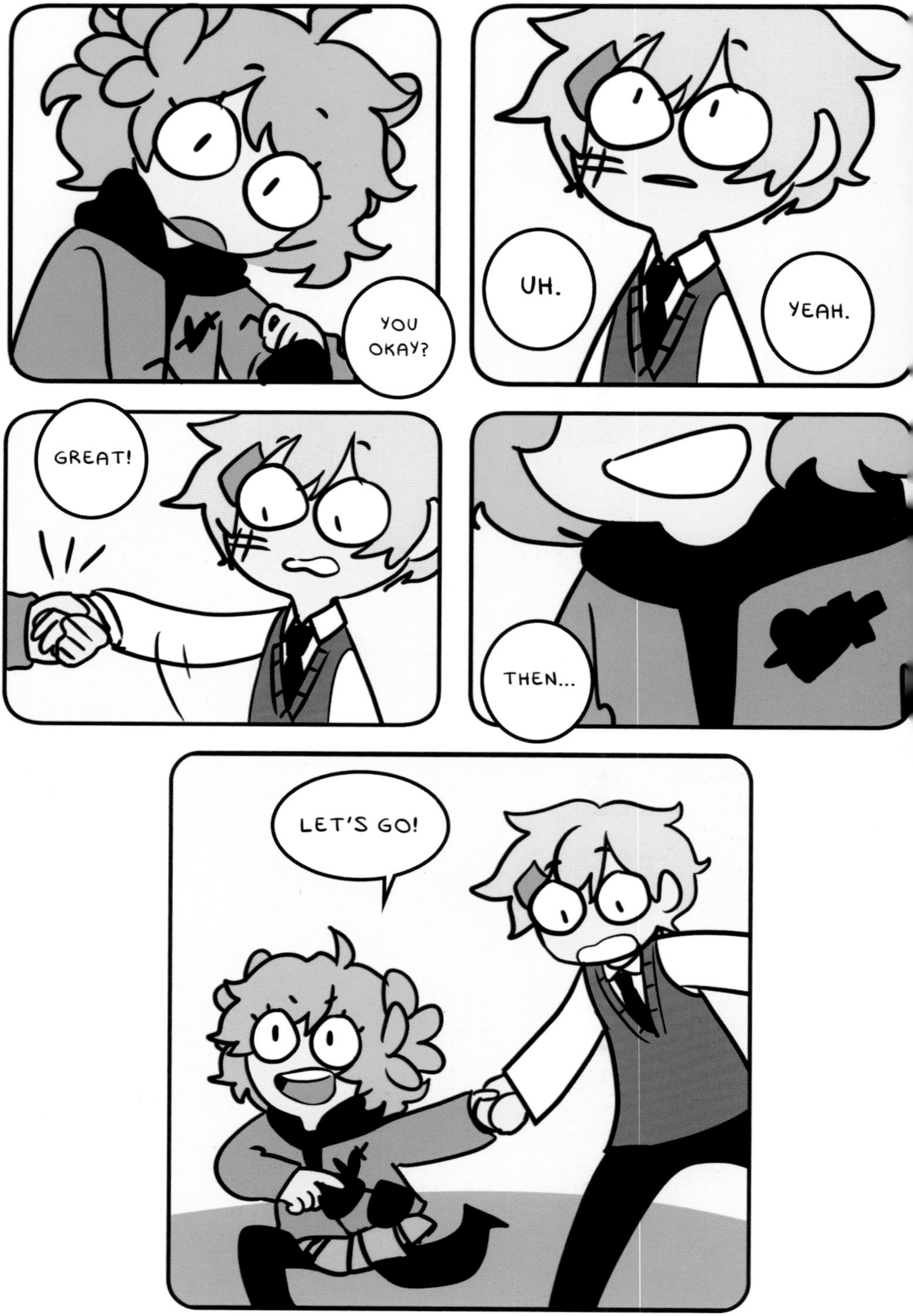
YOU OKAY?
UH.
YEAH.
GREAT!
THEN...
LET'S GO!

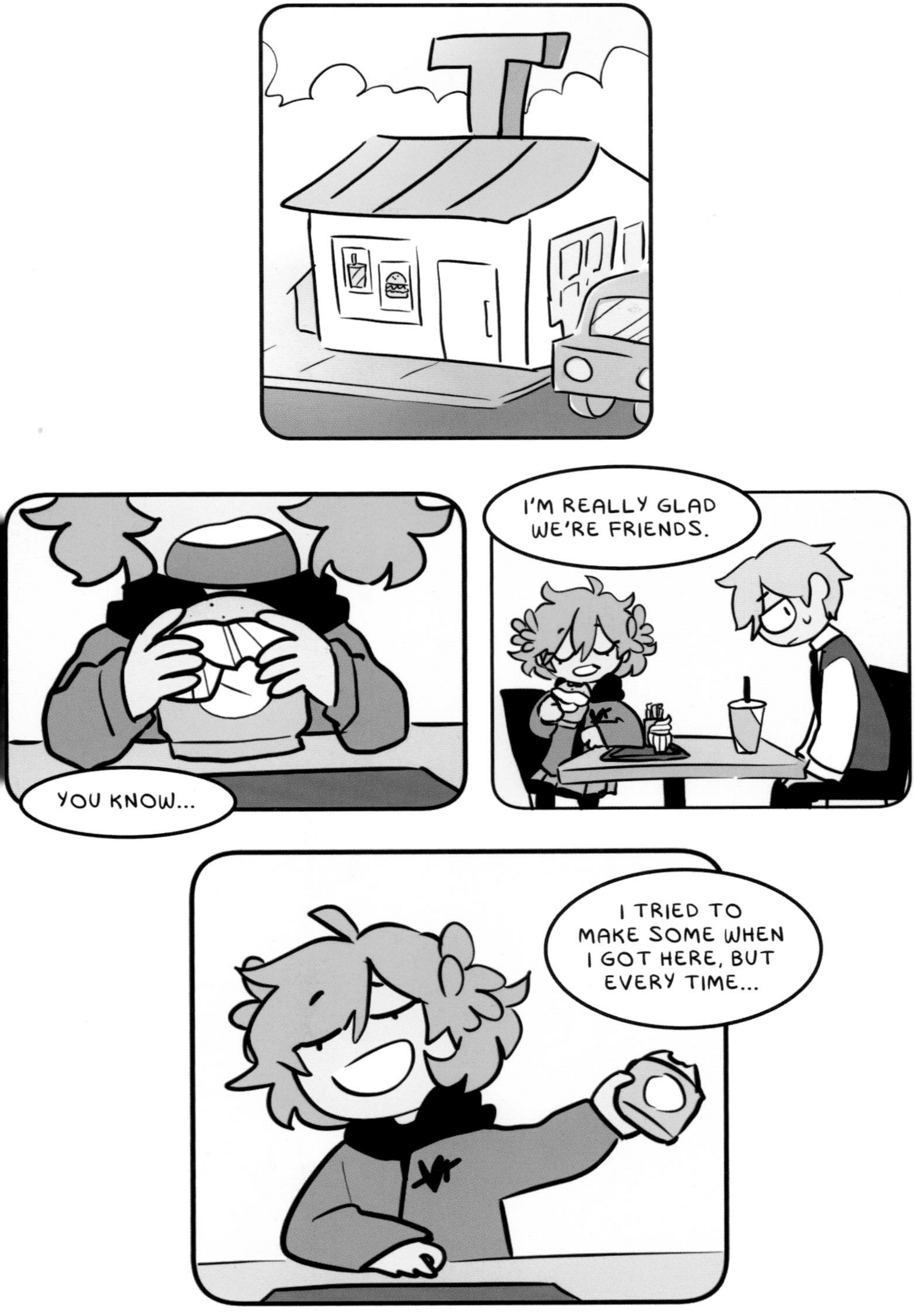
YOU KNOW...
I'M REALLY GLAD WE'RE FRIENDS.
I TRIED TO MAKE SOME WHEN I GOT HERE, BUT EVERY TIME...

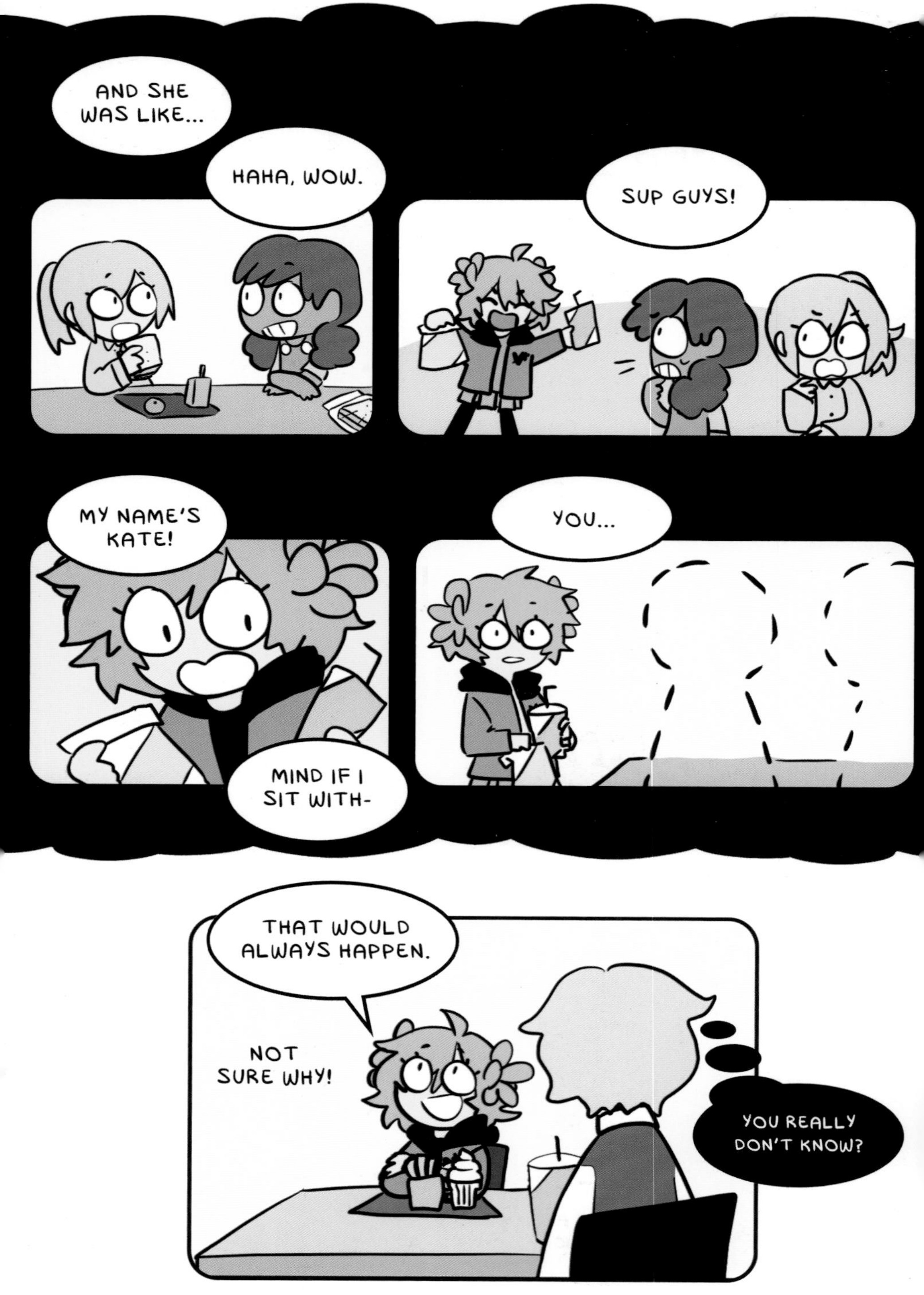
AND SHE WAS LIKE...
HAHA, WOW.
SUP GUYS!
MY NAME'S KATE!
MIND IF I SIT WITH-
YOU...
THAT WOULD ALWAYS HAPPEN.
NOT SURE WHY!
YOU REALLY DON'T KNOW?

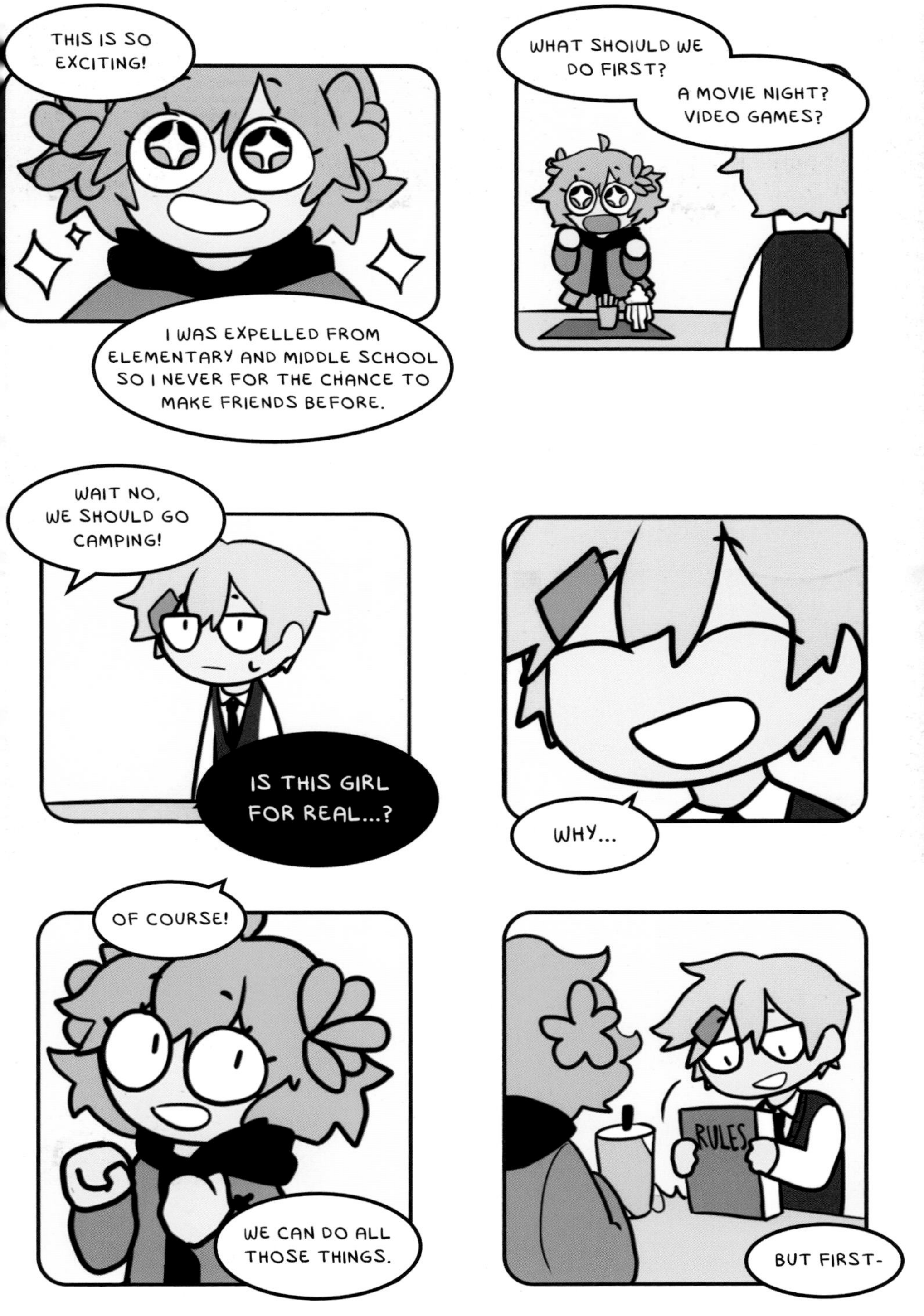
THIS IS SO EXCITING!
I WAS EXPELLED FROM ELEMENTARY AND MIDDLE SCHOOL SO I NEVER FOR THE CHANCE TO MAKE FRIENDS BEFORE.
WHAT SHOIULD WE DO FIRST?
A MOVIE NIGHT? VIDEO GAMES?
WAIT NO, WE SHOULD GO CAMPING!
IS THIS GIRL FOR REAL...?
WHY...
OF COURSE!
WE CAN DO ALL THOSE THINGS.
RULES
BUT FIRST-

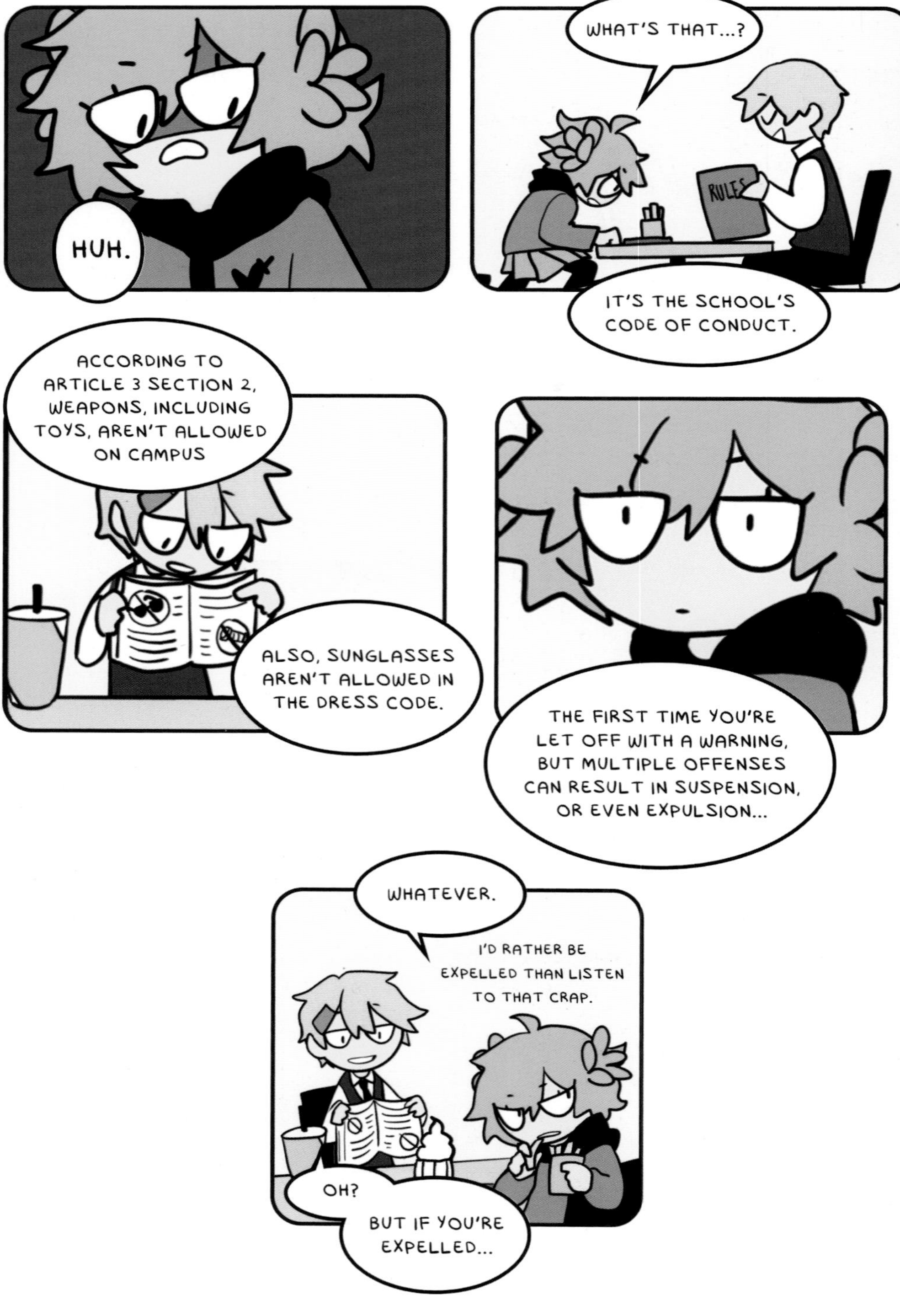
HUH.
WHAT'S THAT...?
RULES
IT'S THE SCHOOL'S CODE OF CONDUCT.
ACCORDING TO ARTICLE 3 SECTION 2, WEAPONS, INCLUDING TOYS, AREN'T ALLOWED ON CAMPUS
ALSO, SUNGLASSES AREN'T ALLOWED IN THE DRESS CODE.
THE FIRST TIME YOU'RE LET OFF WITH A WARNING, BUT MULTIPLE OFFENSES CAN RESULT IN SUSPENSION, OR EVEN EXPULSION...
WHATEVER.
I'D RATHER BE EXPELLED THAN LISTEN TO THAT CRAP.
OH?
BUT IF YOU'RE EXPELLED...

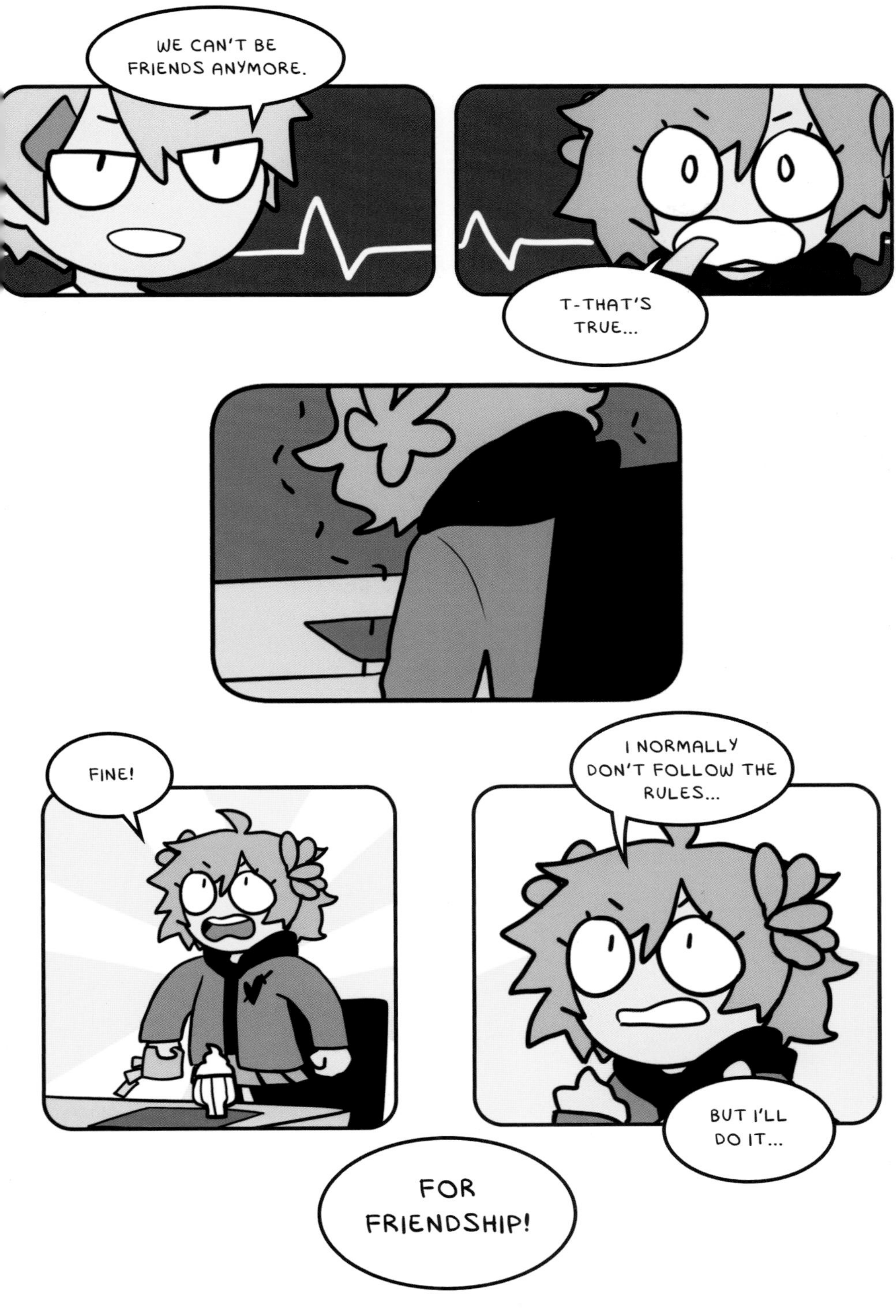
WE CAN'T BE FRIENDS ANYMORE.
T-THAT'S TRUE...
FINE!
I NORMALLY DON'T FOLLOW THE RULES...
BUT I'LL DO IT...
FOR FRIENDSHIP!

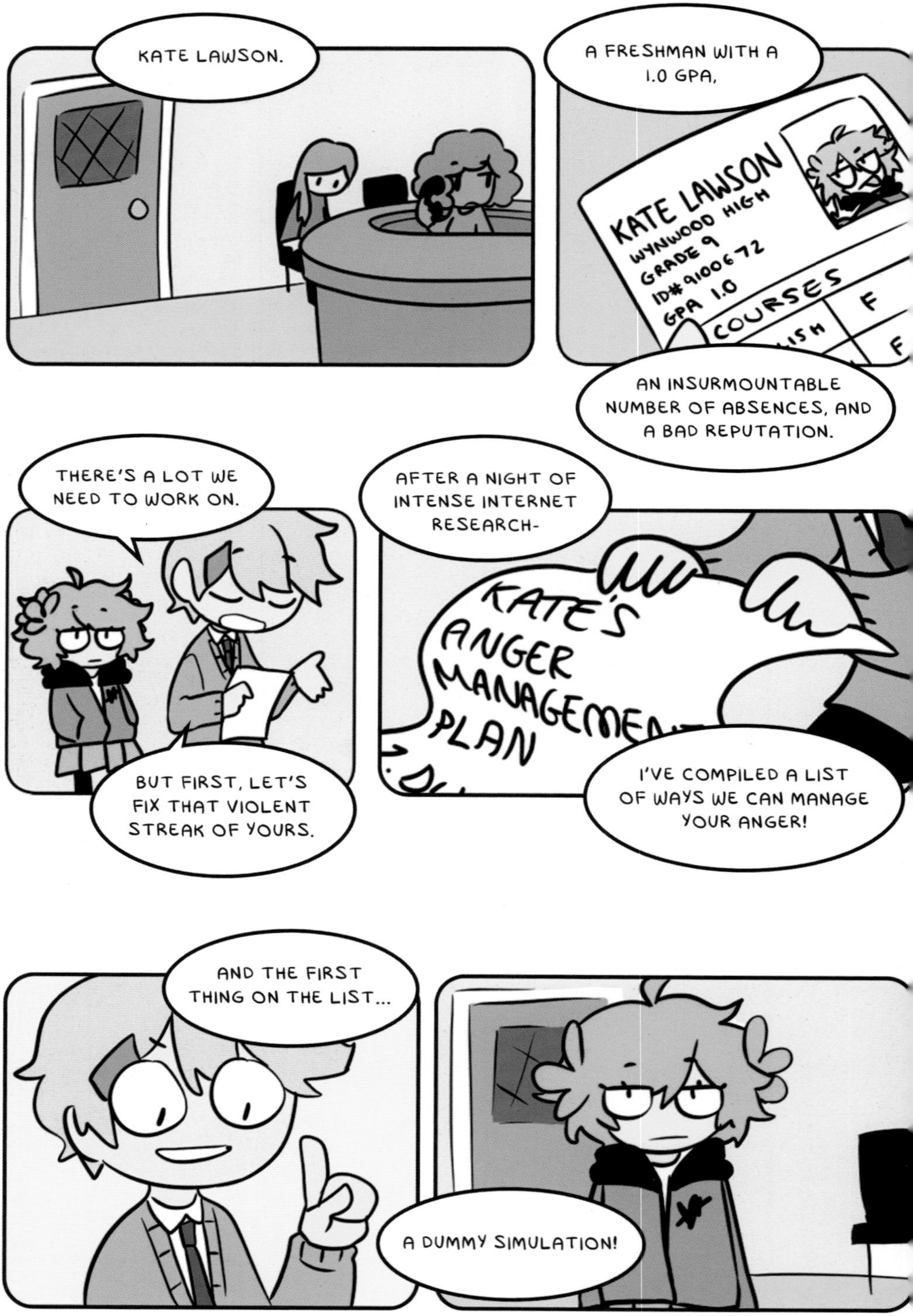
KATE LAWSON.
A FRESHMAN WITH A 1.0 GPA,
KATE LAWSON
WYNWOOD HIGH
GRADE 9
ID# 9100672
GPA 1.0
COURSES
AN INSURMOUNTABLE NUMBER OF ABSENCES, AND A BAD REPUTATION.
THERE'S A LOT WE NEED TO WORK ON.
BUT FIRST, LET'S FIX THAT VIOLENT STREAK OF YOURS.
AFTER A NIGHT OF INTENSE INTERNET RESEARCH-
KATE'S ANGER MANAGEMENT PLAN
I'VE COMPILED A LIST OF WAYS WE CAN MANAGE YOUR ANGER!
AND THE FIRST THING ON THE LIST...
A DUMMY SIMULATION!

OKAY.

THAT'S ALL OF THEM, RIGHT?

NO MORE GADGETS HIDDEN IN YOUR POCKETS OR ANYTHING?

YES...

WONDERFUL!

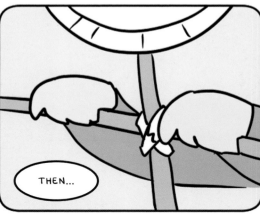

THEN...

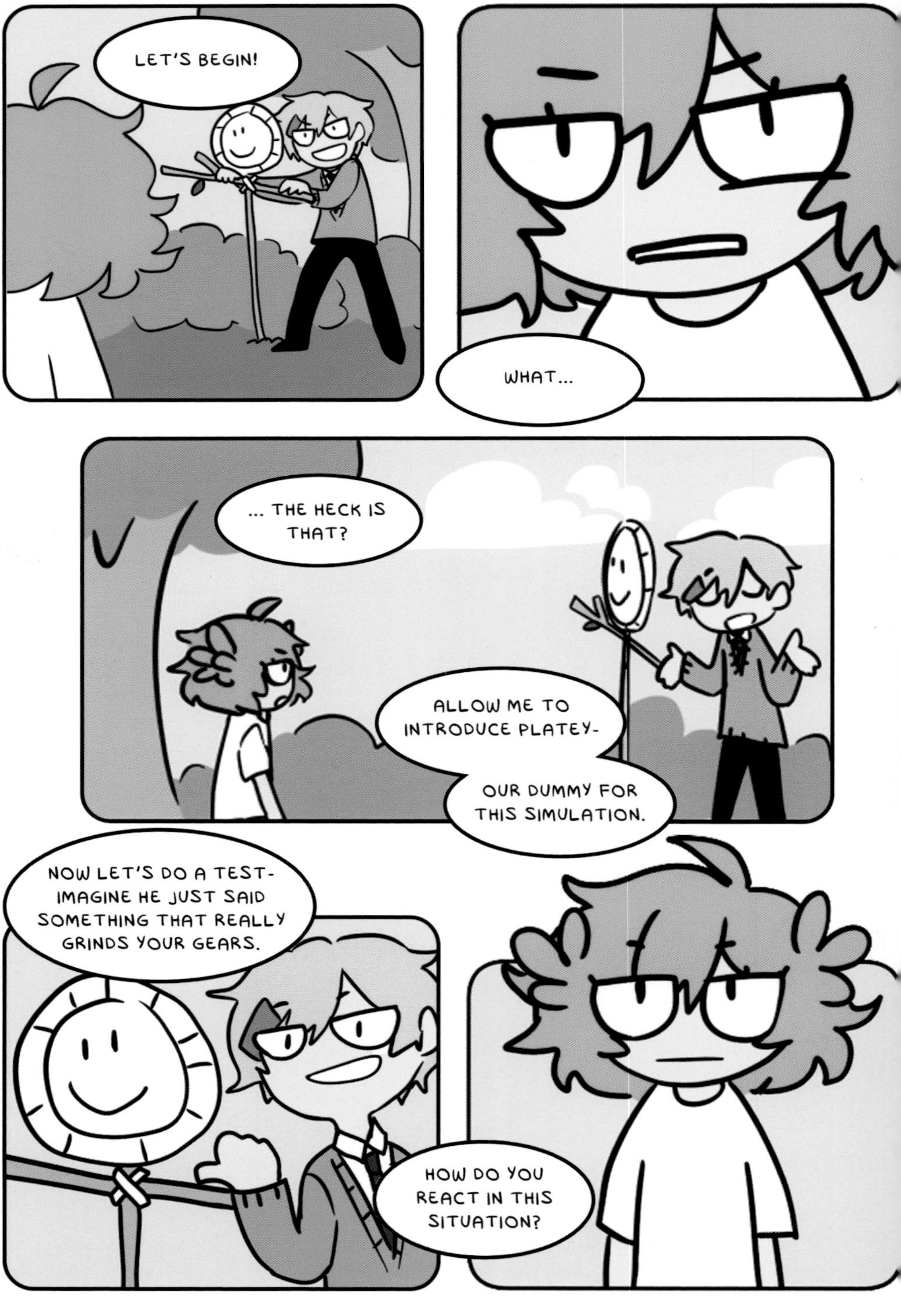
LET'S BEGIN!
WHAT...
... THE HECK IS THAT?
ALLOW ME TO INTRODUCE PLATEY-
OUR DUMMY FOR THIS SIMULATION.
NOW LET'S DO A TEST- IMAGINE HE JUST SAID SOMETHING THAT REALLY GRINDS YOUR GEARS.
HOW DO YOU REACT IN THIS SITUATION?

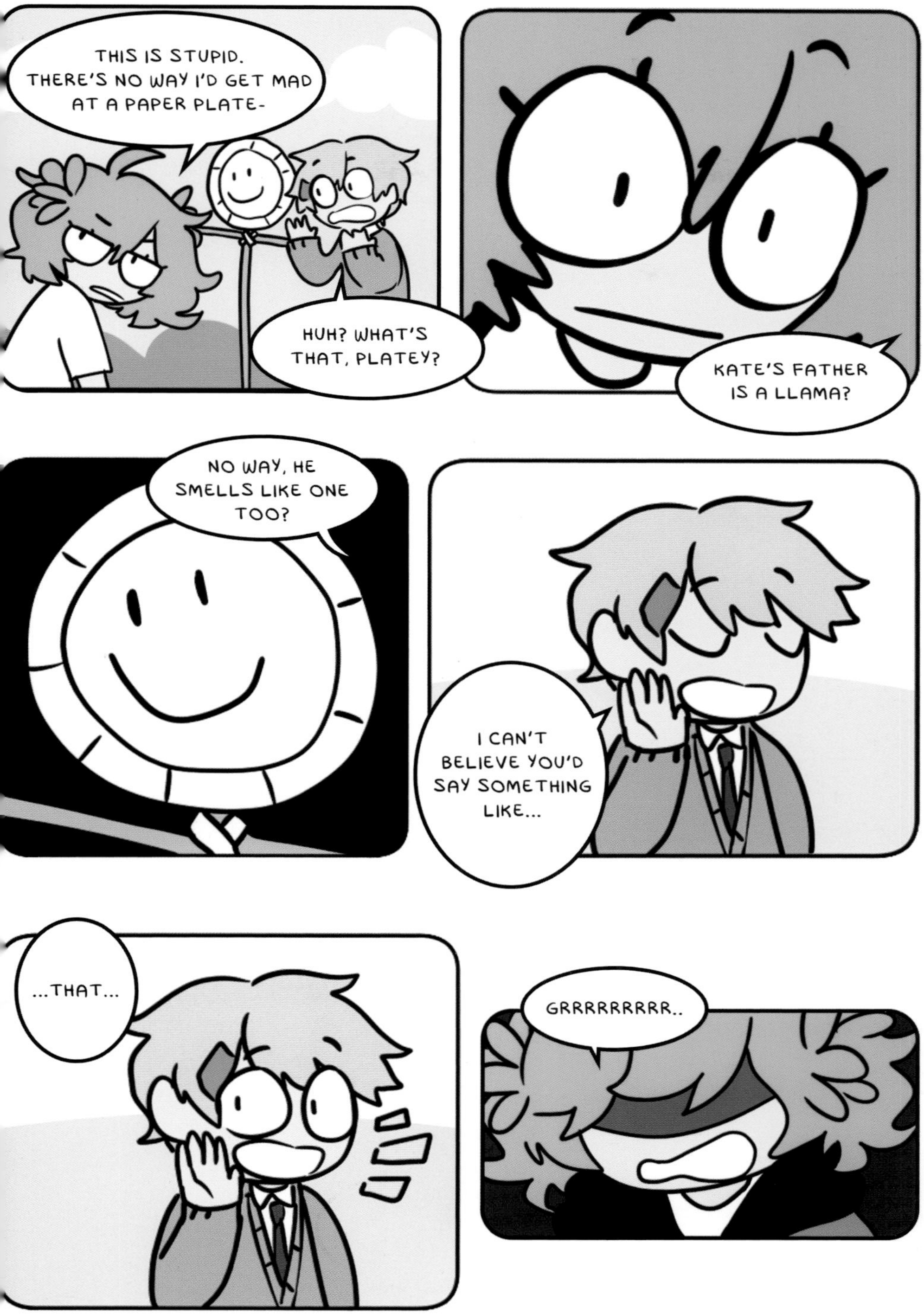
THIS IS STUPID. THERE'S NO WAY I'D GET MAD AT A PAPER PLATE-
HUH? WHAT'S THAT, PLATEY?
KATE'S FATHER IS A LLAMA?
NO WAY, HE SMELLS LIKE ONE TOO?
I CAN'T BELIEVE YOU'D SAY SOMETHING LIKE...
...THAT...
GRRRRRRRRR..

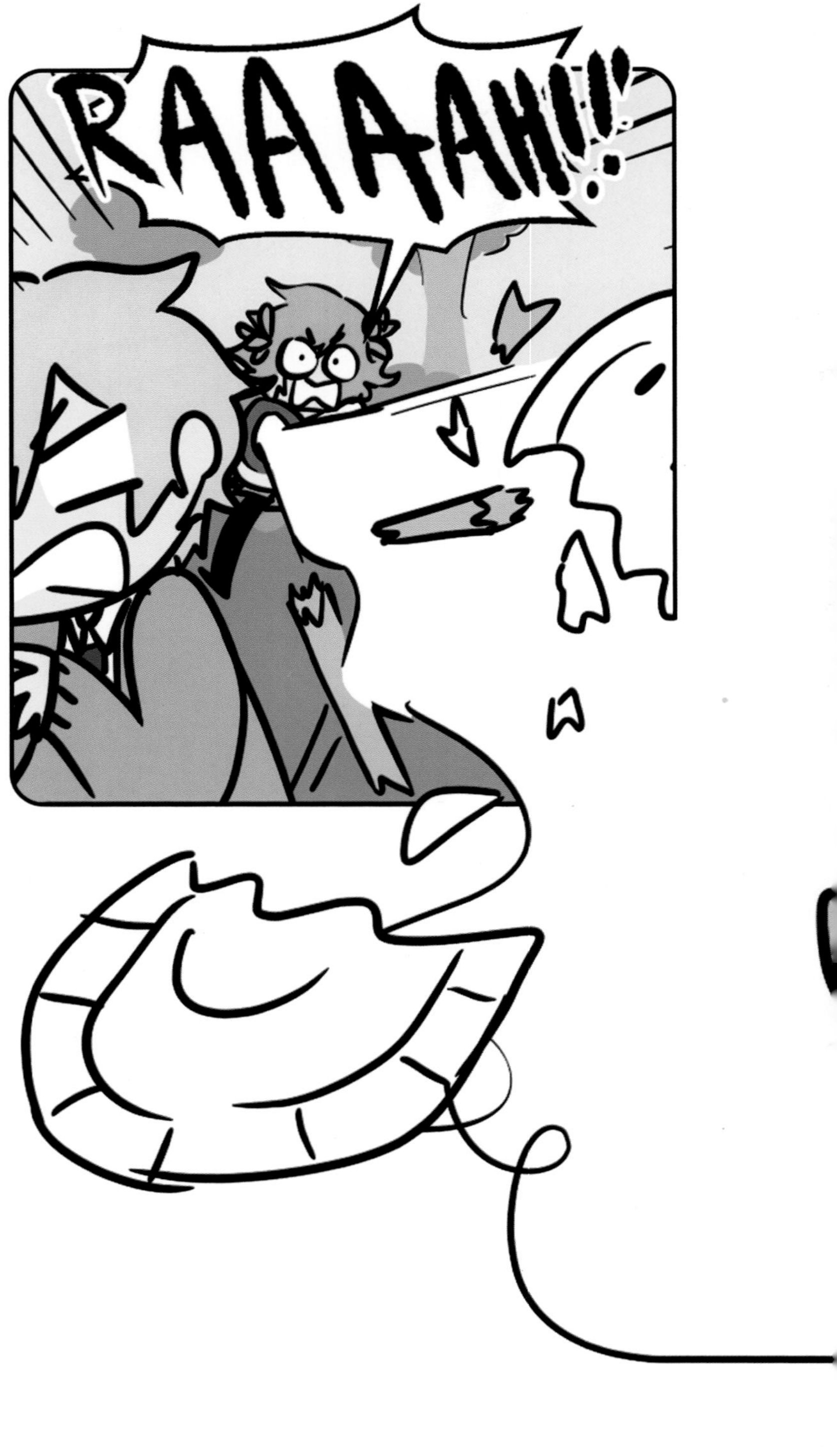
RAAAAH!!!

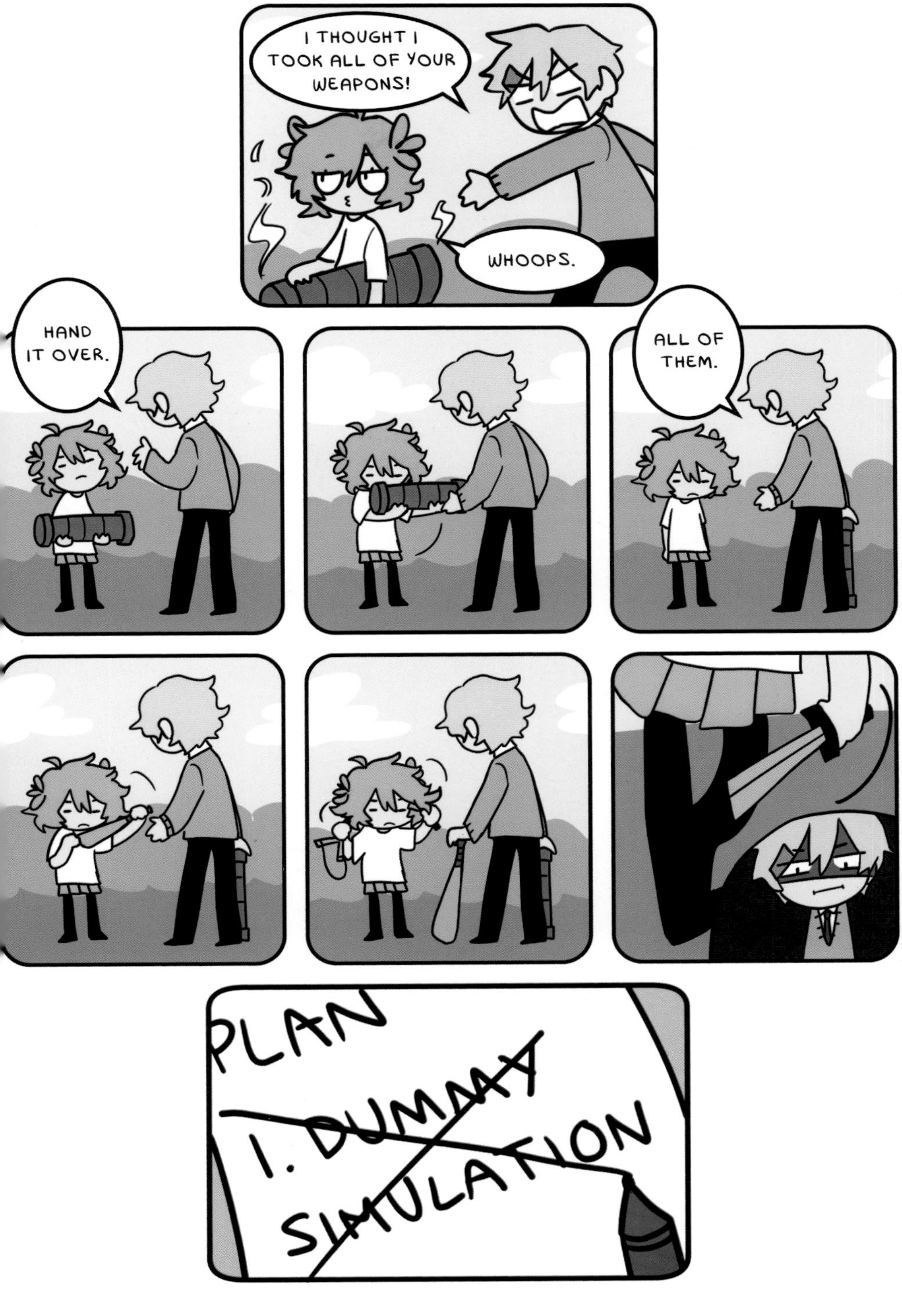
I THOUGHT I TOOK ALL OF YOUR WEAPONS!
WHOOPS.
HAND IT OVER.
ALL OF THEM.
PLAN
1. DUMMY
SIMULATION

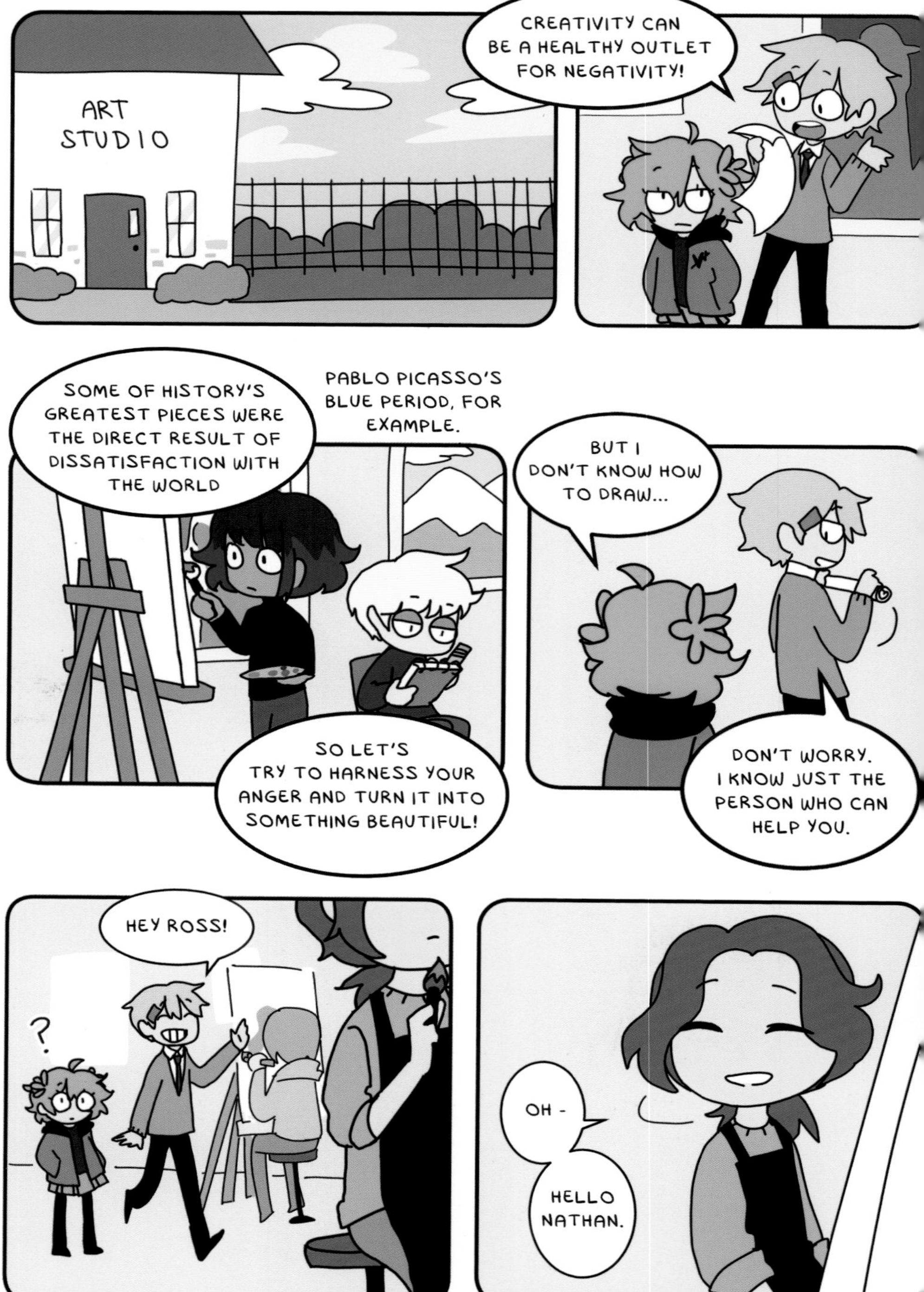
ART STUDIO
CREATIVITY CAN BE A HEALTHY OUTLET FOR NEGATIVITY!
SOME OF HISTORY'S GREATEST PIECES WERE THE DIRECT RESULT OF DISSATISFACTION WITH THE WORLD
PABLO PICASSO'S BLUE PERIOD, FOR EXAMPLE.
SO LET'S TRY TO HARNESS YOUR ANGER AND TURN IT INTO SOMETHING BEAUTIFUL!
BUT I DON'T KNOW HOW TO DRAW...
DON'T WORRY. I KNOW JUST THE PERSON WHO CAN HELP YOU.
HEY ROSS!
?
OH -
HELLO NATHAN.

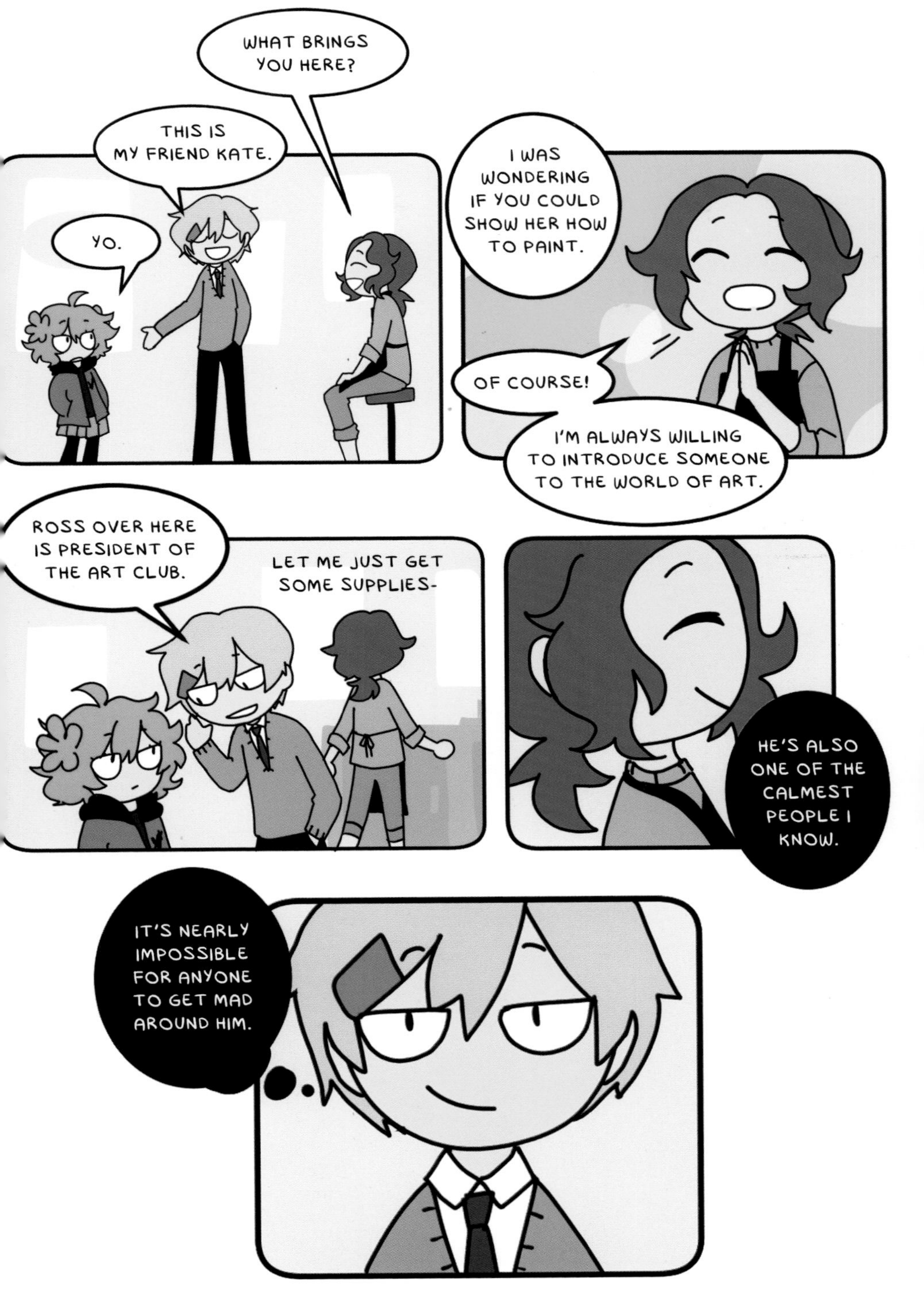
WHAT BRINGS YOU HERE?
THIS IS MY FRIEND KATE.
YO.
I WAS WONDERING IF YOU COULD SHOW HER HOW TO PAINT.
OF COURSE!
I'M ALWAYS WILLING TO INTRODUCE SOMEONE TO THE WORLD OF ART.
ROSS OVER HERE IS PRESIDENT OF THE ART CLUB.
LET ME JUST GET SOME SUPPLIES-
HE'S ALSO ONE OF THE CALMEST PEOPLE I KNOW.
IT'S NEARLY IMPOSSIBLE FOR ANYONE TO GET MAD AROUND HIM.

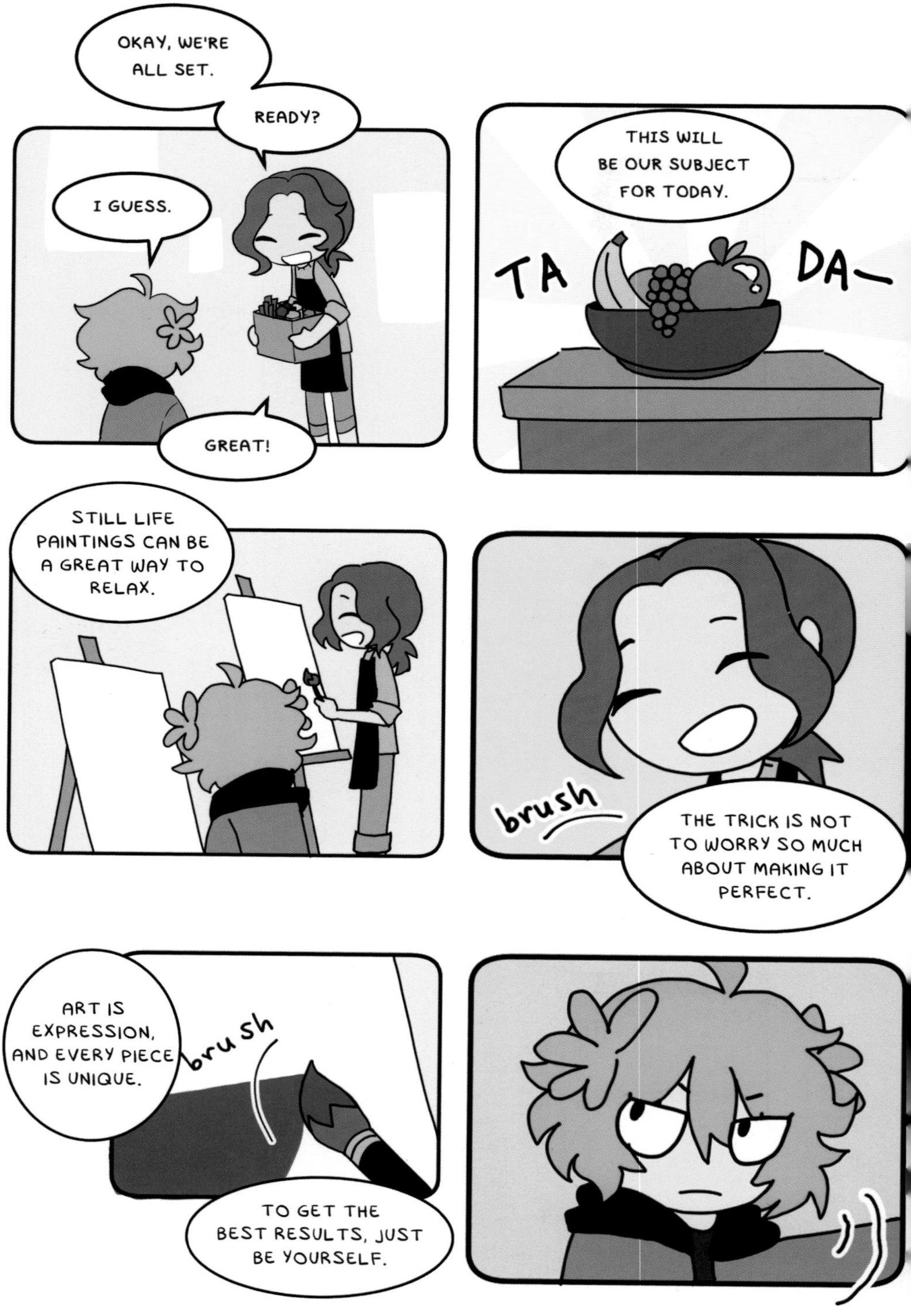

OKAY, WE'RE ALL SET.
READY?
I GUESS.
GREAT!
THIS WILL BE OUR SUBJECT FOR TODAY.
TA
DA—
STILL LIFE PAINTINGS CAN BE A GREAT WAY TO RELAX.
brush
THE TRICK IS NOT TO WORRY SO MUCH ABOUT MAKING IT PERFECT.
ART IS EXPRESSION, AND EVERY PIECE IS UNIQUE.
brush
TO GET THE BEST RESULTS, JUST BE YOURSELF.

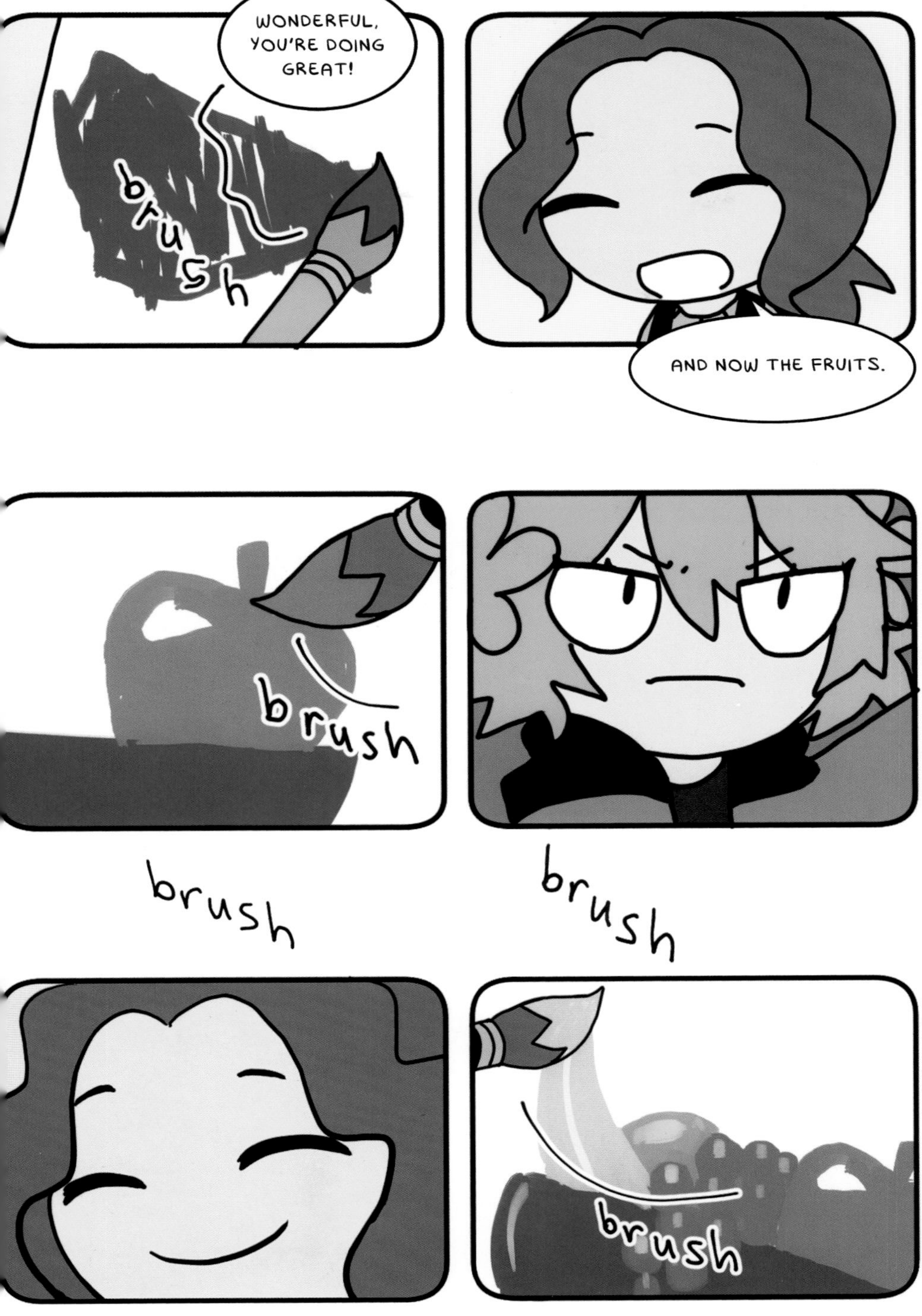
WONDERFUL, YOU'RE DOING GREAT!
brush
AND NOW THE FRUITS.
brush
brush
brush
brush

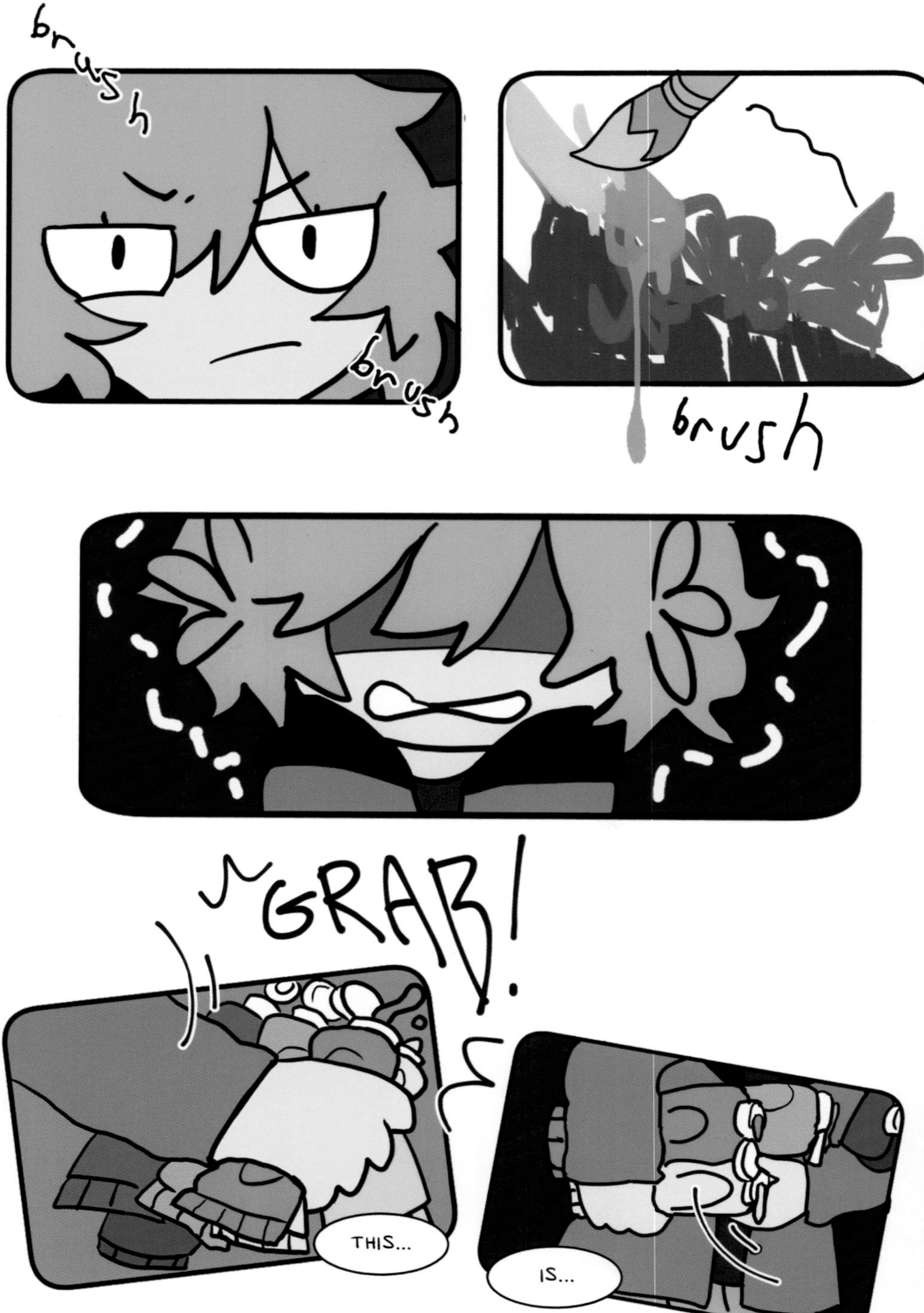
brush
brush
brush
GRAB!
THIS...
IS...

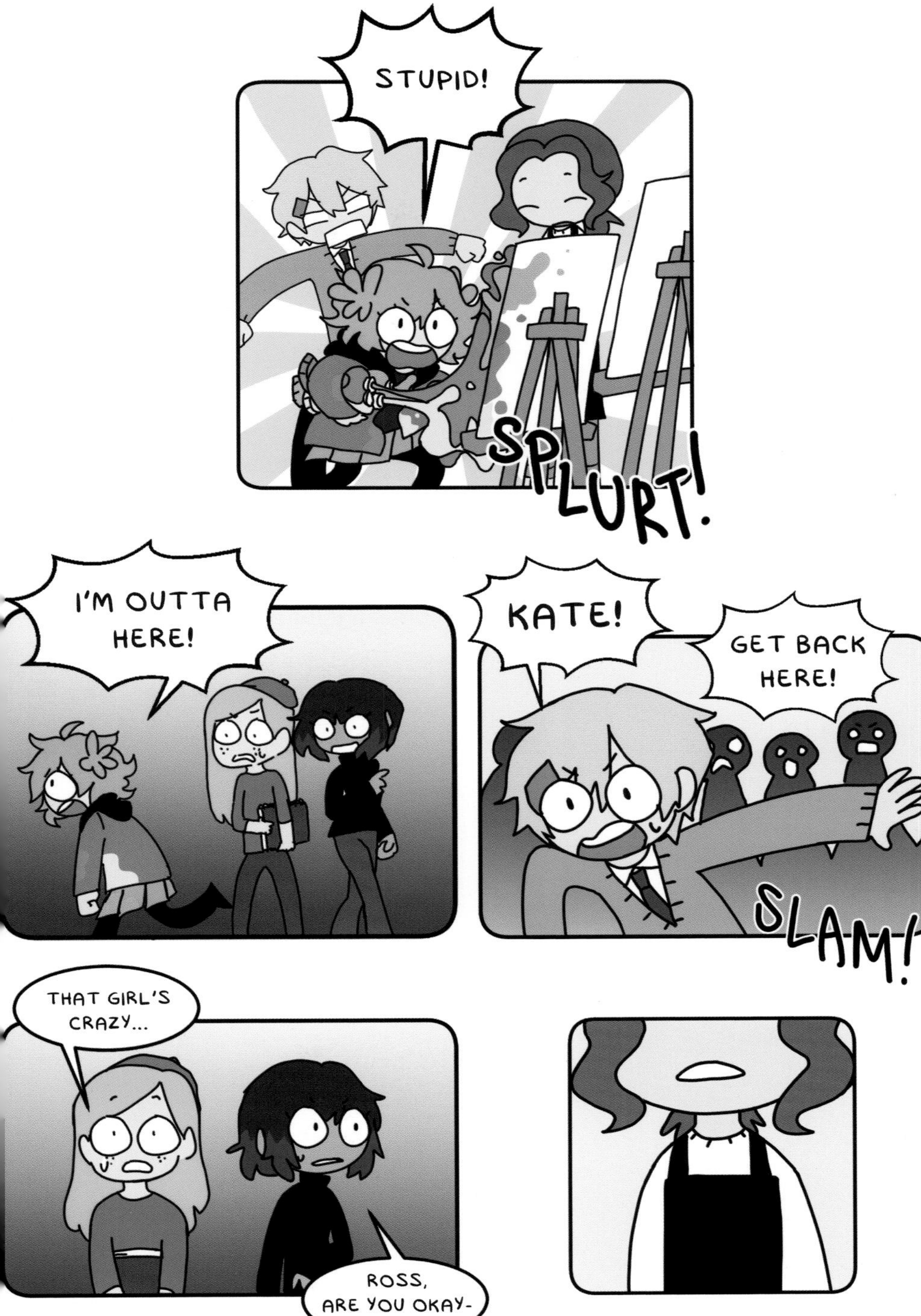
STUPID!
SPLURT!
I'M OUTTA HERE!
KATE!
GET BACK HERE!
SLAM!
THAT GIRL'S CRAZY...
ROSS, ARE YOU OKAY-

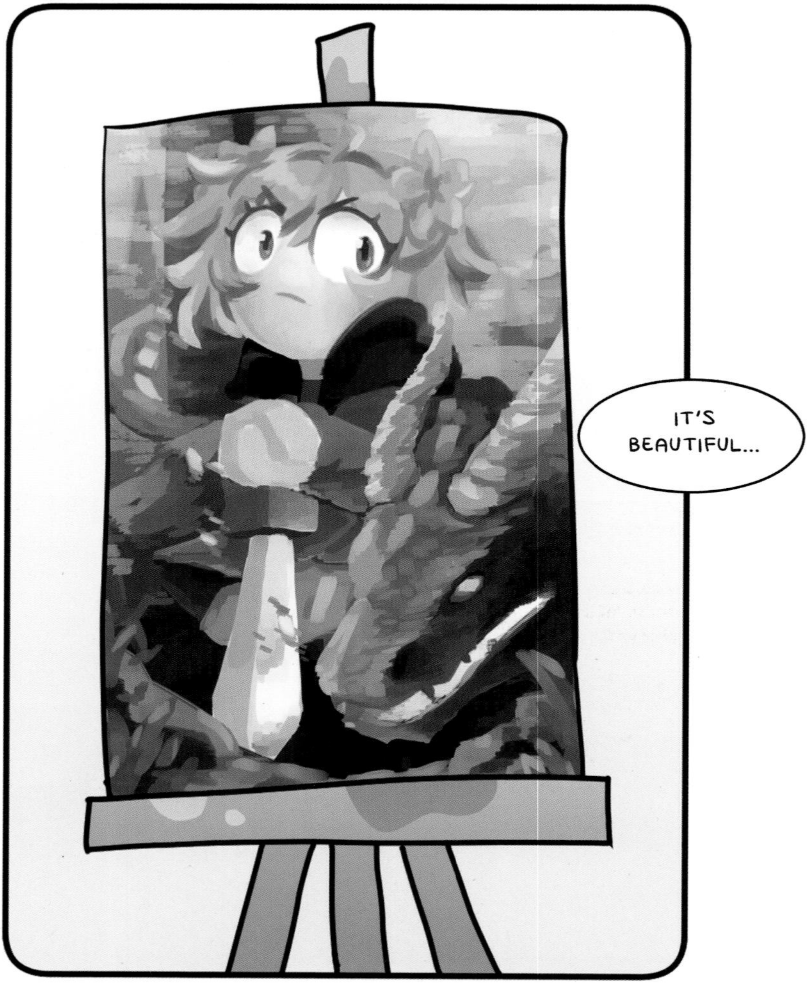
IT'S
BEAUTIFUL...
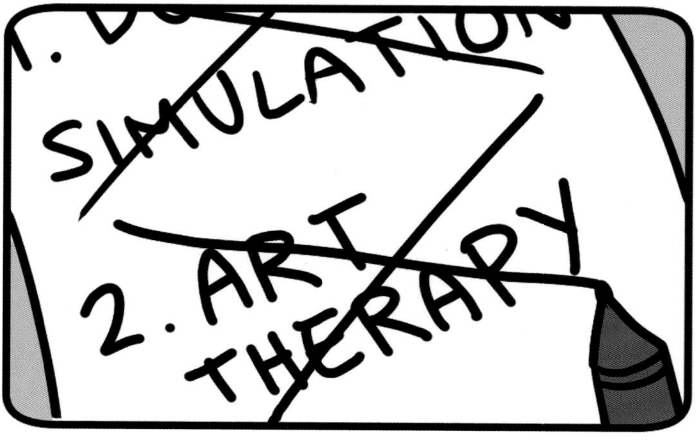
SIMULATION
2. ART THERAPY

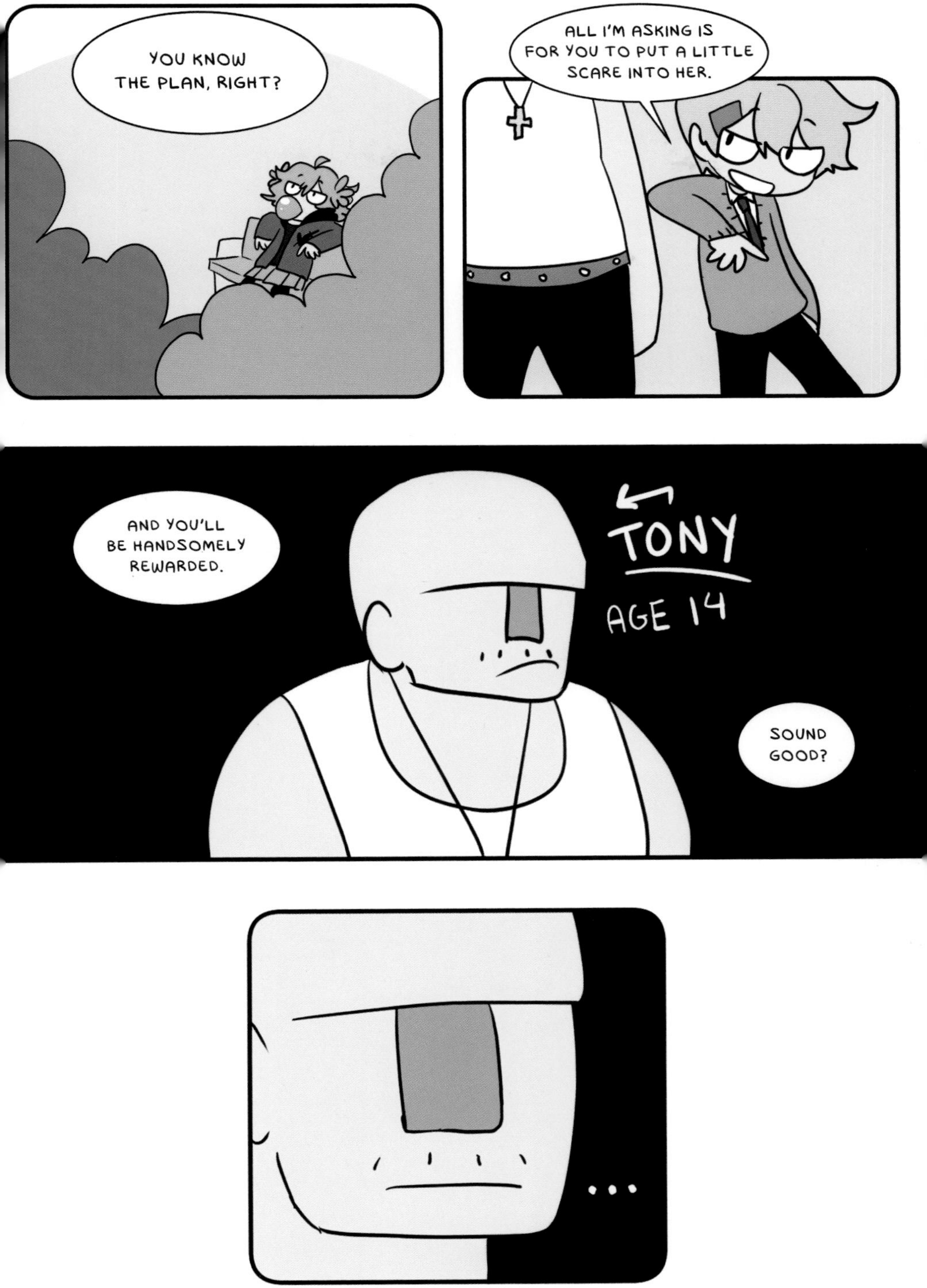
YOU KNOW THE PLAN, RIGHT?
ALL I'M ASKING IS FOR YOU TO PUT A LITTLE SCARE INTO HER.
AND YOU'LL BE HANDSOMELY REWARDED.
TONY
AGE 14
SOUND GOOD?
...

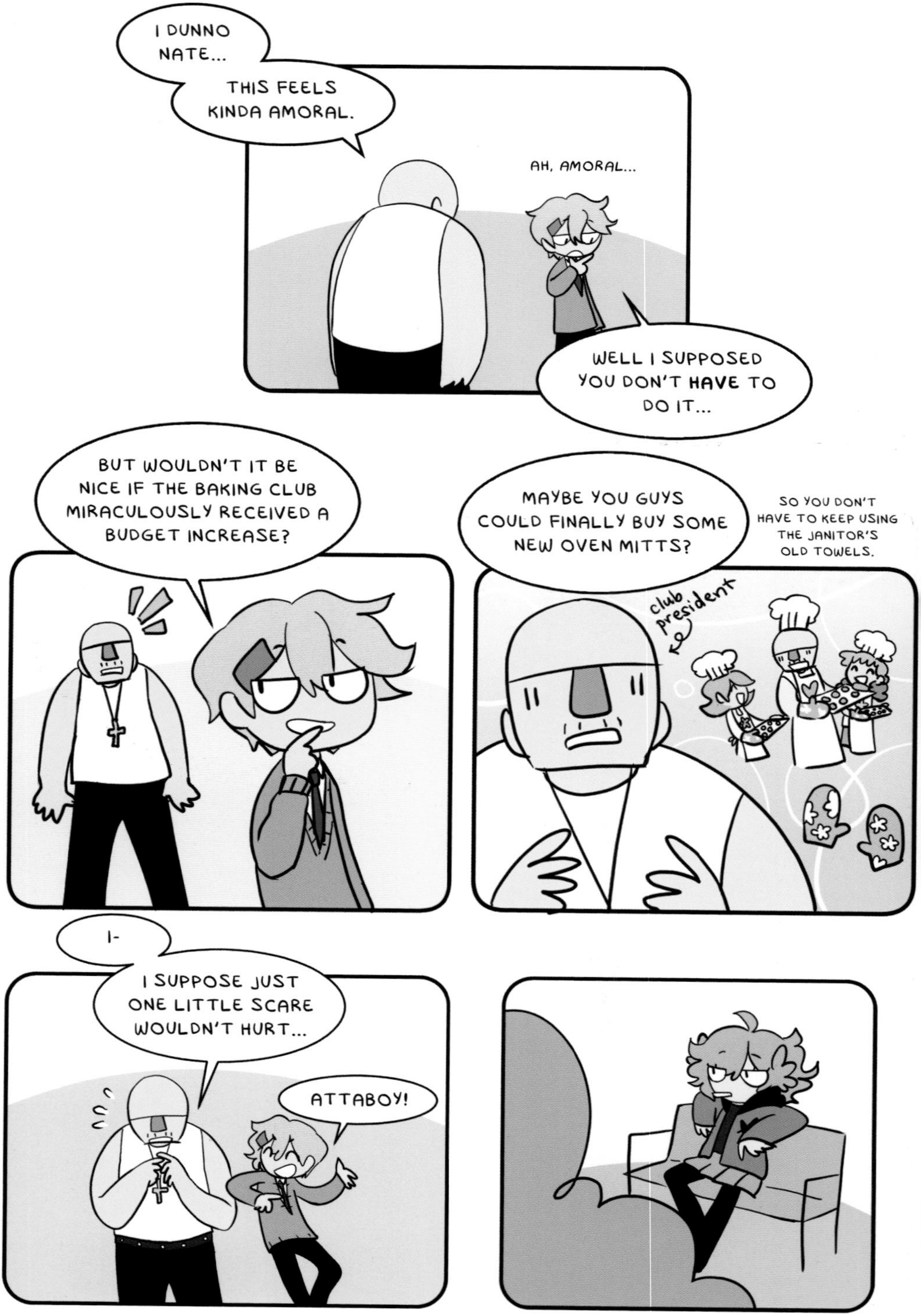
I DUNNO NATE...
THIS FEELS KINDA AMORAL.
AH, AMORAL...
WELL I SUPPOSED YOU DON'T **HAVE** TO DO IT...
BUT WOULDN'T IT BE NICE IF THE BAKING CLUB MIRACULOUSLY RECEIVED A BUDGET INCREASE?
MAYBE YOU GUYS COULD FINALLY BUY SOME NEW OVEN MITTS?
SO YOU DON'T HAVE TO KEEP USING THE JANITOR'S OLD TOWELS.
club president
I-
I SUPPOSE JUST ONE LITTLE SCARE WOULDN'T HURT...
ATTABOY!

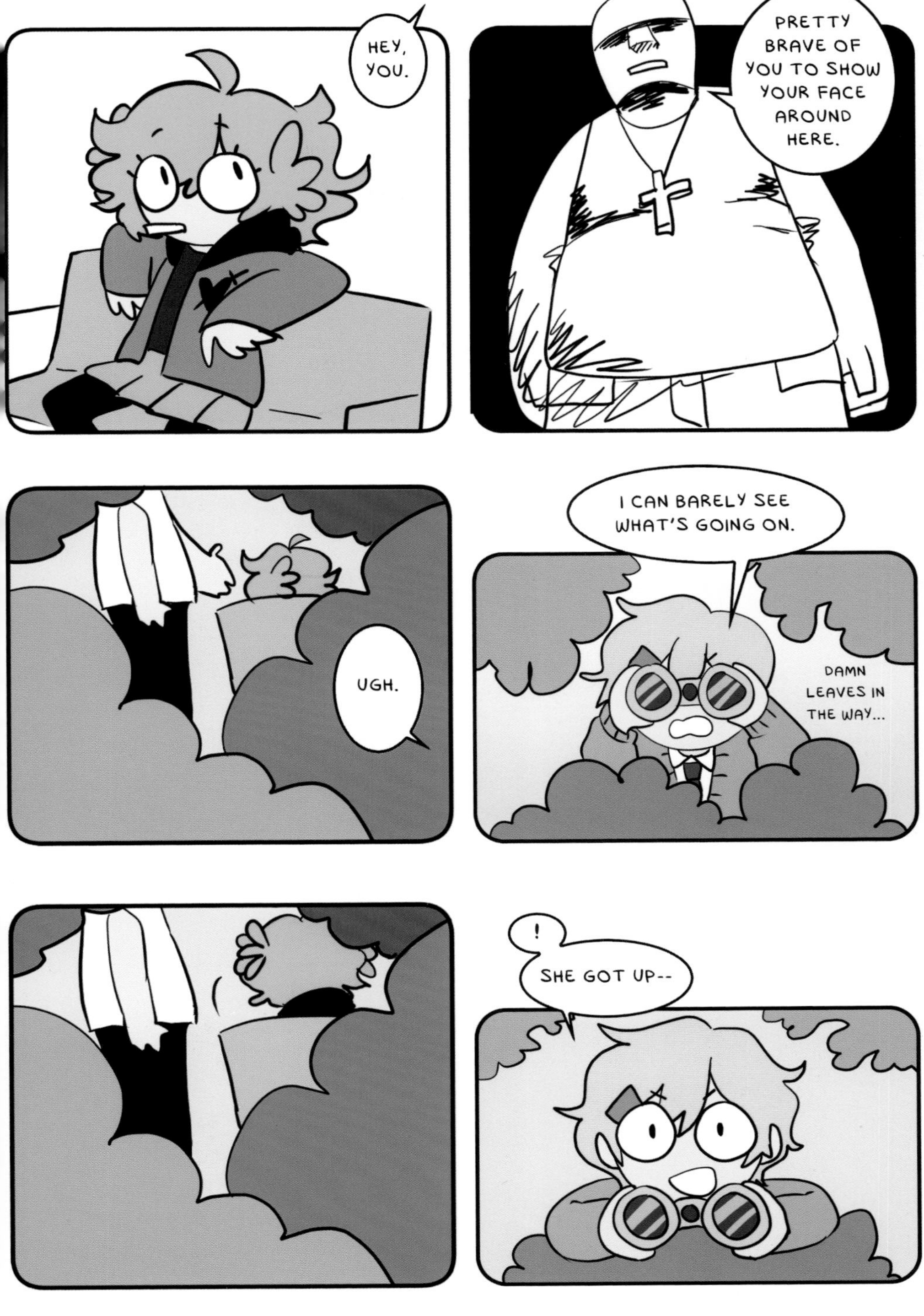
HEY, YOU.
PRETTY BRAVE OF YOU TO SHOW YOUR FACE AROUND HERE.
UGH.
I CAN BARELY SEE WHAT'S GOING ON.
DAMN LEAVES IN THE WAY...
!
SHE GOT UP--

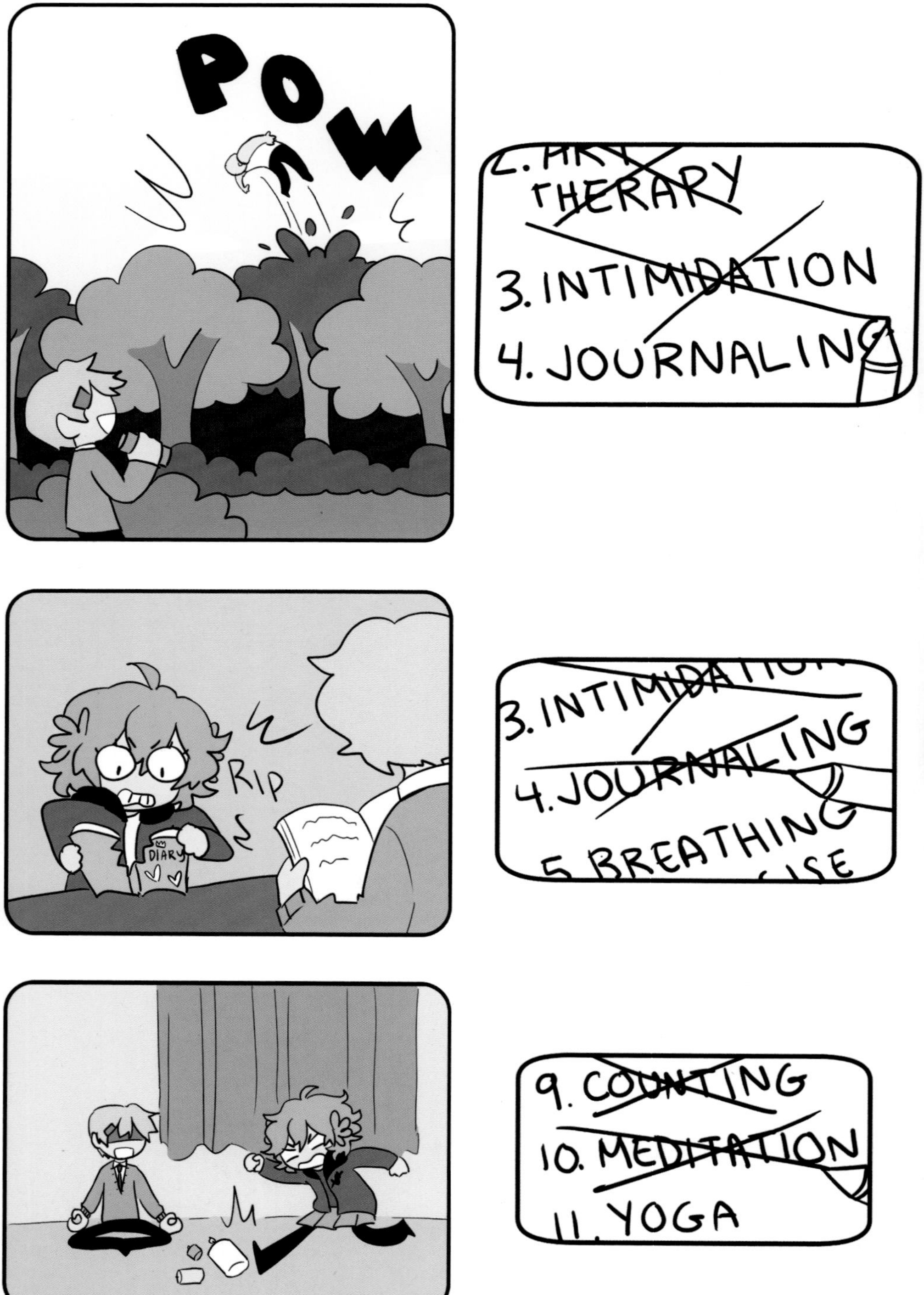
POW
THERAPY
3. INTIMIDATION
4. JOURNALING
Rip
DIARY
3. INTIMI
4. JOURNALING
5. BREATHING
9. COUNTING
10. MEDITATION
11. YOGA

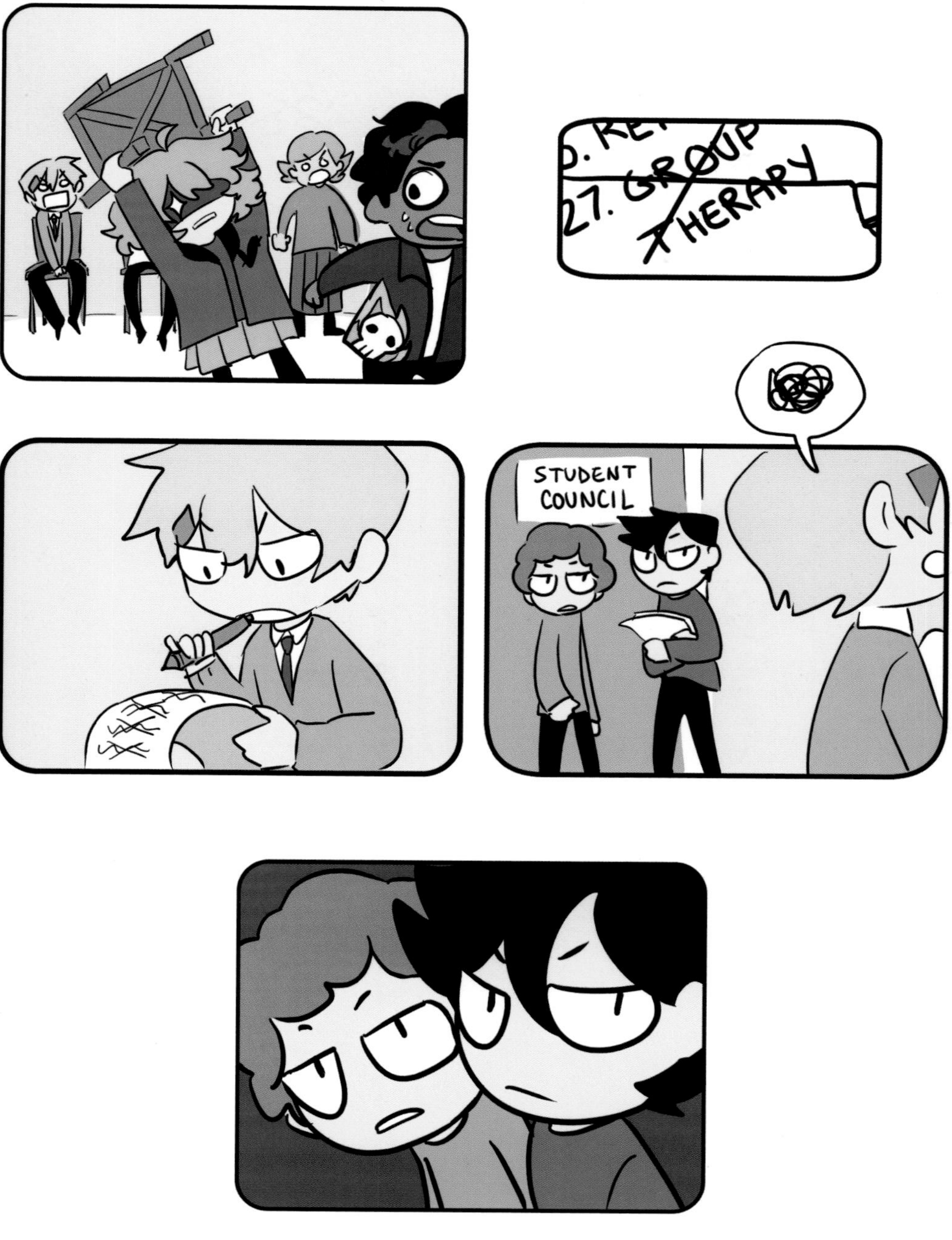
27. GROUP THERAPY
STUDENT COUNCIL

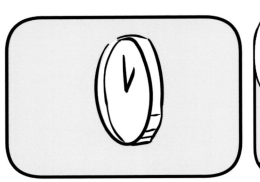

THAT CONCLUDES TODAY'S COUNCIL MEETING!

THANKS FOR COMING!

shuffle

glance

. . . .

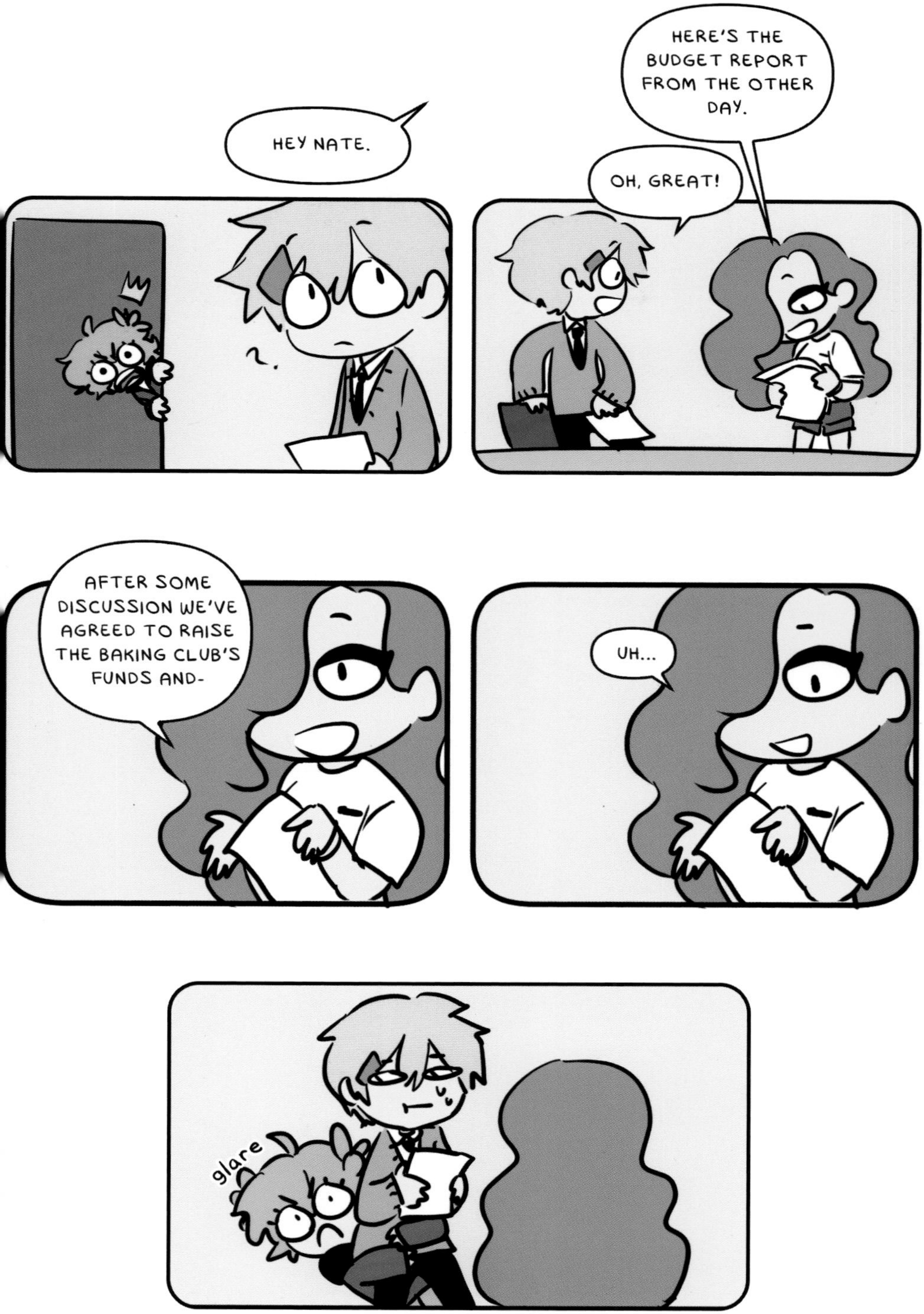
HEY NATE.
HERE'S THE BUDGET REPORT FROM THE OTHER DAY.
OH, GREAT!
AFTER SOME DISCUSSION WE'VE AGREED TO RAISE THE BAKING CLUB'S FUNDS AND-
UH...
glare

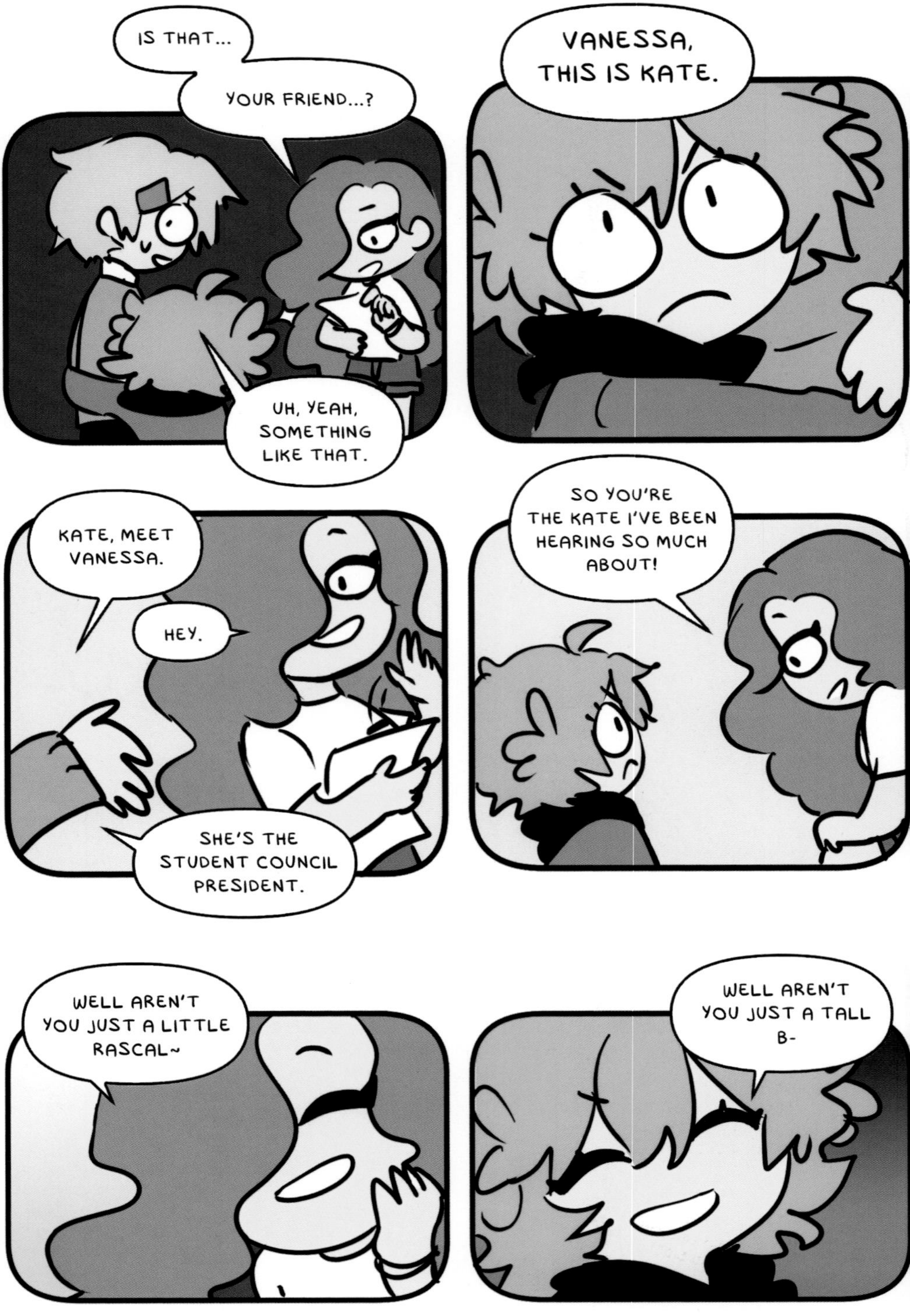
IS THAT...
YOUR FRIEND...?
UH, YEAH, SOMETHING LIKE THAT.
VANESSA, THIS IS KATE.
KATE, MEET VANESSA.
HEY.
SHE'S THE STUDENT COUNCIL PRESIDENT.
SO YOU'RE THE KATE I'VE BEEN HEARING SO MUCH ABOUT!
WELL AREN'T YOU JUST A LITTLE RASCAL~
WELL AREN'T YOU JUST A TALL B-

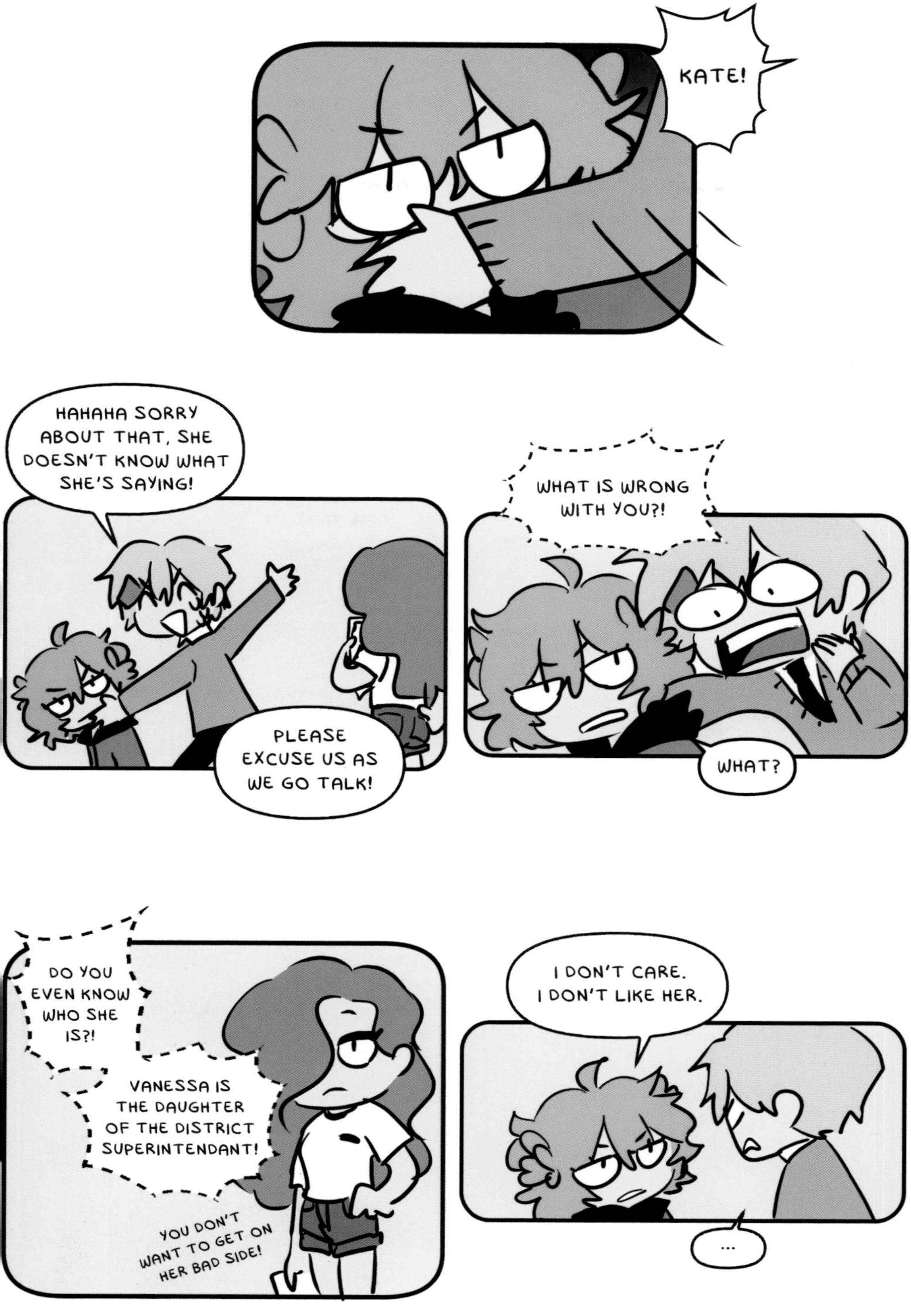
KATE!
HAHAHA SORRY ABOUT THAT, SHE DOESN'T KNOW WHAT SHE'S SAYING!
PLEASE EXCUSE US AS WE GO TALK!
WHAT IS WRONG WITH YOU?!
WHAT?
DO YOU EVEN KNOW WHO SHE IS?!
VANESSA IS THE DAUGHTER OF THE DISTRICT SUPERINTENDANT!
YOU DON'T WANT TO GET ON HER BAD SIDE!
I DON'T CARE. I DON'T LIKE HER.
...

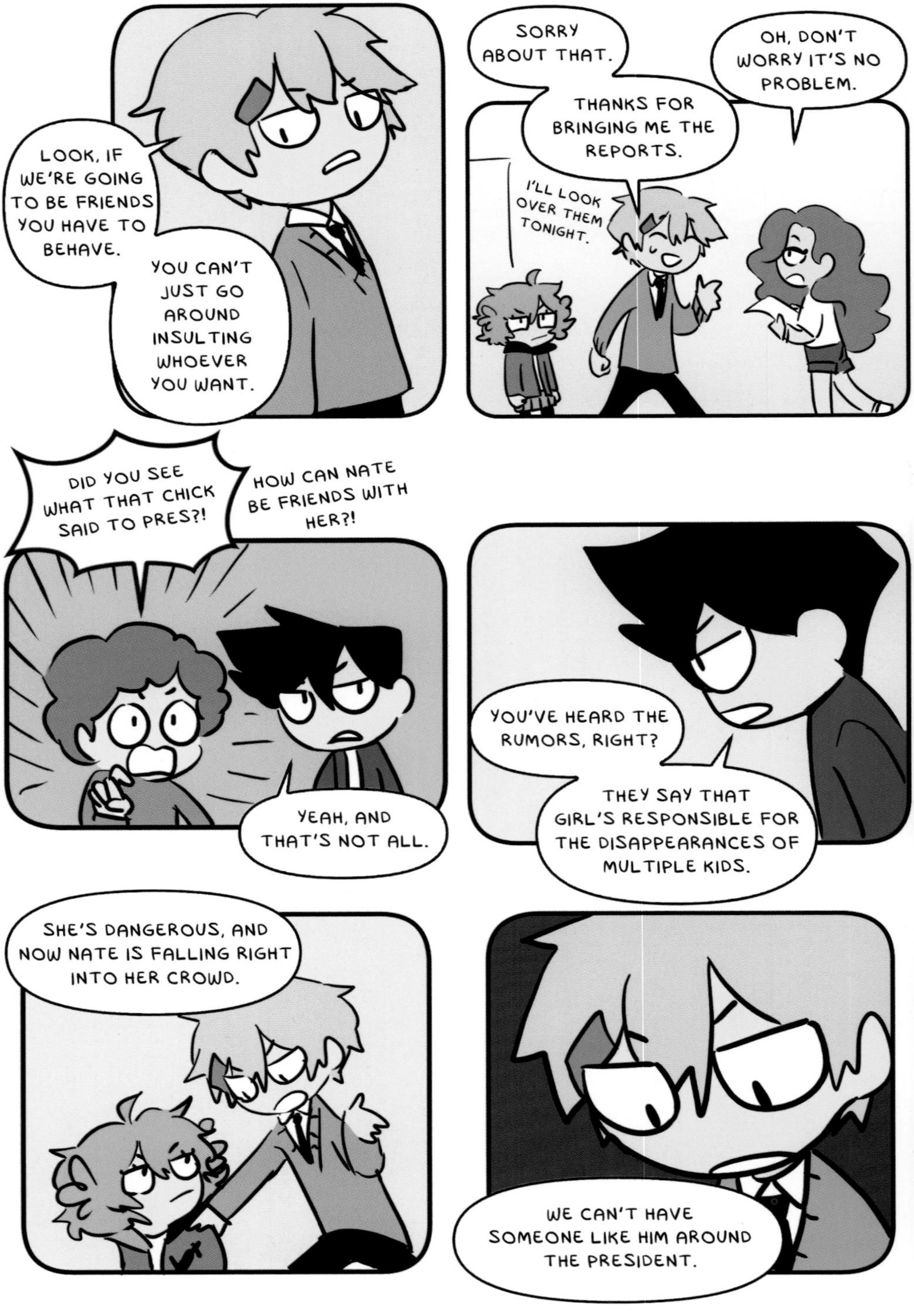
LOOK, IF WE'RE GOING TO BE FRIENDS YOU HAVE TO BEHAVE.
YOU CAN'T JUST GO AROUND INSULTING WHOEVER YOU WANT.
SORRY ABOUT THAT.
THANKS FOR BRINGING ME THE REPORTS.
I'LL LOOK OVER THEM TONIGHT.
OH, DON'T WORRY IT'S NO PROBLEM.
DID YOU SEE WHAT THAT CHICK SAID TO PRES?!
HOW CAN NATE BE FRIENDS WITH HER?!
YEAH, AND THAT'S NOT ALL.
YOU'VE HEARD THE RUMORS, RIGHT?
THEY SAY THAT GIRL'S RESPONSIBLE FOR THE DISAPPEARANCES OF MULTIPLE KIDS.
SHE'S DANGEROUS, AND NOW NATE IS FALLING RIGHT INTO HER CROWD.
WE CAN'T HAVE SOMEONE LIKE HIM AROUND THE PRESIDENT.

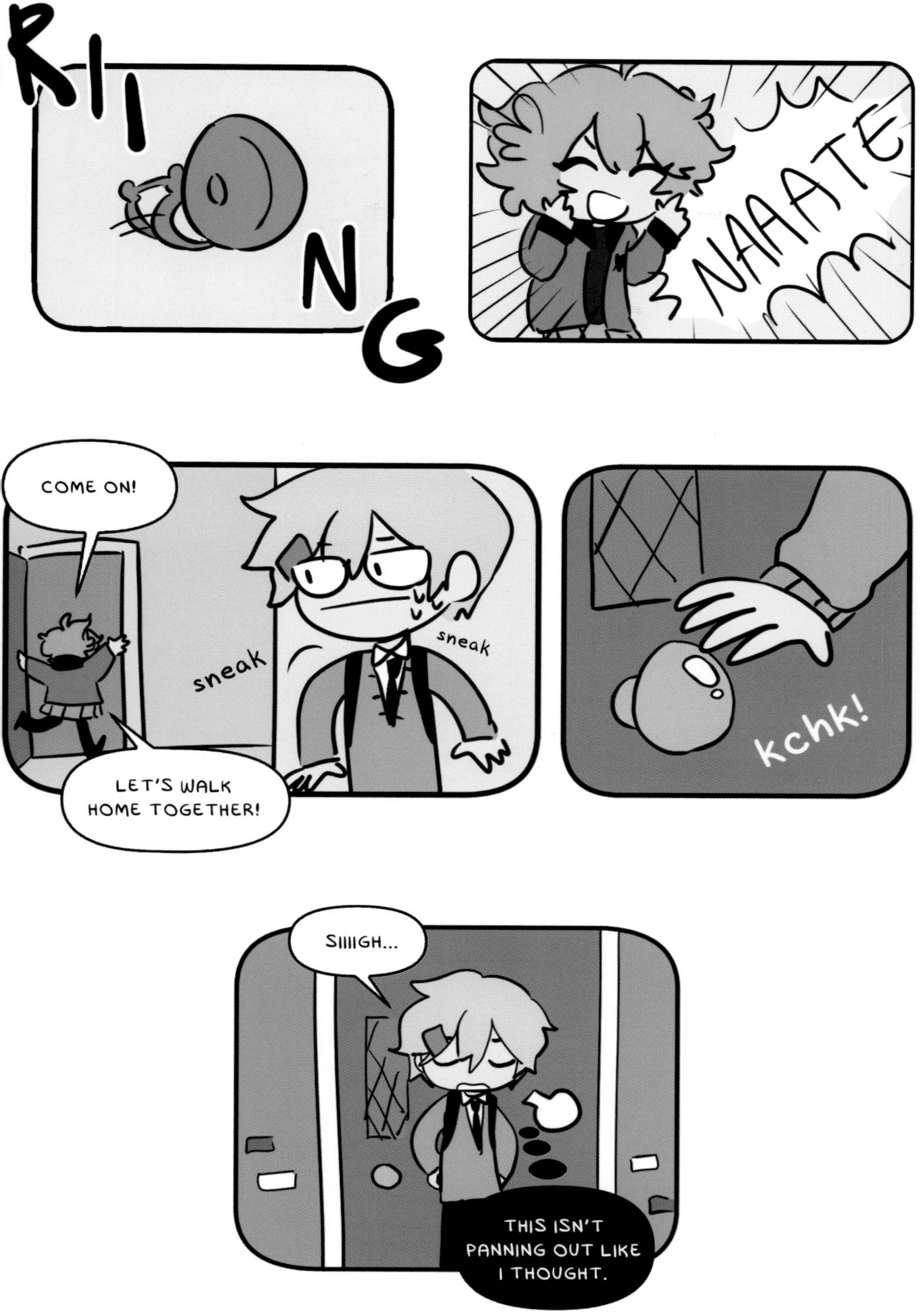
RIING
NAAATE
COME ON!
LET'S WALK HOME TOGETHER!
sneak
sneak
kchk!
SIIIGH...
THIS ISN'T PANNING OUT LIKE I THOUGHT.

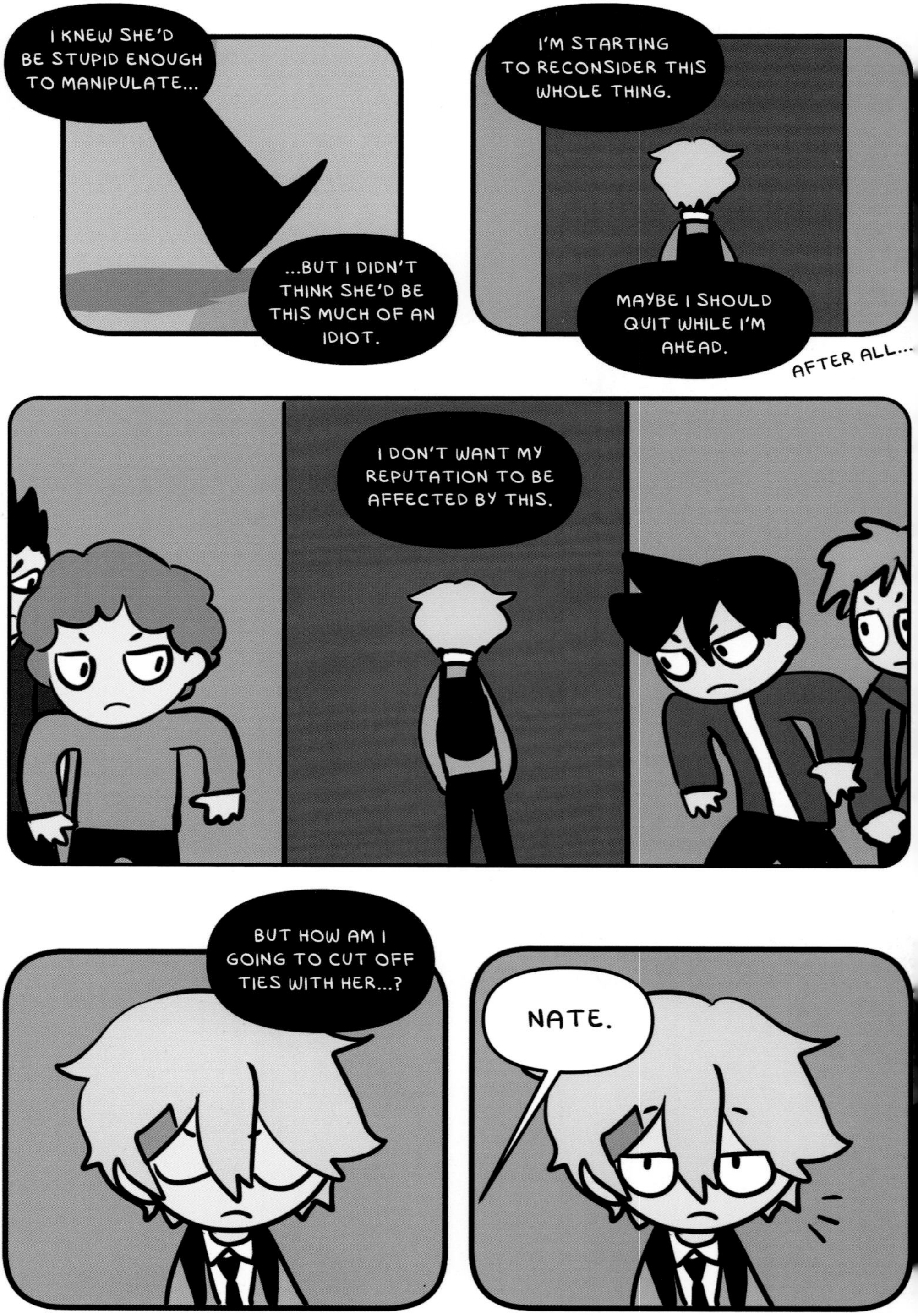
I KNEW SHE'D BE STUPID ENOUGH TO MANIPULATE...
...BUT I DIDN'T THINK SHE'D BE THIS MUCH OF AN IDIOT.
I'M STARTING TO RECONSIDER THIS WHOLE THING.
MAYBE I SHOULD QUIT WHILE I'M AHEAD.
AFTER ALL...
I DON'T WANT MY REPUTATION TO BE AFFECTED BY THIS.
BUT HOW AM I GOING TO CUT OFF TIES WITH HER...?
NATE.

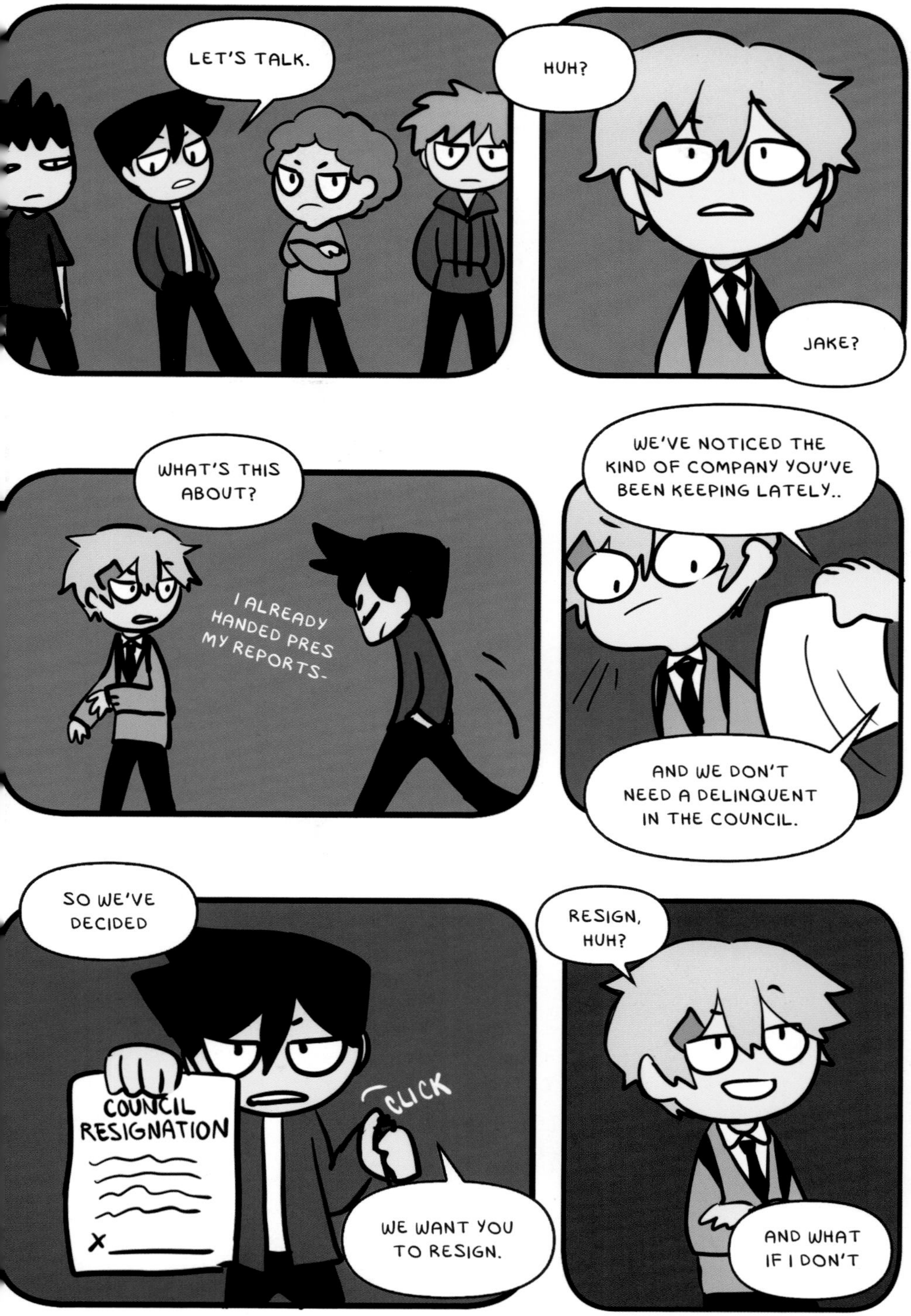
LET'S TALK.
HUH?
JAKE?
WHAT'S THIS ABOUT?
I ALREADY HANDED PRES MY REPORTS-
WE'VE NOTICED THE KIND OF COMPANY YOU'VE BEEN KEEPING LATELY..
AND WE DON'T NEED A DELINQUENT IN THE COUNCIL.
SO WE'VE DECIDED
COUNCIL RESIGNATION
X
CLICK
WE WANT YOU TO RESIGN.
RESIGN, HUH?
AND WHAT IF I DON'T

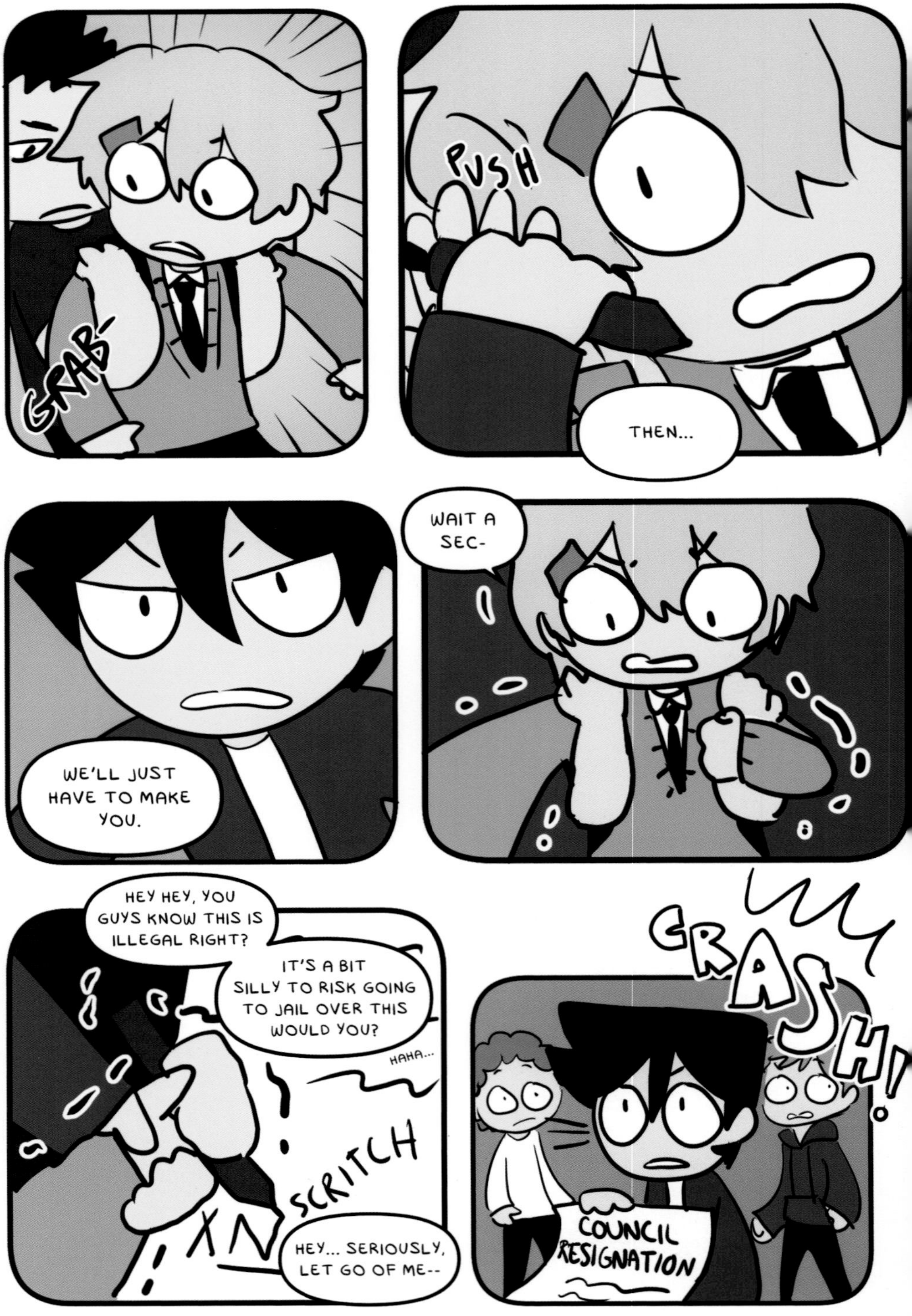
GRAB
PUSH
THEN...
WE'LL JUST HAVE TO MAKE YOU.
WAIT A SEC-
HEY HEY, YOU GUYS KNOW THIS IS ILLEGAL RIGHT?
IT'S A BIT SILLY TO RISK GOING TO JAIL OVER THIS WOULD YOU?
HAHA...
SCRITCH
HEY... SERIOUSLY, LET GO OF ME--
CRASH!
COUNCIL RESIGNATION

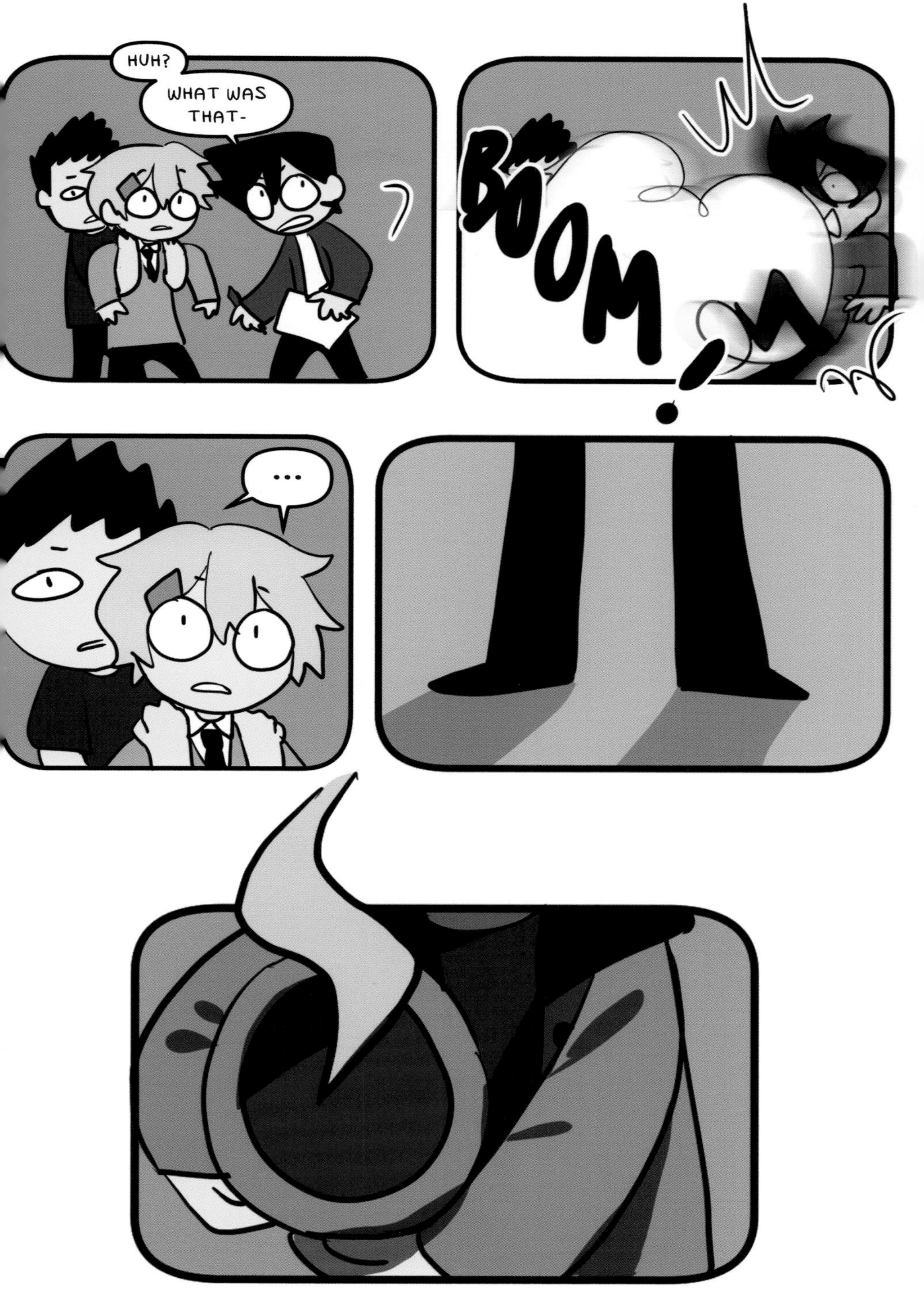
HUH?
WHAT WAS THAT-
BOOM!
...

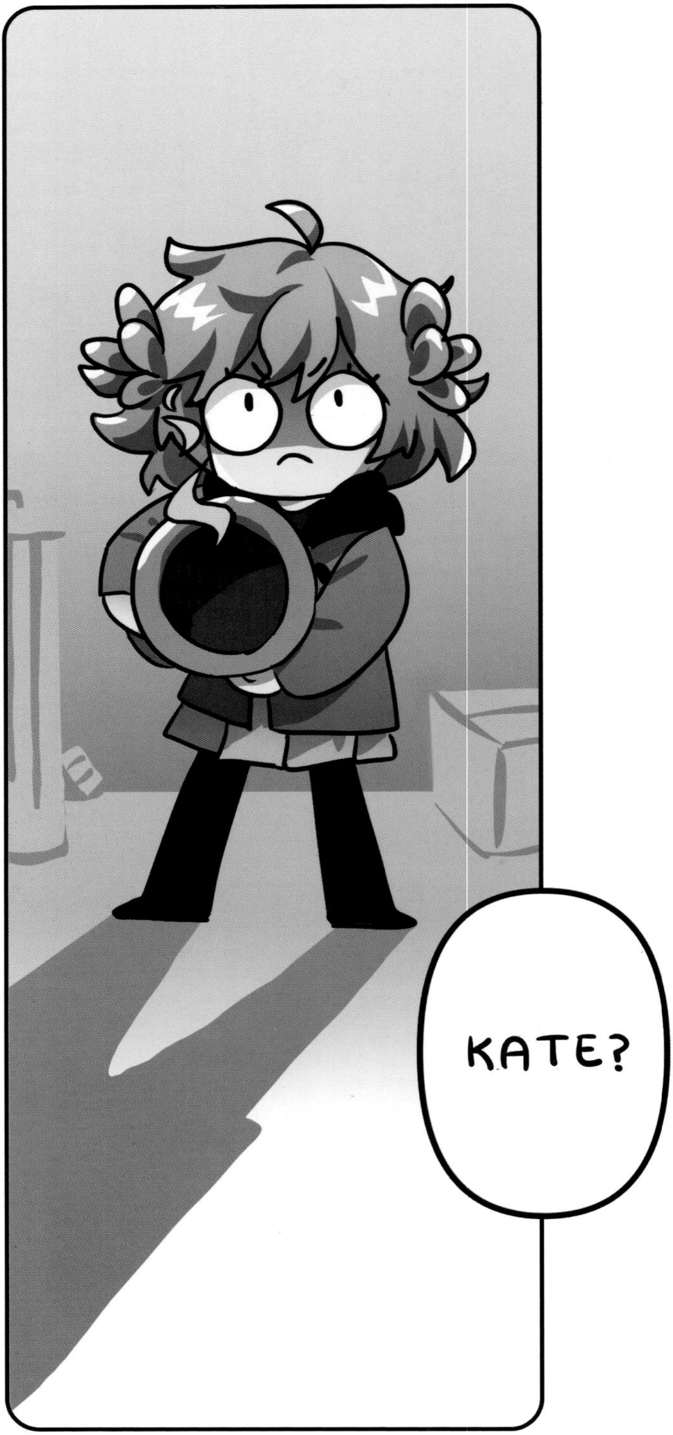
KATE?

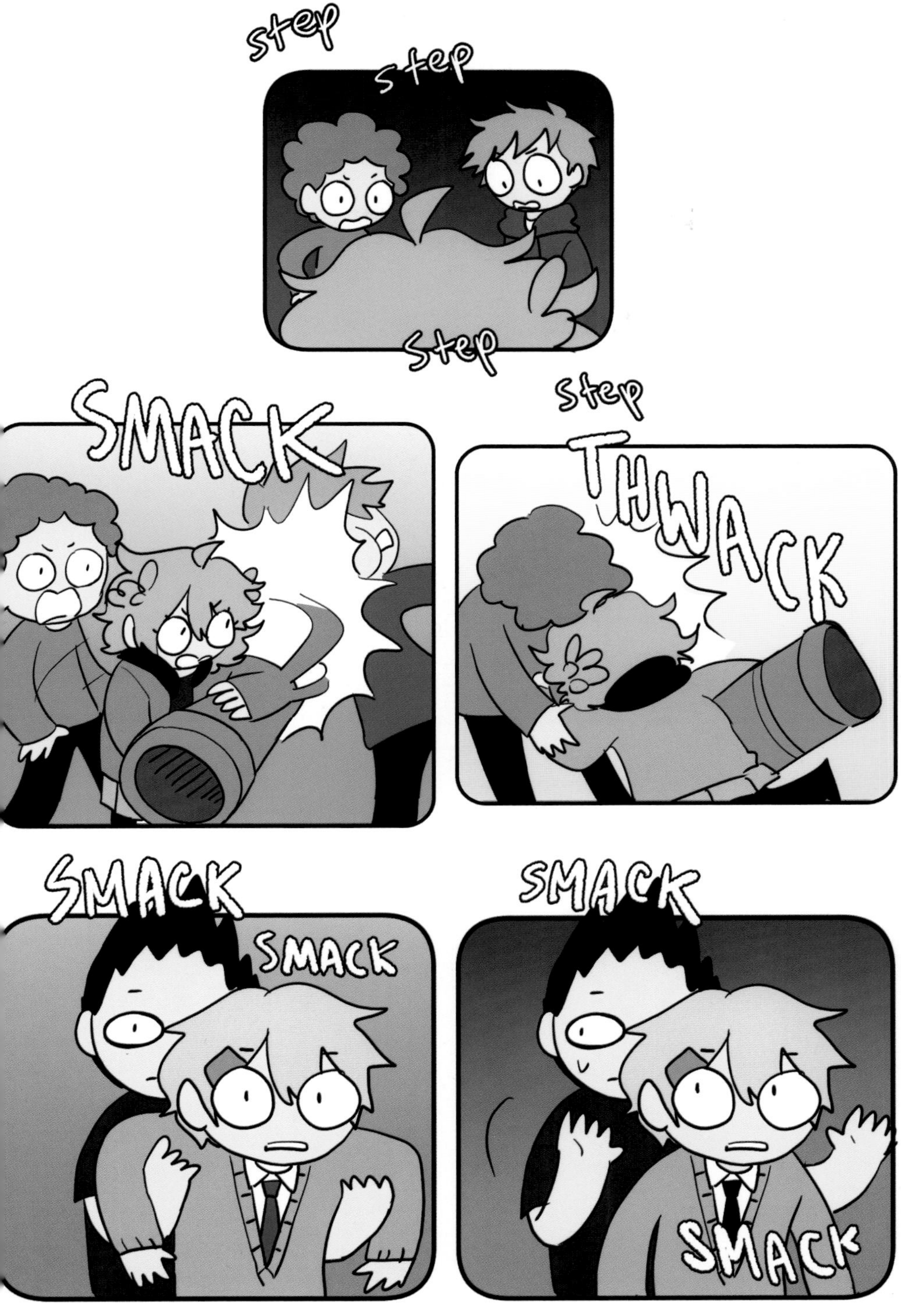
step
step
Step
SMACK
step
THWACK
SMACK
SMACK
SMACK
SMACK

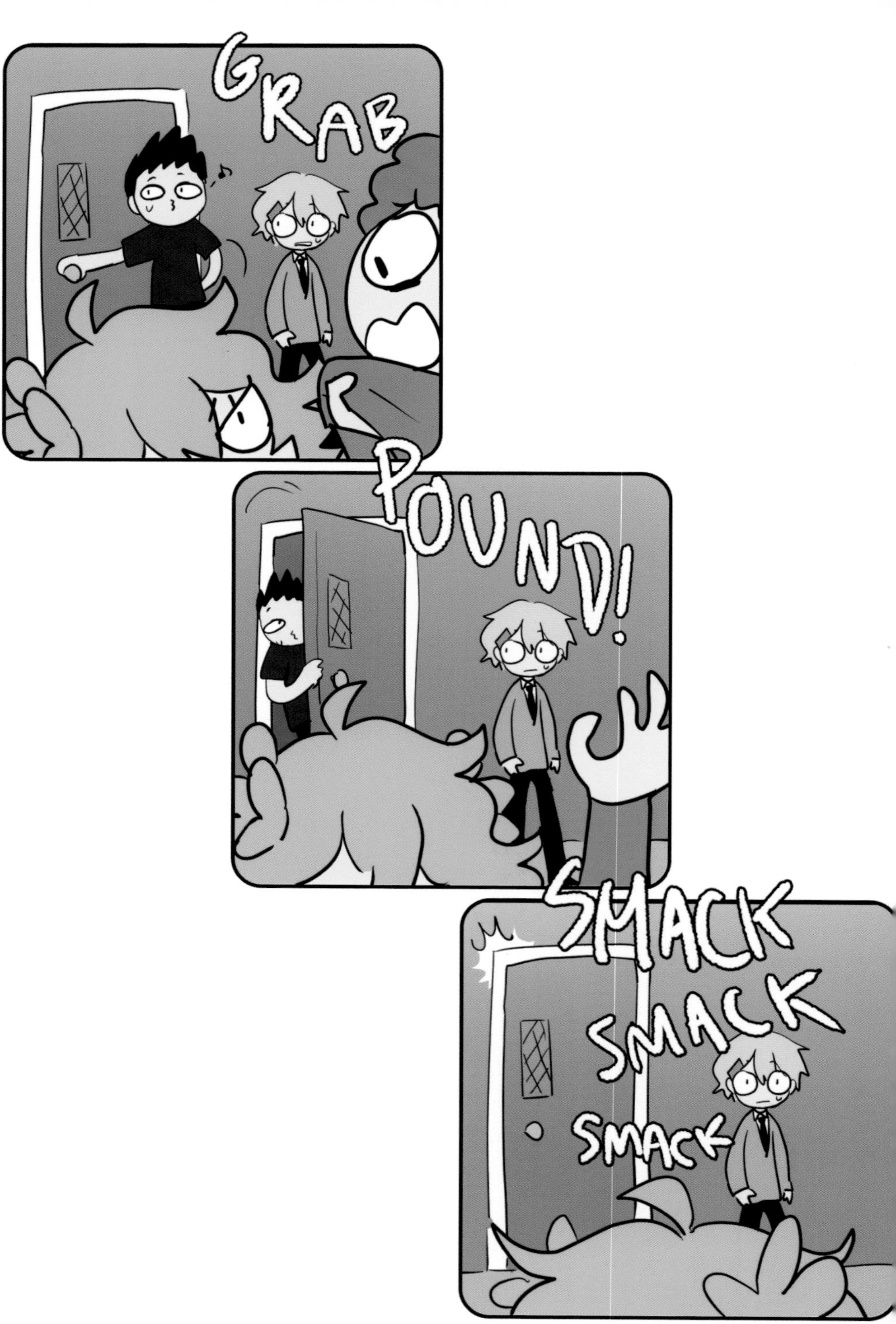
GRAB
POUND!
SMACK
SMACK
SMACK

TCH.

I DON'T CARE IF YOU ARE A GIRL...

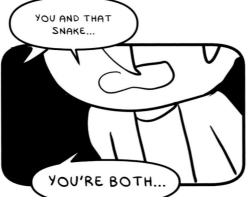

YOU AND THAT SNAKE...

YOU'RE BOTH...

GOING DOWN!

GRAB

SLAM

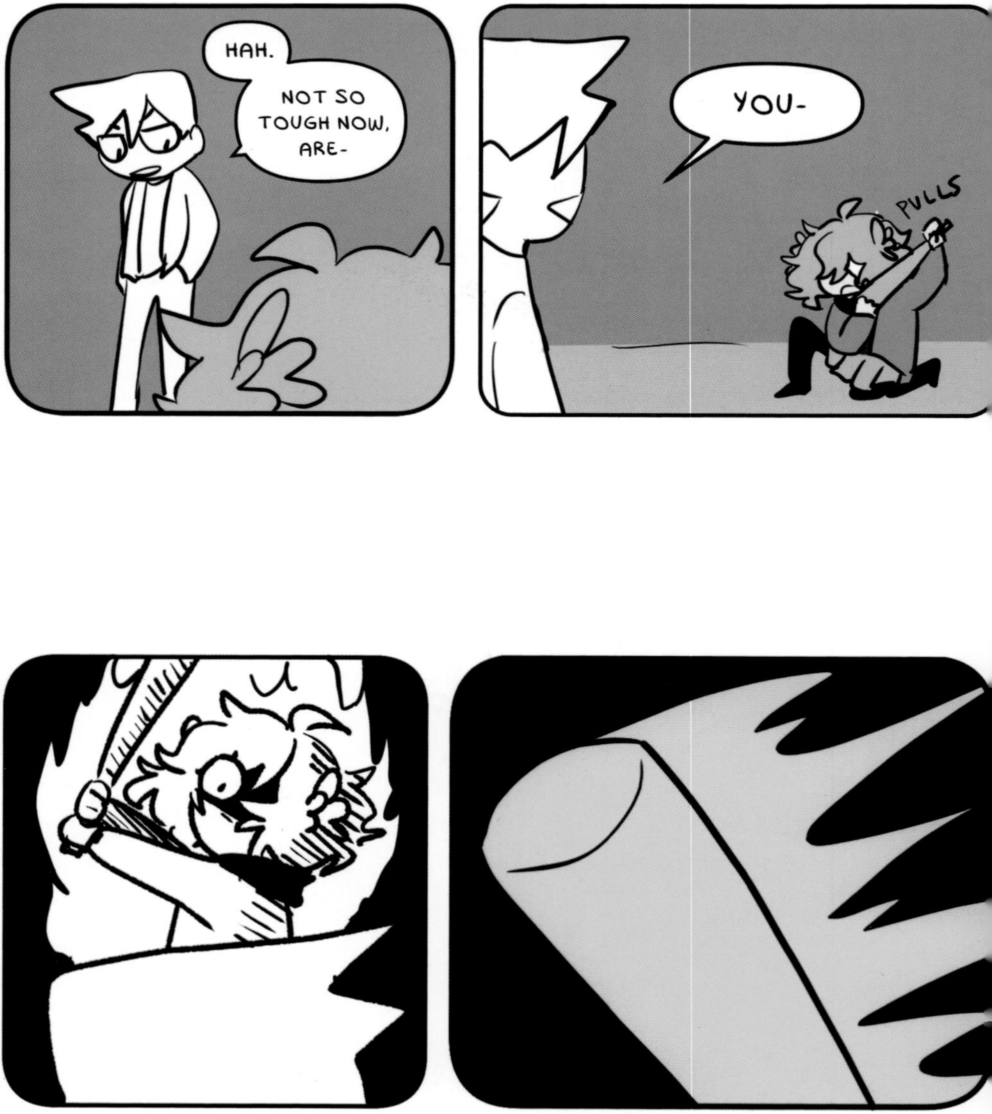
HAH.
NOT SO TOUGH NOW, ARE-
YOU-
PULLS

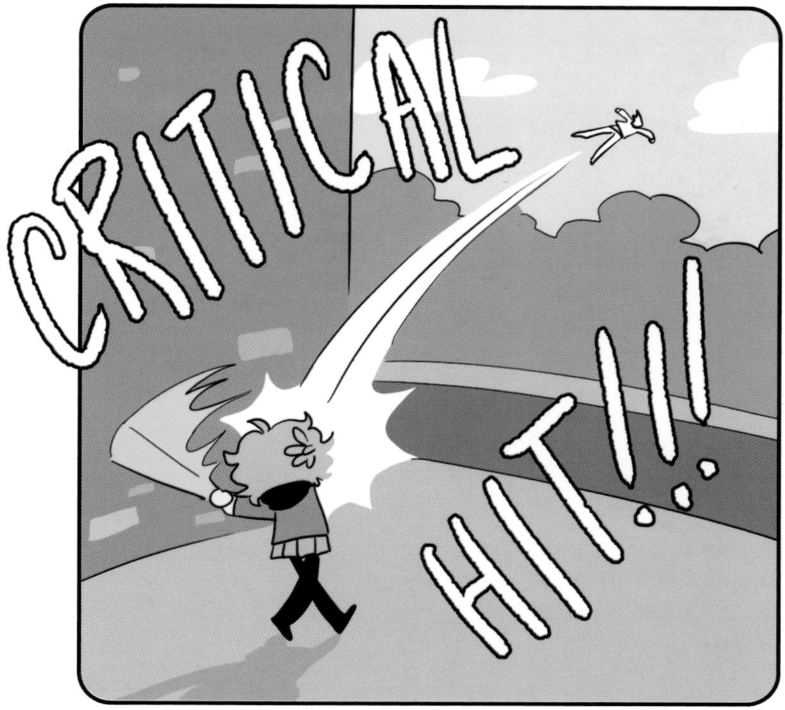
CRITICAL
HIT!!!

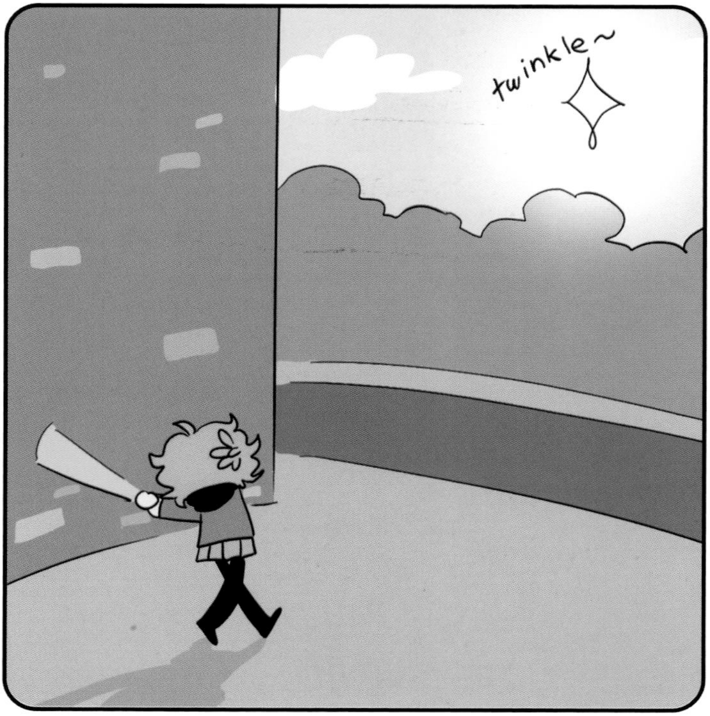
twinkle~

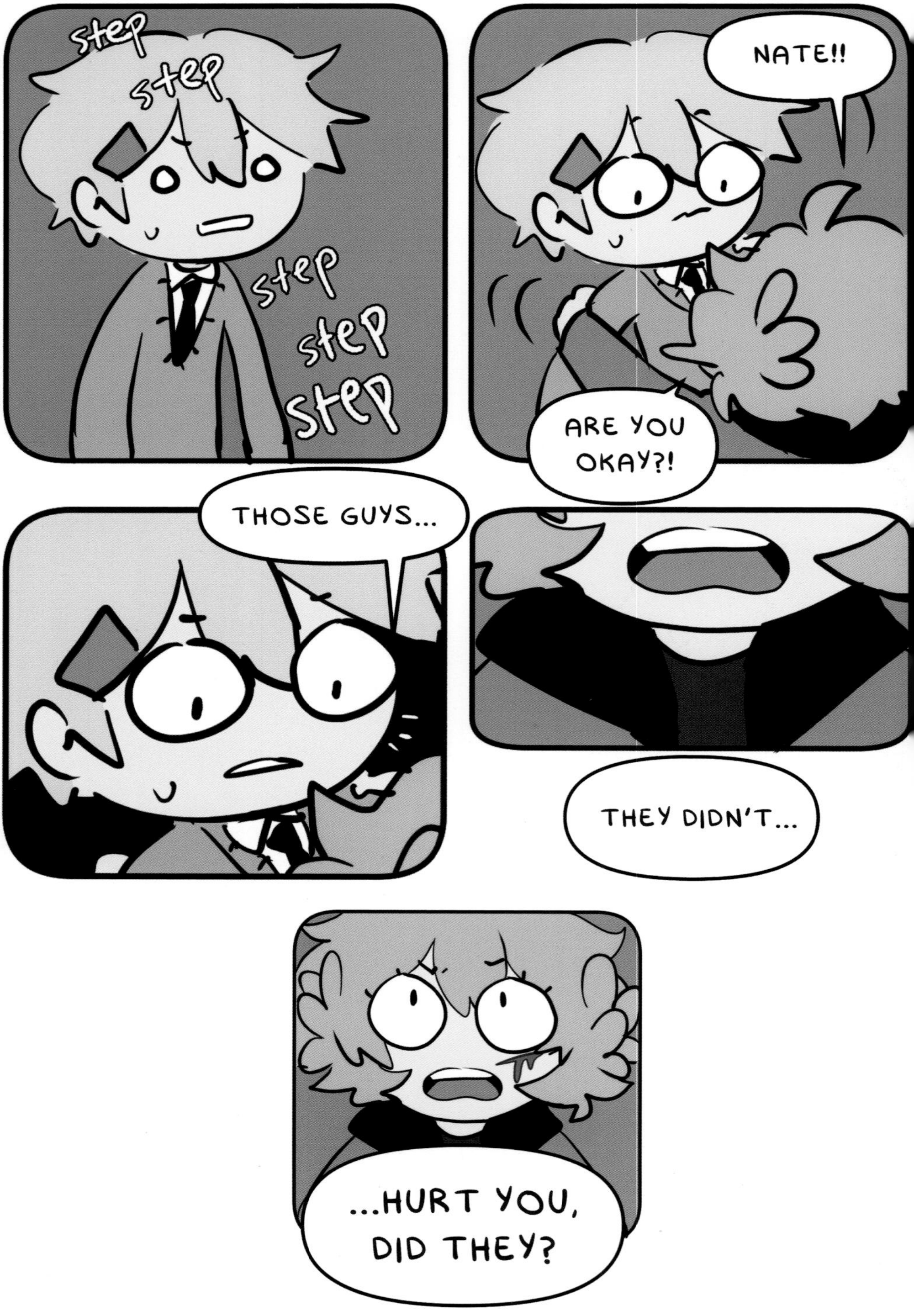
step
step
step
step
step
NATE!!
ARE YOU OKAY?!
THOSE GUYS...
THEY DIDN'T...
...HURT YOU, DID THEY?

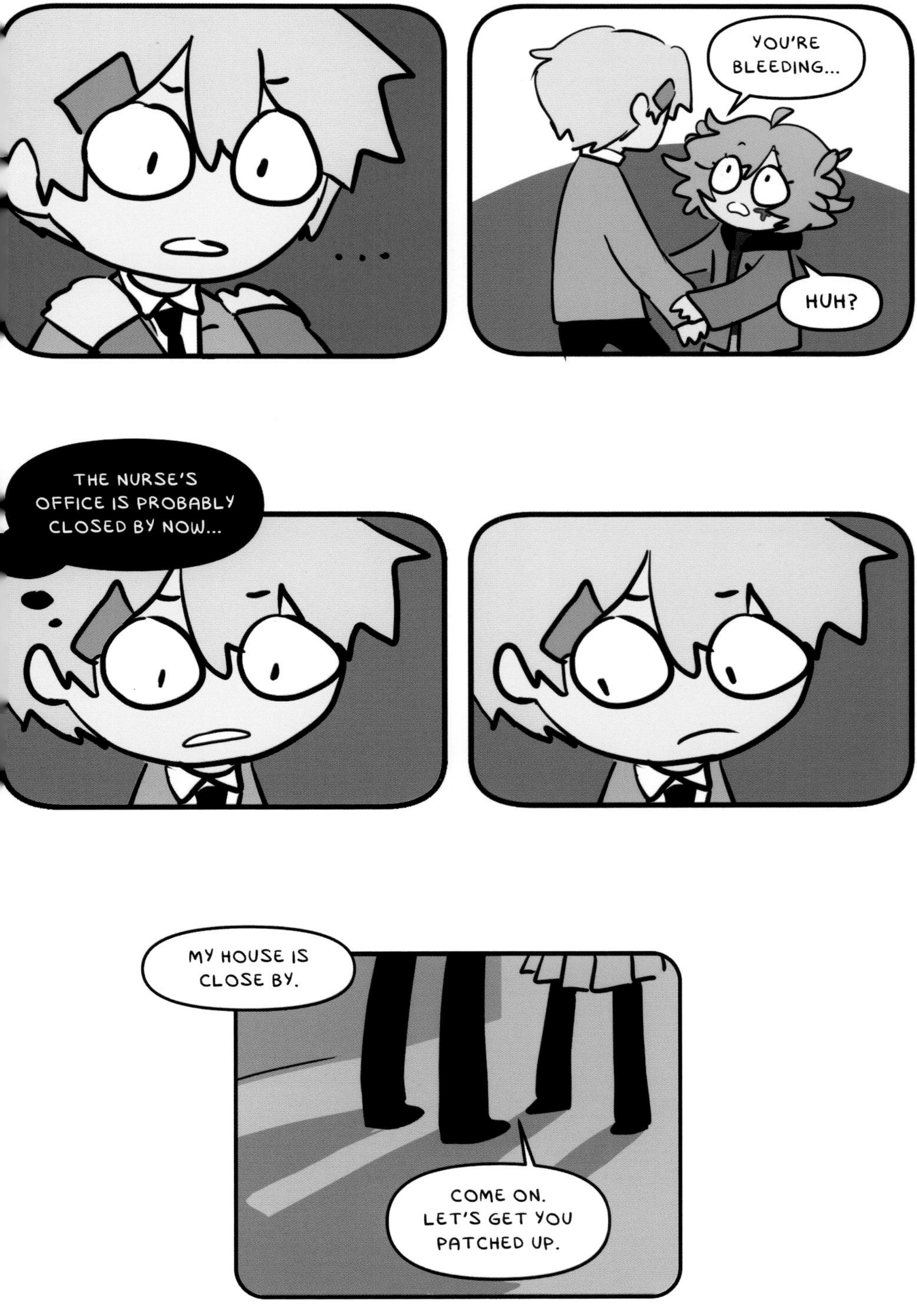
...
YOU'RE BLEEDING...
HUH?
THE NURSE'S OFFICE IS PROBABLY CLOSED BY NOW...
MY HOUSE IS CLOSE BY.
COME ON. LET'S GET YOU PATCHED UP.

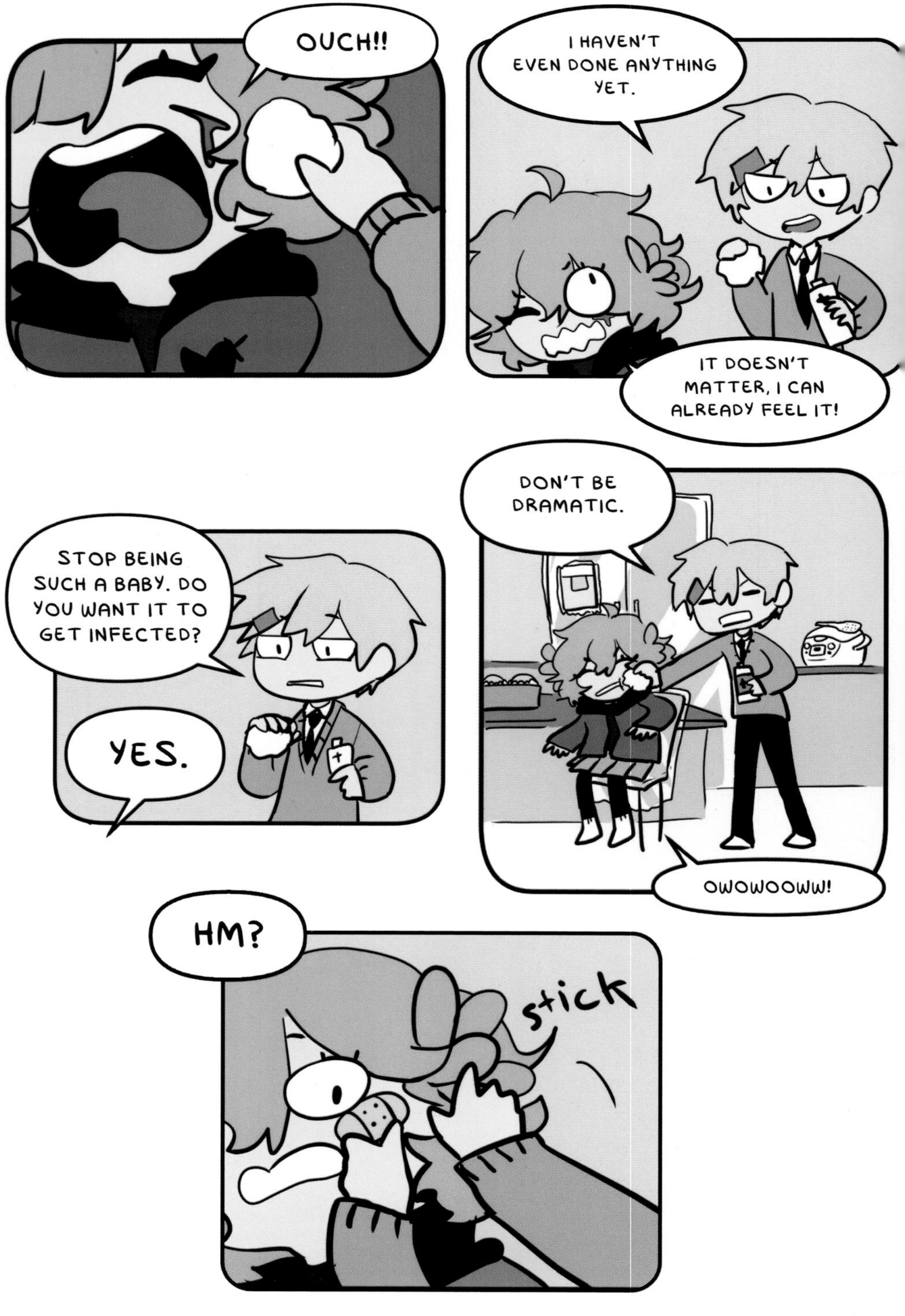
OUCH!!
I HAVEN'T EVEN DONE ANYTHING YET.
IT DOESN'T MATTER, I CAN ALREADY FEEL IT!
STOP BEING SUCH A BABY. DO YOU WANT IT TO GET INFECTED?
YES.
DON'T BE DRAMATIC.
OWOWOOWW!
HM?
stick

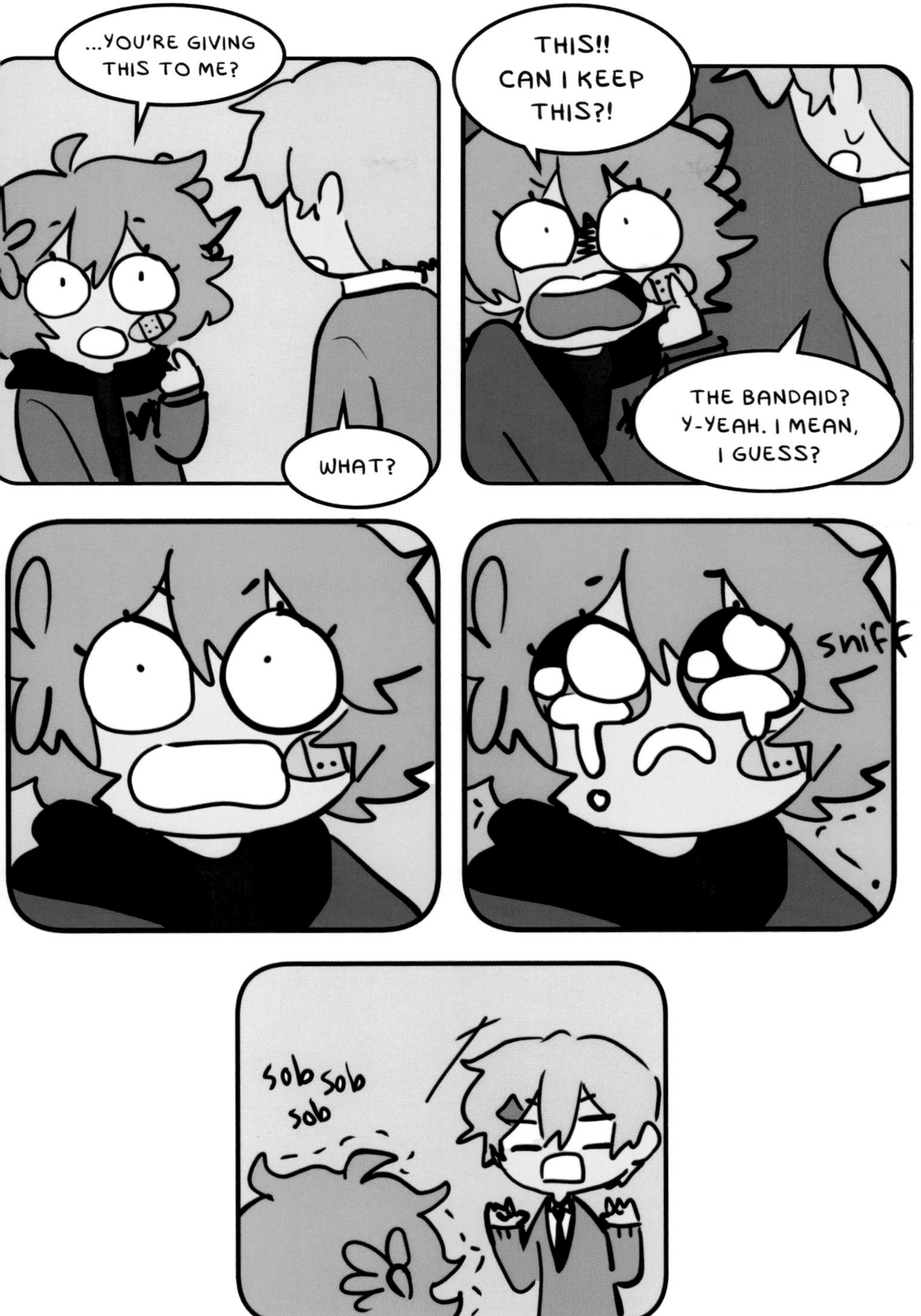
...YOU'RE GIVING THIS TO ME?
WHAT?
THIS!! CAN I KEEP THIS?!
THE BANDAID? Y-YEAH. I MEAN, I GUESS?
sniff
sob sob sob

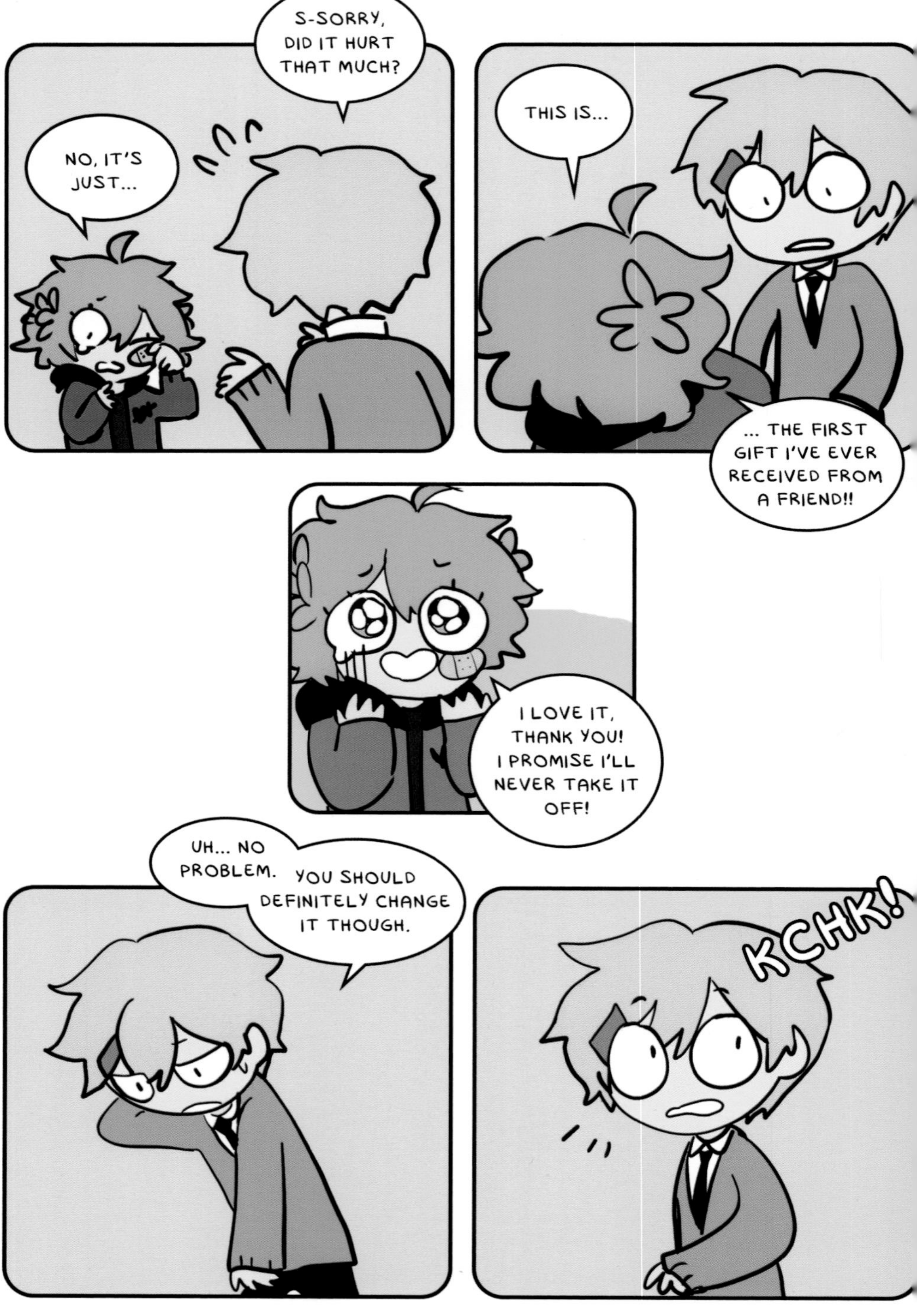
NO, IT'S JUST...
S-SORRY, DID IT HURT THAT MUCH?
THIS IS...
... THE FIRST GIFT I'VE EVER RECEIVED FROM A FRIEND!!
I LOVE IT, THANK YOU! I PROMISE I'LL NEVER TAKE IT OFF!
UH... NO PROBLEM.
YOU SHOULD DEFINITELY CHANGE IT THOUGH.
KCHK!

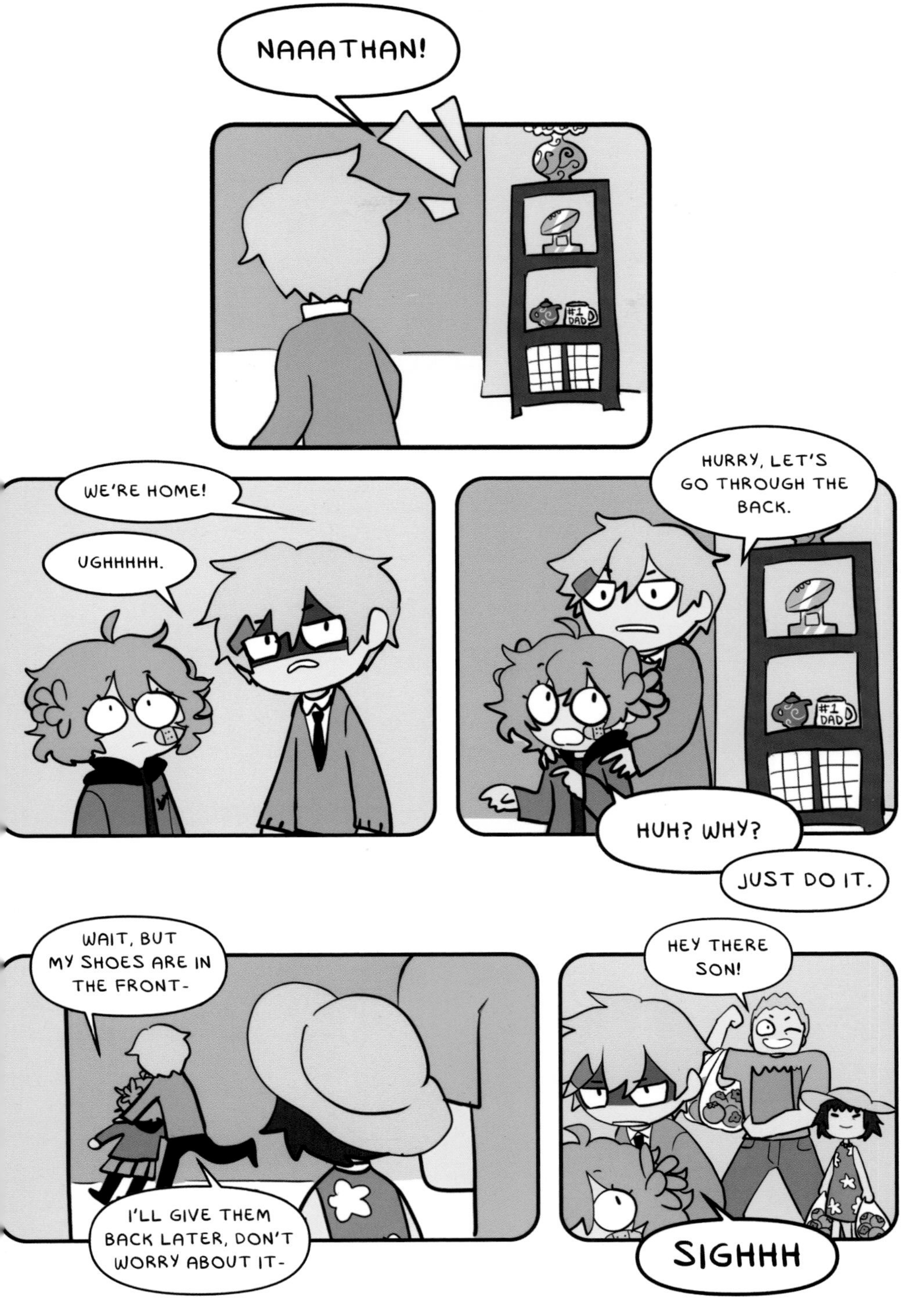
NAAATHAN!
WE'RE HOME!
UGHHHHH.
HURRY, LET'S GO THROUGH THE BACK.
HUH? WHY?
JUST DO IT.
WAIT, BUT MY SHOES ARE IN THE FRONT-
I'LL GIVE THEM BACK LATER, DON'T WORRY ABOUT IT-
HEY THERE SON!
SIGHHH

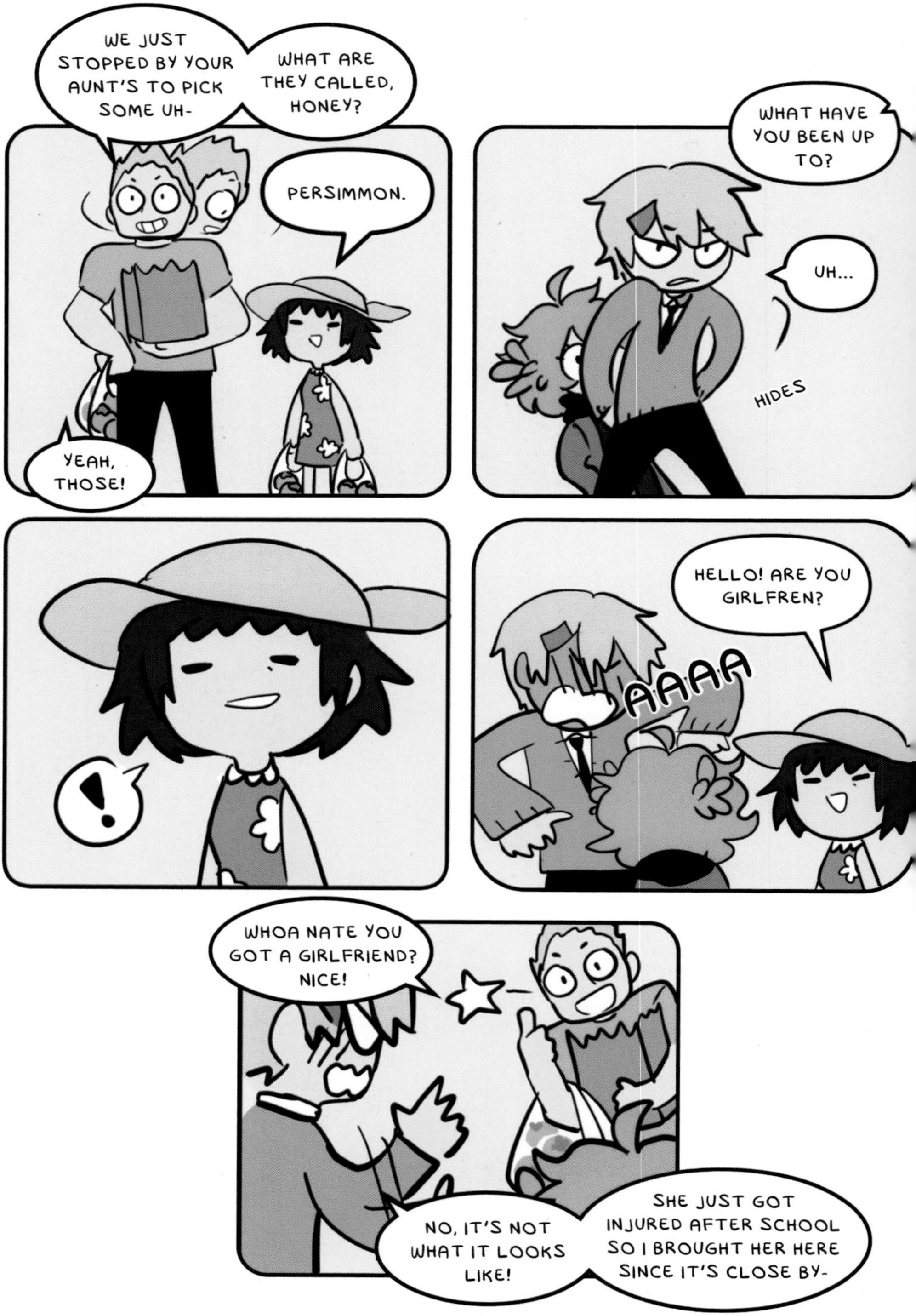
WE JUST STOPPED BY YOUR AUNT'S TO PICK SOME UH-
WHAT ARE THEY CALLED, HONEY?
PERSIMMON.
YEAH, THOSE!
WHAT HAVE YOU BEEN UP TO?
UH...
HIDES
!
HELLO! ARE YOU GIRLFREN?
AAAA
WHOA NATE YOU GOT A GIRLFRIEND? NICE!
NO, IT'S NOT WHAT IT LOOKS LIKE!
SHE JUST GOT INJURED AFTER SCHOOL SO I BROUGHT HER HERE SINCE IT'S CLOSE BY-

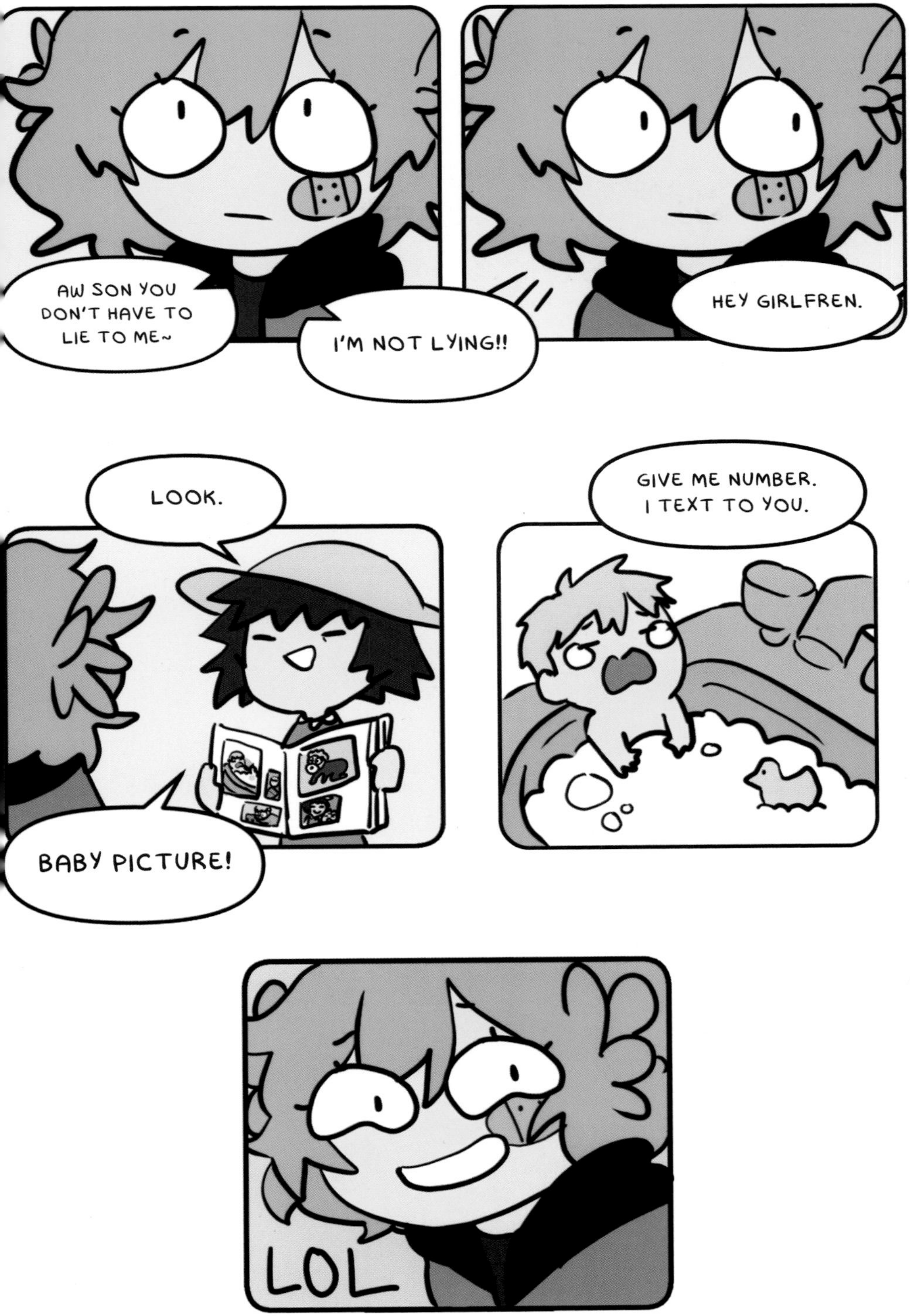
AW SON YOU DON'T HAVE TO LIE TO ME~
I'M NOT LYING!!
HEY GIRLFREN.
LOOK.
BABY PICTURE!
GIVE ME NUMBER. I TEXT TO YOU.
LOL

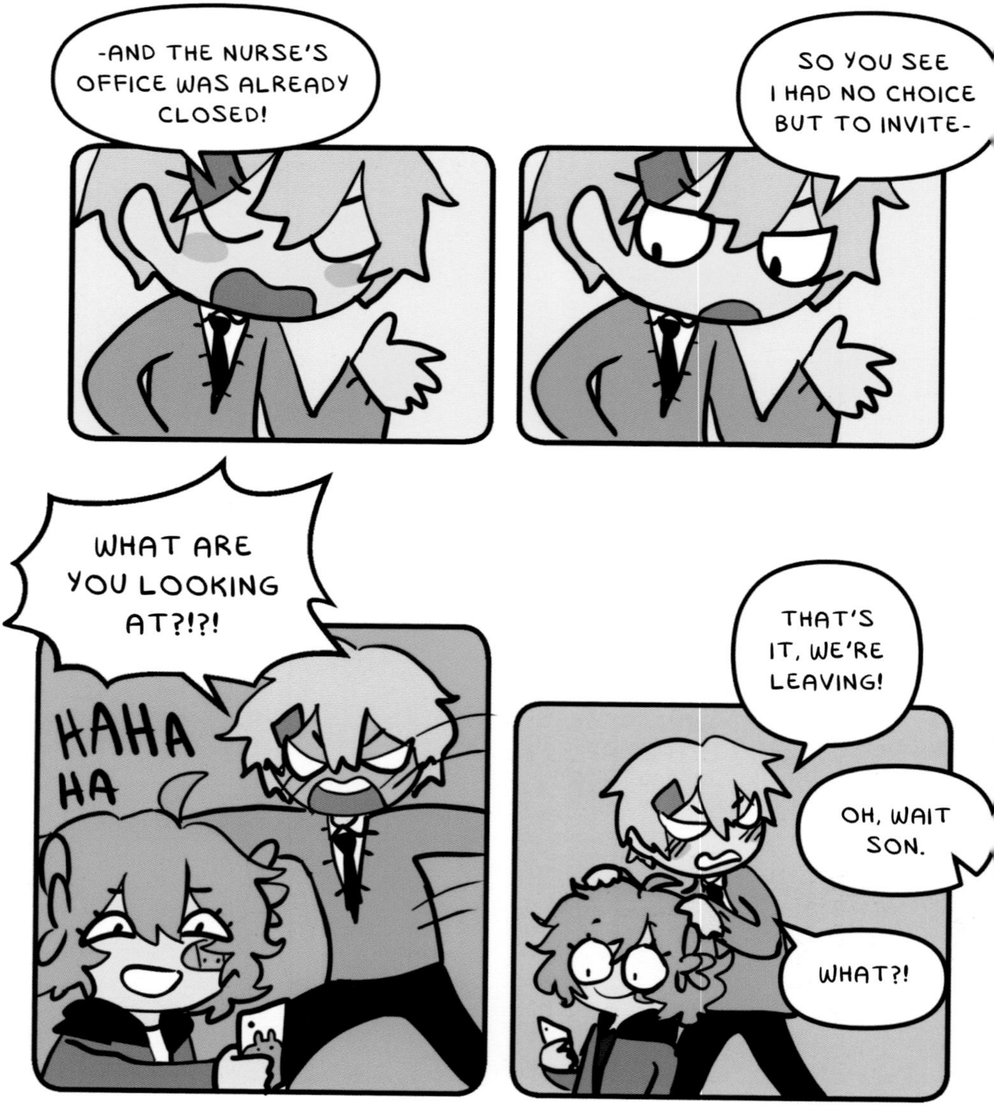
-AND THE NURSE'S OFFICE WAS ALREADY CLOSED!
SO YOU SEE I HAD NO CHOICE BUT TO INVITE-
WHAT ARE YOU LOOKING AT?!?!
HAHA HA
THAT'S IT, WE'RE LEAVING!
OH, WAIT SON.
WHAT?!

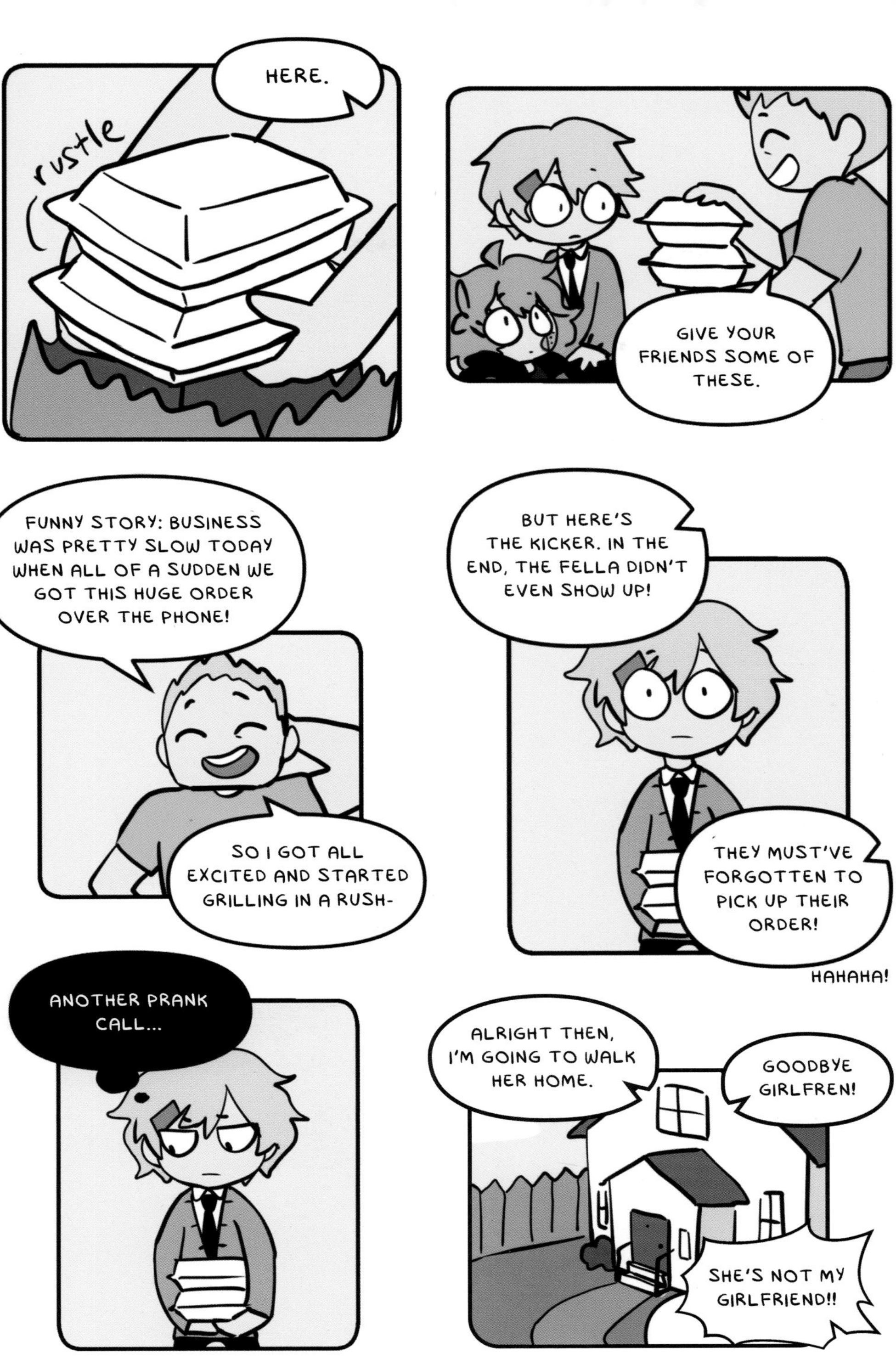
HERE.
rustle
GIVE YOUR FRIENDS SOME OF THESE.
FUNNY STORY: BUSINESS WAS PRETTY SLOW TODAY WHEN ALL OF A SUDDEN WE GOT THIS HUGE ORDER OVER THE PHONE!
SO I GOT ALL EXCITED AND STARTED GRILLING IN A RUSH-
BUT HERE'S THE KICKER. IN THE END, THE FELLA DIDN'T EVEN SHOW UP!
THEY MUST'VE FORGOTTEN TO PICK UP THEIR ORDER!
HAHAHA!
ANOTHER PRANK CALL...
ALRIGHT THEN, I'M GOING TO WALK HER HOME.
GOODBYE GIRLFREN!
SHE'S NOT MY GIRLFRIEND!!

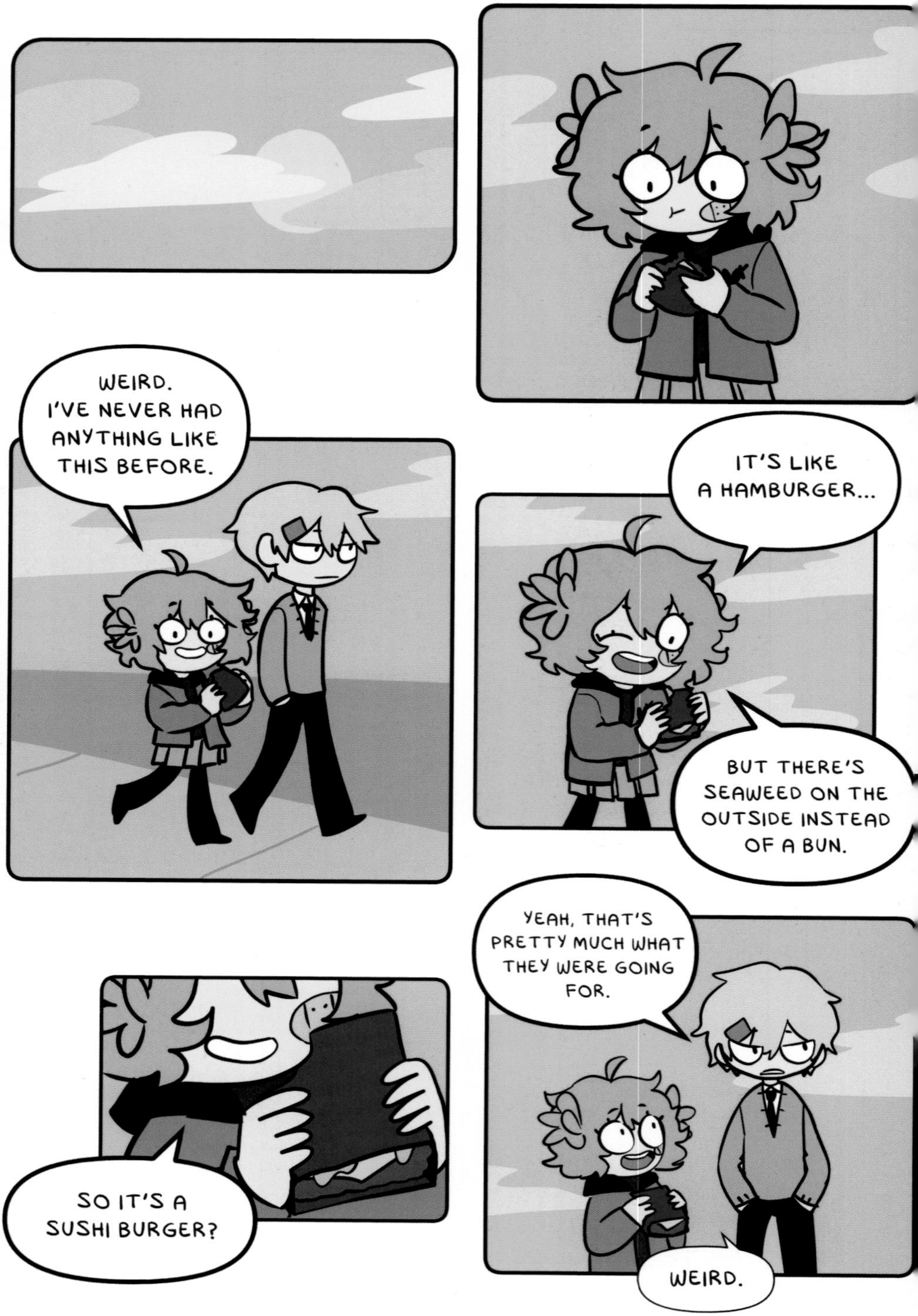
WEIRD. I'VE NEVER HAD ANYTHING LIKE THIS BEFORE.
IT'S LIKE A HAMBURGER...
BUT THERE'S SEAWEED ON THE OUTSIDE INSTEAD OF A BUN.
SO IT'S A SUSHI BURGER?
YEAH, THAT'S PRETTY MUCH WHAT THEY WERE GOING FOR.
WEIRD.

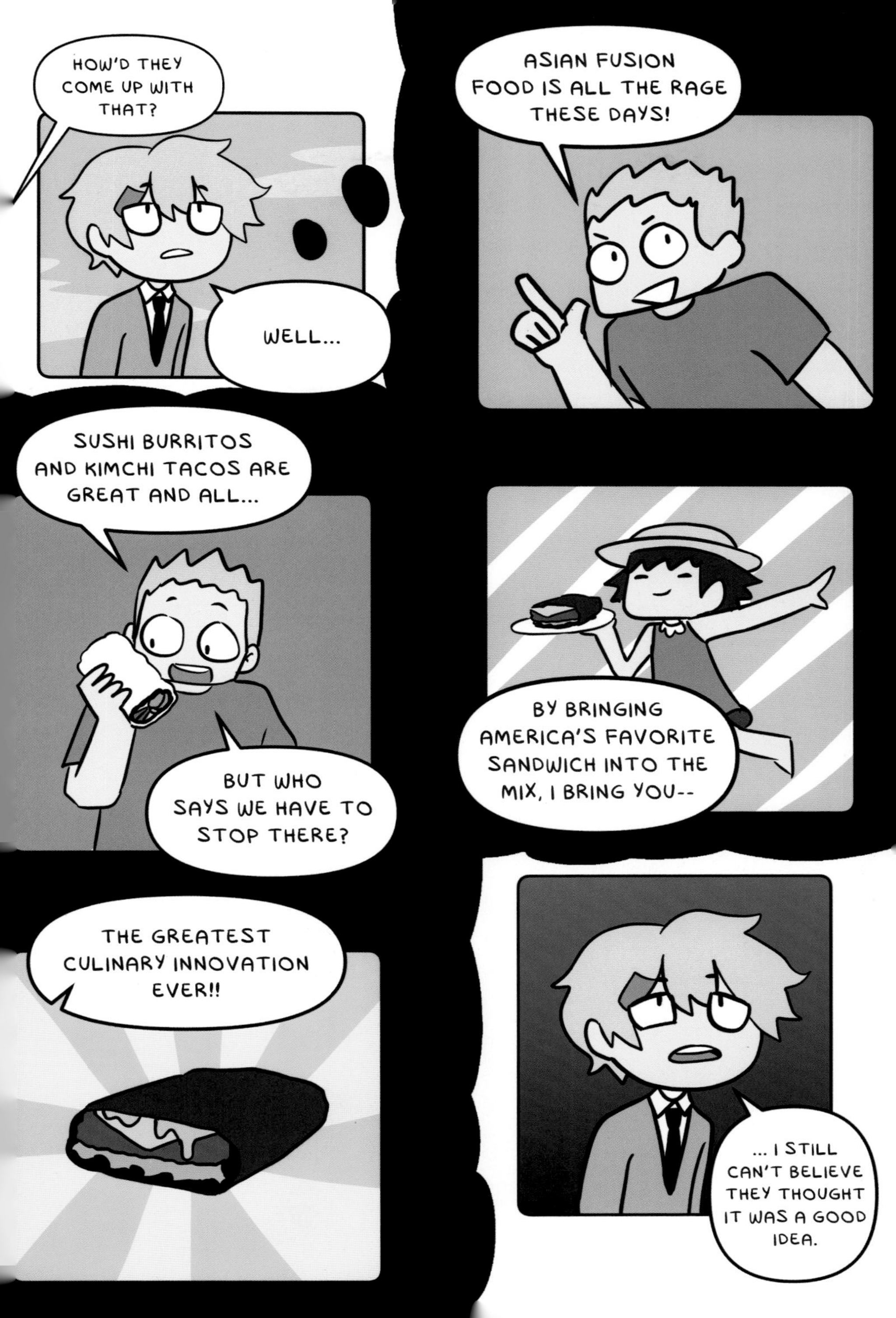
HOW'D THEY COME UP WITH THAT?
WELL...
ASIAN FUSION FOOD IS ALL THE RAGE THESE DAYS!
SUSHI BURRITOS AND KIMCHI TACOS ARE GREAT AND ALL...
BUT WHO SAYS WE HAVE TO STOP THERE?
BY BRINGING AMERICA'S FAVORITE SANDWICH INTO THE MIX, I BRING YOU--
THE GREATEST CULINARY INNOVATION EVER!!
... I STILL CAN'T BELIEVE THEY THOUGHT IT WAS A GOOD IDEA.

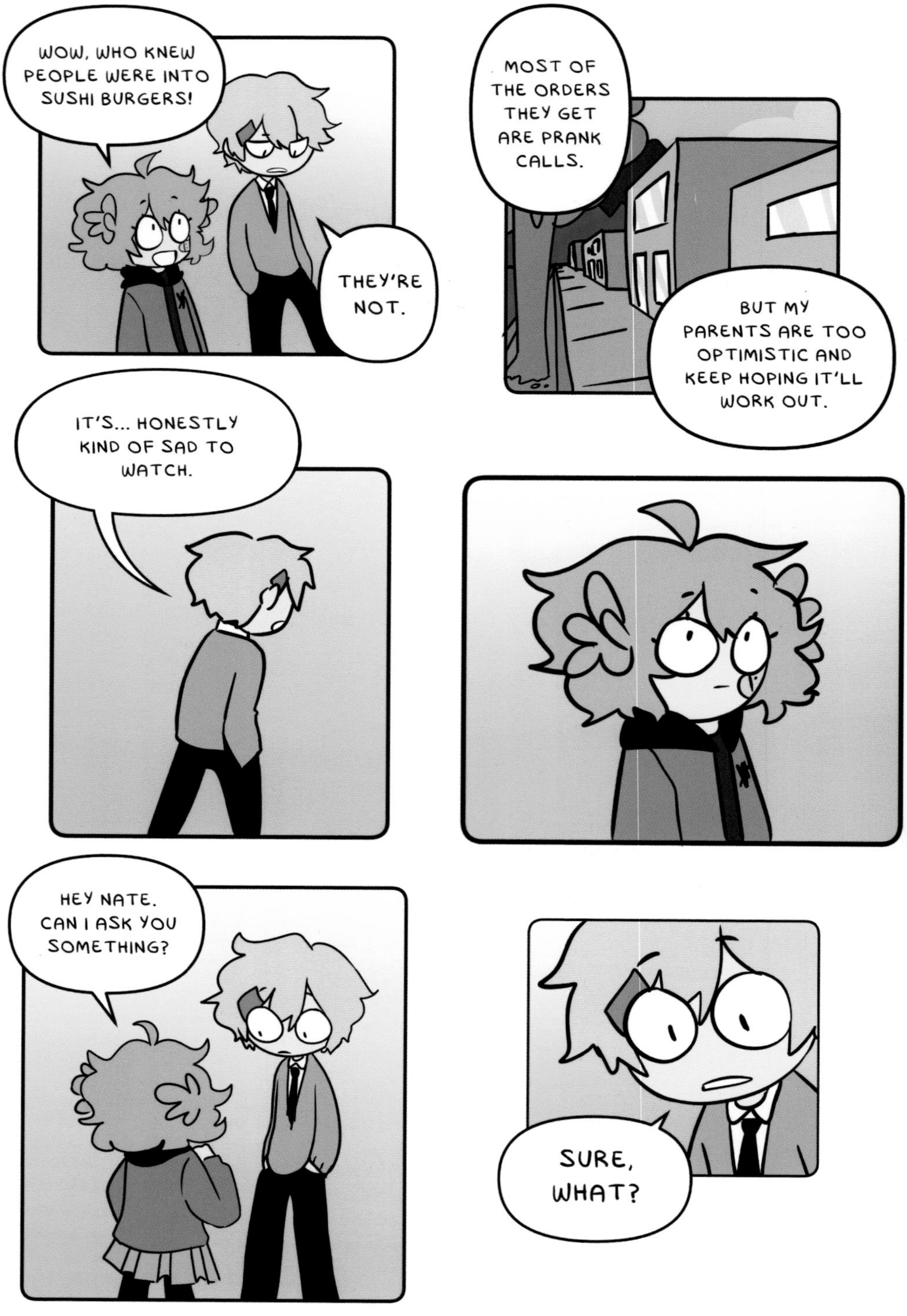
WOW, WHO KNEW PEOPLE WERE INTO SUSHI BURGERS!
THEY'RE NOT.
MOST OF THE ORDERS THEY GET ARE PRANK CALLS.
BUT MY PARENTS ARE TOO OPTIMISTIC AND KEEP HOPING IT'LL WORK OUT.
IT'S... HONESTLY KIND OF SAD TO WATCH.
HEY NATE. CAN I ASK YOU SOMETHING?
SURE, WHAT?

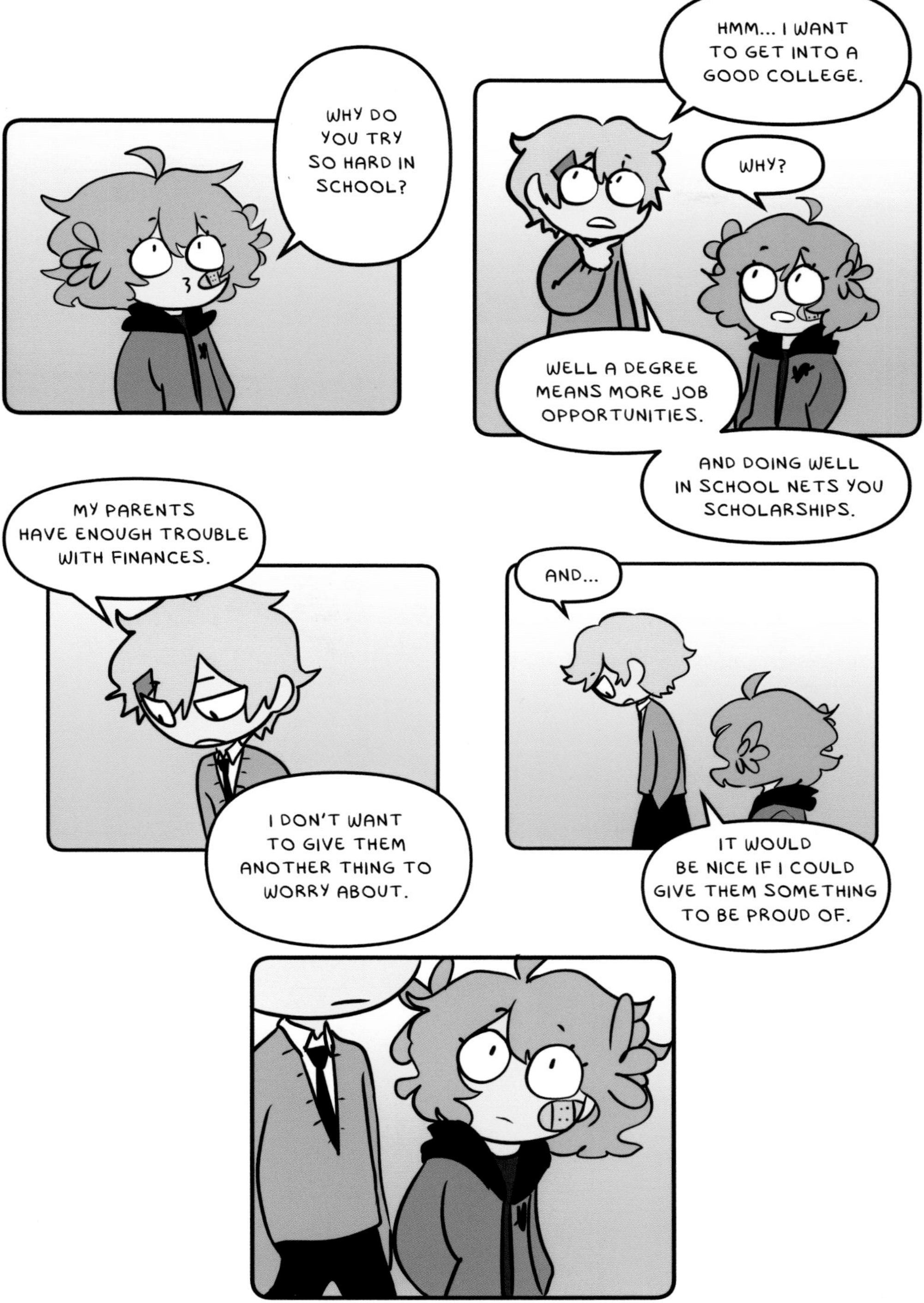
WHY DO YOU TRY SO HARD IN SCHOOL?
HMM... I WANT TO GET INTO A GOOD COLLEGE.
WHY?
WELL A DEGREE MEANS MORE JOB OPPORTUNITIES.
AND DOING WELL IN SCHOOL NETS YOU SCHOLARSHIPS.
MY PARENTS HAVE ENOUGH TROUBLE WITH FINANCES.
I DON'T WANT TO GIVE THEM ANOTHER THING TO WORRY ABOUT.
AND...
IT WOULD BE NICE IF I COULD GIVE THEM SOMETHING TO BE PROUD OF.

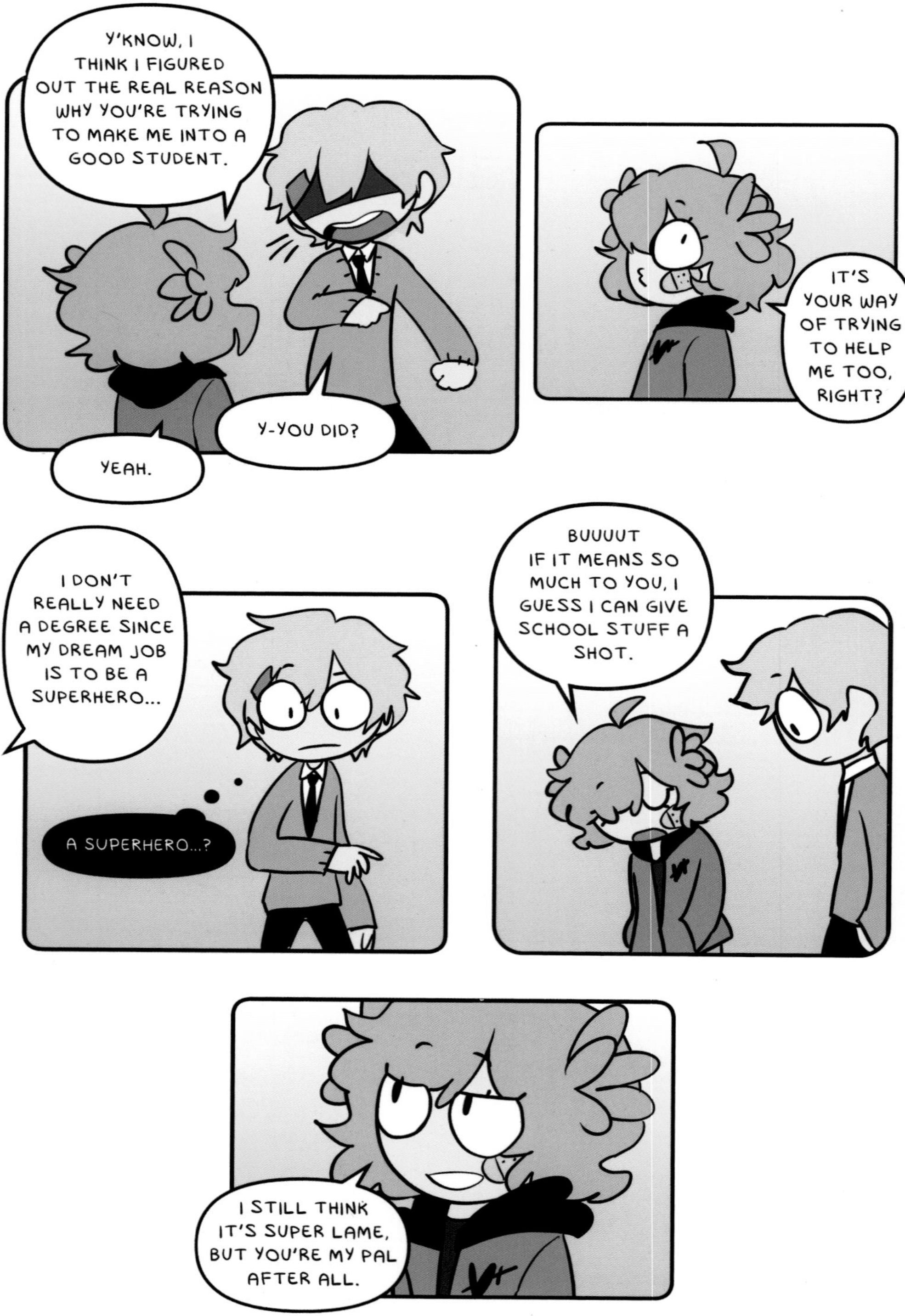
Y'KNOW, I THINK I FIGURED OUT THE REAL REASON WHY YOU'RE TRYING TO MAKE ME INTO A GOOD STUDENT.
Y-YOU DID?
YEAH.
IT'S YOUR WAY OF TRYING TO HELP ME TOO, RIGHT?
I DON'T REALLY NEED A DEGREE SINCE MY DREAM JOB IS TO BE A SUPERHERO...
A SUPERHERO...?
BUUUUT IF IT MEANS SO MUCH TO YOU, I GUESS I CAN GIVE SCHOOL STUFF A SHOT.
I STILL THINK IT'S SUPER LAME, BUT YOU'RE MY PAL AFTER ALL.

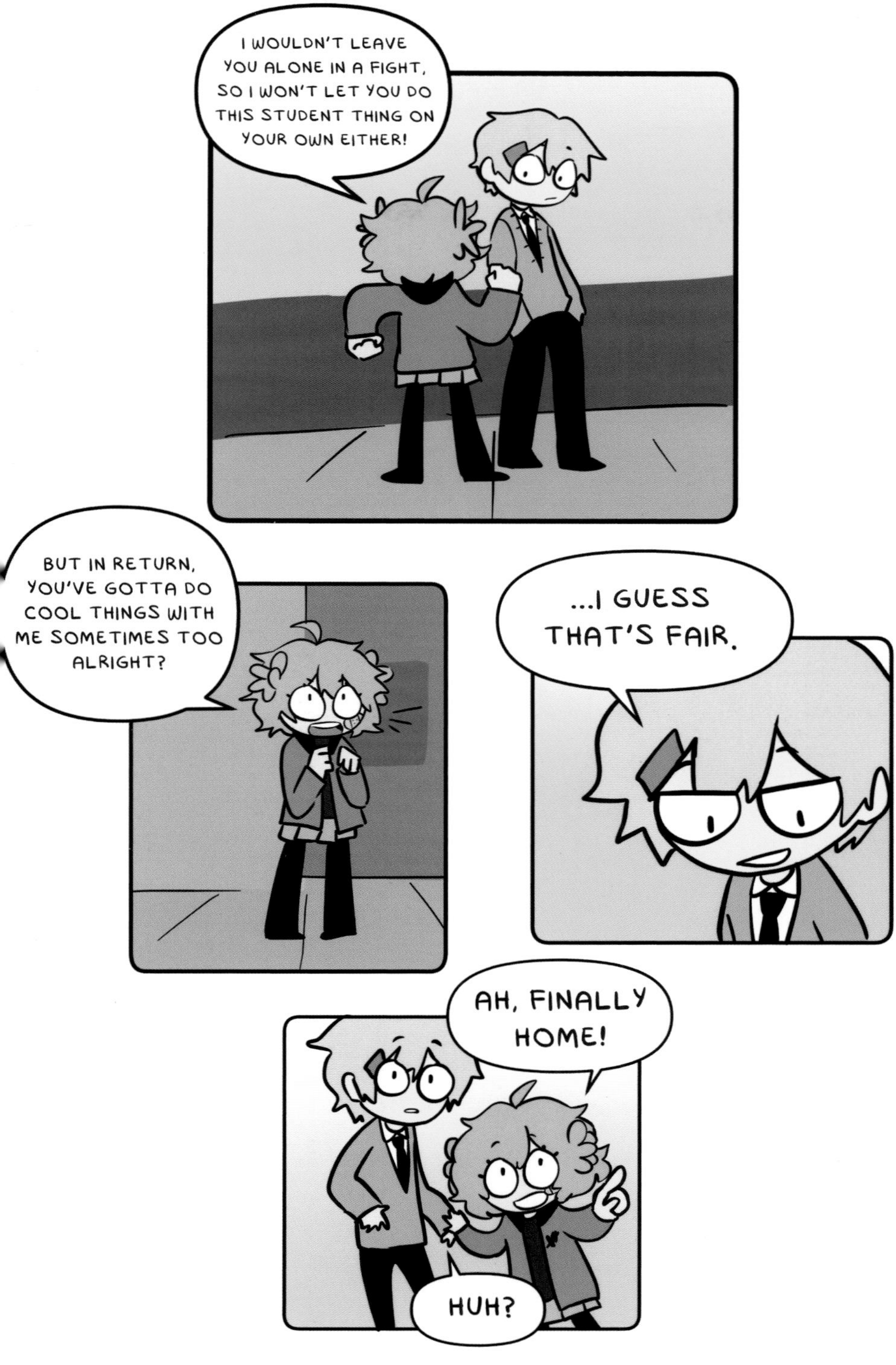
I WOULDN'T LEAVE YOU ALONE IN A FIGHT, SO I WON'T LET YOU DO THIS STUDENT THING ON YOUR OWN EITHER!
BUT IN RETURN, YOU'VE GOTTA DO COOL THINGS WITH ME SOMETIMES TOO ALRIGHT?
...I GUESS THAT'S FAIR.
AH, FINALLY HOME!
HUH?

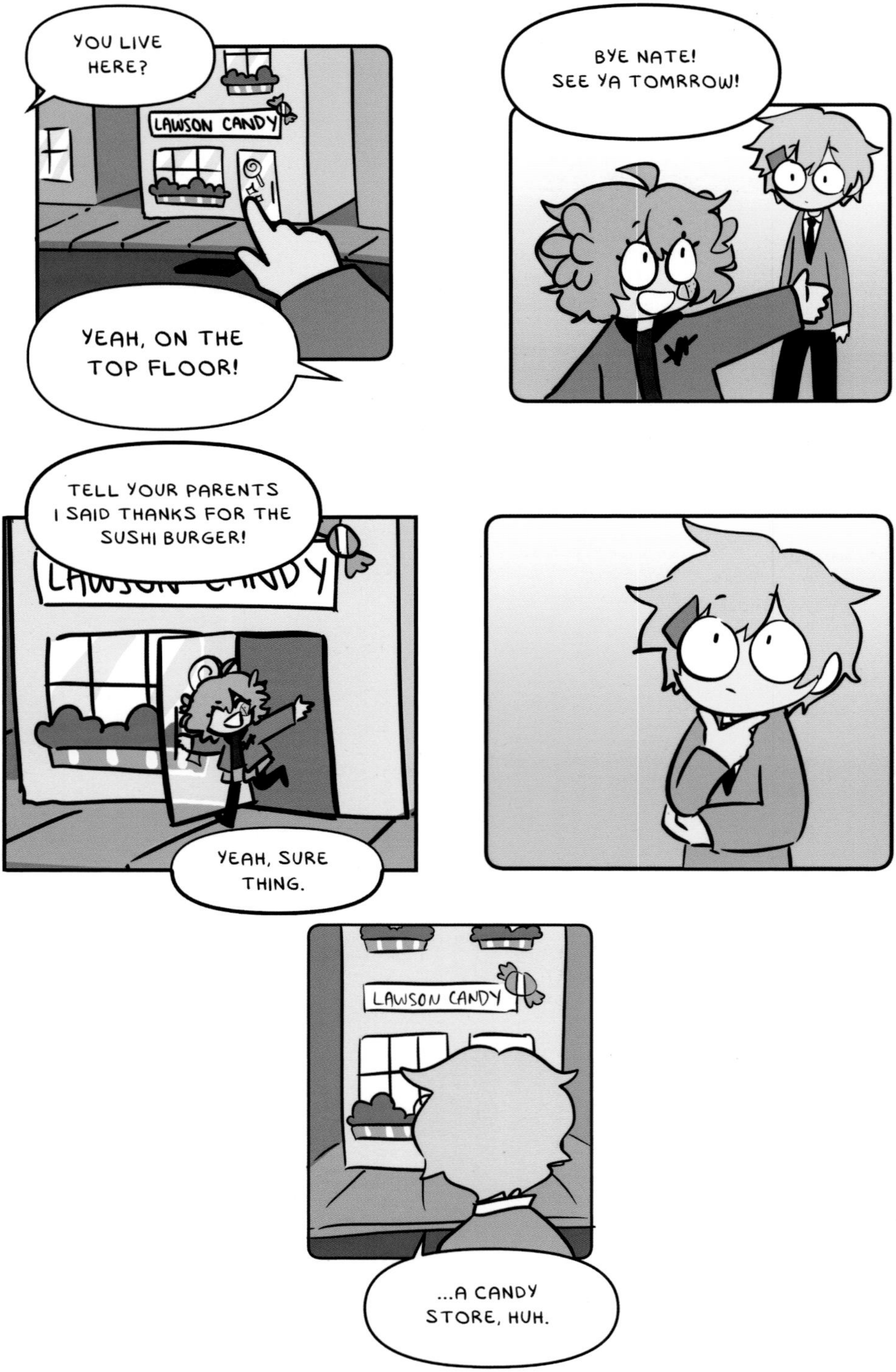
YOU LIVE HERE?
LAWSON CANDY
YEAH, ON THE TOP FLOOR!
BYE NATE! SEE YA TOMRROW!
TELL YOUR PARENTS I SAID THANKS FOR THE SUSHI BURGER!
YEAH, SURE THING.
LAWSON CANDY
...A CANDY STORE, HUH.

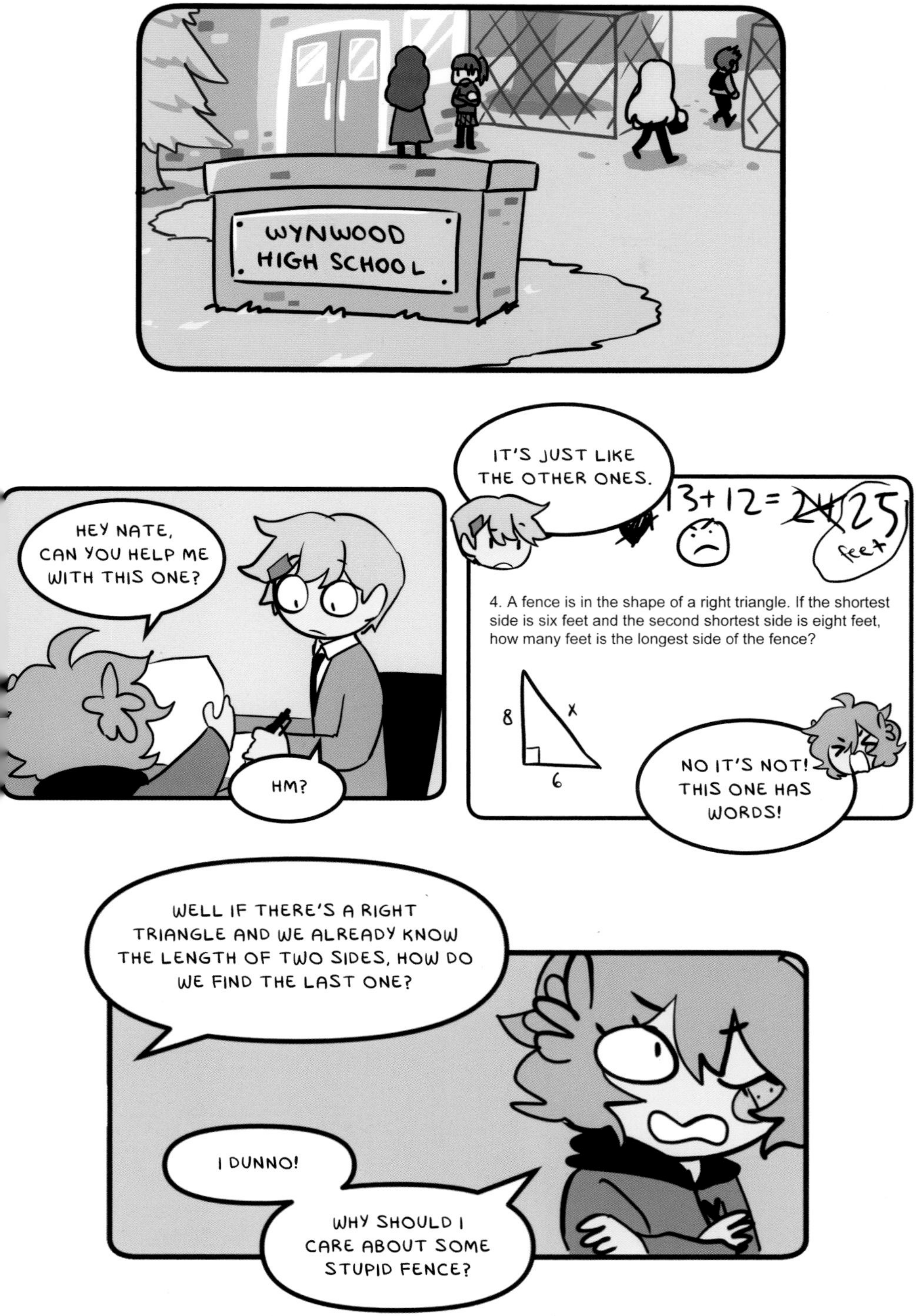
WYNWOOD HIGH SCHOOL
HEY NATE, CAN YOU HELP ME WITH THIS ONE?
HM?
IT'S JUST LIKE THE OTHER ONES.
13+12= 24 25 feet
4. A fence is in the shape of a right triangle. If the shortest side is six feet and the second shortest side is eight feet, how many feet is the longest side of the fence?
8
x
6
NO IT'S NOT! THIS ONE HAS WORDS!
WELL IF THERE'S A RIGHT TRIANGLE AND WE ALREADY KNOW THE LENGTH OF TWO SIDES, HOW DO WE FIND THE LAST ONE?
I DUNNO!
WHY SHOULD I CARE ABOUT SOME STUPID FENCE?

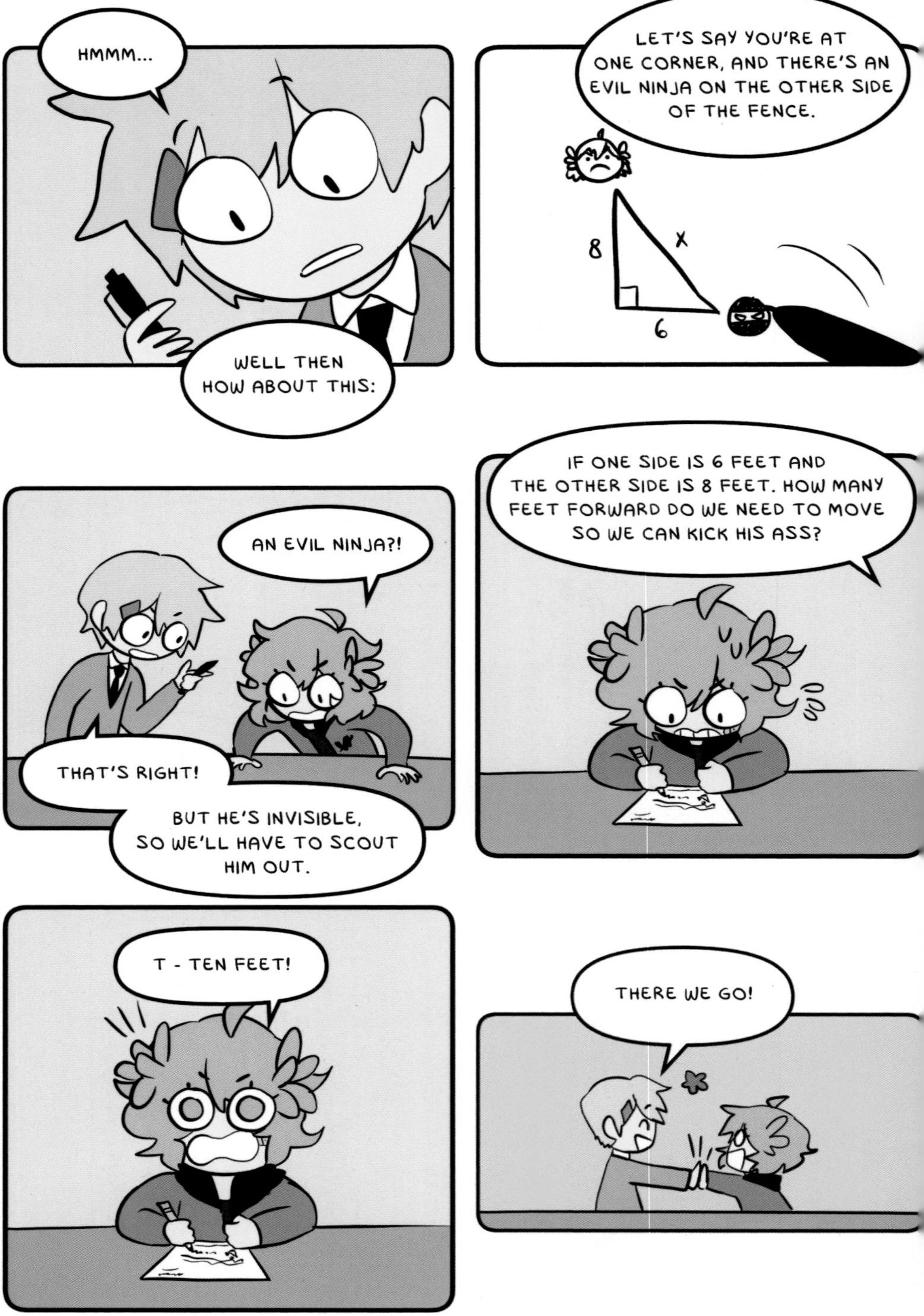
HMMM...
WELL THEN HOW ABOUT THIS:
LET'S SAY YOU'RE AT ONE CORNER, AND THERE'S AN EVIL NINJA ON THE OTHER SIDE OF THE FENCE.
8
X
6
AN EVIL NINJA?!
THAT'S RIGHT!
BUT HE'S INVISIBLE, SO WE'LL HAVE TO SCOUT HIM OUT.
IF ONE SIDE IS 6 FEET AND THE OTHER SIDE IS 8 FEET. HOW MANY FEET FORWARD DO WE NEED TO MOVE SO WE CAN KICK HIS ASS?
T - TEN FEET!
THERE WE GO!

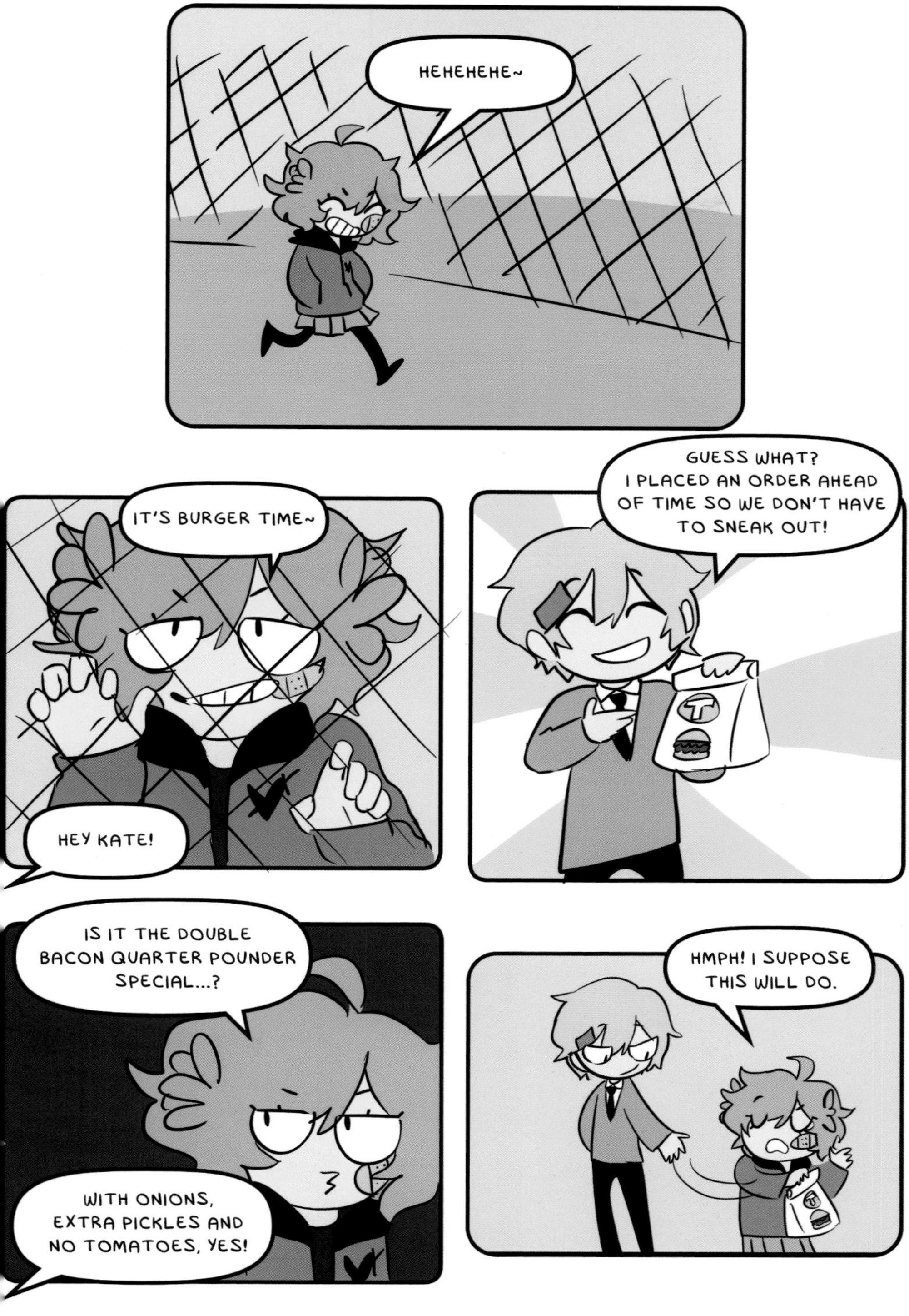
HEHEHEHE~
IT'S BURGER TIME~
HEY KATE!
GUESS WHAT? I PLACED AN ORDER AHEAD OF TIME SO WE DON'T HAVE TO SNEAK OUT!
IS IT THE DOUBLE BACON QUARTER POUNDER SPECIAL...?
WITH ONIONS, EXTRA PICKLES AND NO TOMATOES, YES!
HMPH! I SUPPOSE THIS WILL DO.

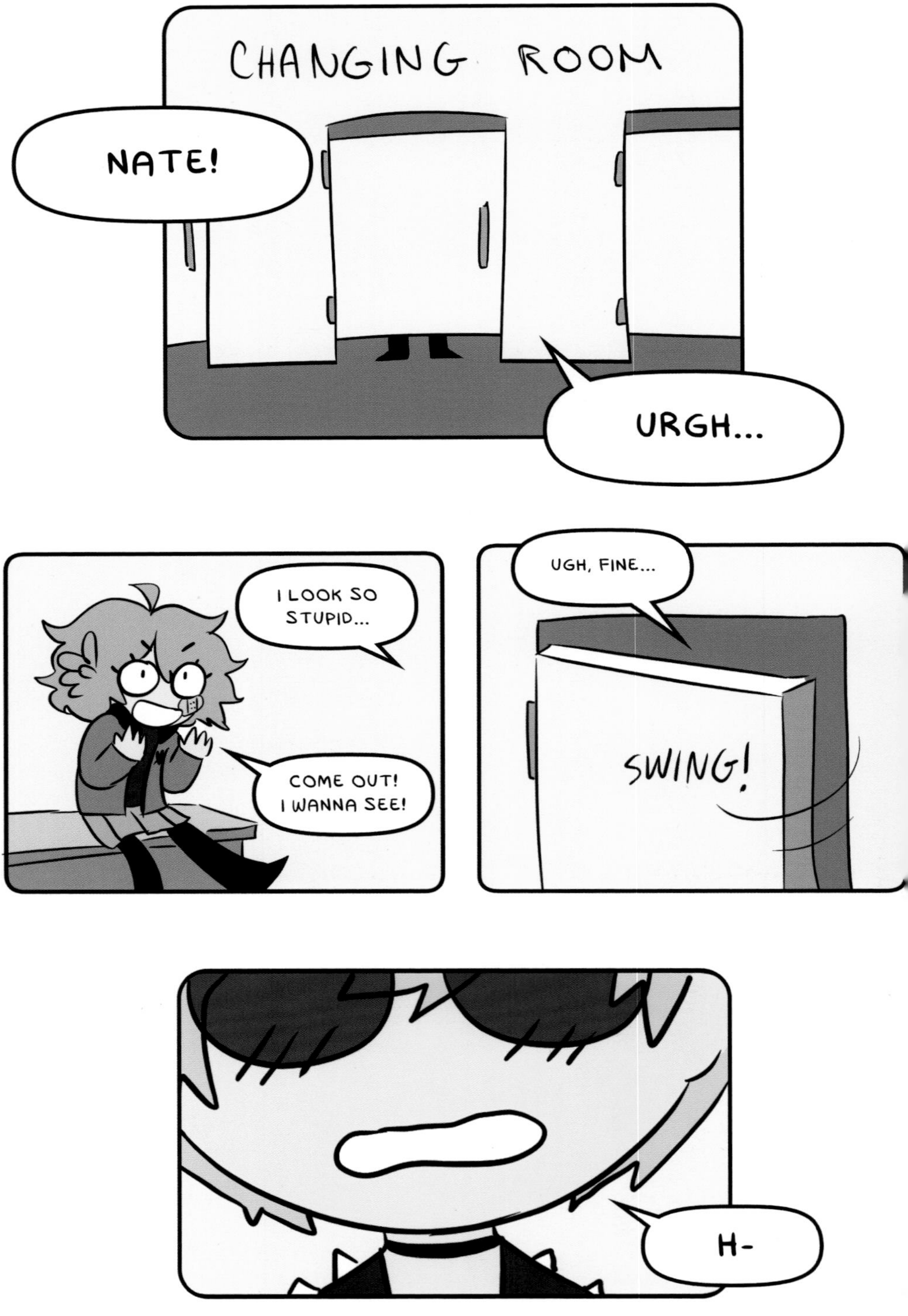
CHANGING ROOM
NATE!
URGH...
I LOOK SO STUPID...
COME OUT! I WANNA SEE!
UGH, FINE...
SWING!
H-

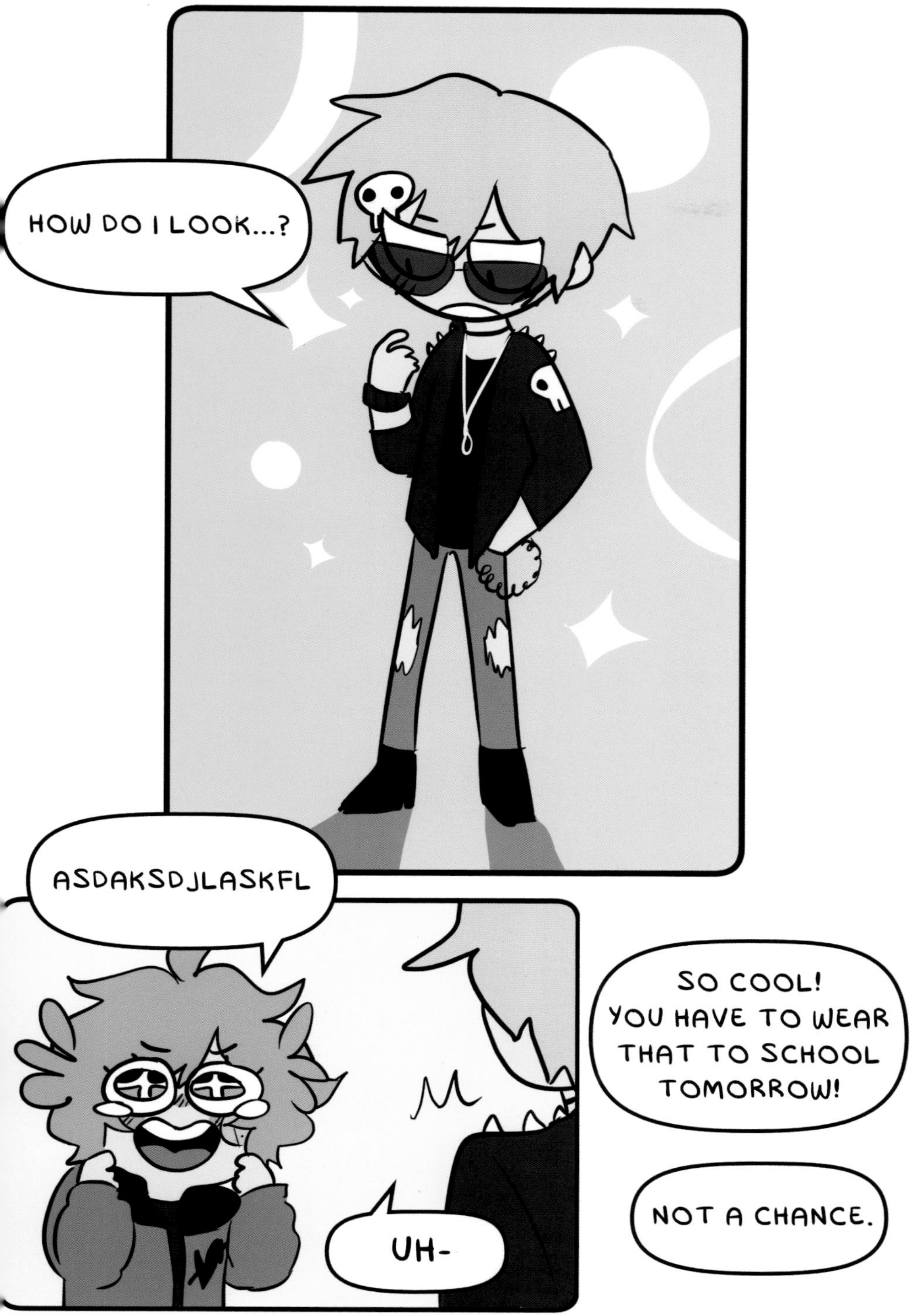
HOW DO I LOOK...?
ASDAKSDJLASKFL
SO COOL! YOU HAVE TO WEAR THAT TO SCHOOL TOMORROW!
UH-
NOT A CHANCE.

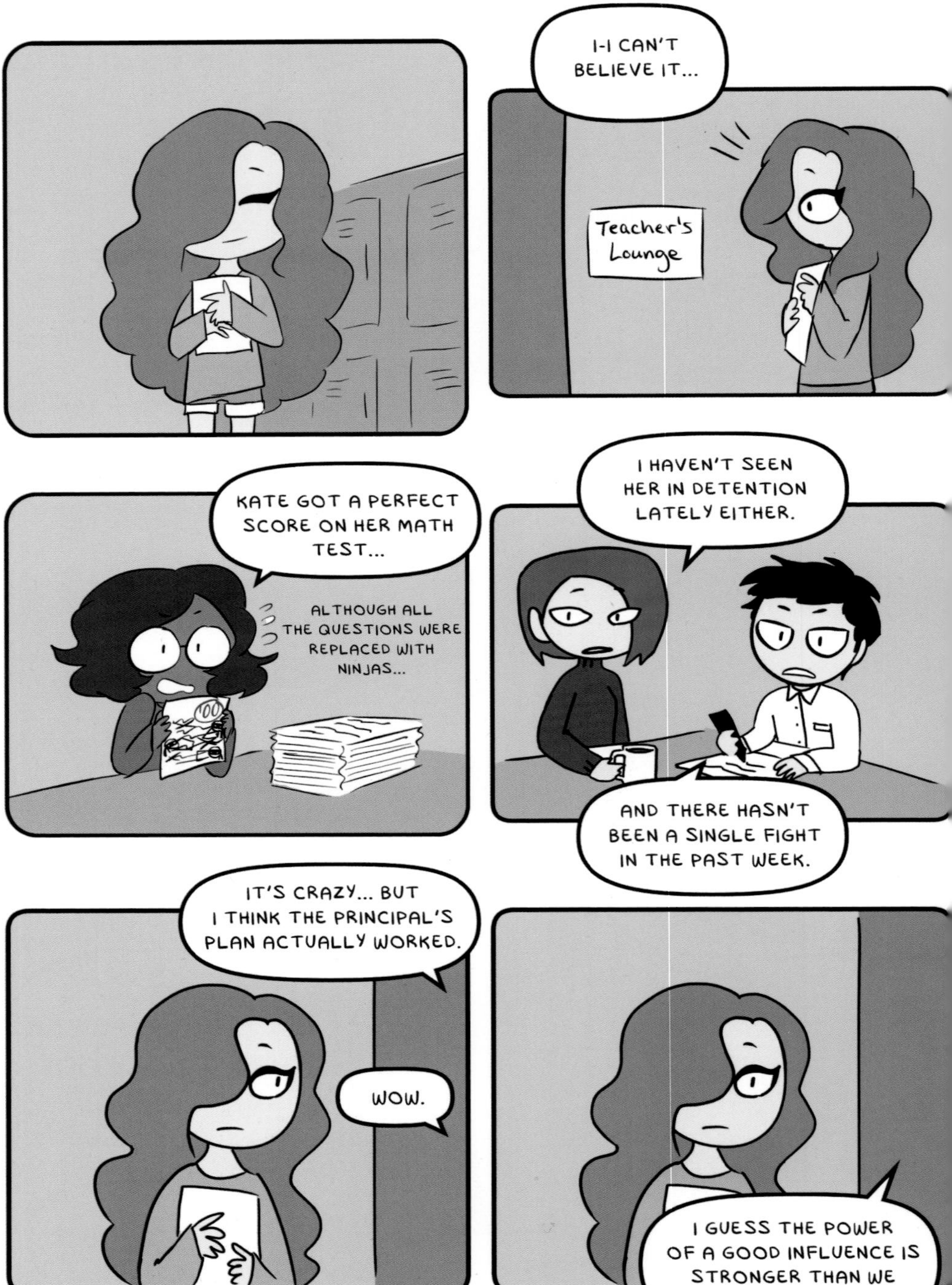
I-I CAN'T BELIEVE IT...
Teacher's Lounge
KATE GOT A PERFECT SCORE ON HER MATH TEST...
ALTHOUGH ALL THE QUESTIONS WERE REPLACED WITH NINJAS...
100
I HAVEN'T SEEN HER IN DETENTION LATELY EITHER.
AND THERE HASN'T BEEN A SINGLE FIGHT IN THE PAST WEEK.
IT'S CRAZY... BUT I THINK THE PRINCIPAL'S PLAN ACTUALLY WORKED.
WOW.
I GUESS THE POWER OF A GOOD INFLUENCE IS STRONGER THAN WE THOUGHT.

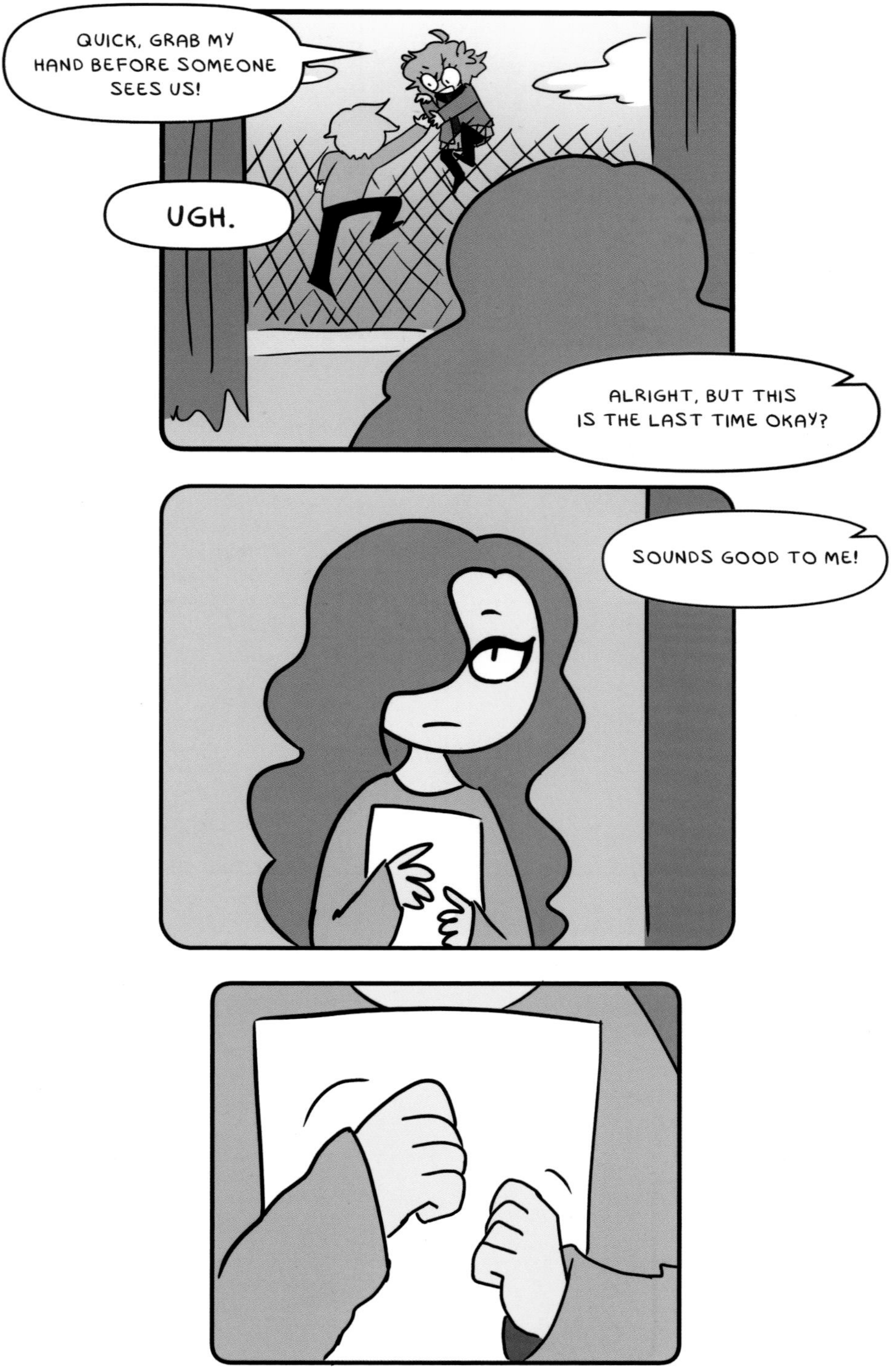
QUICK, GRAB MY HAND BEFORE SOMEONE SEES US!
UGH.
ALRIGHT, BUT THIS IS THE LAST TIME OKAY?
SOUNDS GOOD TO ME!

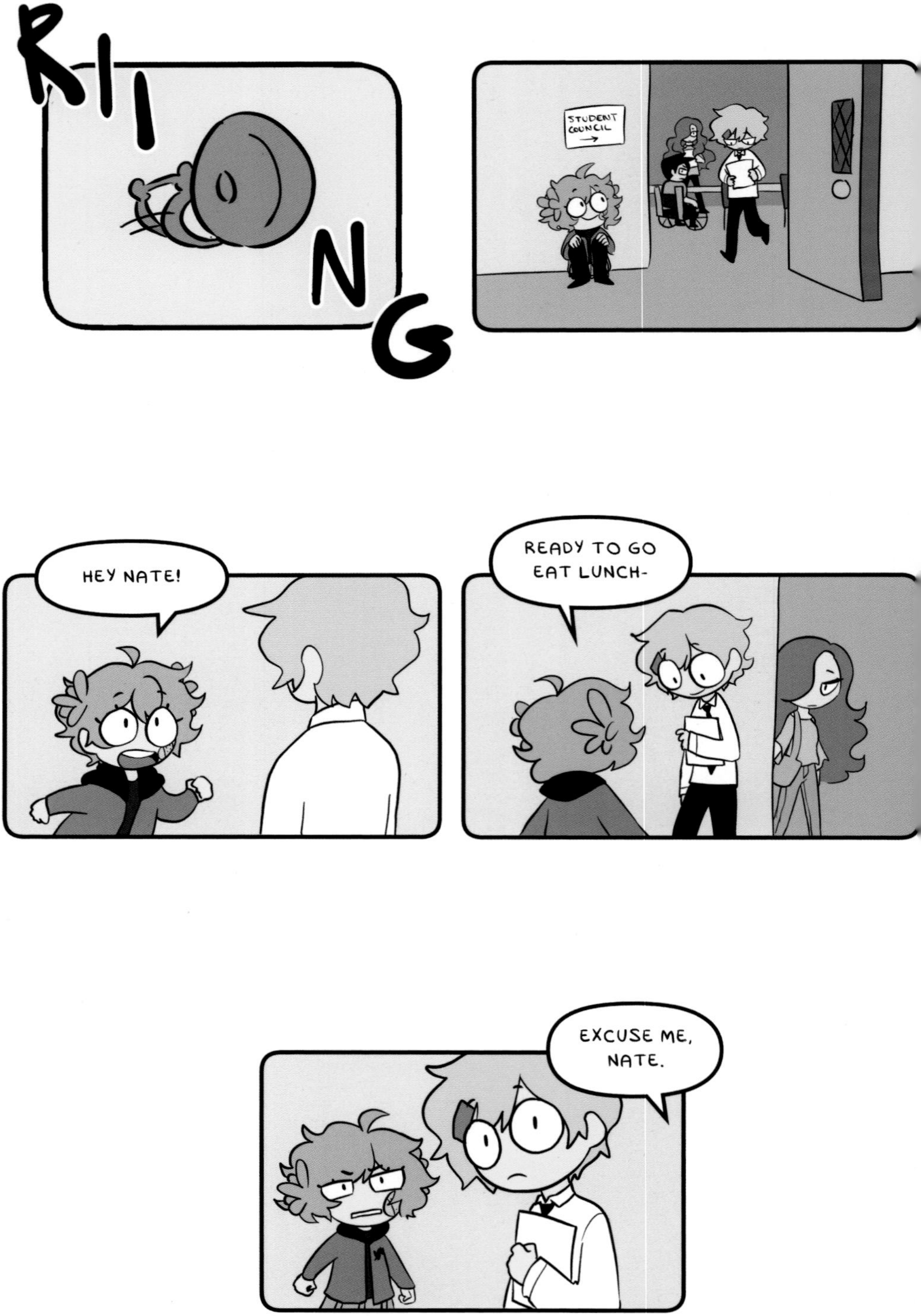
RIIING
STUDENT COUNCIL →
HEY NATE!
READY TO GO EAT LUNCH-
EXCUSE ME, NATE.

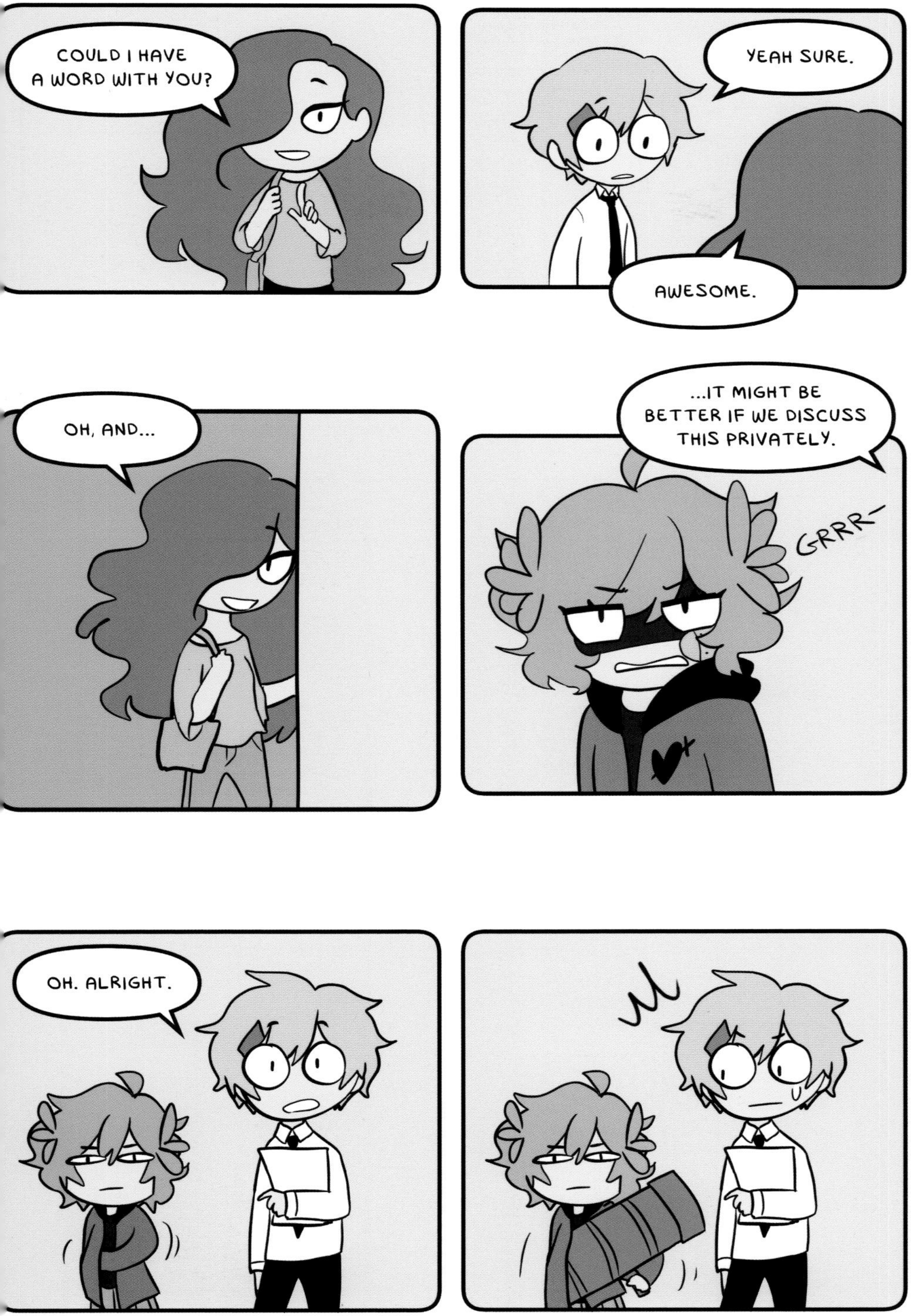
COULD I HAVE A WORD WITH YOU?
YEAH SURE.
AWESOME.
OH, AND...
...IT MIGHT BE BETTER IF WE DISCUSS THIS PRIVATELY.
GRRR-
OH. ALRIGHT.

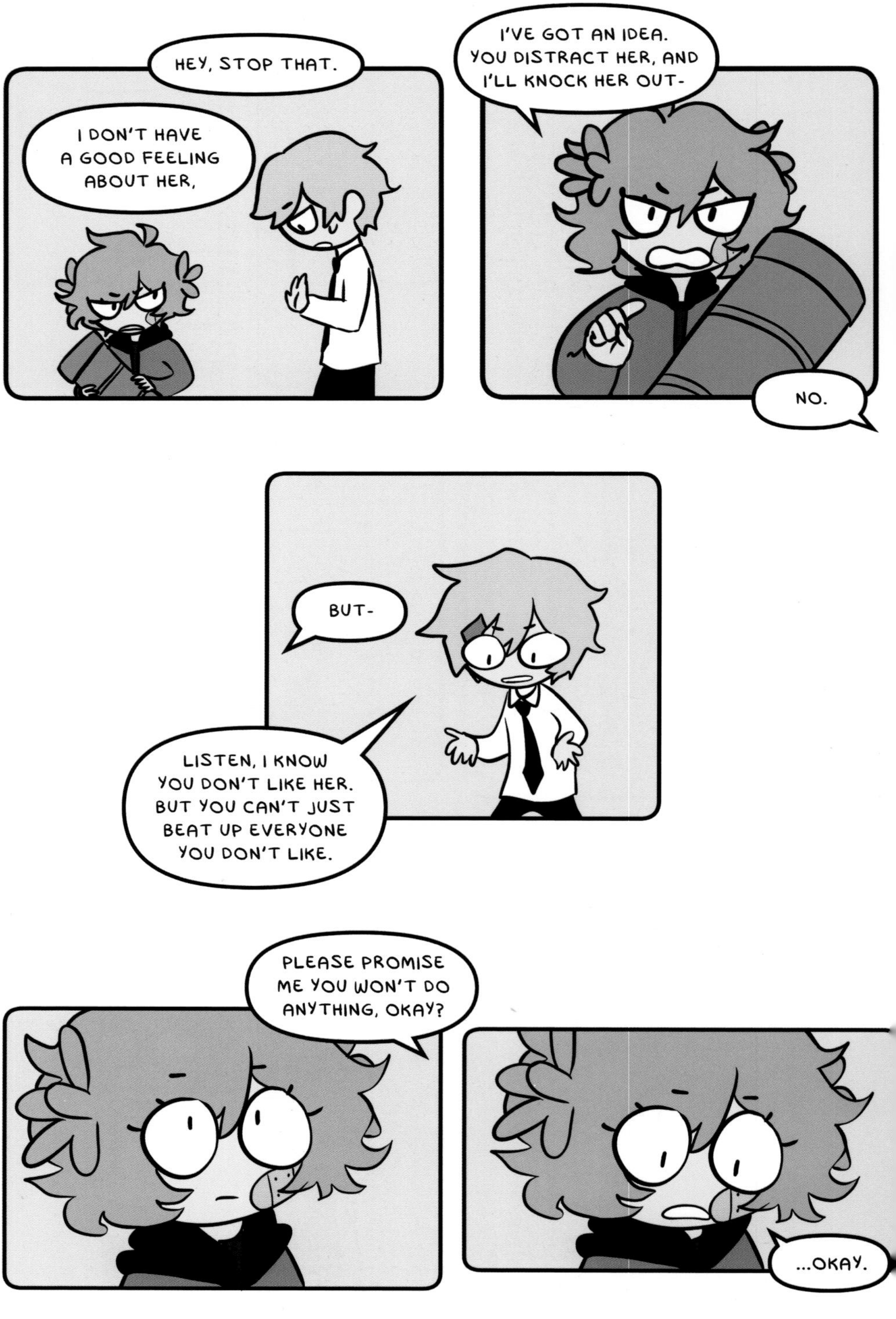
HEY, STOP THAT.
I DON'T HAVE A GOOD FEELING ABOUT HER,
I'VE GOT AN IDEA. YOU DISTRACT HER, AND I'LL KNOCK HER OUT-
NO.
BUT-
LISTEN, I KNOW YOU DON'T LIKE HER. BUT YOU CAN'T JUST BEAT UP EVERYONE YOU DON'T LIKE.
PLEASE PROMISE ME YOU WON'T DO ANYTHING, OKAY?
...OKAY.

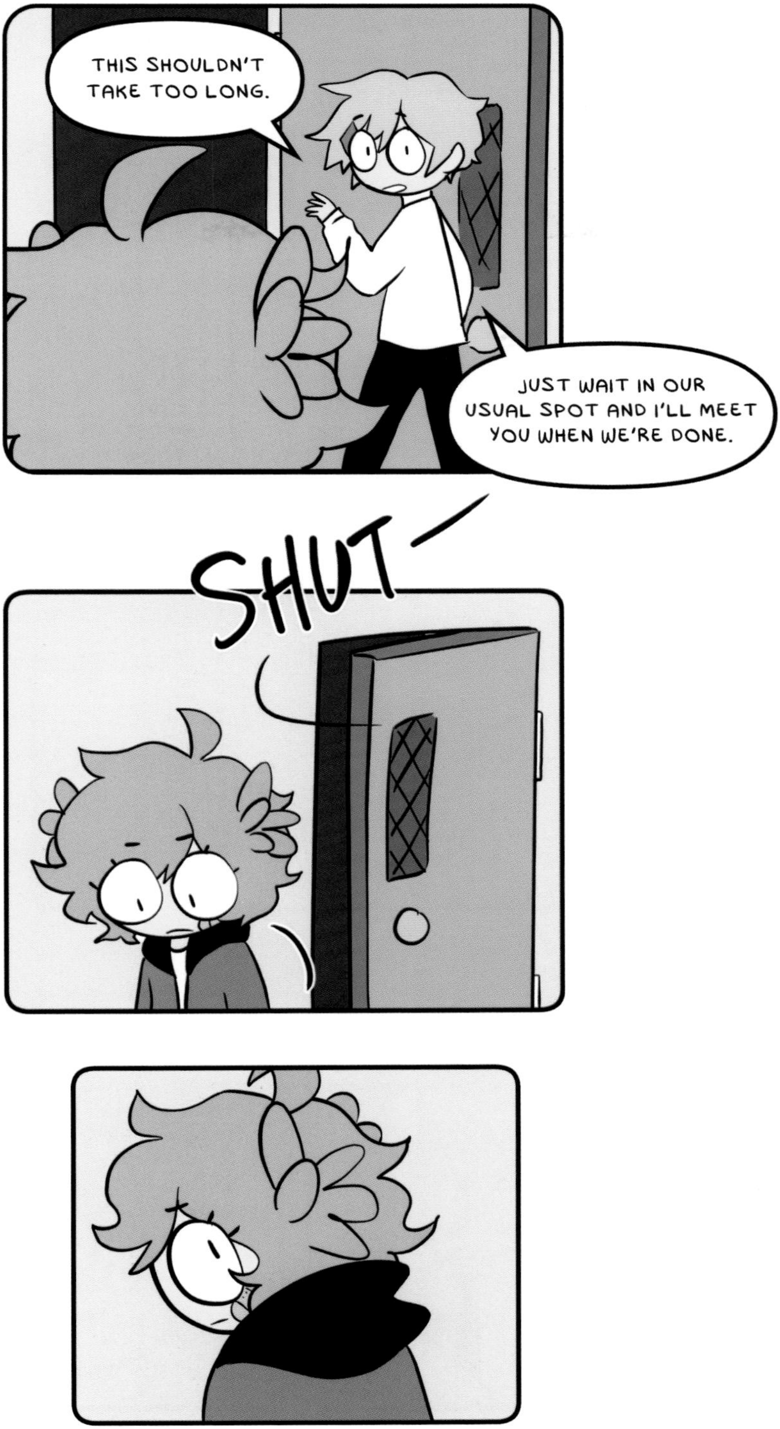
THIS SHOULDN'T TAKE TOO LONG.
JUST WAIT IN OUR USUAL SPOT AND I'LL MEET YOU WHEN WE'RE DONE.
SHUT—

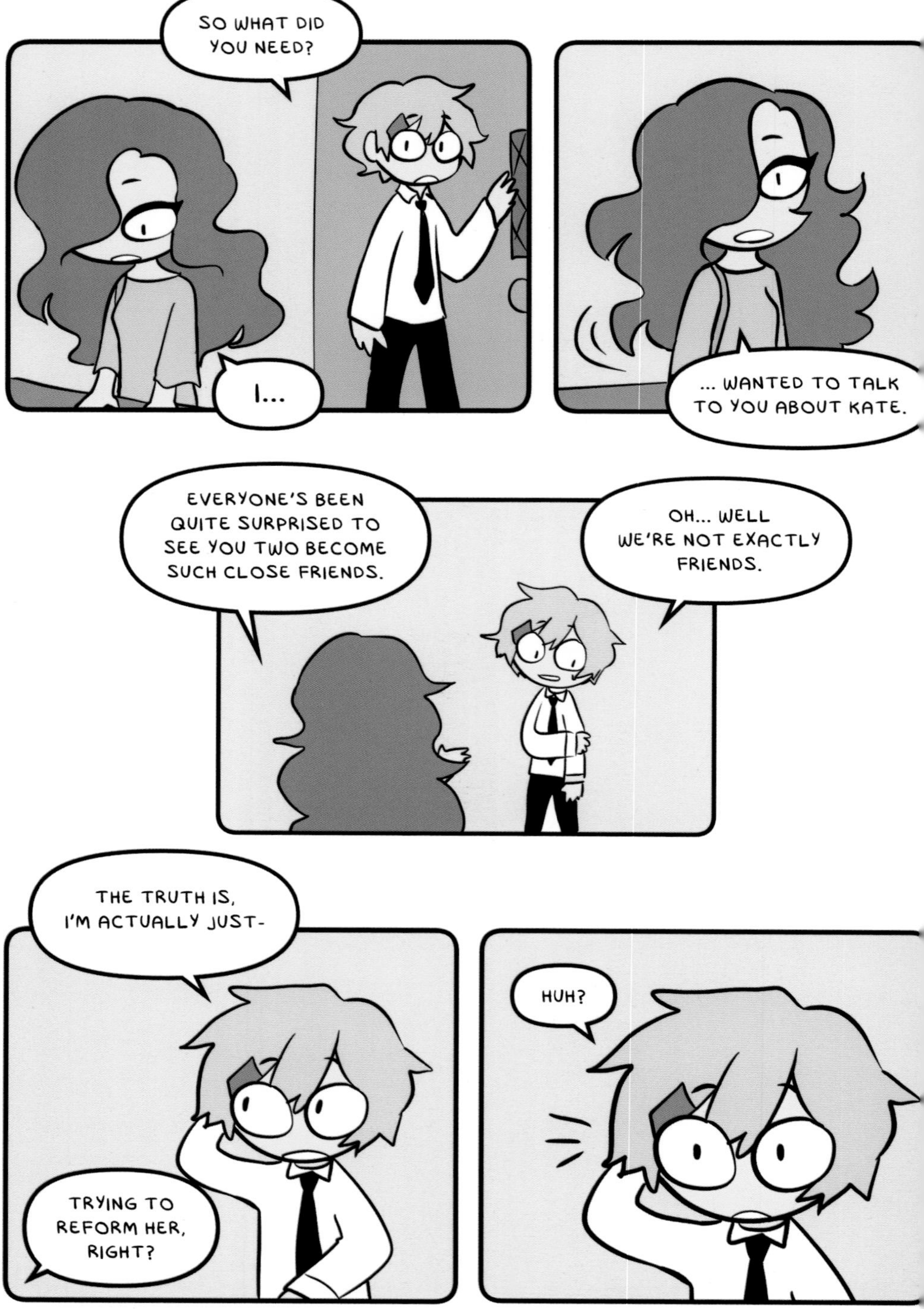
SO WHAT DID YOU NEED?
I...
... WANTED TO TALK TO YOU ABOUT KATE.
EVERYONE'S BEEN QUITE SURPRISED TO SEE YOU TWO BECOME SUCH CLOSE FRIENDS.
OH... WELL WE'RE NOT EXACTLY FRIENDS.
THE TRUTH IS, I'M ACTUALLY JUST-
TRYING TO REFORM HER, RIGHT?
HUH?

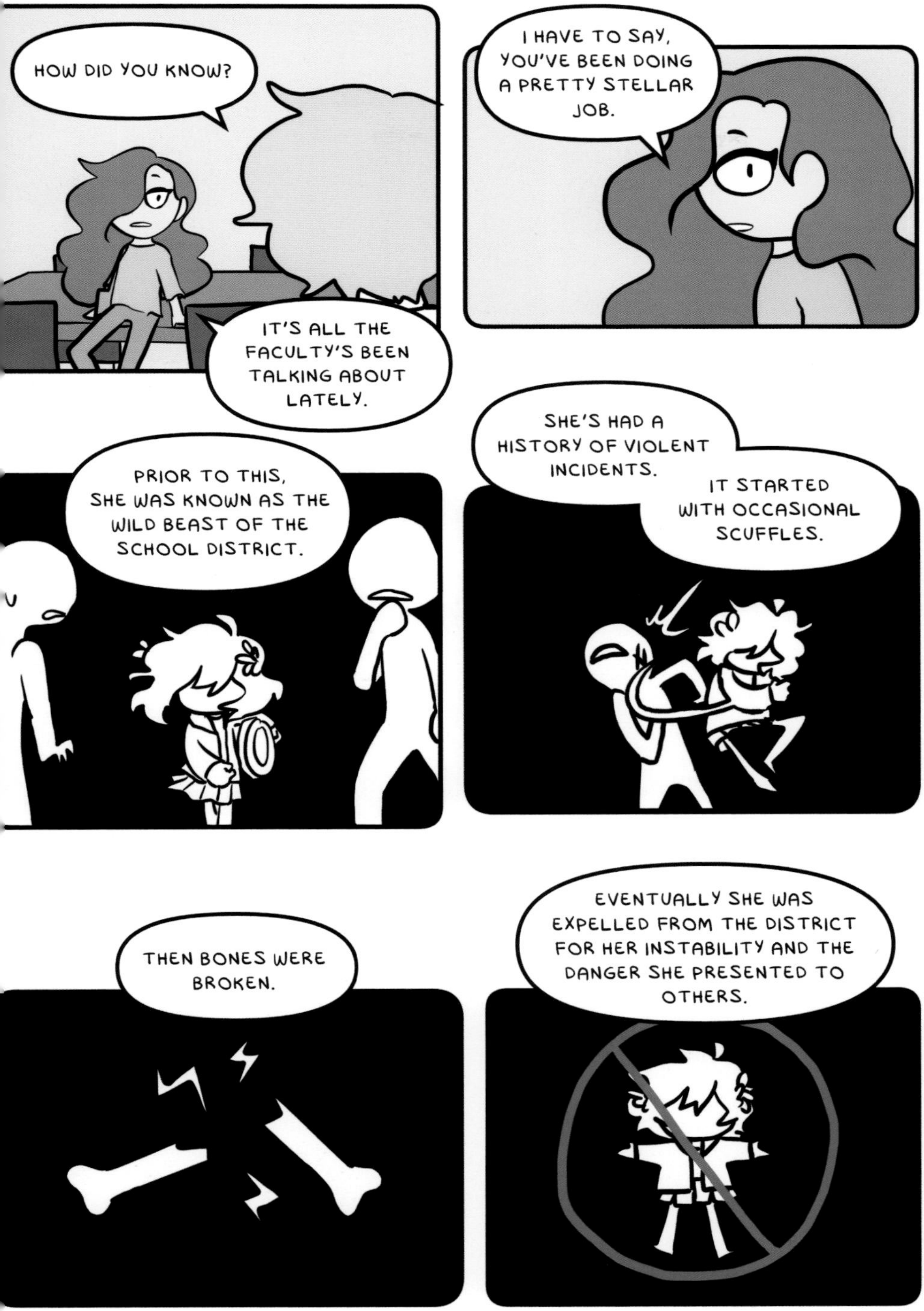
HOW DID YOU KNOW?
IT'S ALL THE FACULTY'S BEEN TALKING ABOUT LATELY.
I HAVE TO SAY, YOU'VE BEEN DOING A PRETTY STELLAR JOB.
PRIOR TO THIS, SHE WAS KNOWN AS THE WILD BEAST OF THE SCHOOL DISTRICT.
SHE'S HAD A HISTORY OF VIOLENT INCIDENTS.
IT STARTED WITH OCCASIONAL SCUFFLES.
THEN BONES WERE BROKEN.
EVENTUALLY SHE WAS EXPELLED FROM THE DISTRICT FOR HER INSTABILITY AND THE DANGER SHE PRESENTED TO OTHERS.

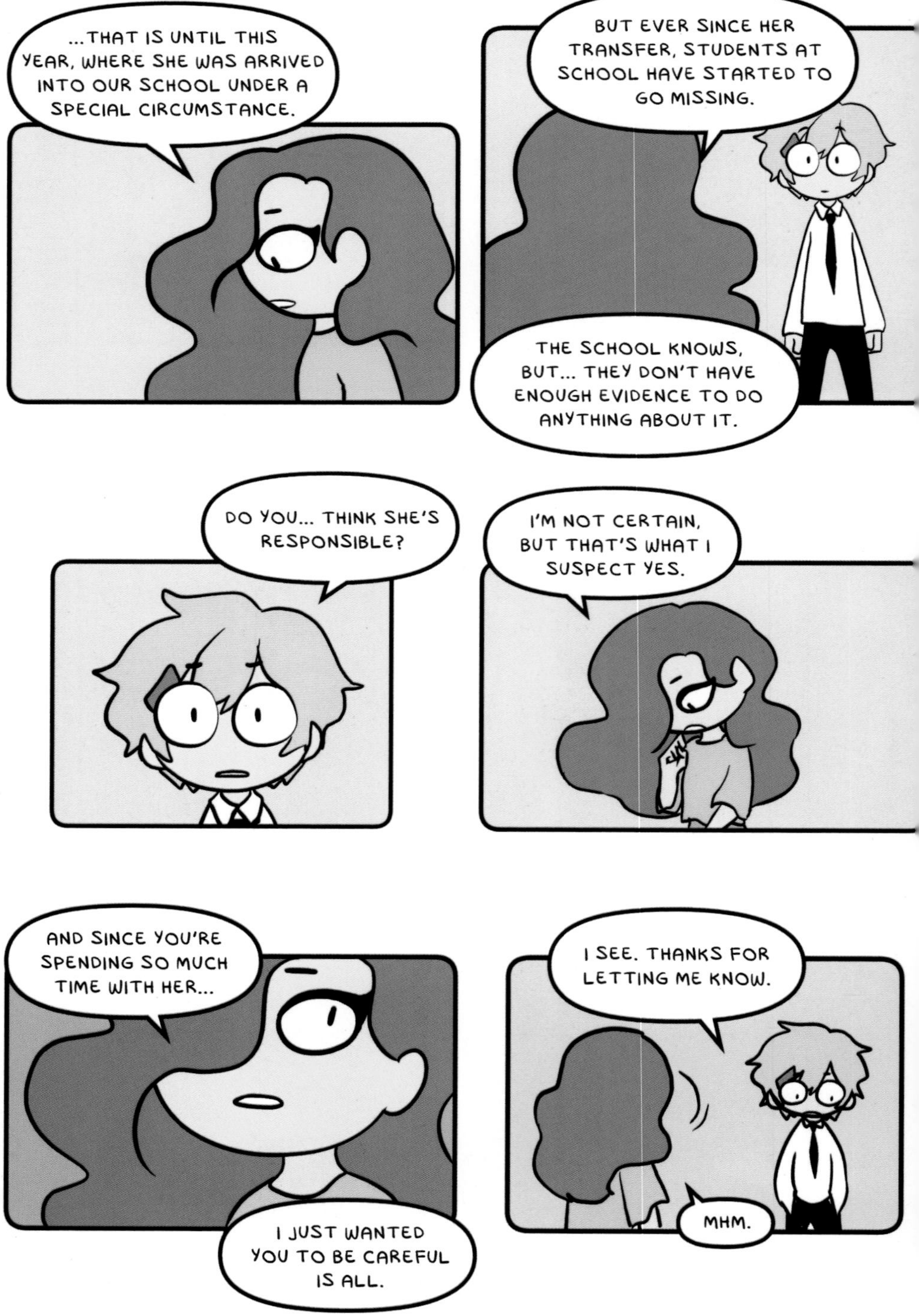
...THAT IS UNTIL THIS YEAR, WHERE SHE WAS ARRIVED INTO OUR SCHOOL UNDER A SPECIAL CIRCUMSTANCE.
BUT EVER SINCE HER TRANSFER, STUDENTS AT SCHOOL HAVE STARTED TO GO MISSING.
THE SCHOOL KNOWS, BUT... THEY DON'T HAVE ENOUGH EVIDENCE TO DO ANYTHING ABOUT IT.
DO YOU... THINK SHE'S RESPONSIBLE?
I'M NOT CERTAIN, BUT THAT'S WHAT I SUSPECT YES.
AND SINCE YOU'RE SPENDING SO MUCH TIME WITH HER...
I JUST WANTED YOU TO BE CAREFUL IS ALL.
I SEE. THANKS FOR LETTING ME KNOW.
MHM.

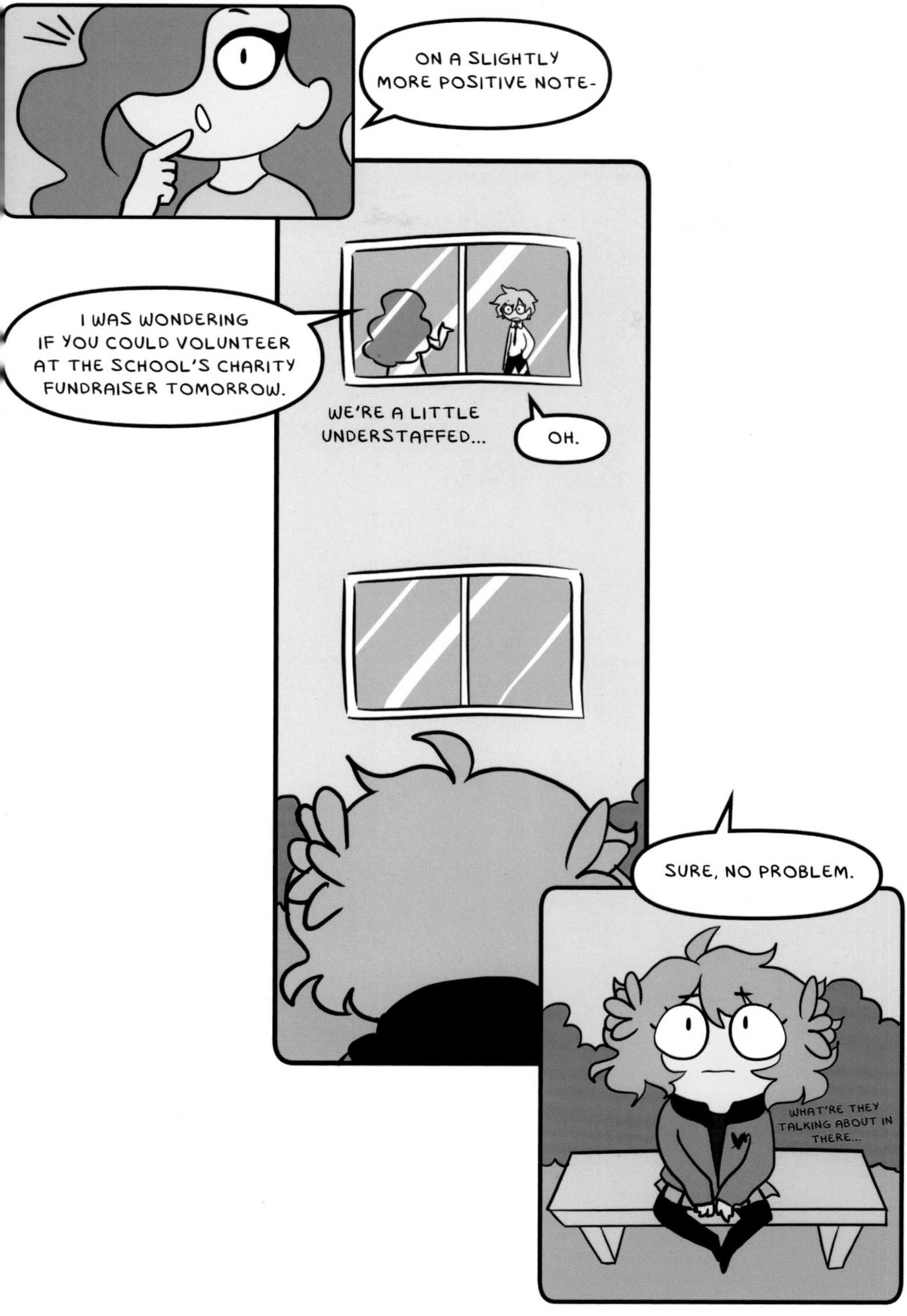
ON A SLIGHTLY MORE POSITIVE NOTE-
I WAS WONDERING IF YOU COULD VOLUNTEER AT THE SCHOOL'S CHARITY FUNDRAISER TOMORROW.
WE'RE A LITTLE UNDERSTAFFED...
OH.
SURE, NO PROBLEM.
WHAT'RE THEY TALKING ABOUT IN THERE...

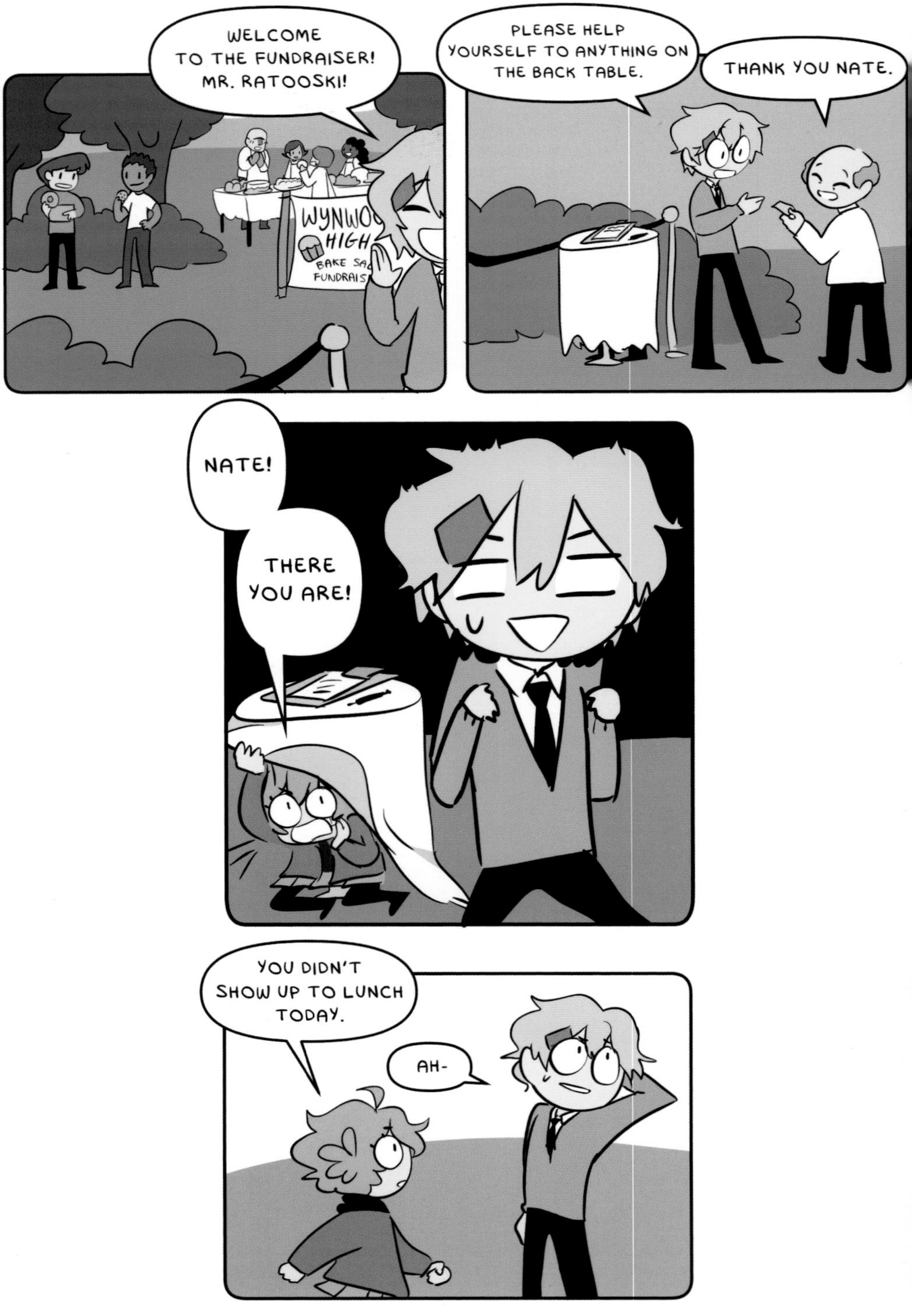
WELCOME TO THE FUNDRAISER! MR. RATOOSKI!
WYNWO HIGH BAKE SA FUNDRAIS
PLEASE HELP YOURSELF TO ANYTHING ON THE BACK TABLE.
THANK YOU NATE.
NATE!
THERE YOU ARE!
YOU DIDN'T SHOW UP TO LUNCH TODAY.
AH-

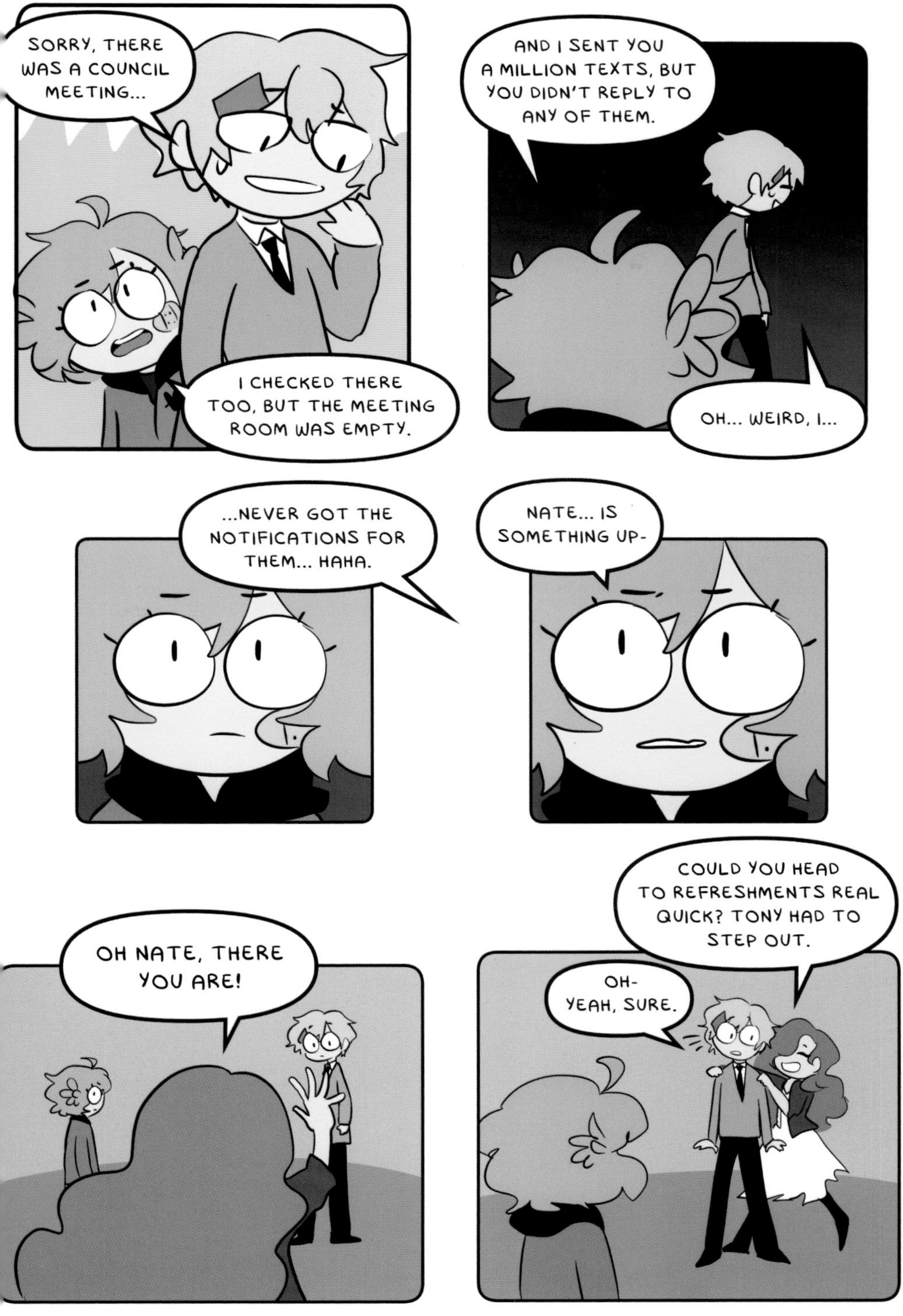
SORRY, THERE WAS A COUNCIL MEETING...
I CHECKED THERE TOO, BUT THE MEETING ROOM WAS EMPTY.
AND I SENT YOU A MILLION TEXTS, BUT YOU DIDN'T REPLY TO ANY OF THEM.
OH... WEIRD, I...
...NEVER GOT THE NOTIFICATIONS FOR THEM... HAHA.
NATE... IS SOMETHING UP-
OH NATE, THERE YOU ARE!
COULD YOU HEAD TO REFRESHMENTS REAL QUICK? TONY HAD TO STEP OUT.
OH- YEAH, SURE.

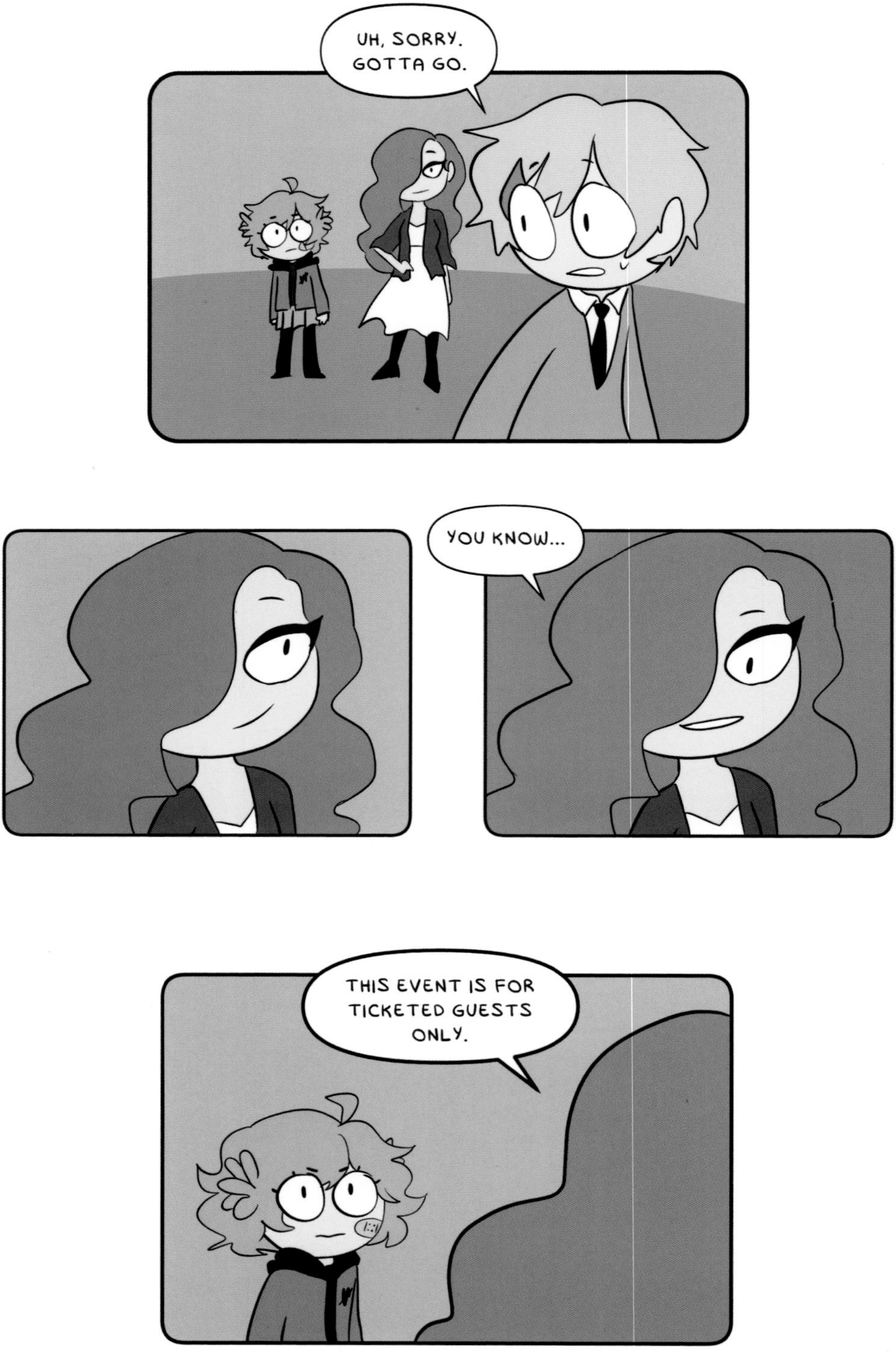
UH, SORRY. GOTTA GO.
YOU KNOW...
THIS EVENT IS FOR TICKETED GUESTS ONLY.

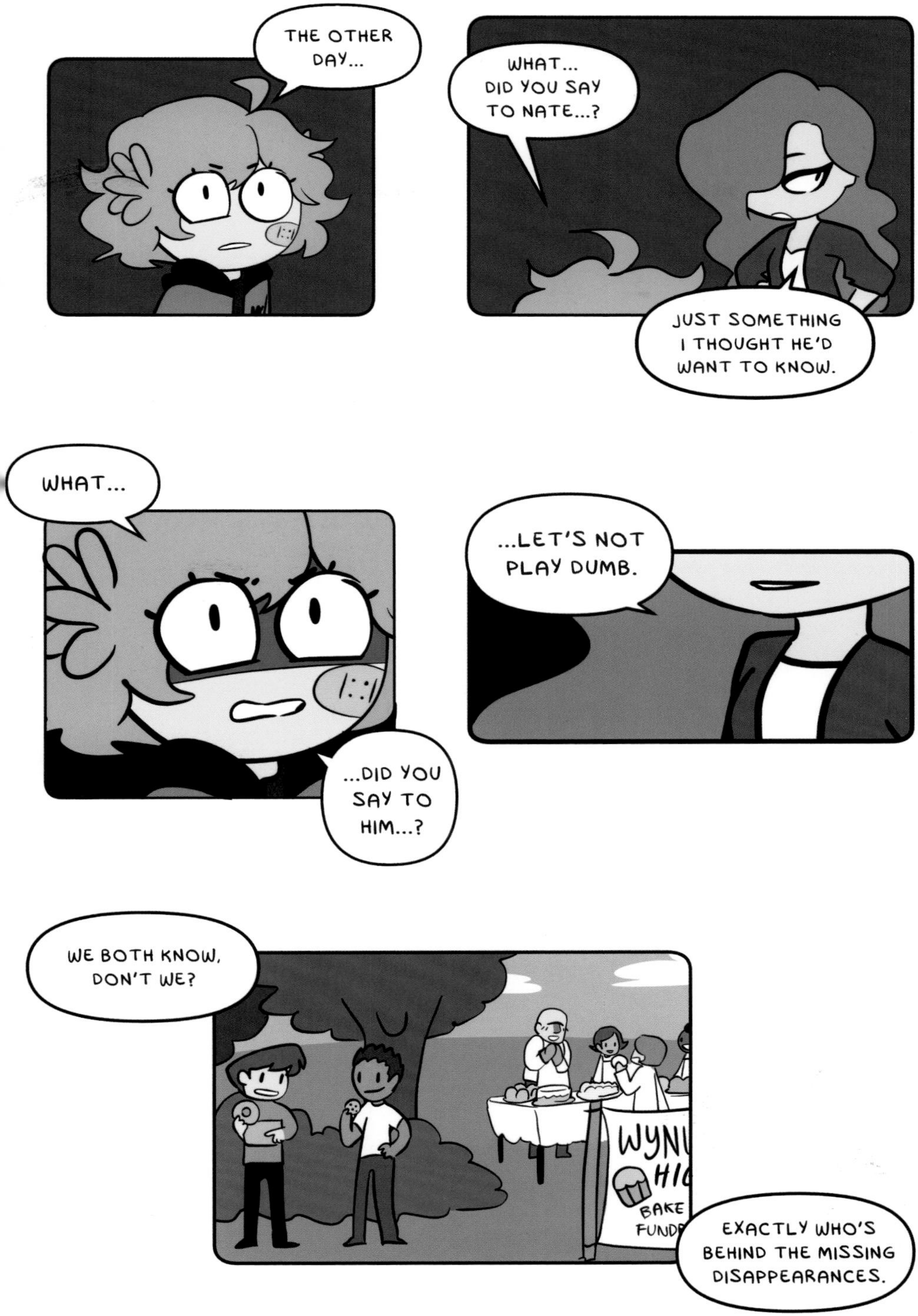
THE OTHER DAY...
WHAT... DID YOU SAY TO NATE...?
JUST SOMETHING I THOUGHT HE'D WANT TO KNOW.
WHAT...
...DID YOU SAY TO HIM...?
...LET'S NOT PLAY DUMB.
WE BOTH KNOW, DON'T WE?
BAKE
EXACTLY WHO'S BEHIND THE MISSING DISAPPEARANCES.

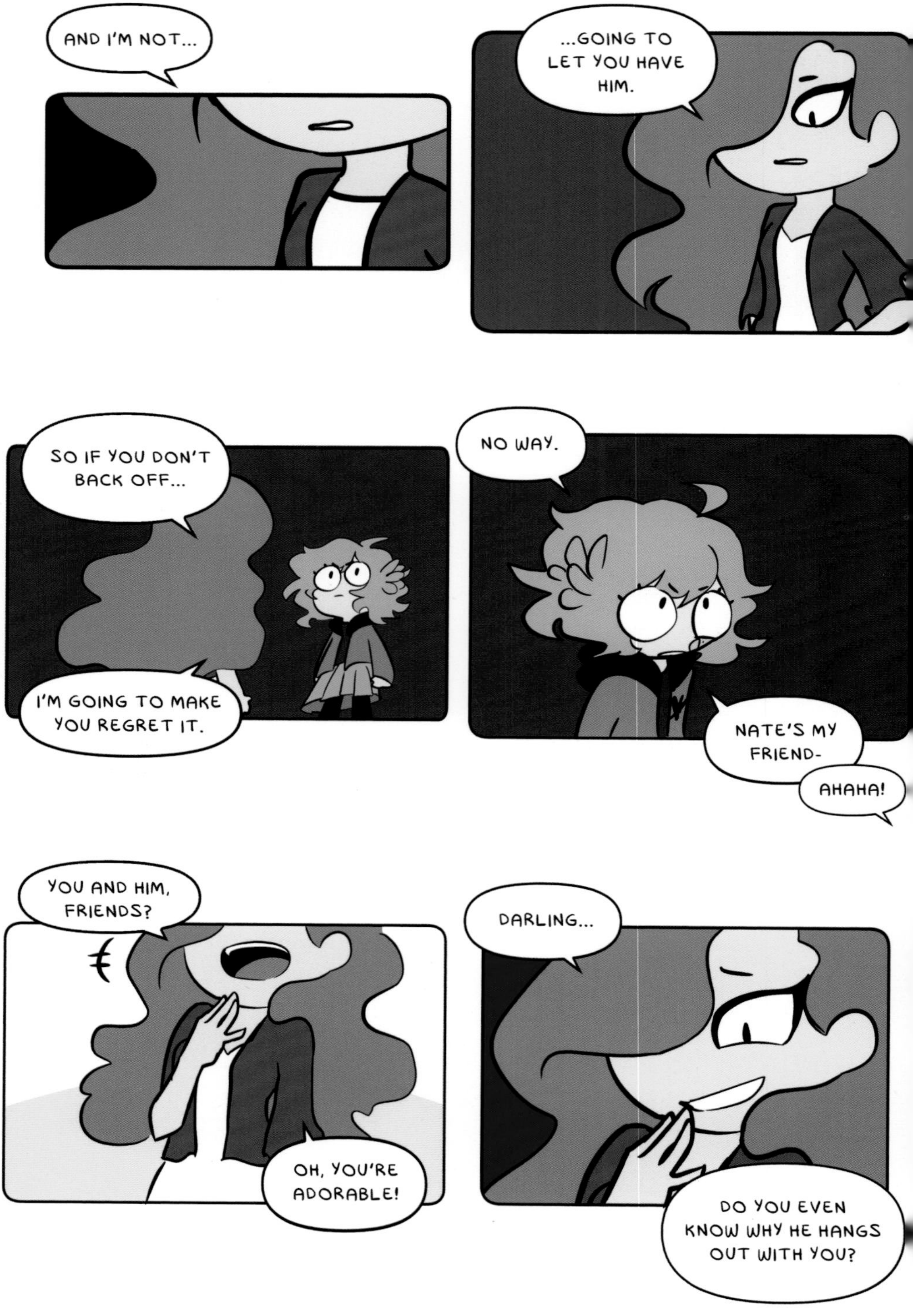
AND I'M NOT...
...GOING TO LET YOU HAVE HIM.
SO IF YOU DON'T BACK OFF...
I'M GOING TO MAKE YOU REGRET IT.
NO WAY.
NATE'S MY FRIEND-
AHAHA!
YOU AND HIM, FRIENDS?
OH, YOU'RE ADORABLE!
DARLING...
DO YOU EVEN KNOW WHY HE HANGS OUT WITH YOU?

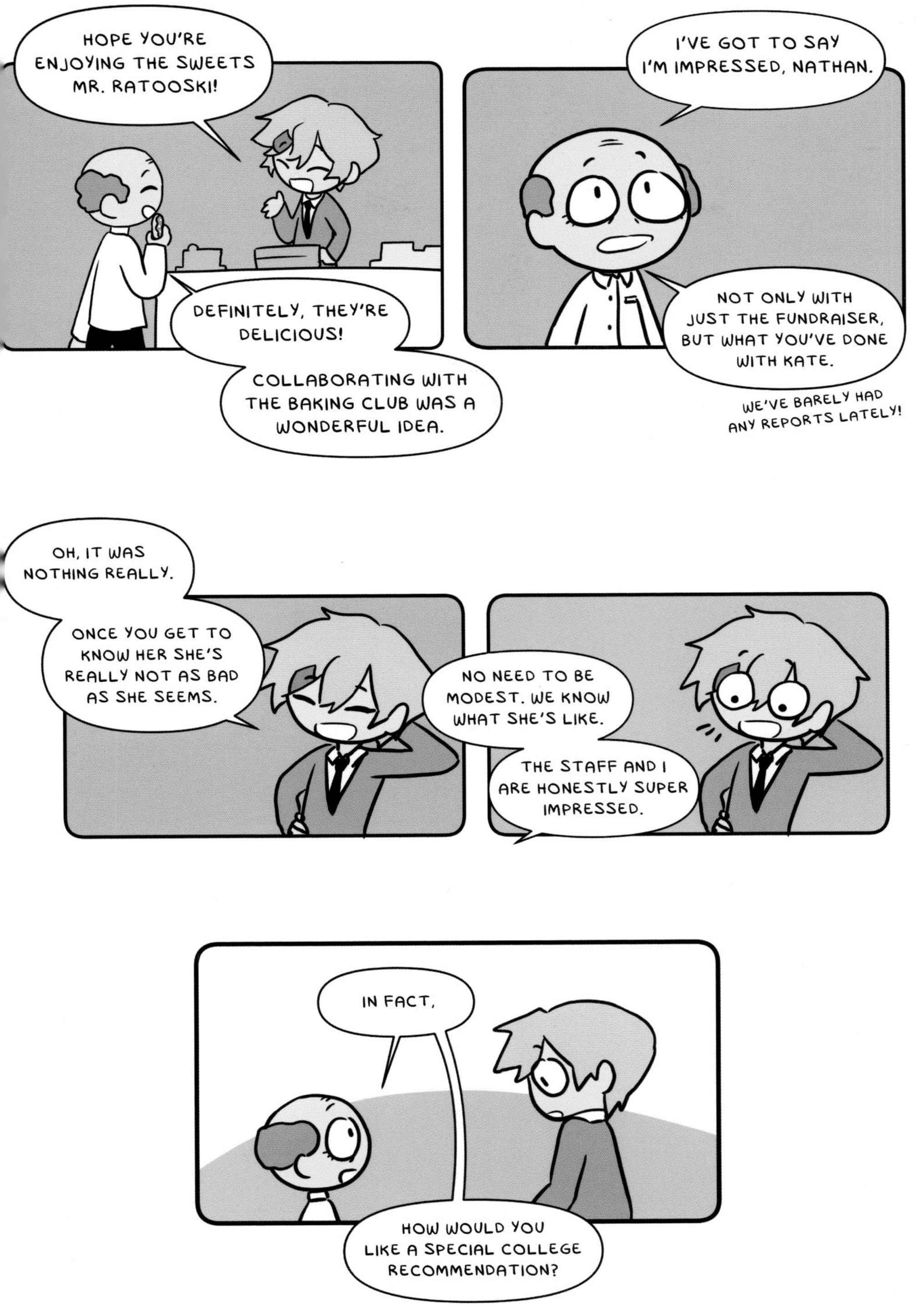
HOPE YOU'RE ENJOYING THE SWEETS MR. RATOOSKI!
DEFINITELY, THEY'RE DELICIOUS!
COLLABORATING WITH THE BAKING CLUB WAS A WONDERFUL IDEA.
I'VE GOT TO SAY I'M IMPRESSED, NATHAN.
NOT ONLY WITH JUST THE FUNDRAISER, BUT WHAT YOU'VE DONE WITH KATE.
WE'VE BARELY HAD ANY REPORTS LATELY!
OH, IT WAS NOTHING REALLY.
ONCE YOU GET TO KNOW HER SHE'S REALLY NOT AS BAD AS SHE SEEMS.
NO NEED TO BE MODEST. WE KNOW WHAT SHE'S LIKE.
THE STAFF AND I ARE HONESTLY SUPER IMPRESSED.
IN FACT,
HOW WOULD YOU LIKE A SPECIAL COLLEGE RECOMMENDATION?

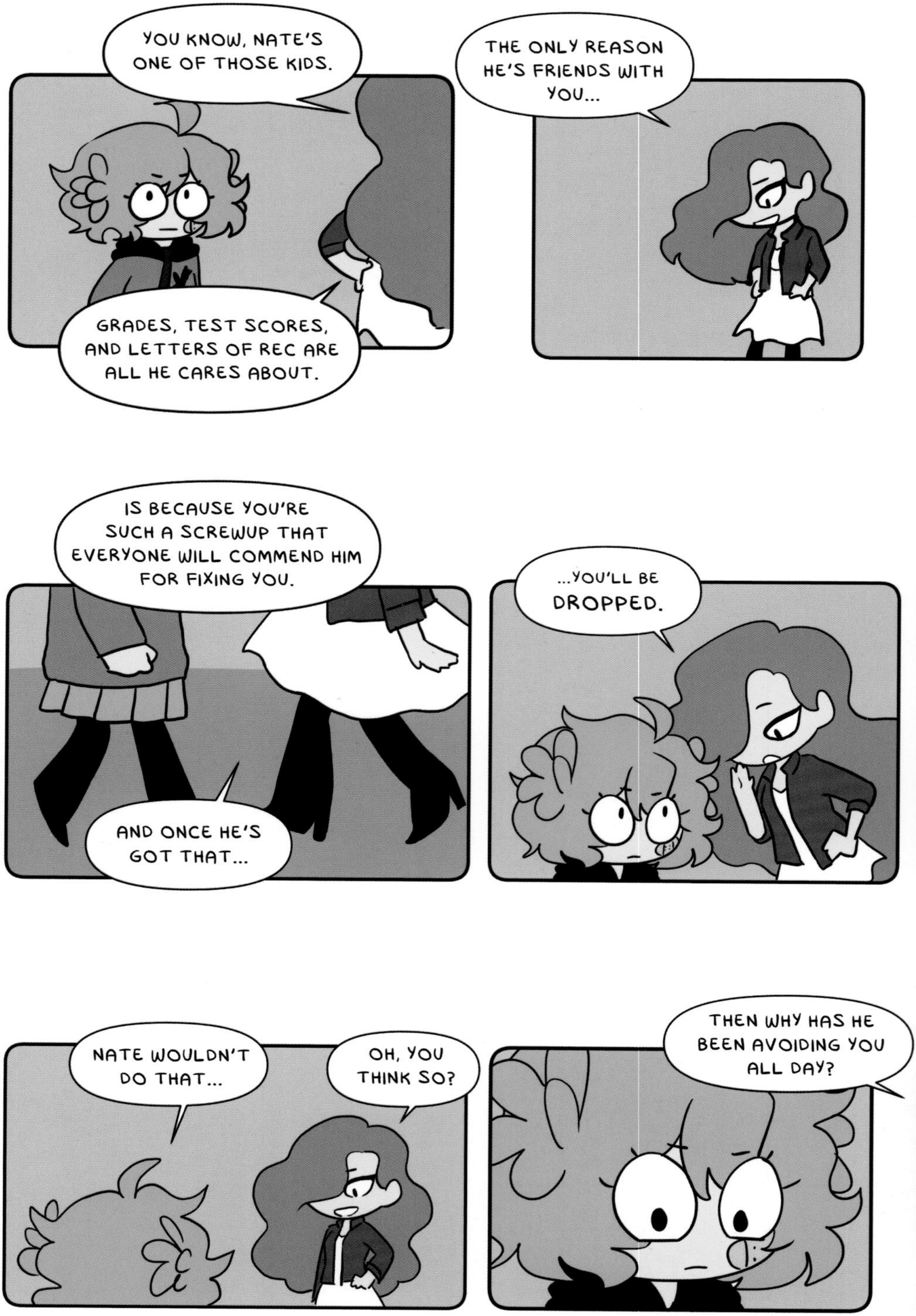
YOU KNOW, NATE'S ONE OF THOSE KIDS.
GRADES, TEST SCORES, AND LETTERS OF REC ARE ALL HE CARES ABOUT.
THE ONLY REASON HE'S FRIENDS WITH YOU...
IS BECAUSE YOU'RE SUCH A SCREWUP THAT EVERYONE WILL COMMEND HIM FOR FIXING YOU.
AND ONCE HE'S GOT THAT...
...YOU'LL BE DROPPED.
NATE WOULDN'T DO THAT...
OH, YOU THINK SO?
THEN WHY HAS HE BEEN AVOIDING YOU ALL DAY?

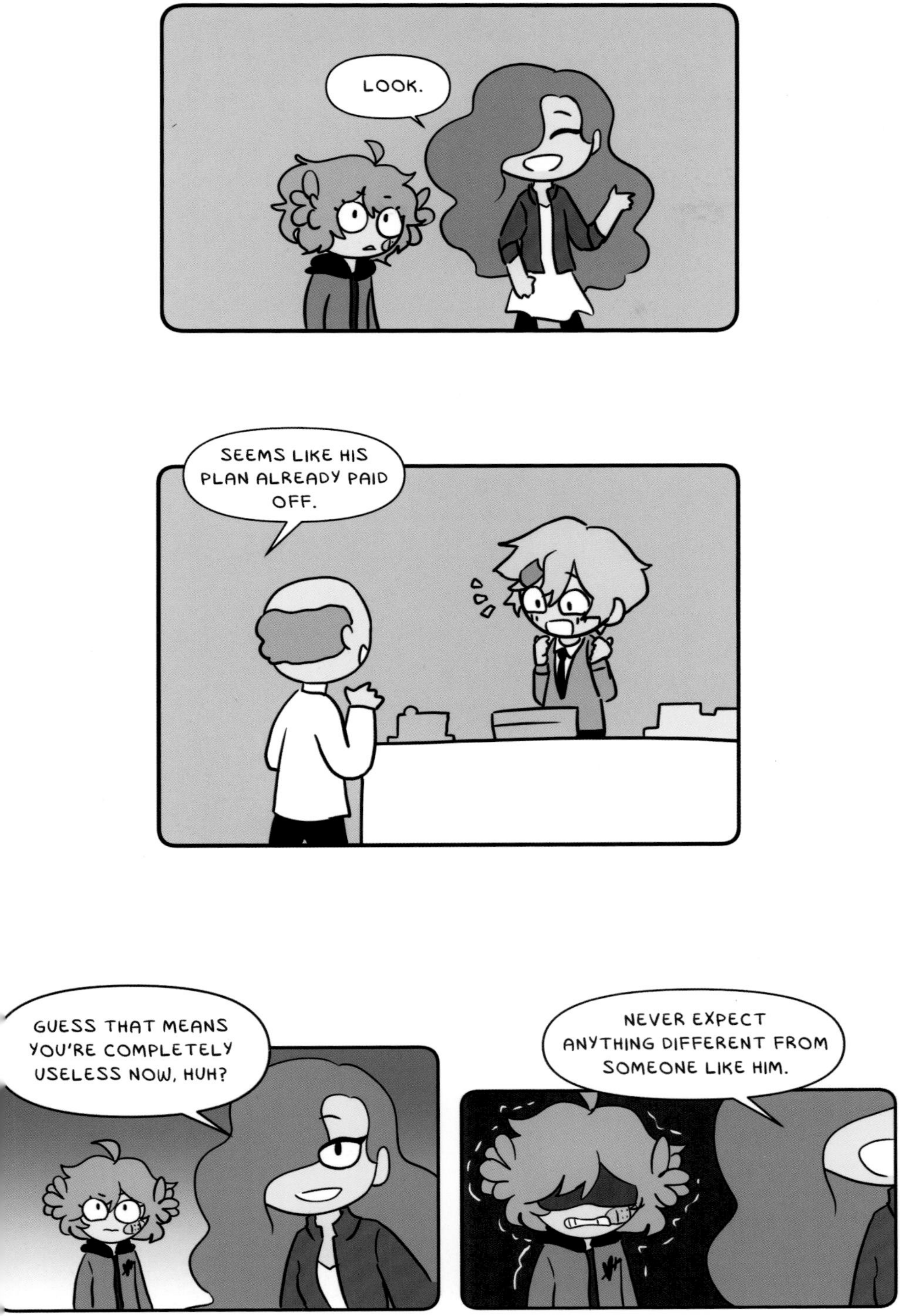
LOOK.
SEEMS LIKE HIS PLAN ALREADY PAID OFF.
GUESS THAT MEANS YOU'RE COMPLETELY USELESS NOW, HUH?
NEVER EXPECT ANYTHING DIFFERENT FROM SOMEONE LIKE HIM.

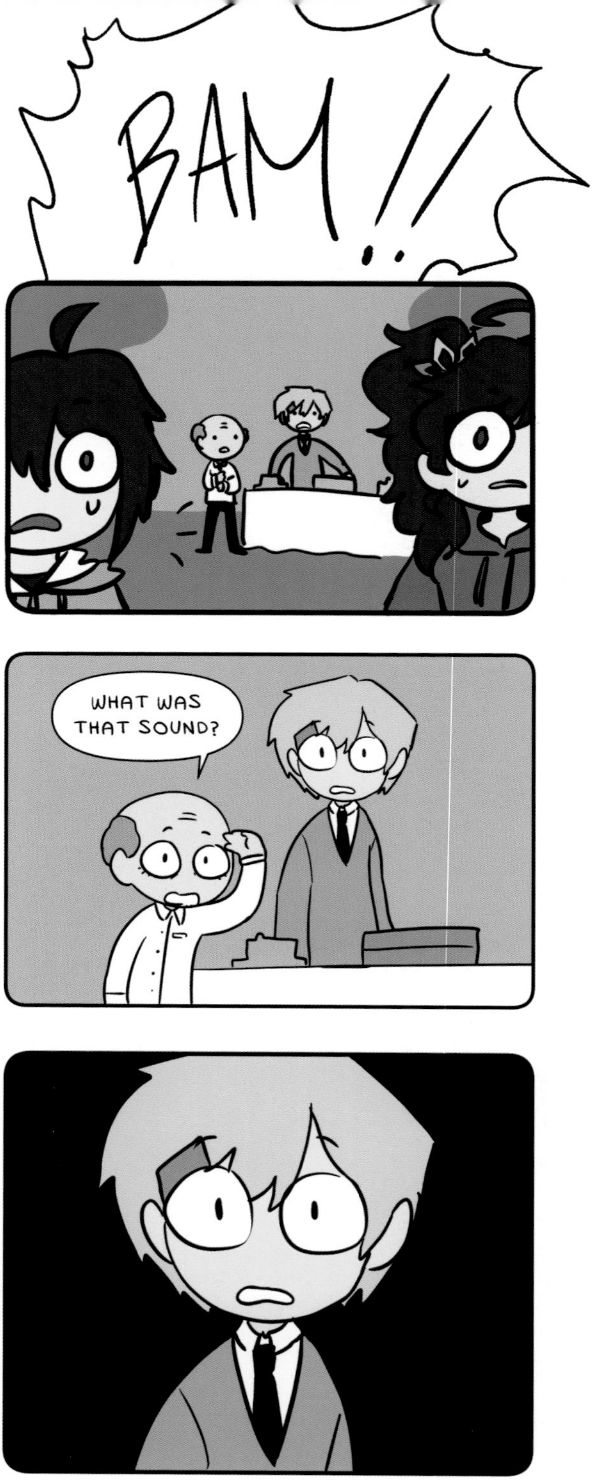
BAM!!
WHAT WAS THAT SOUND?

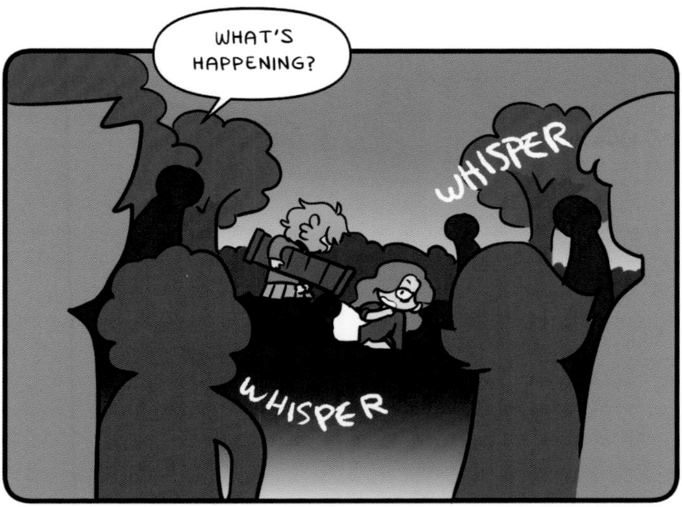
WHAT'S HAPPENING?
WHISPER
WHISPER

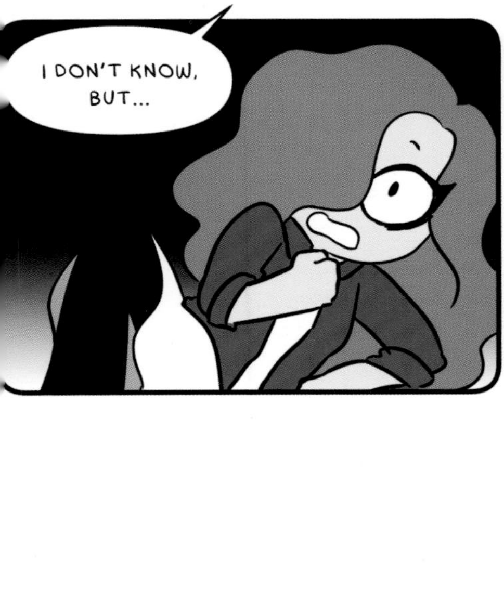
I DON'T KNOW, BUT...

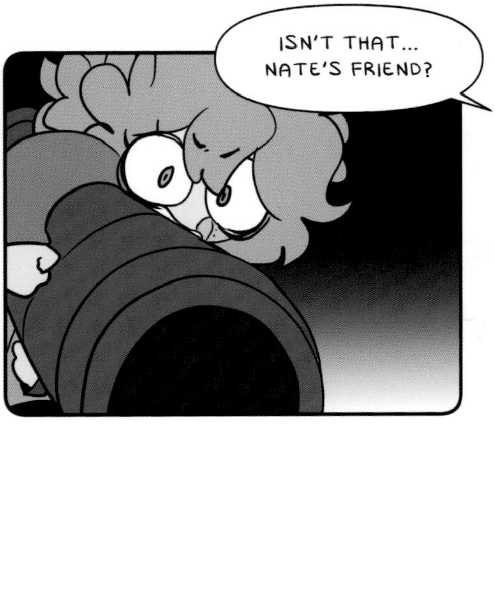
ISN'T THAT... NATE'S FRIEND?

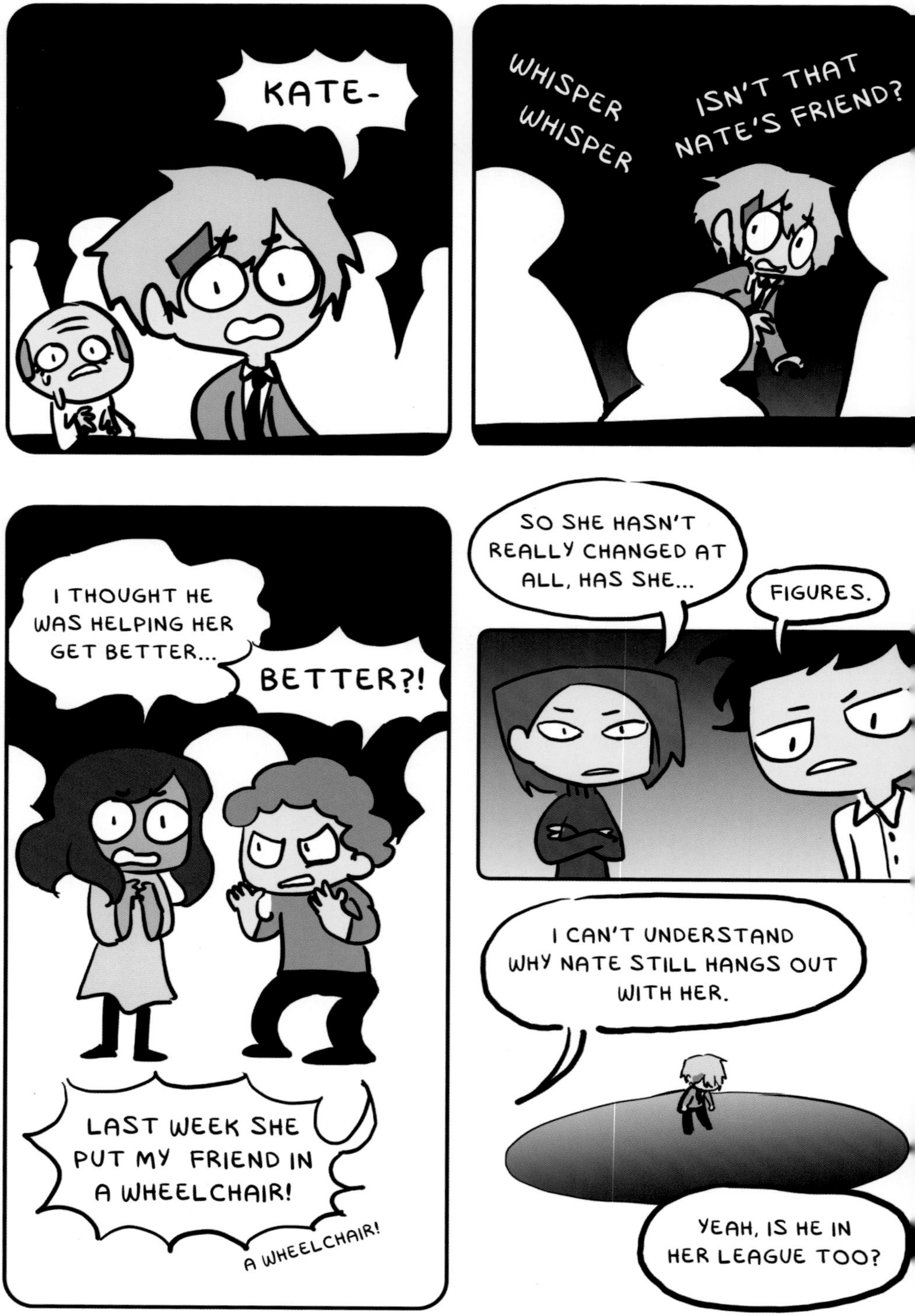
KATE-
WHISPER
WHISPER
ISN'T THAT NATE'S FRIEND?
I THOUGHT HE WAS HELPING HER GET BETTER...
BETTER?!
LAST WEEK SHE PUT MY FRIEND IN A WHEELCHAIR!
A WHEELCHAIR!
SO SHE HASN'T REALLY CHANGED AT ALL, HAS SHE...
FIGURES.
I CAN'T UNDERSTAND WHY NATE STILL HANGS OUT WITH HER.
YEAH, IS HE IN HER LEAGUE TOO?

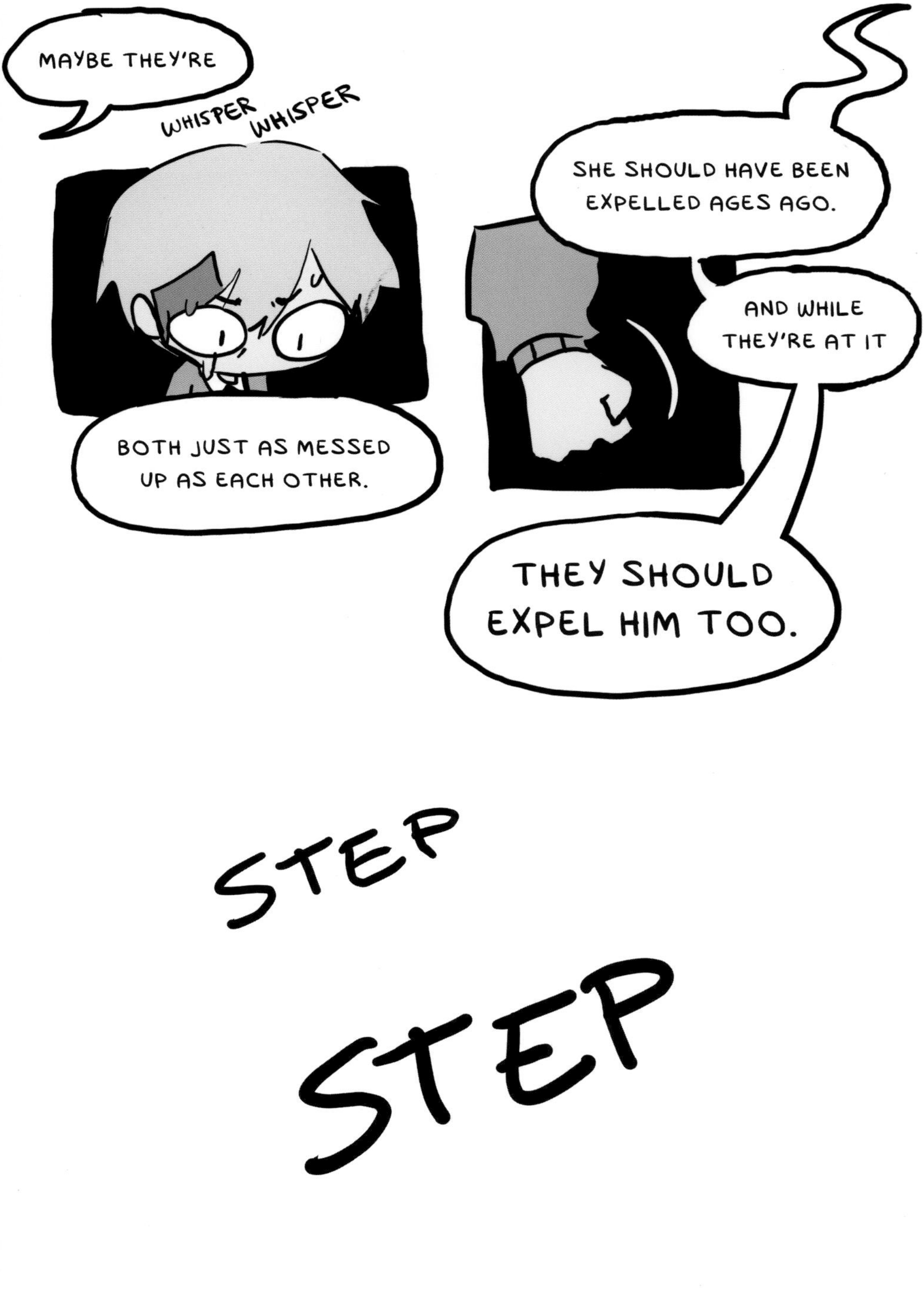
MAYBE THEY'RE
WHISPER WHISPER
BOTH JUST AS MESSED UP AS EACH OTHER.
SHE SHOULD HAVE BEEN EXPELLED AGES AGO.
AND WHILE THEY'RE AT IT
THEY SHOULD EXPEL HIM TOO.
STEP
STEP

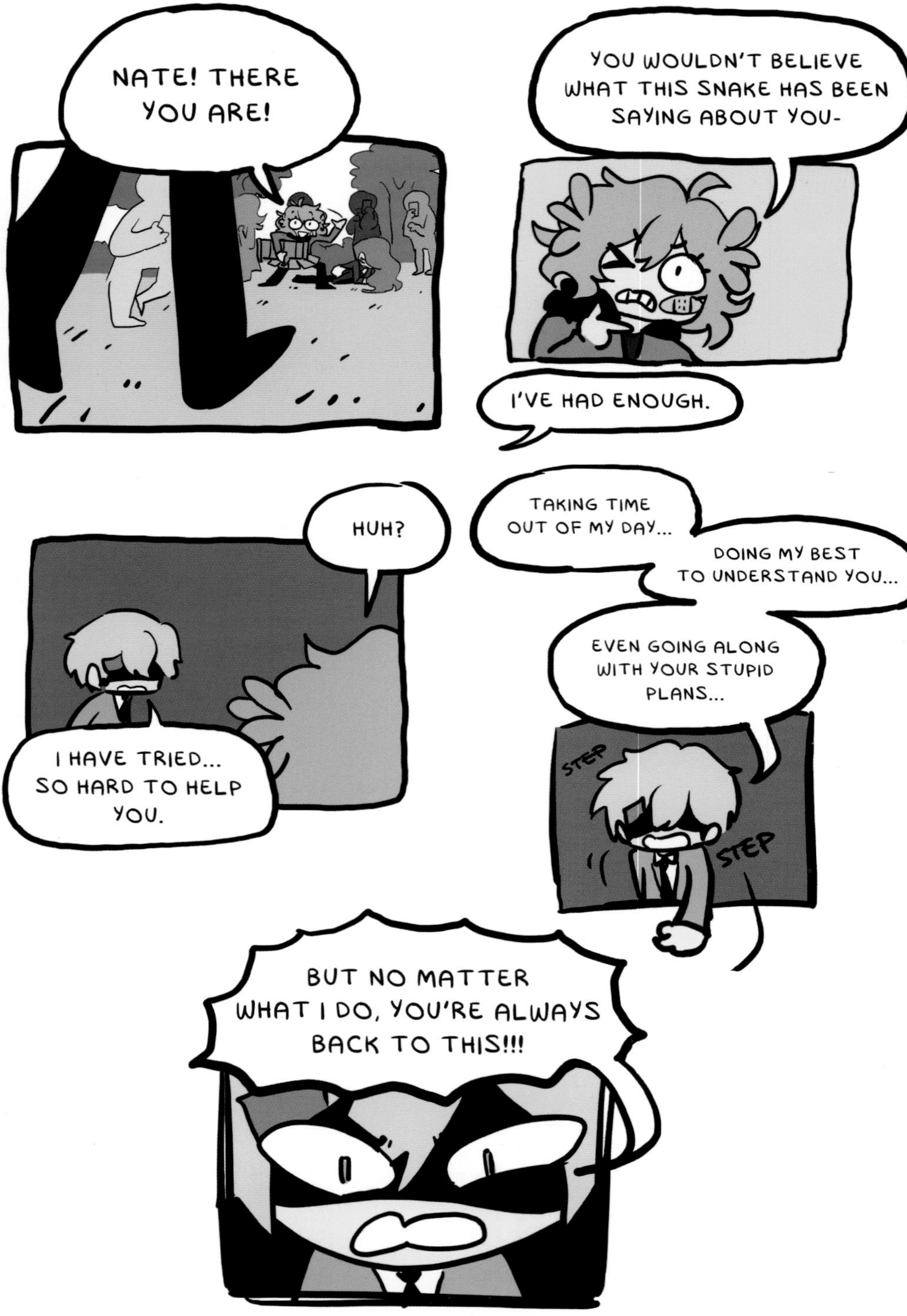

NATE! THERE YOU ARE!
YOU WOULDN'T BELIEVE WHAT THIS SNAKE HAS BEEN SAYING ABOUT YOU-
I'VE HAD ENOUGH.
HUH?
I HAVE TRIED... SO HARD TO HELP YOU.
TAKING TIME OUT OF MY DAY...
DOING MY BEST TO UNDERSTAND YOU...
EVEN GOING ALONG WITH YOUR STUPID PLANS...
STEP
STEP
BUT NO MATTER WHAT I DO, YOU'RE ALWAYS BACK TO THIS!!!

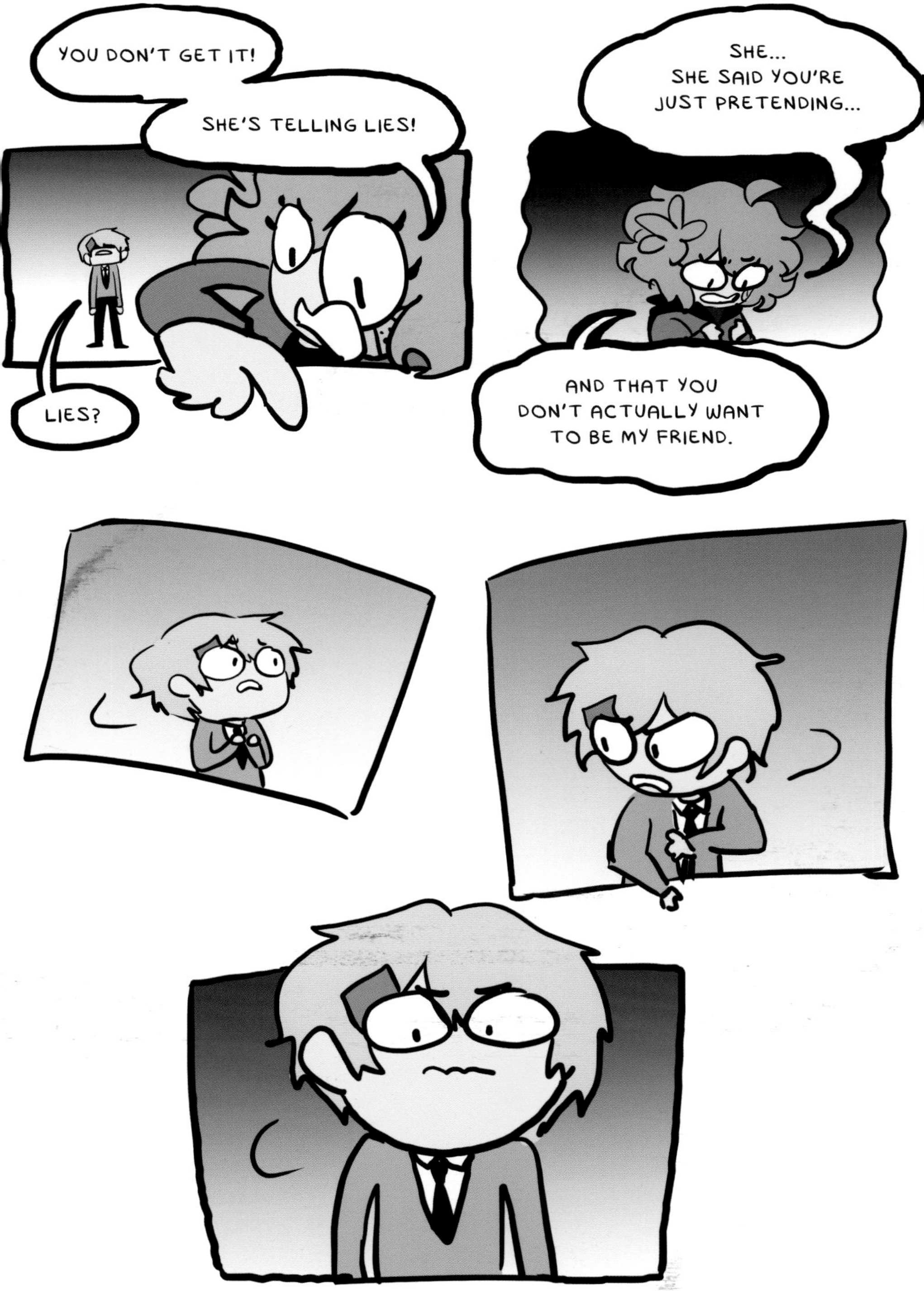
YOU DON'T GET IT!
SHE'S TELLING LIES!
LIES?
SHE...
SHE SAID YOU'RE
JUST PRETENDING...
AND THAT YOU
DON'T ACTUALLY WANT
TO BE MY FRIEND.

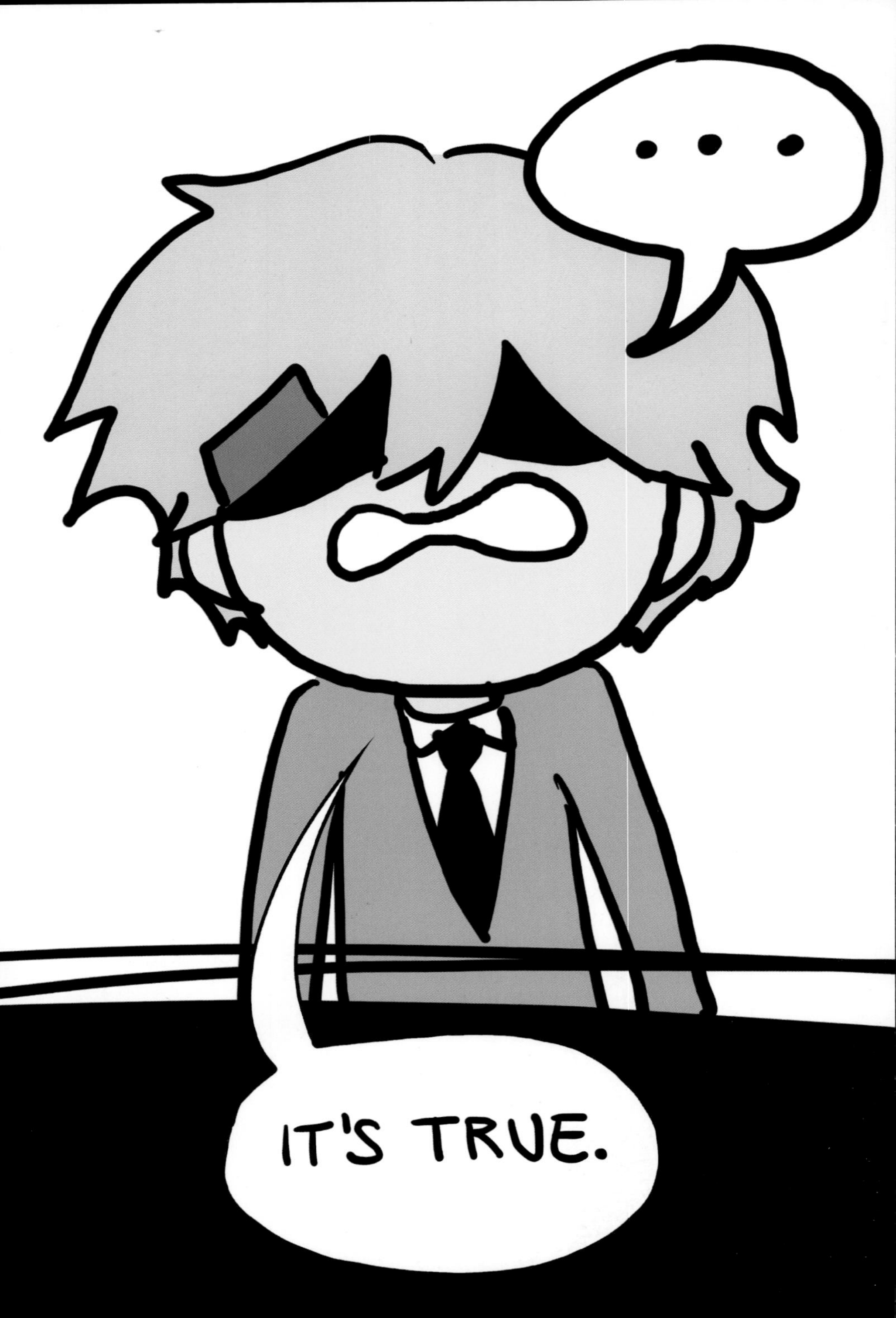
...
IT'S TRUE.

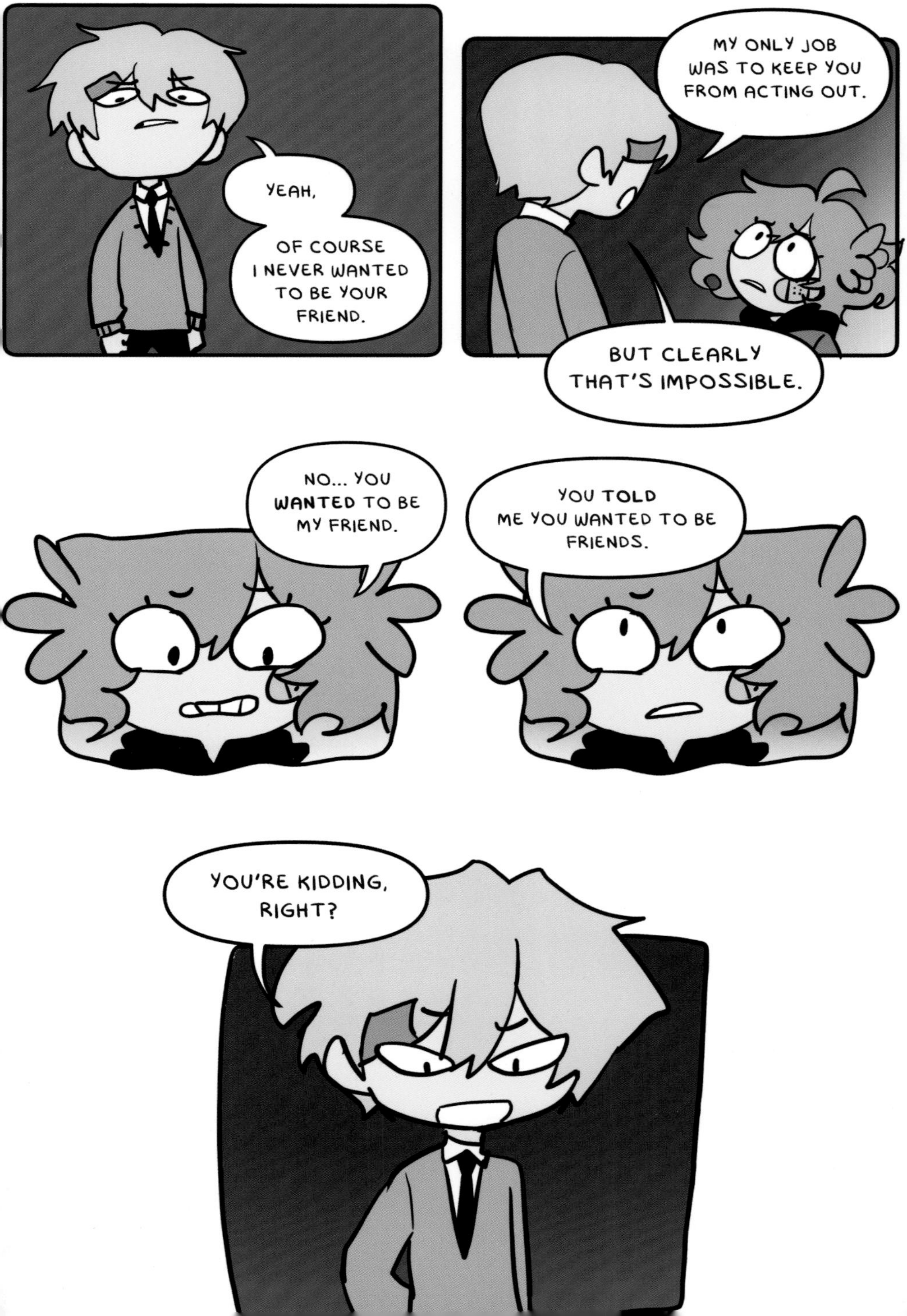
YEAH,
OF COURSE I NEVER WANTED TO BE YOUR FRIEND.
MY ONLY JOB WAS TO KEEP YOU FROM ACTING OUT.
BUT CLEARLY THAT'S IMPOSSIBLE.
NO... YOU WANTED TO BE MY FRIEND.
YOU TOLD ME YOU WANTED TO BE FRIENDS.
YOU'RE KIDDING, RIGHT?

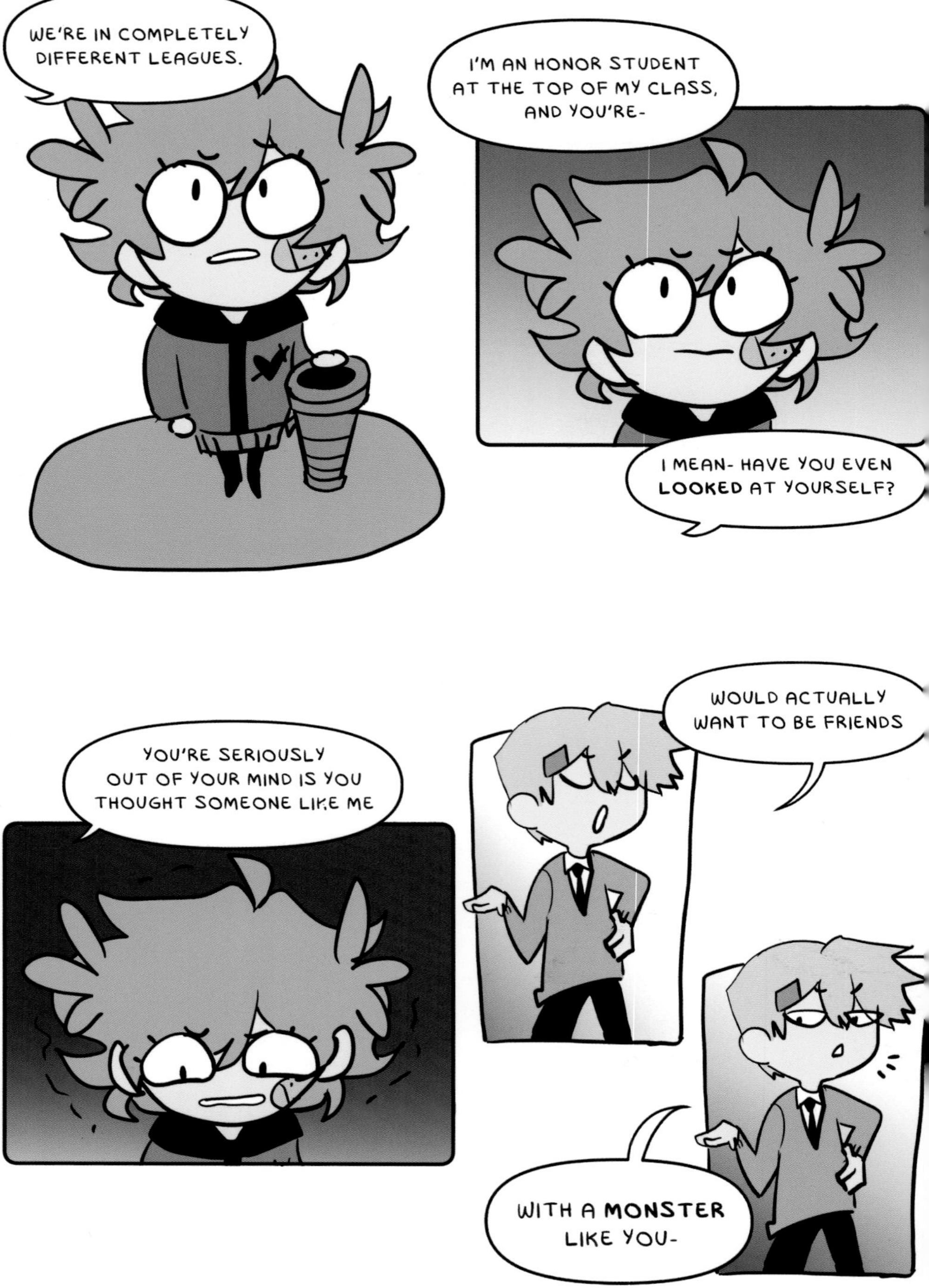
WE'RE IN COMPLETELY DIFFERENT LEAGUES.
I'M AN HONOR STUDENT AT THE TOP OF MY CLASS, AND YOU'RE-
I MEAN- HAVE YOU EVEN **LOOKED** AT YOURSELF?
YOU'RE SERIOUSLY OUT OF YOUR MIND IS YOU THOUGHT SOMEONE LIKE ME
WOULD ACTUALLY WANT TO BE FRIENDS
WITH A **MONSTER** LIKE YOU-

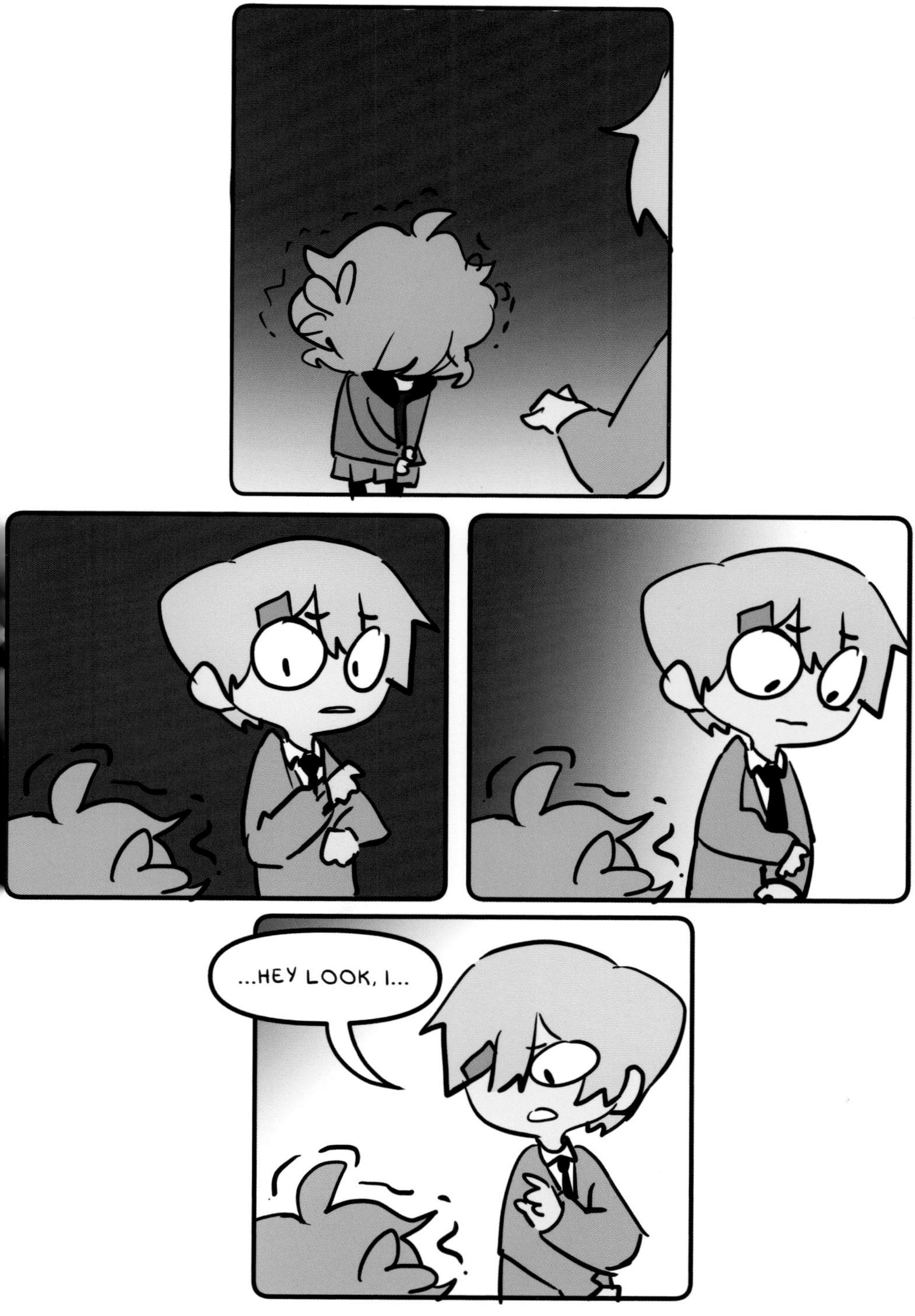
...HEY LOOK, I...

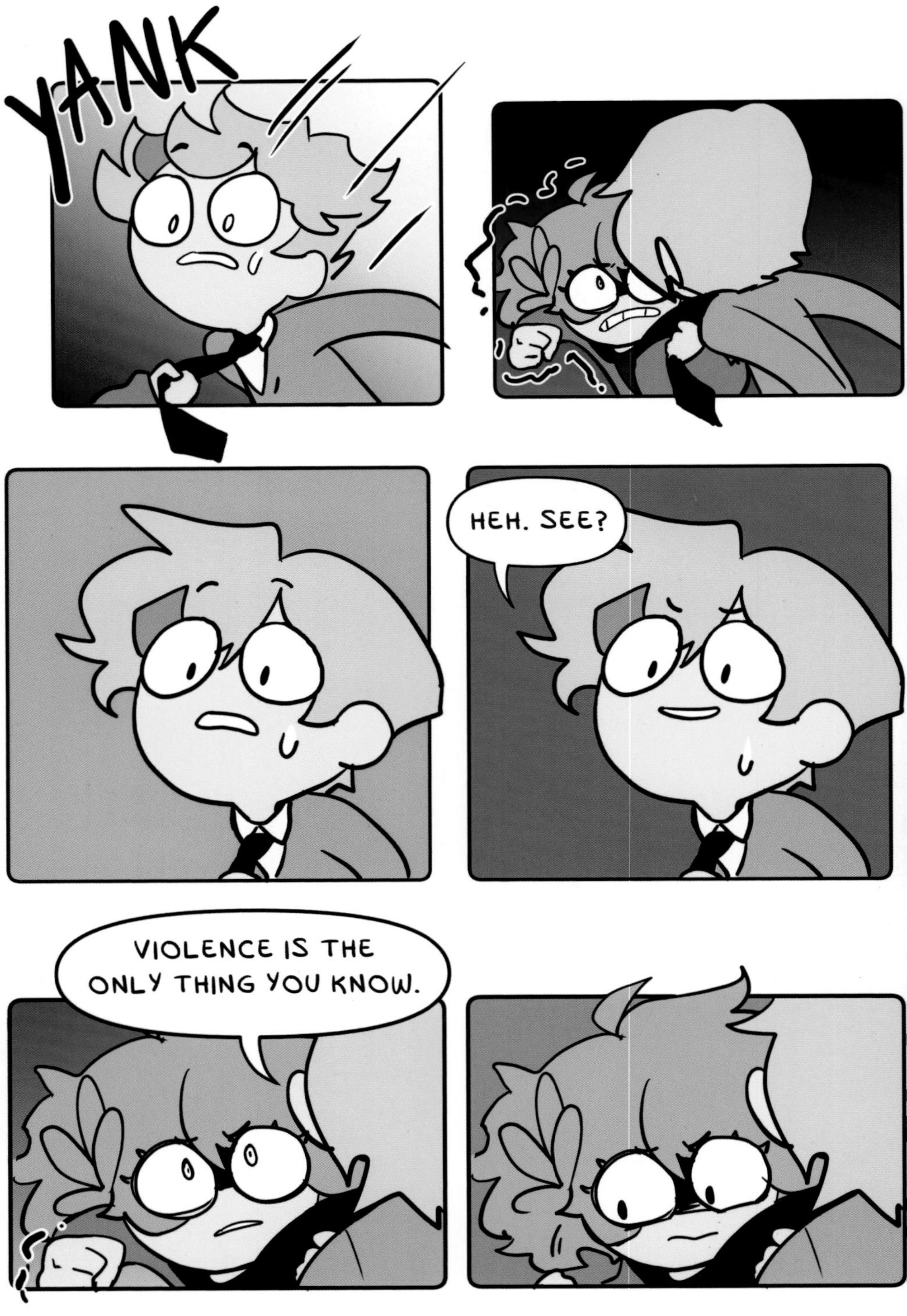
YANK
HEH. SEE?
VIOLENCE IS THE ONLY THING YOU KNOW.

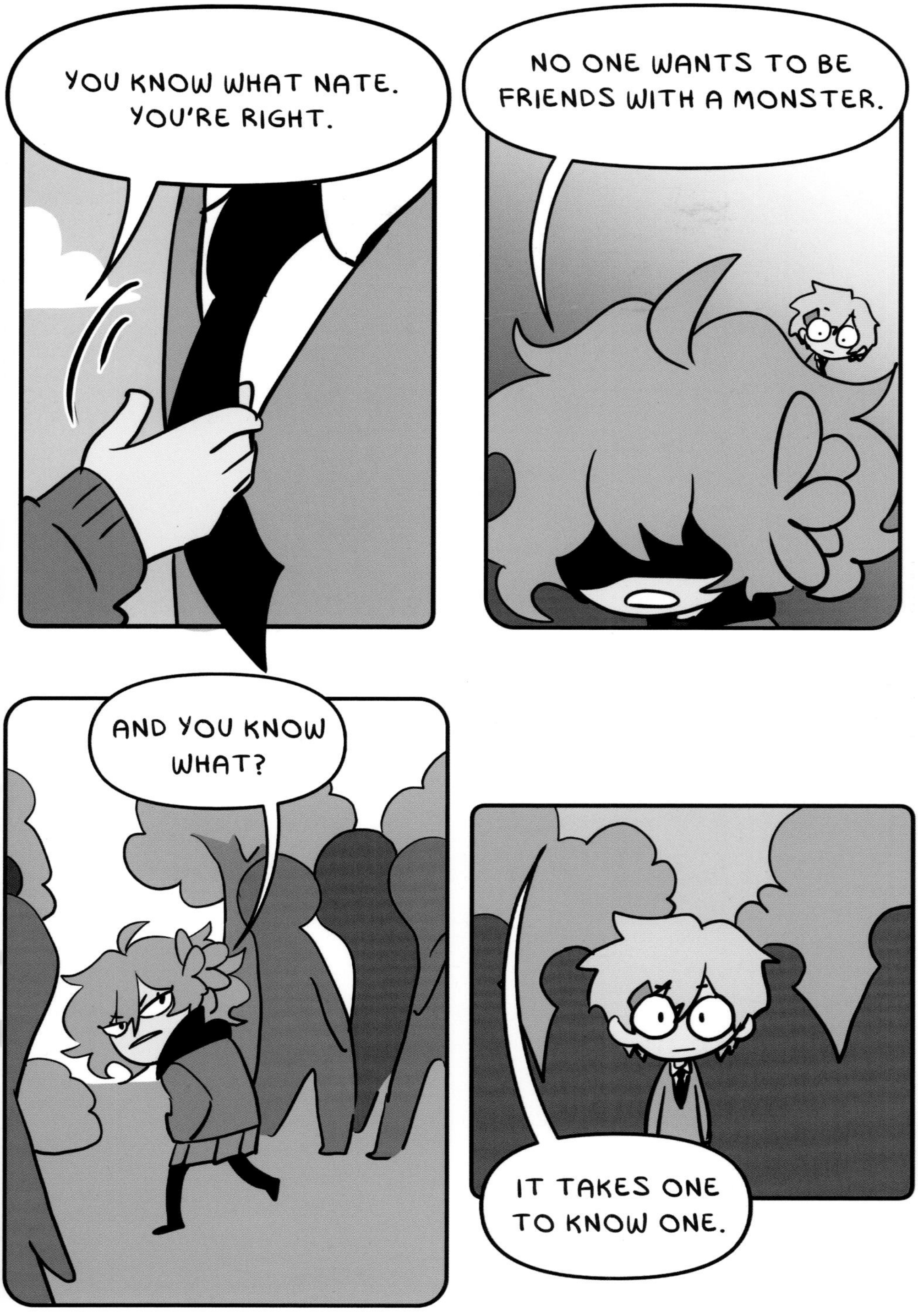
YOU KNOW WHAT NATE. YOU'RE RIGHT.
NO ONE WANTS TO BE FRIENDS WITH A MONSTER.
AND YOU KNOW WHAT?
IT TAKES ONE TO KNOW ONE.

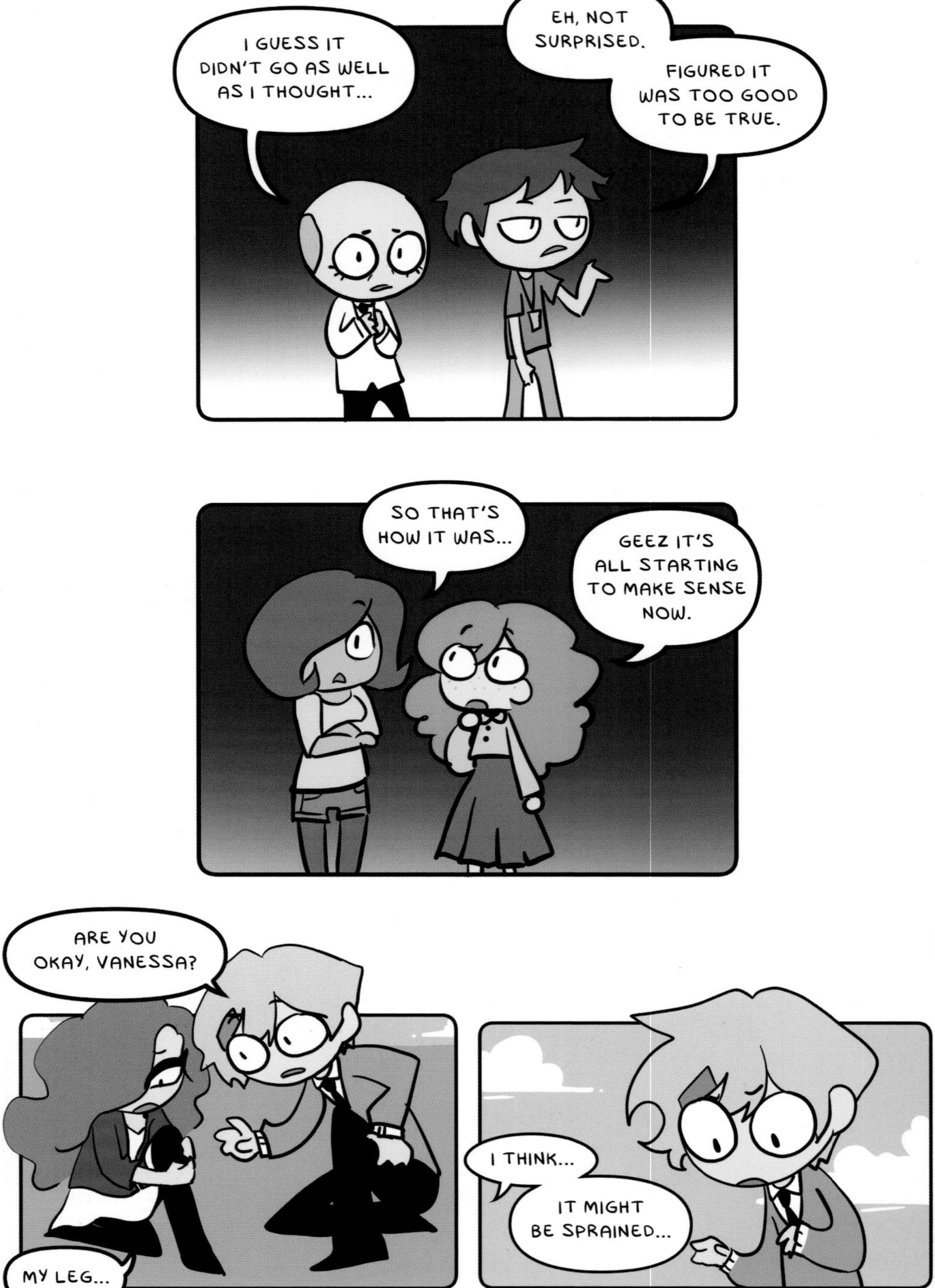
I GUESS IT DIDN'T GO AS WELL AS I THOUGHT...
EH, NOT SURPRISED.
FIGURED IT WAS TOO GOOD TO BE TRUE.
SO THAT'S HOW IT WAS...
GEEZ IT'S ALL STARTING TO MAKE SENSE NOW.
ARE YOU OKAY, VANESSA?
MY LEG...
I THINK...
IT MIGHT BE SPRAINED...

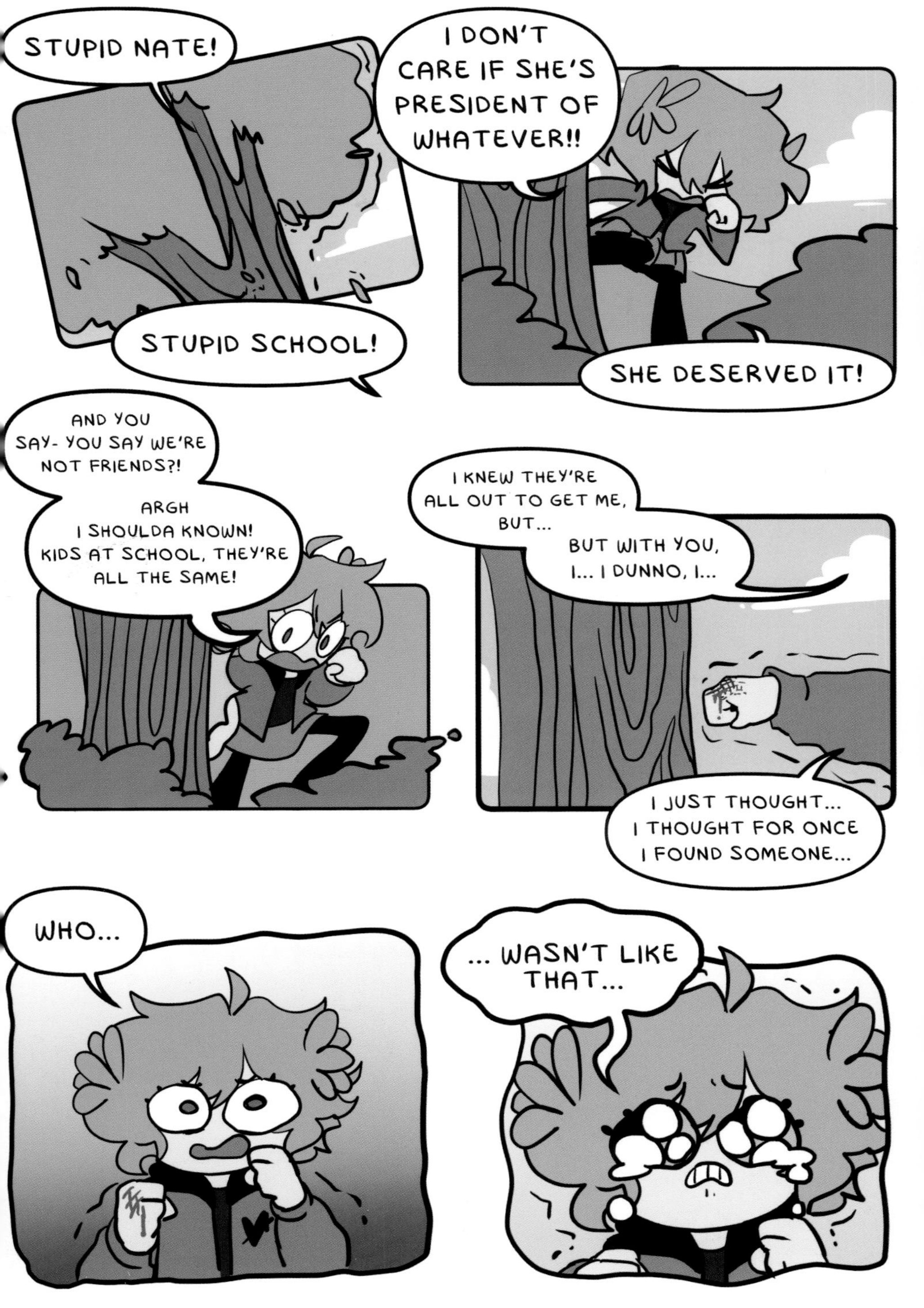
STUPID NATE!
STUPID SCHOOL!
I DON'T CARE IF SHE'S PRESIDENT OF WHATEVER!!
SHE DESERVED IT!
AND YOU SAY- YOU SAY WE'RE NOT FRIENDS?!
ARGH I SHOULDA KNOWN! KIDS AT SCHOOL, THEY'RE ALL THE SAME!
I KNEW THEY'RE ALL OUT TO GET ME, BUT...
BUT WITH YOU, I... I DUNNO, I...
I JUST THOUGHT... I THOUGHT FOR ONCE I FOUND SOMEONE...
WHO...
... WASN'T LIKE THAT...

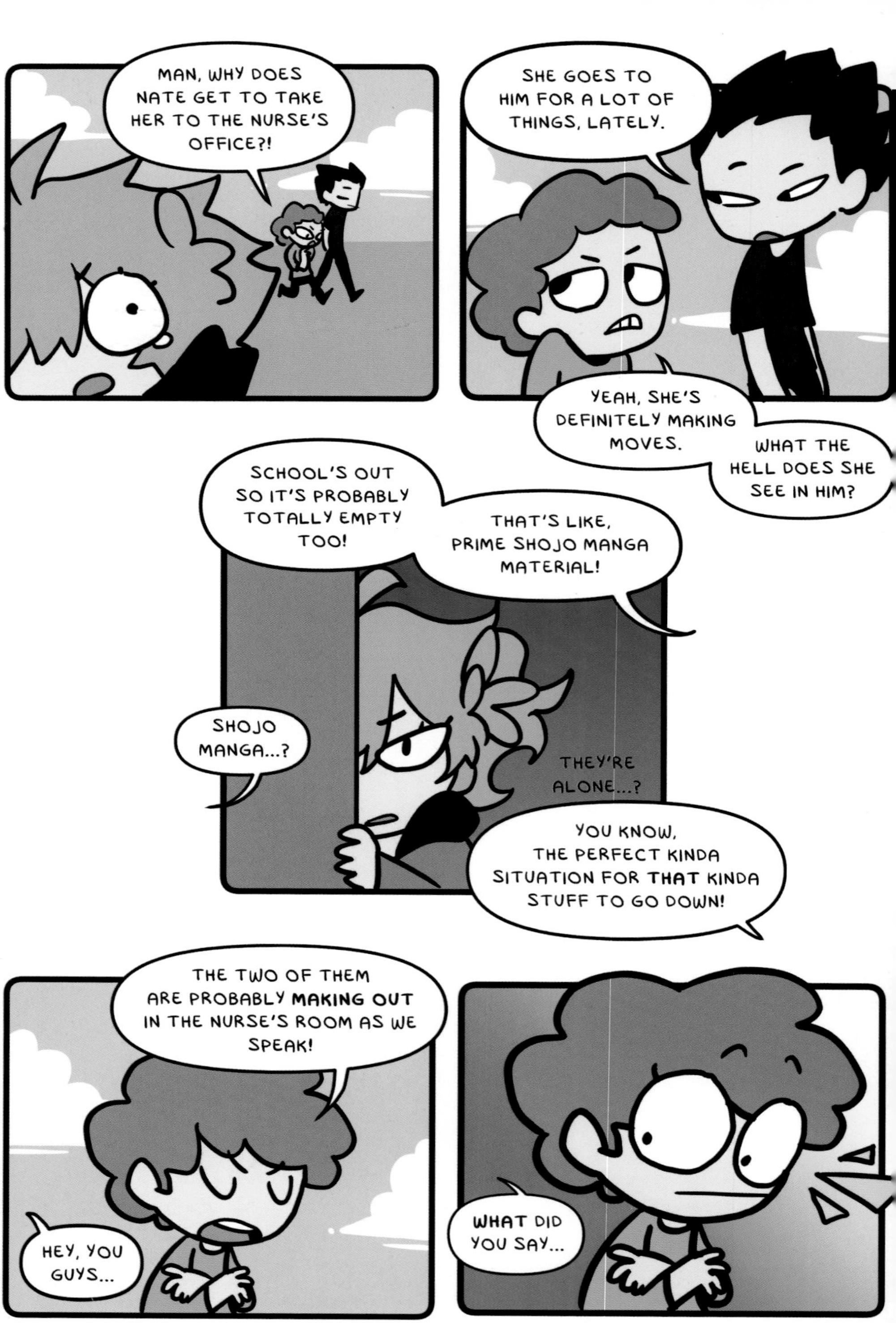
MAN, WHY DOES NATE GET TO TAKE HER TO THE NURSE'S OFFICE?!
SHE GOES TO HIM FOR A LOT OF THINGS, LATELY.
YEAH, SHE'S DEFINITELY MAKING MOVES.
WHAT THE HELL DOES SHE SEE IN HIM?
SCHOOL'S OUT SO IT'S PROBABLY TOTALLY EMPTY TOO!
THAT'S LIKE, PRIME SHOJO MANGA MATERIAL!
SHOJO MANGA...?
THEY'RE ALONE...?
YOU KNOW, THE PERFECT KINDA SITUATION FOR THAT KINDA STUFF TO GO DOWN!
THE TWO OF THEM ARE PROBABLY MAKING OUT IN THE NURSE'S ROOM AS WE SPEAK!
HEY, YOU GUYS...
WHAT DID YOU SAY...

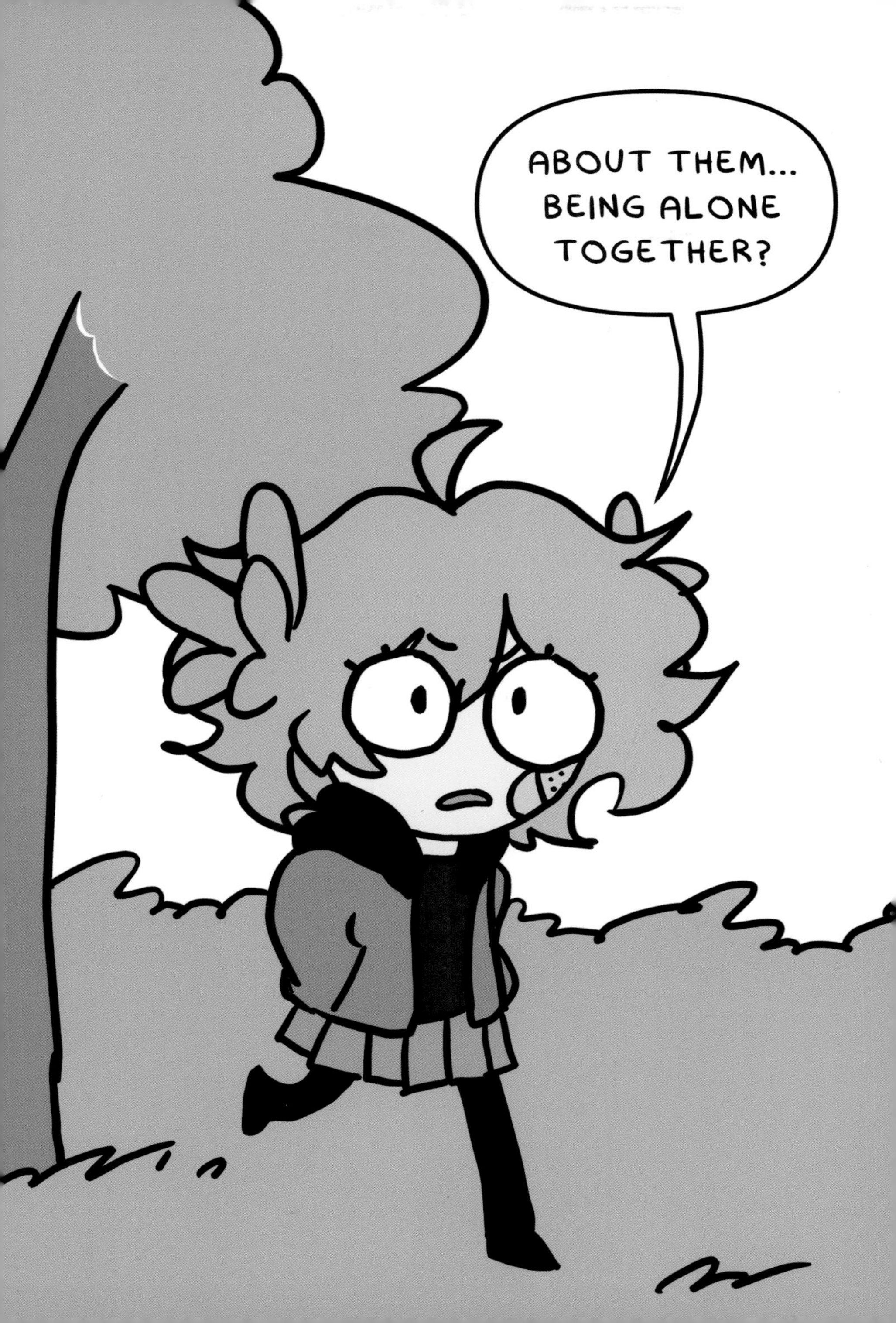
ABOUT THEM... BEING ALONE TOGETHER?

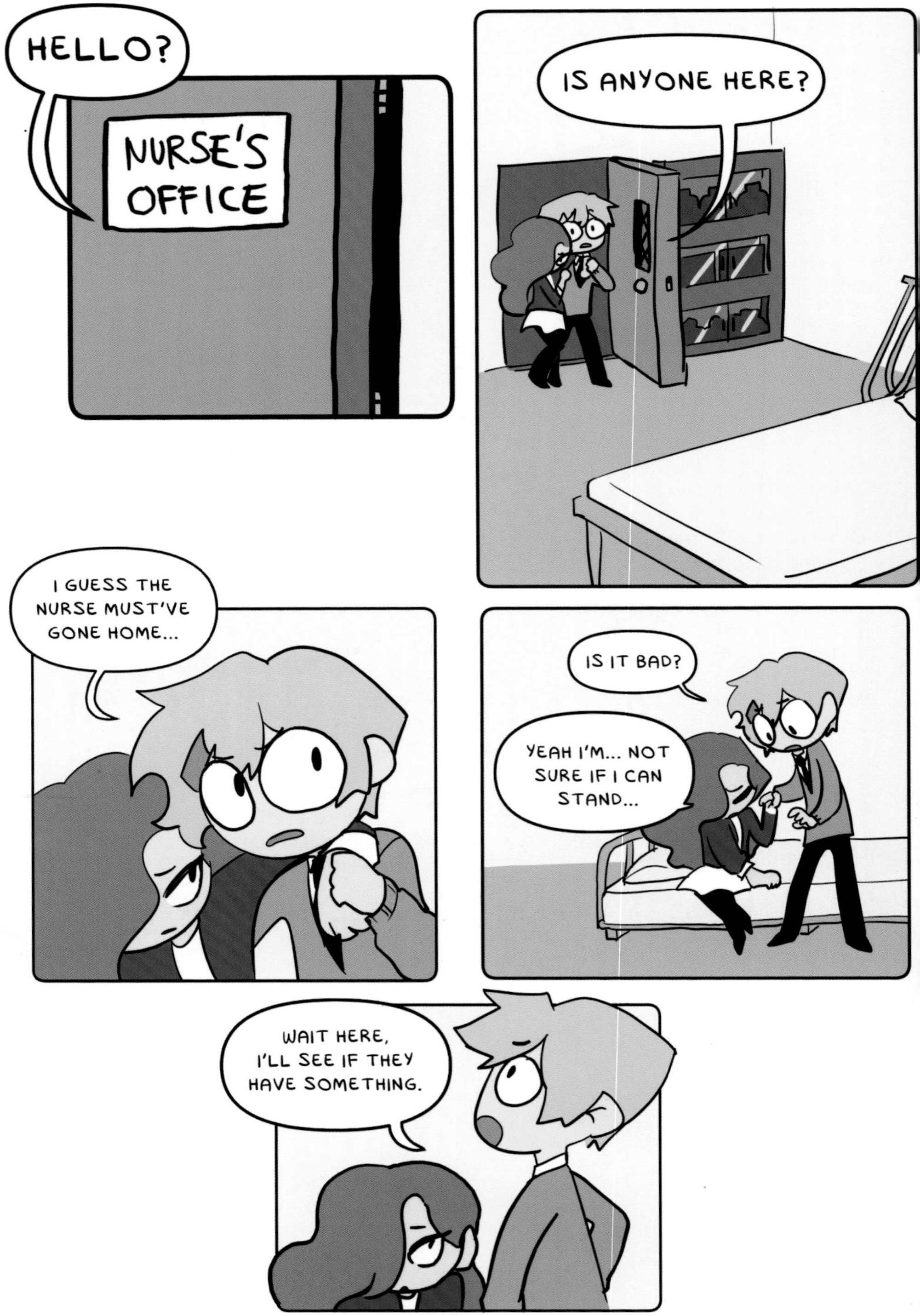
HELLO?
NURSE'S OFFICE
IS ANYONE HERE?
I GUESS THE NURSE MUST'VE GONE HOME...
IS IT BAD?
YEAH I'M... NOT SURE IF I CAN STAND...
WAIT HERE, I'LL SEE IF THEY HAVE SOMETHING.

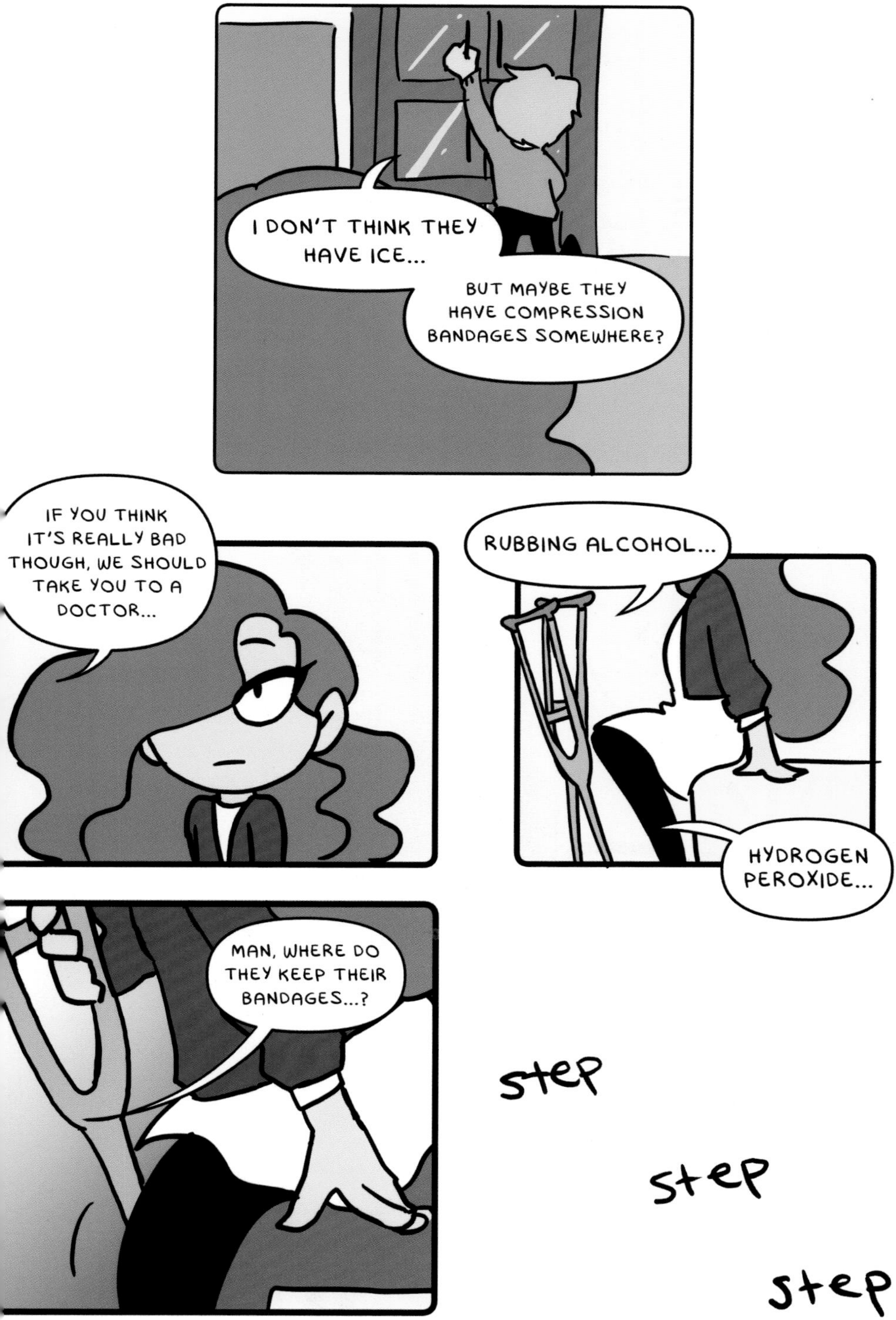
I DON'T THINK THEY HAVE ICE...
BUT MAYBE THEY HAVE COMPRESSION BANDAGES SOMEWHERE?
IF YOU THINK IT'S REALLY BAD THOUGH, WE SHOULD TAKE YOU TO A DOCTOR...
RUBBING ALCOHOL...
HYDROGEN PEROXIDE...
MAN, WHERE DO THEY KEEP THEIR BANDAGES...?
step
step
step

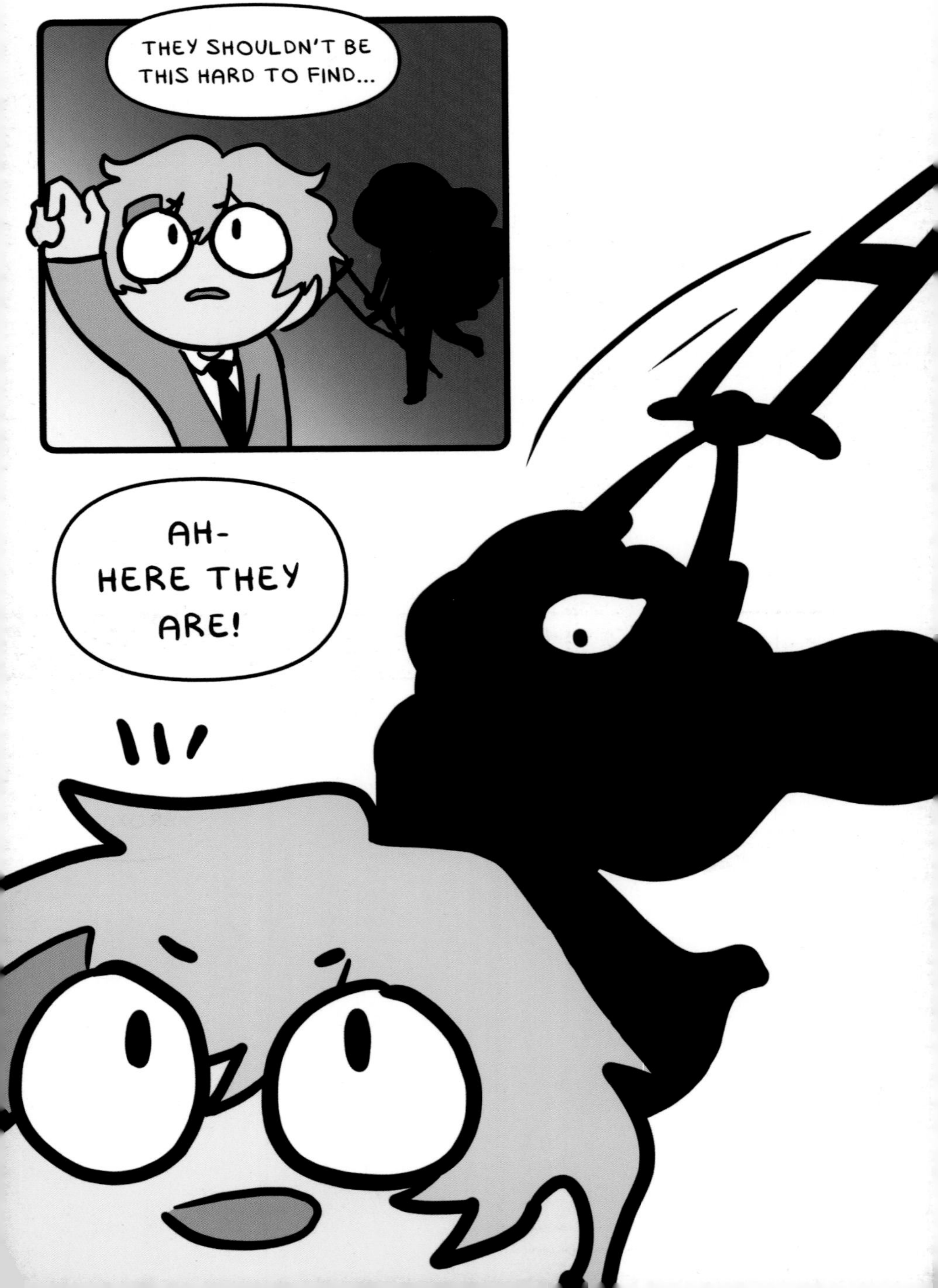
THEY SHOULDN'T BE THIS HARD TO FIND...
AH- HERE THEY ARE!

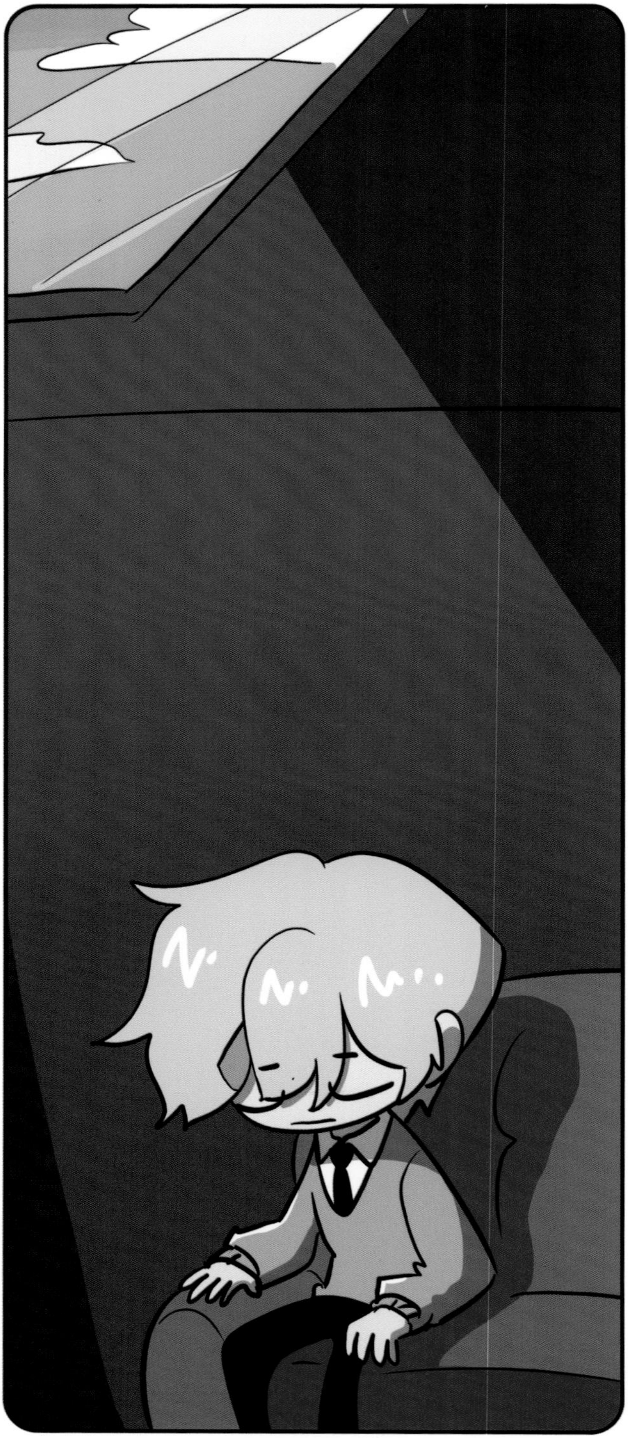

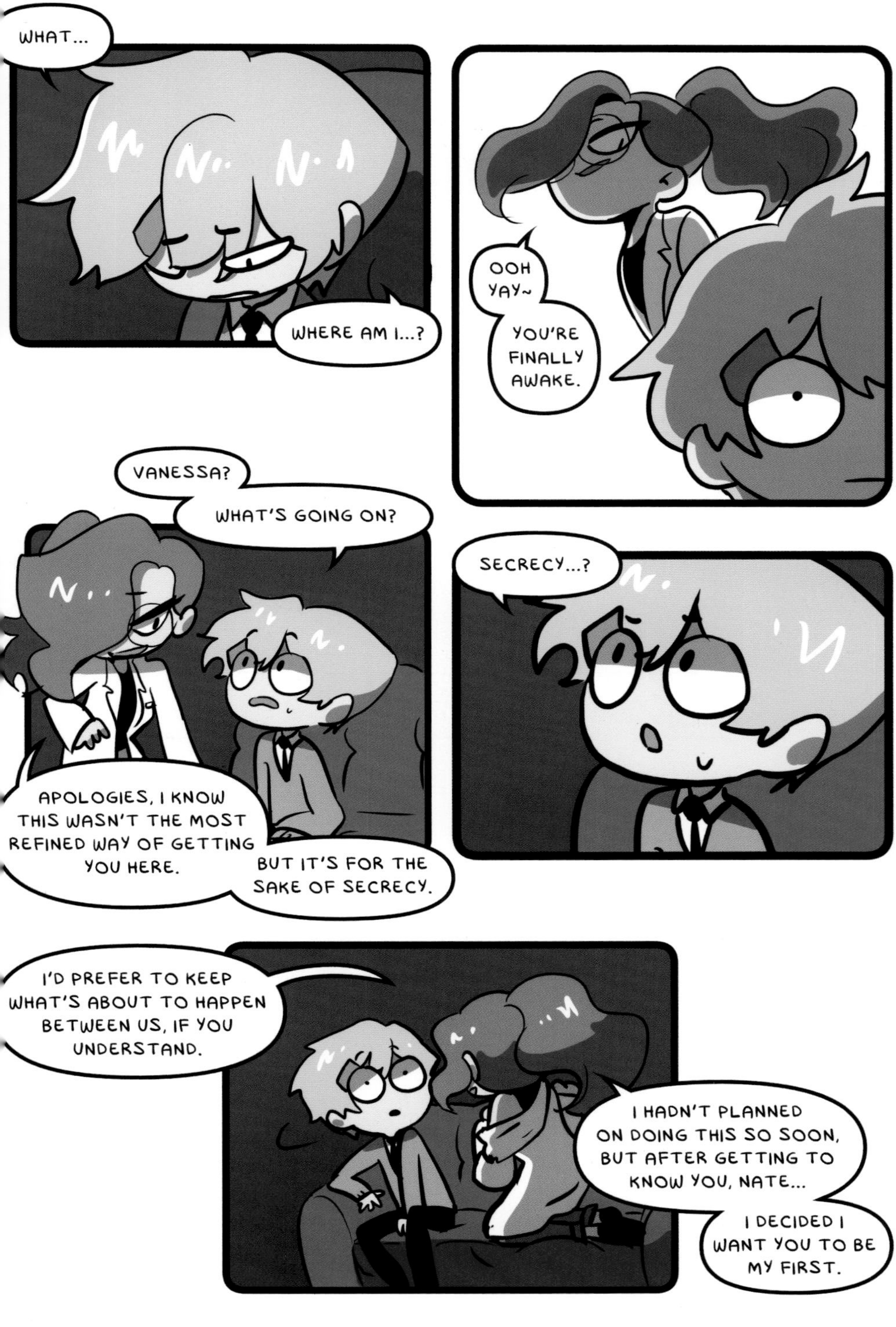
WHAT...
WHERE AM I...?
OOH YAY~
YOU'RE FINALLY AWAKE.
VANESSA?
WHAT'S GOING ON?
APOLOGIES, I KNOW THIS WASN'T THE MOST REFINED WAY OF GETTING YOU HERE.
BUT IT'S FOR THE SAKE OF SECRECY.
SECRECY...?
I'D PREFER TO KEEP WHAT'S ABOUT TO HAPPEN BETWEEN US, IF YOU UNDERSTAND.
I HADN'T PLANNED ON DOING THIS SO SOON, BUT AFTER GETTING TO KNOW YOU, NATE...
I DECIDED I WANT YOU TO BE MY FIRST.

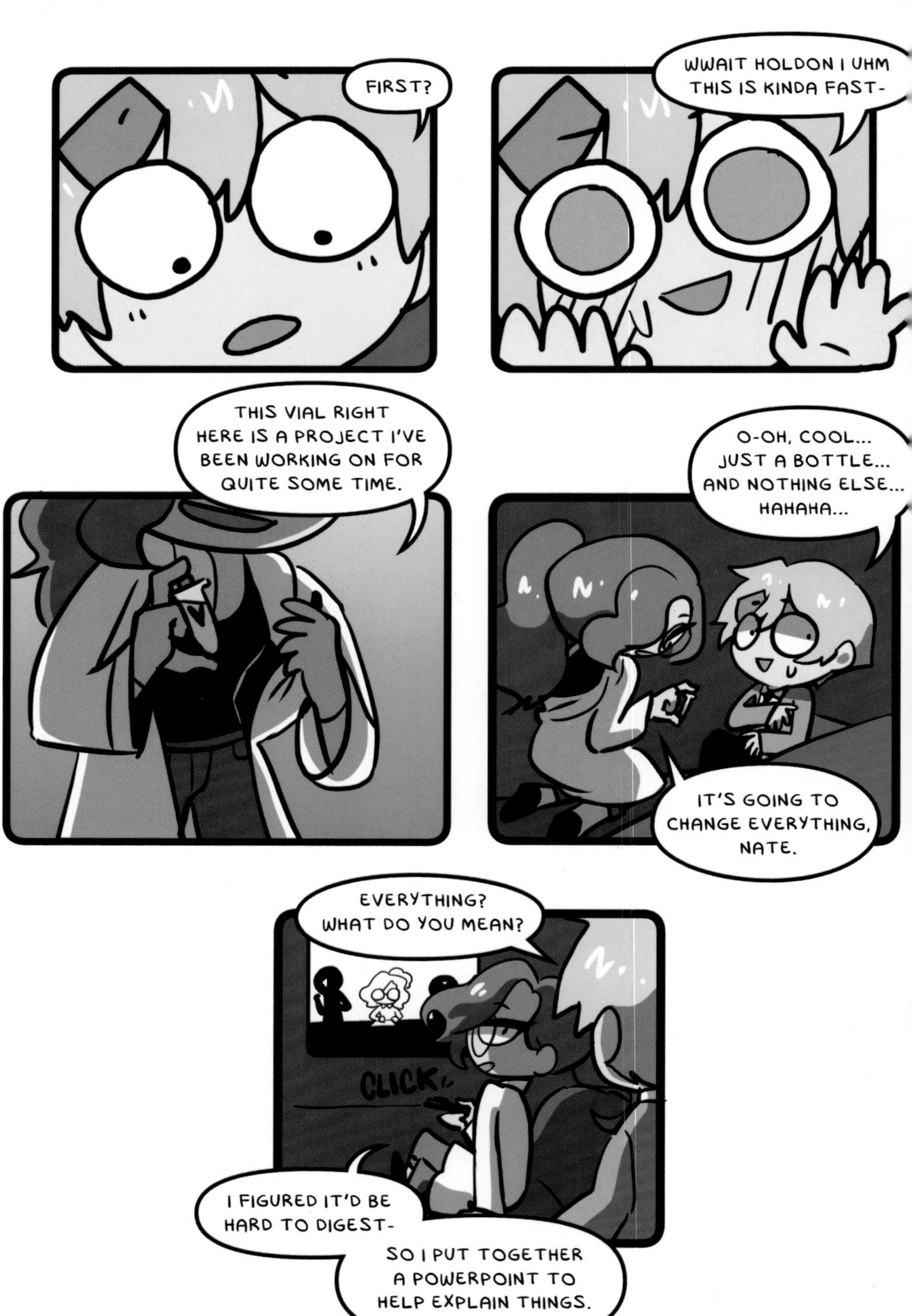
FIRST?
WWAIT HOLDON I UHM THIS IS KINDA FAST-
THIS VIAL RIGHT HERE IS A PROJECT I'VE BEEN WORKING ON FOR QUITE SOME TIME.
O-OH, COOL... JUST A BOTTLE... AND NOTHING ELSE... HAHAHA...
IT'S GOING TO CHANGE EVERYTHING, NATE.
EVERYTHING? WHAT DO YOU MEAN?
CLICK
I FIGURED IT'D BE HARD TO DIGEST-
SO I PUT TOGETHER A POWERPOINT TO HELP EXPLAIN THINGS.

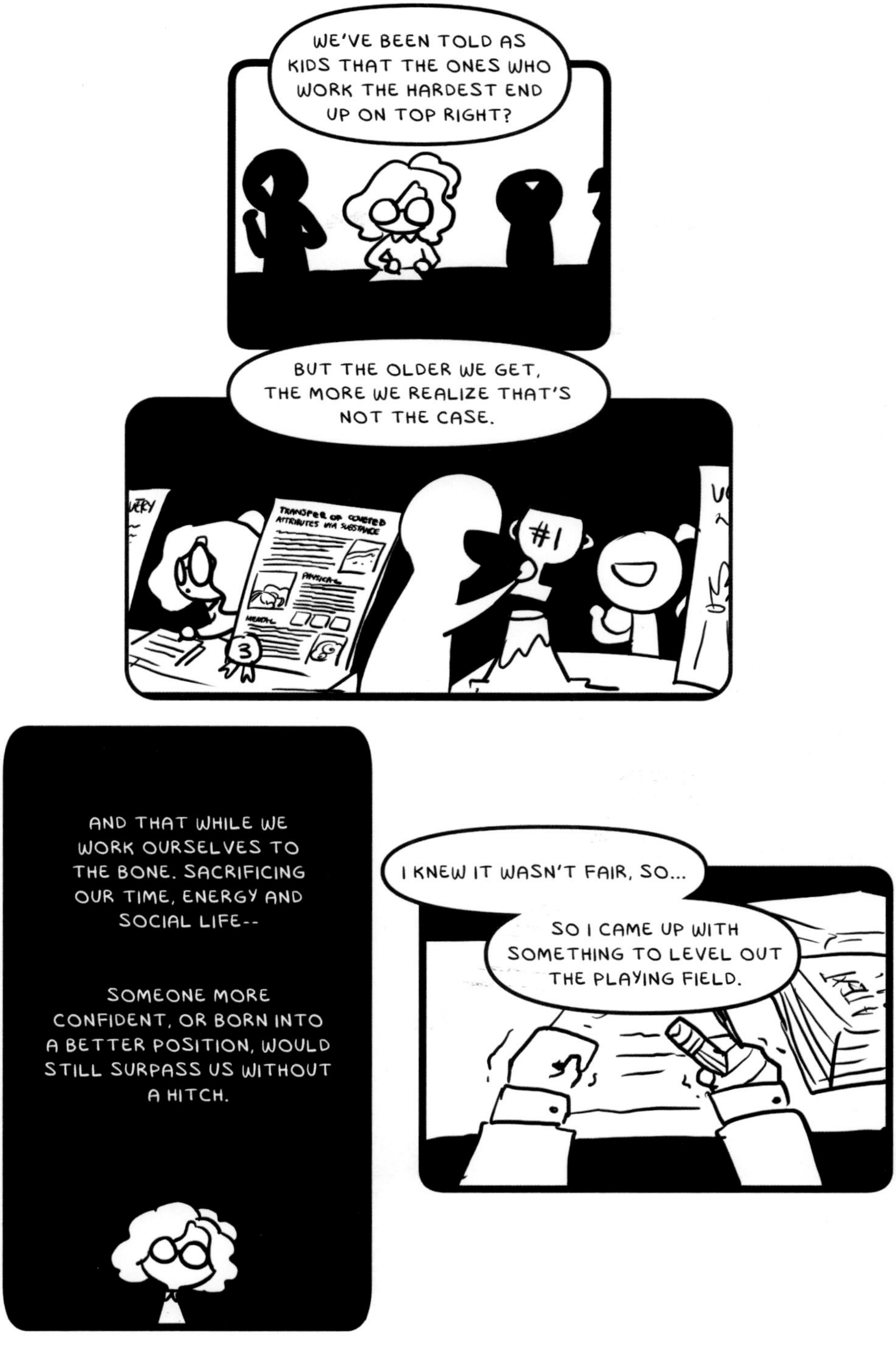
WE'VE BEEN TOLD AS KIDS THAT THE ONES WHO WORK THE HARDEST END UP ON TOP RIGHT?
BUT THE OLDER WE GET, THE MORE WE REALIZE THAT'S NOT THE CASE.
#1
AND THAT WHILE WE WORK OURSELVES TO THE BONE. SACRIFICING OUR TIME, ENERGY AND SOCIAL LIFE--
SOMEONE MORE CONFIDENT, OR BORN INTO A BETTER POSITION, WOULD STILL SURPASS US WITHOUT A HITCH.
I KNEW IT WASN'T FAIR, SO...
SO I CAME UP WITH SOMETHING TO LEVEL OUT THE PLAYING FIELD.

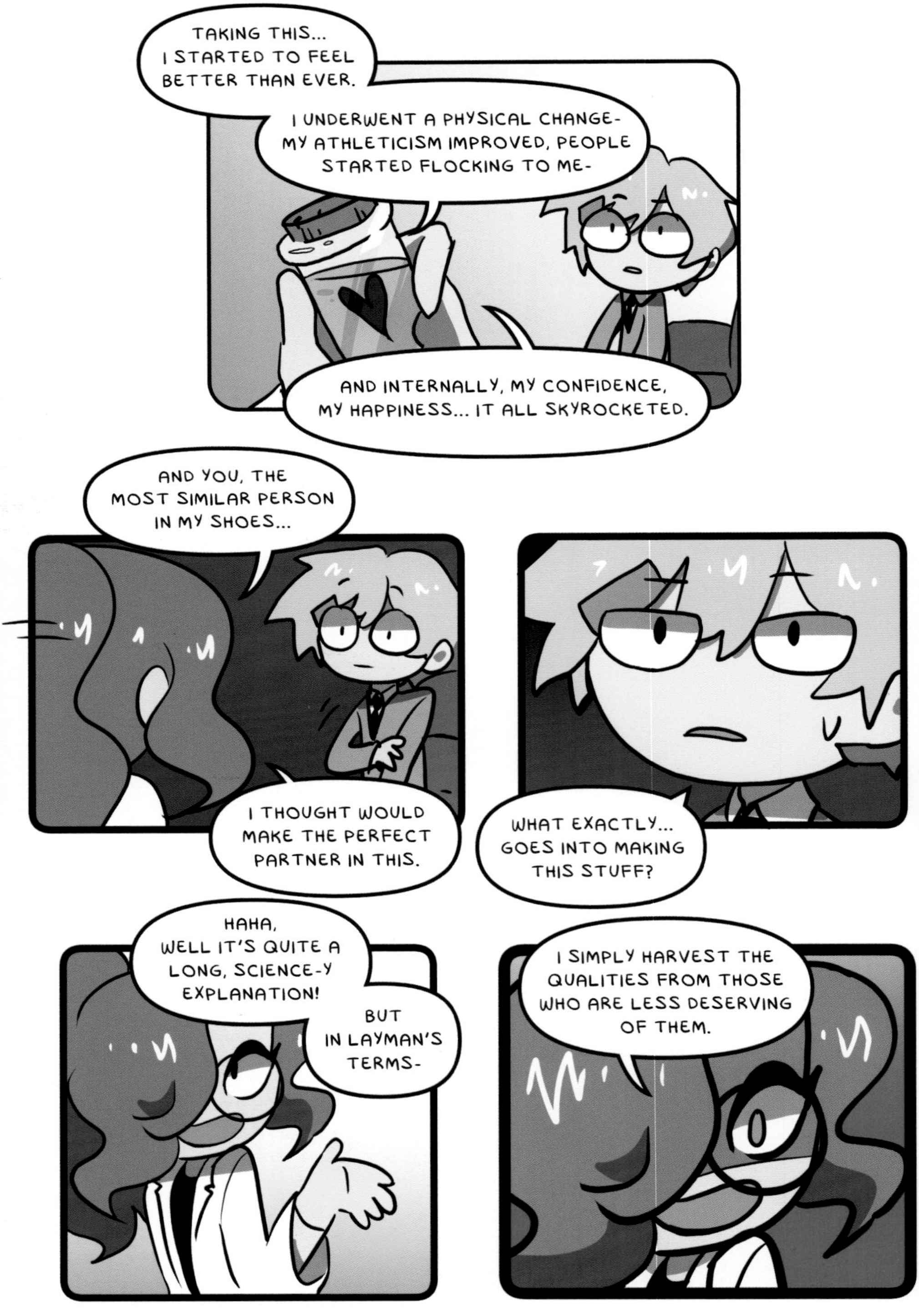
TAKING THIS... I STARTED TO FEEL BETTER THAN EVER.
I UNDERWENT A PHYSICAL CHANGE- MY ATHLETICISM IMPROVED, PEOPLE STARTED FLOCKING TO ME-
AND INTERNALLY, MY CONFIDENCE, MY HAPPINESS... IT ALL SKYROCKETED.
AND YOU, THE MOST SIMILAR PERSON IN MY SHOES...
I THOUGHT WOULD MAKE THE PERFECT PARTNER IN THIS.
WHAT EXACTLY... GOES INTO MAKING THIS STUFF?
HAHA, WELL IT'S QUITE A LONG, SCIENCE-Y EXPLANATION!
BUT IN LAYMAN'S TERMS-
I SIMPLY HARVEST THE QUALITIES FROM THOSE WHO ARE LESS DESERVING OF THEM.

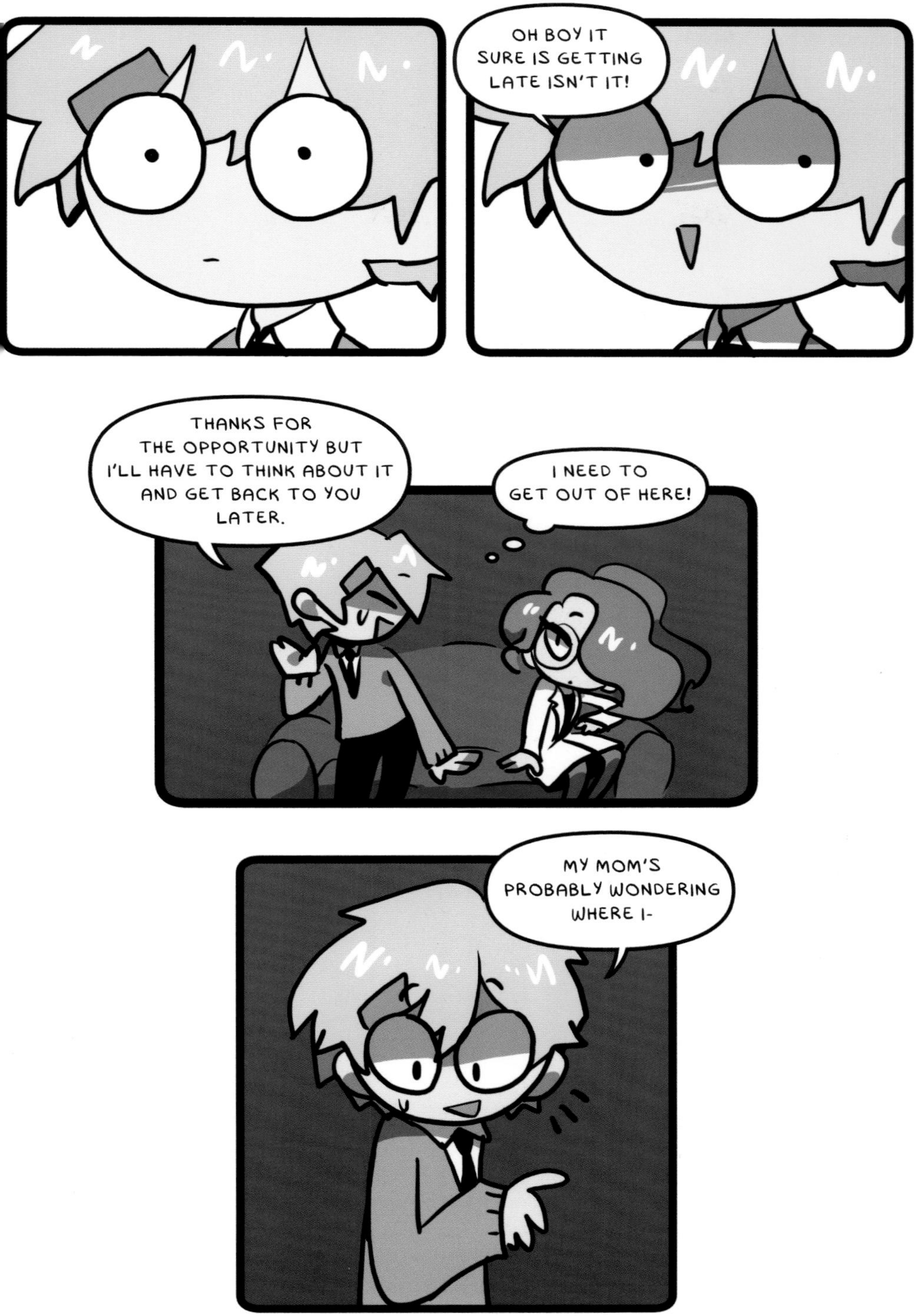
OH BOY IT SURE IS GETTING LATE ISN'T IT!
THANKS FOR THE OPPORTUNITY BUT I'LL HAVE TO THINK ABOUT IT AND GET BACK TO YOU LATER.
I NEED TO GET OUT OF HERE!
MY MOM'S PROBABLY WONDERING WHERE I-

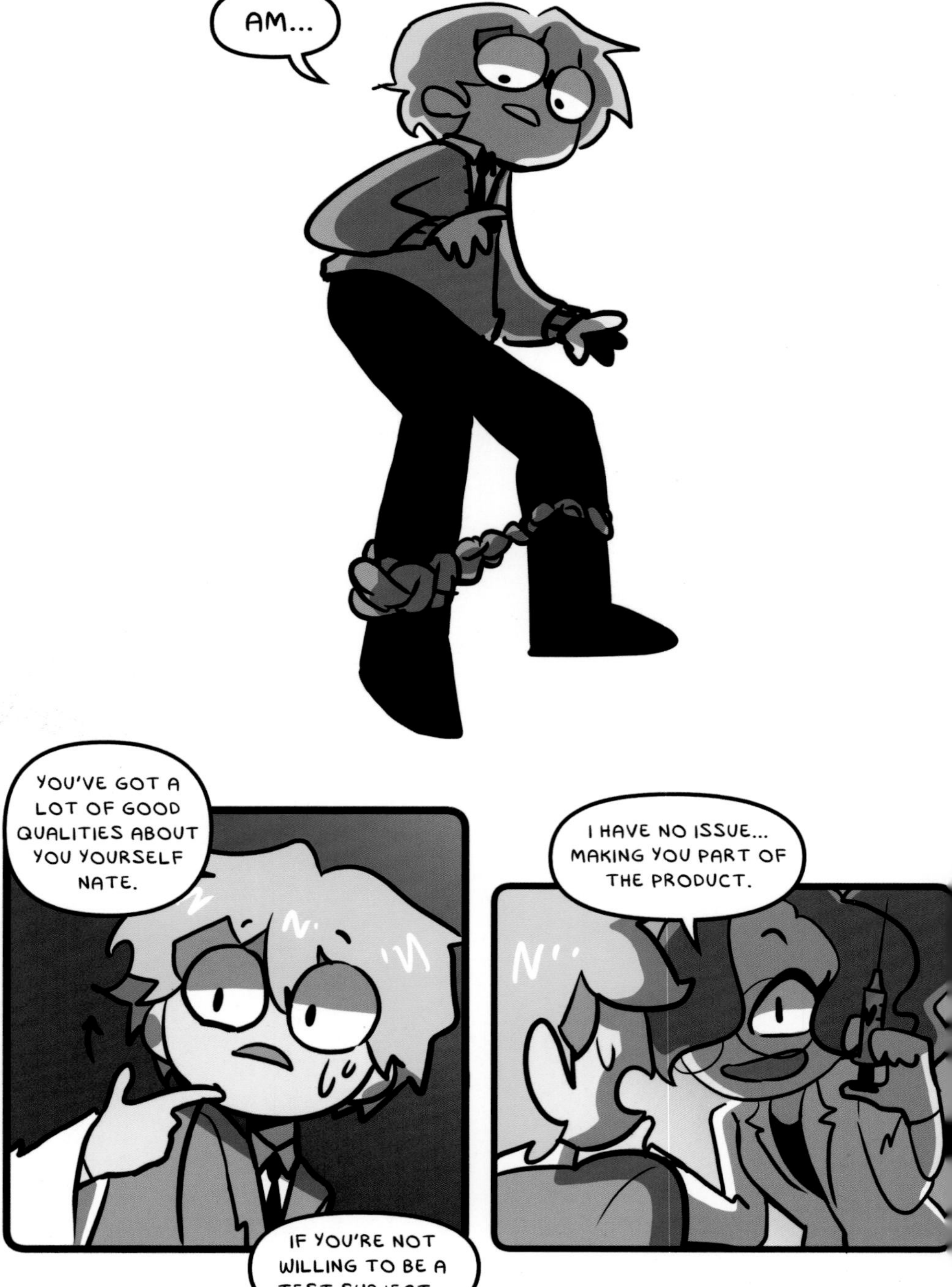
AM...
YOU'VE GOT A LOT OF GOOD QUALITIES ABOUT YOU YOURSELF NATE.
IF YOU'RE NOT WILLING TO BE A TEST SUBJECT...
I HAVE NO ISSUE... MAKING YOU PART OF THE PRODUCT.

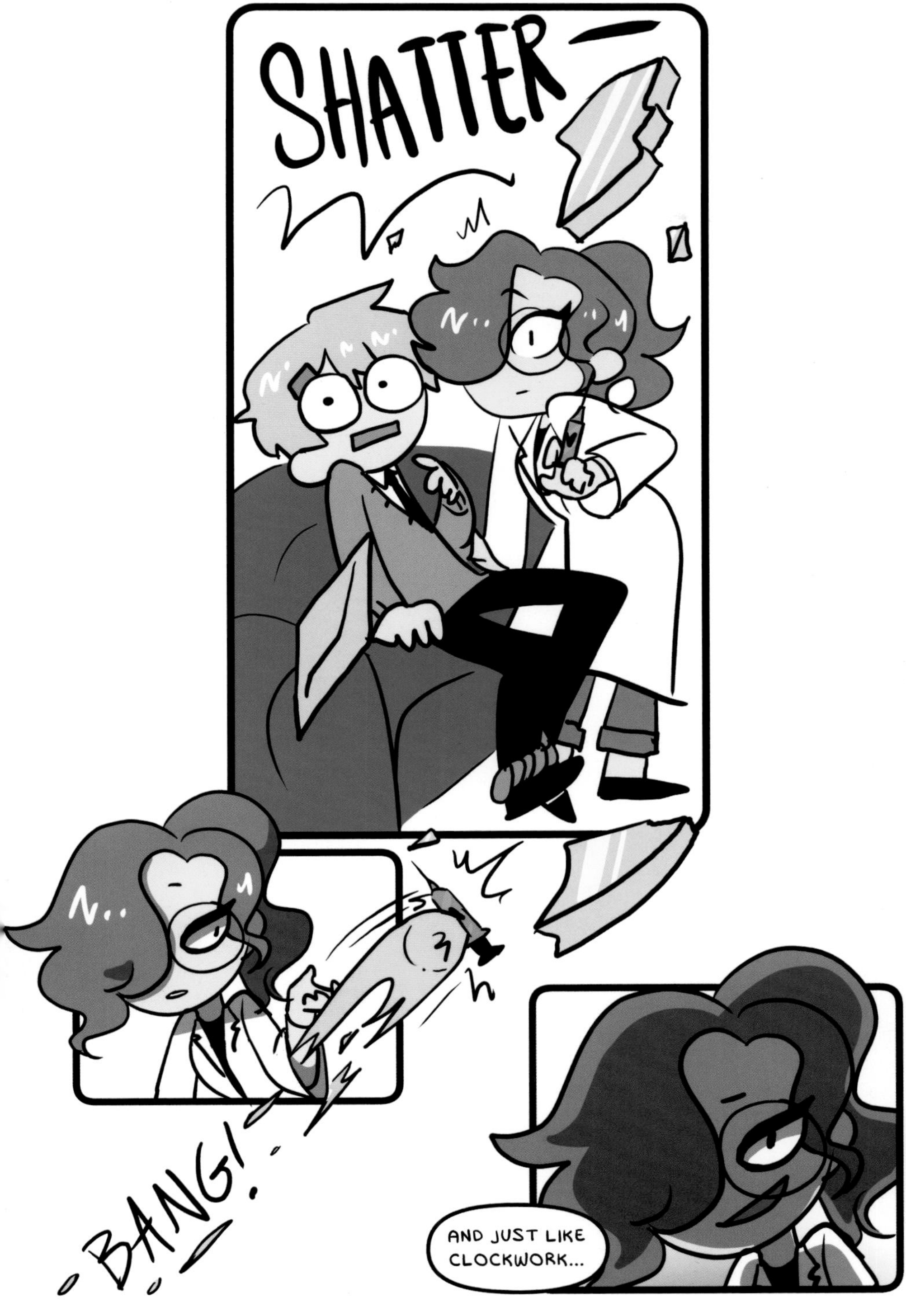
SHATTER
BANG!
AND JUST LIKE CLOCKWORK...

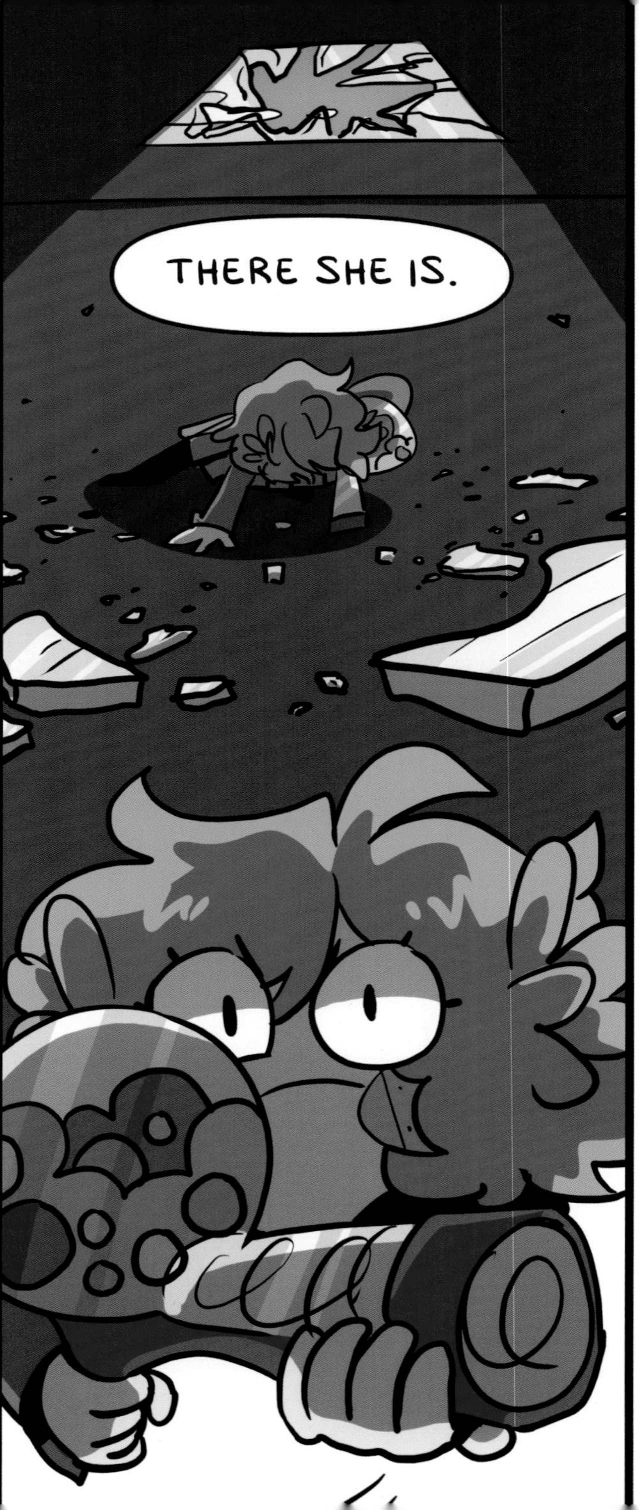
THERE SHE IS.

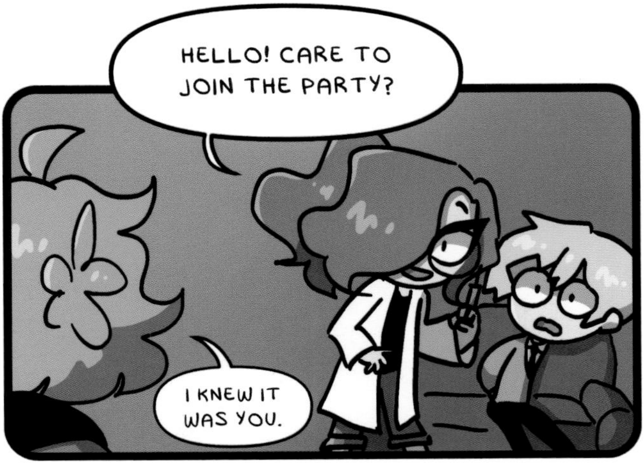
HELLO! CARE TO JOIN THE PARTY?
I KNEW IT WAS YOU.

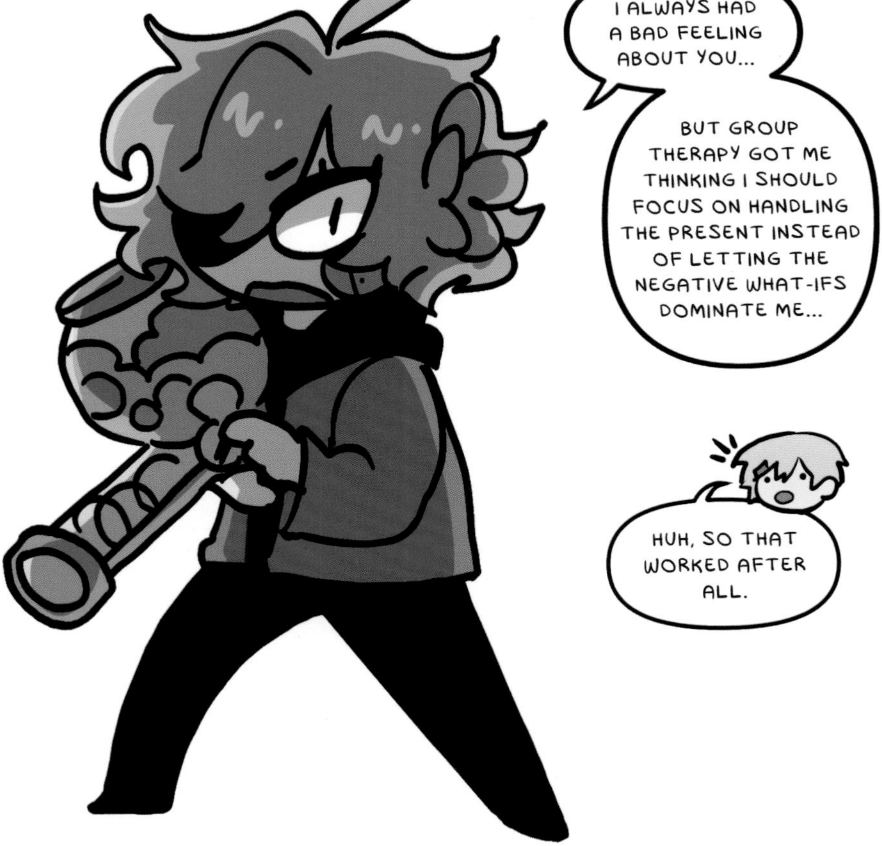
I ALWAYS HAD A BAD FEELING ABOUT YOU...
BUT GROUP THERAPY GOT ME THINKING I SHOULD FOCUS ON HANDLING THE PRESENT INSTEAD OF LETTING THE NEGATIVE WHAT-IFS DOMINATE ME...
HUH, SO THAT WORKED AFTER ALL.

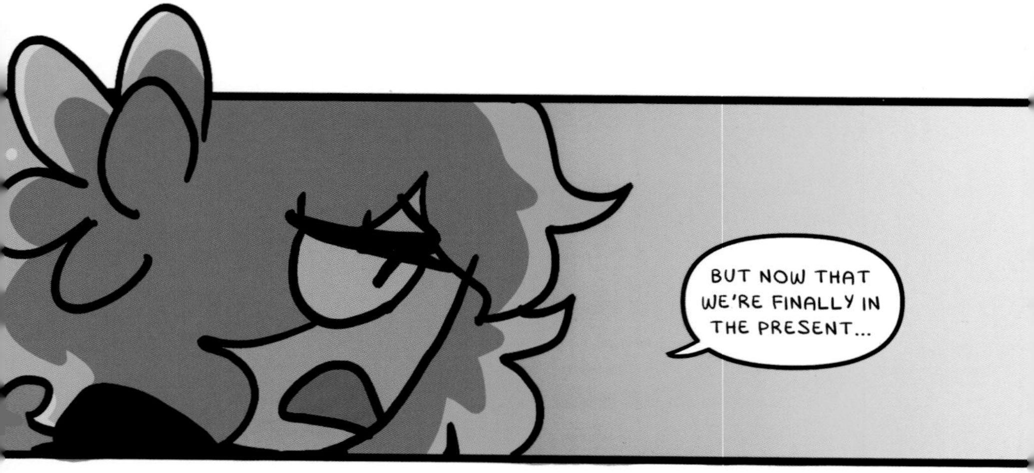
BUT NOW THAT WE'RE FINALLY IN THE PRESENT...

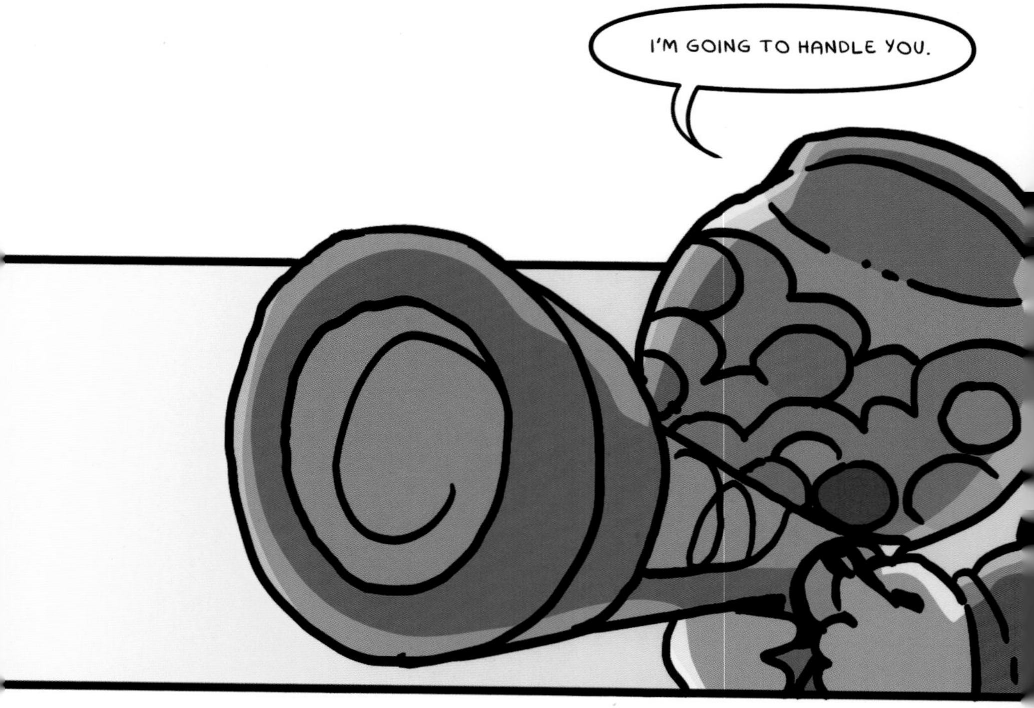
I'M GOING TO HANDLE YOU.

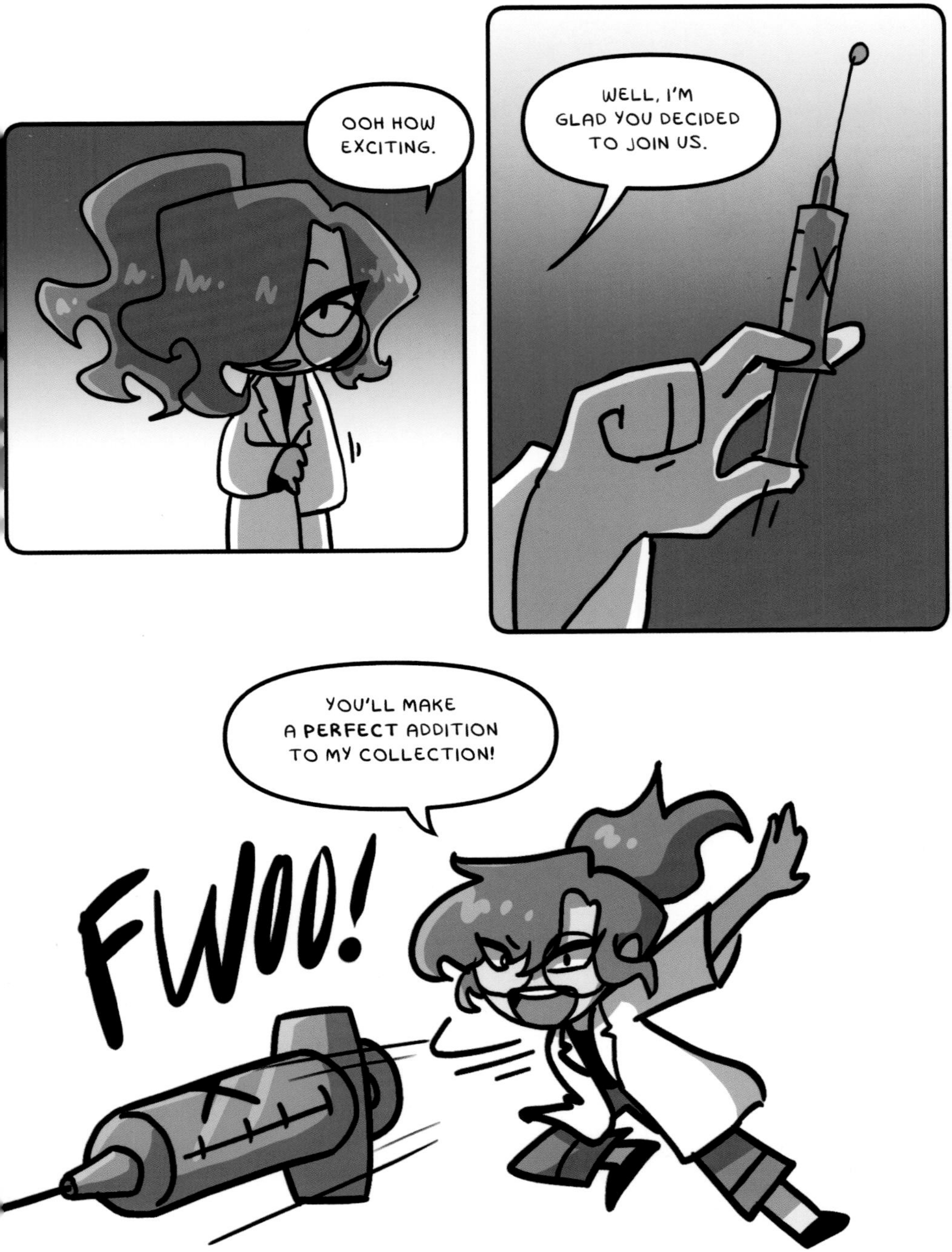
OOH HOW EXCITING.
WELL, I'M GLAD YOU DECIDED TO JOIN US.
YOU'LL MAKE A **PERFECT** ADDITION TO MY COLLECTION!
FWOO!

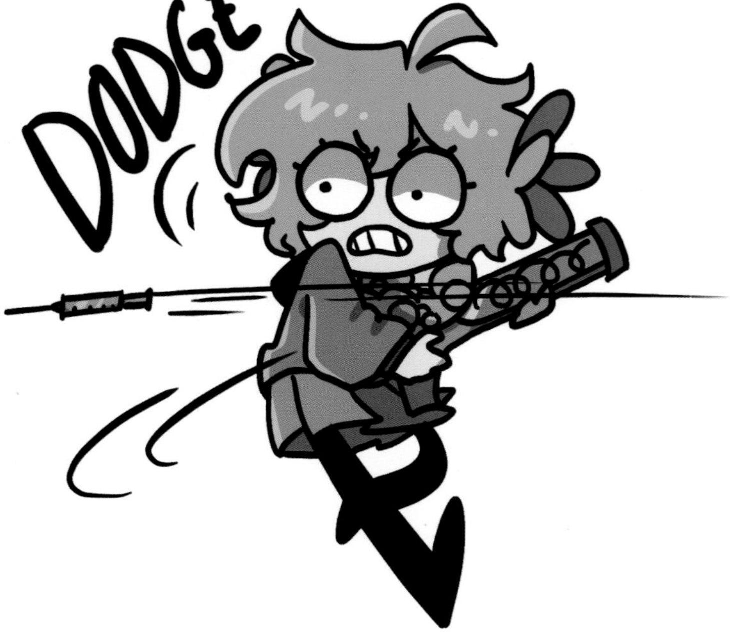
DODGE

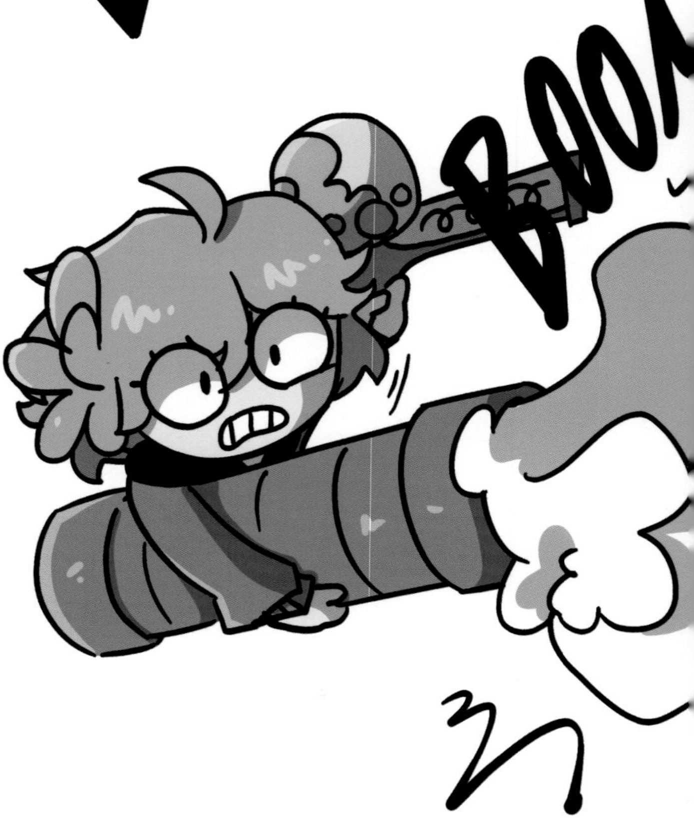
BOO

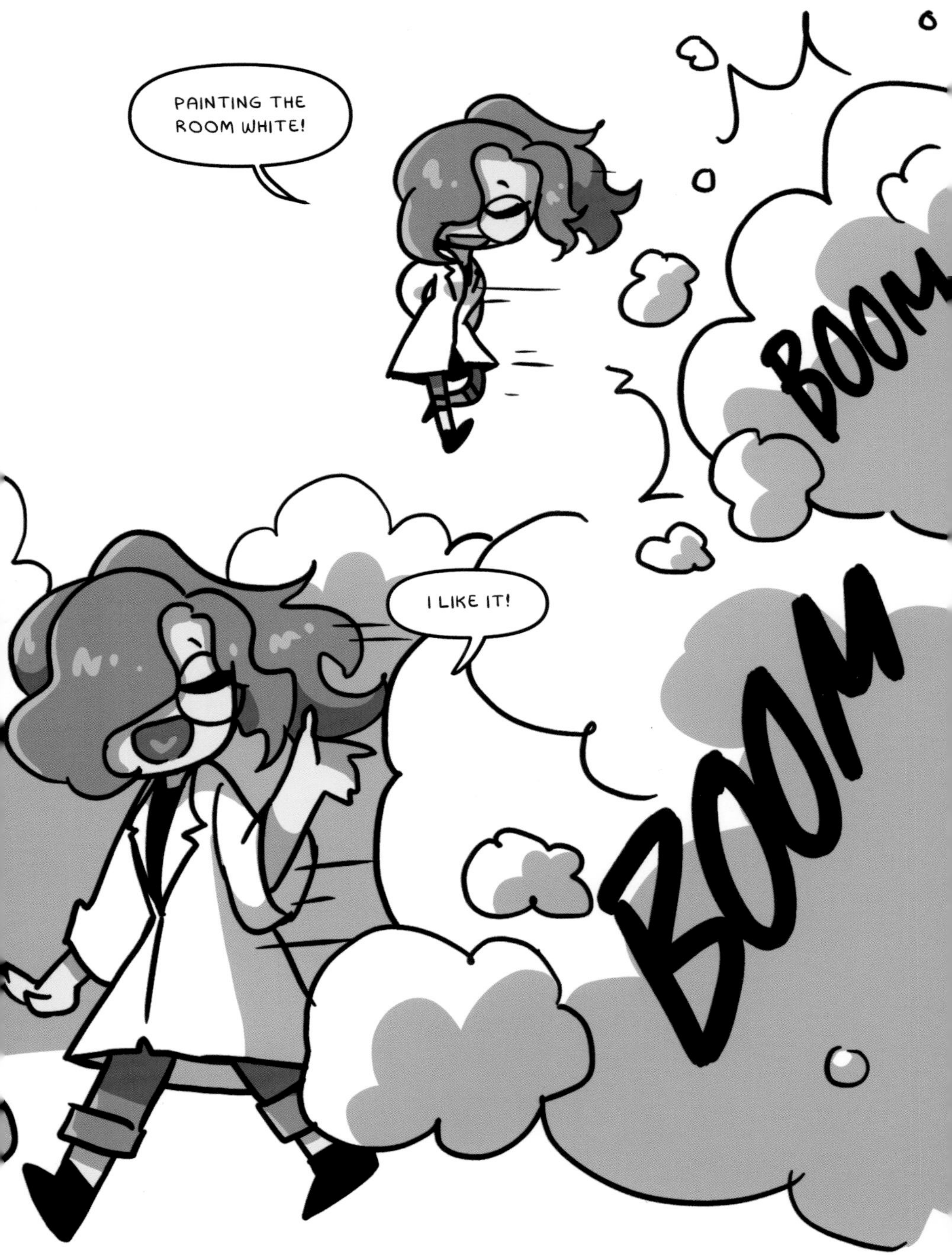
PAINTING THE ROOM WHITE!
BOOM
I LIKE IT!
BOOM

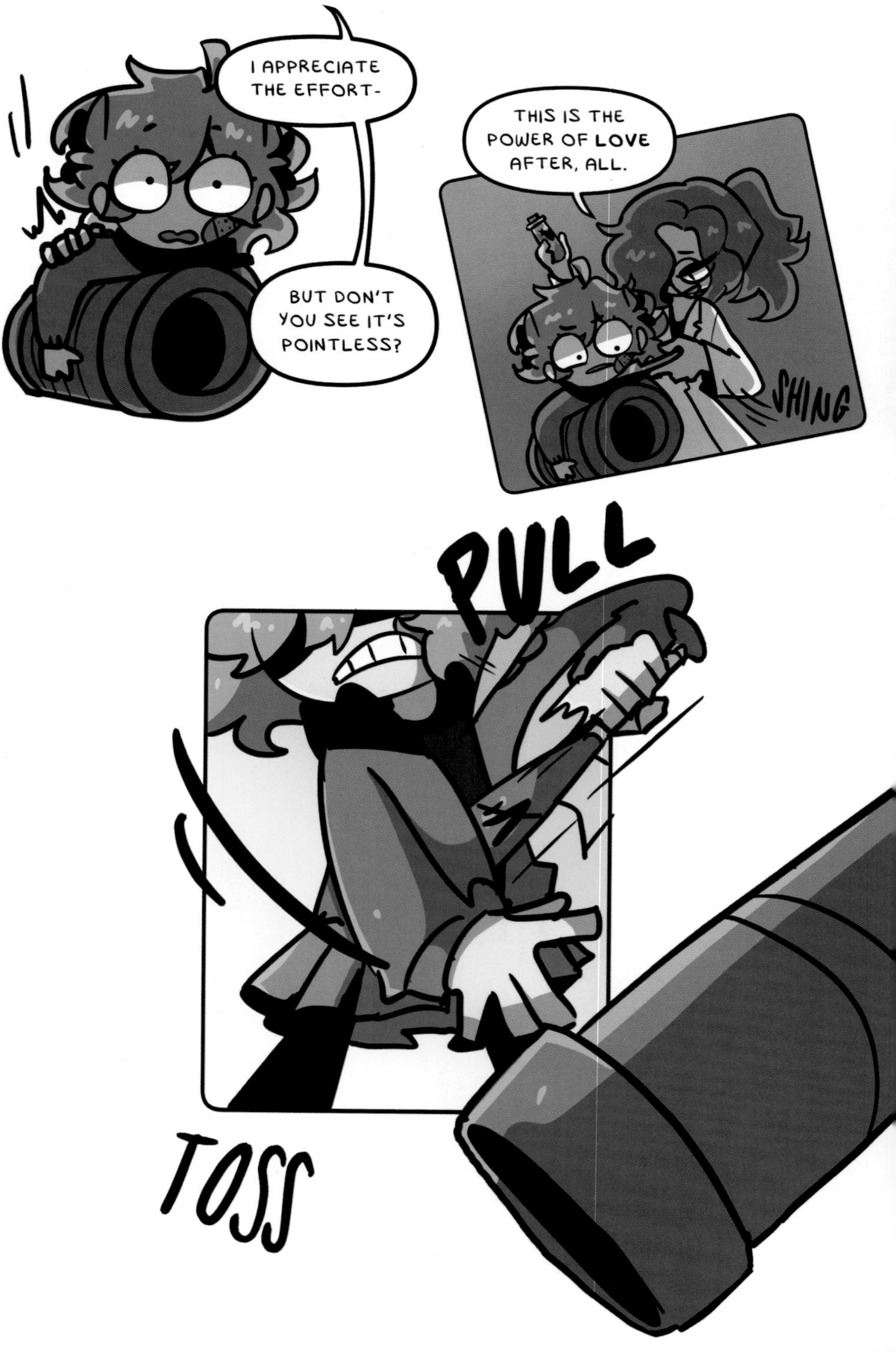
I APPRECIATE THE EFFORT-
BUT DON'T YOU SEE IT'S POINTLESS?
THIS IS THE POWER OF **LOVE** AFTER, ALL.
SHING
PULL
TOSS

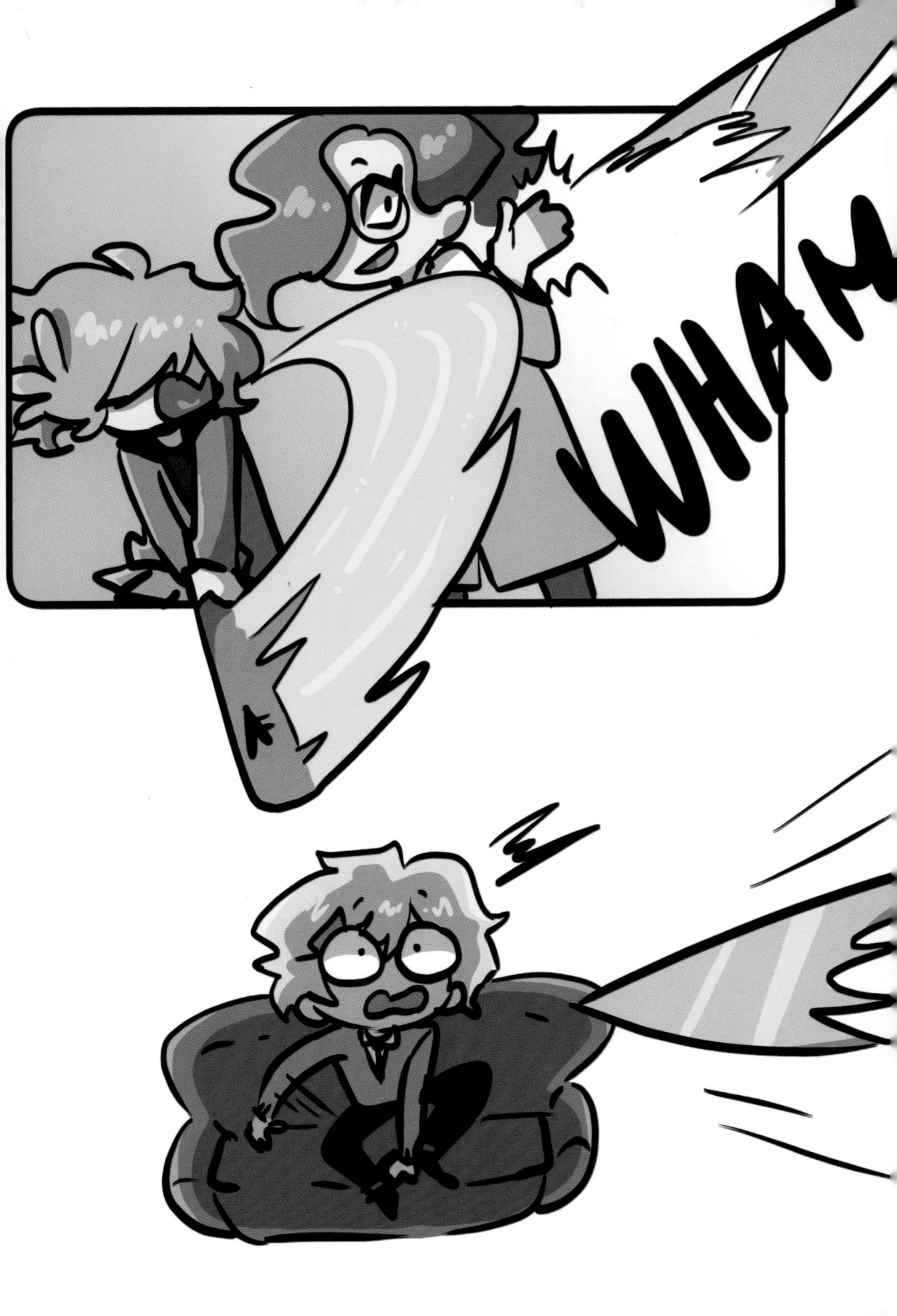
WHAM

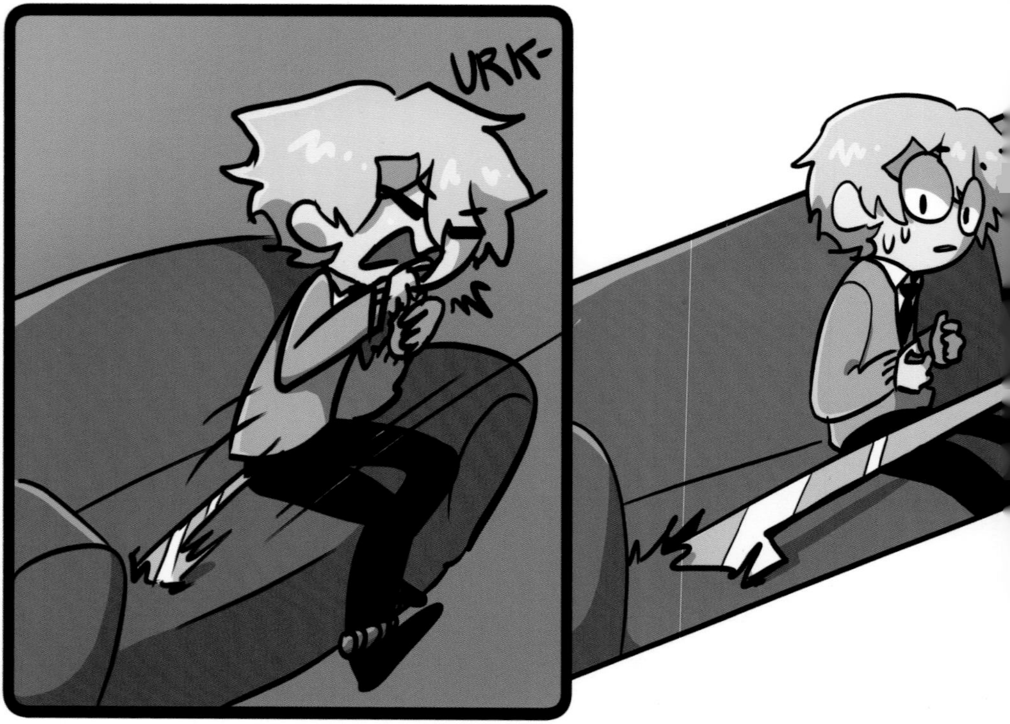
URK-

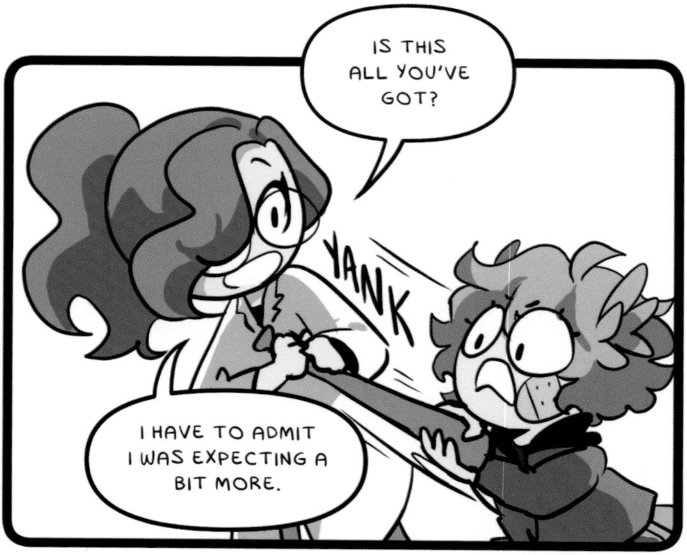
IS THIS ALL YOU'VE GOT?
YANK
I HAVE TO ADMIT I WAS EXPECTING A BIT MORE.

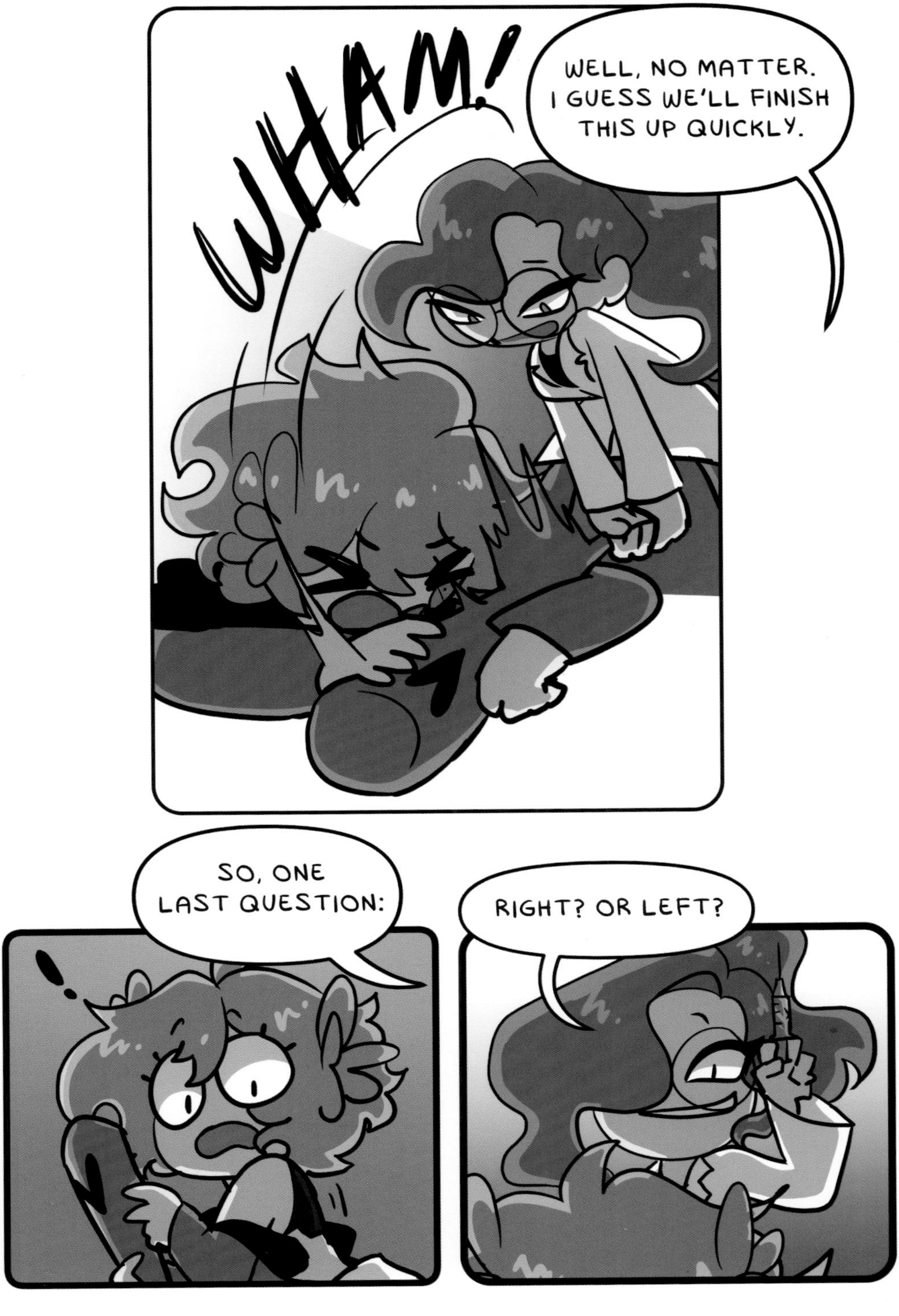
WHAM!
WELL, NO MATTER. I GUESS WE'LL FINISH THIS UP QUICKLY.
SO, ONE LAST QUESTION:
RIGHT? OR LEFT?

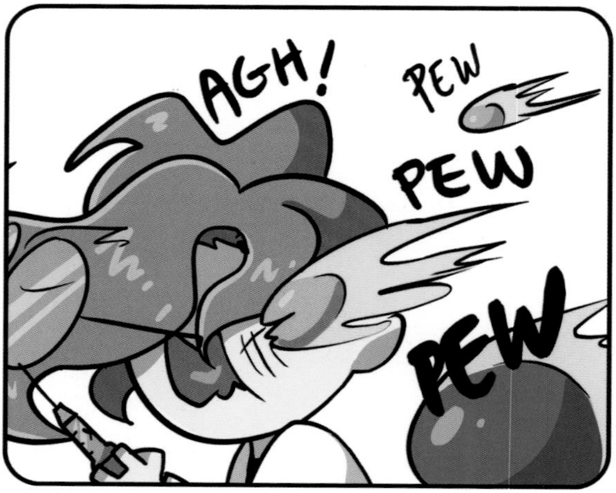
AGH!
PEW
PEW
PEW

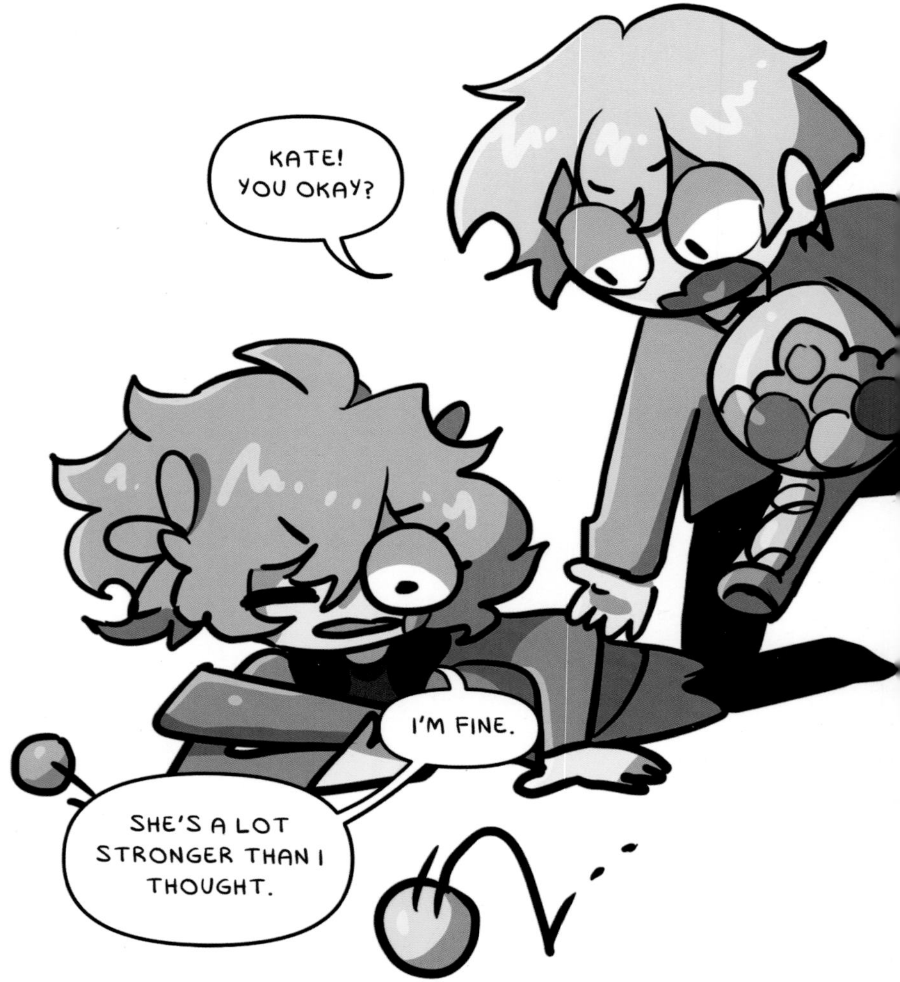
KATE! YOU OKAY?
I'M FINE.
SHE'S A LOT STRONGER THAN I THOUGHT.

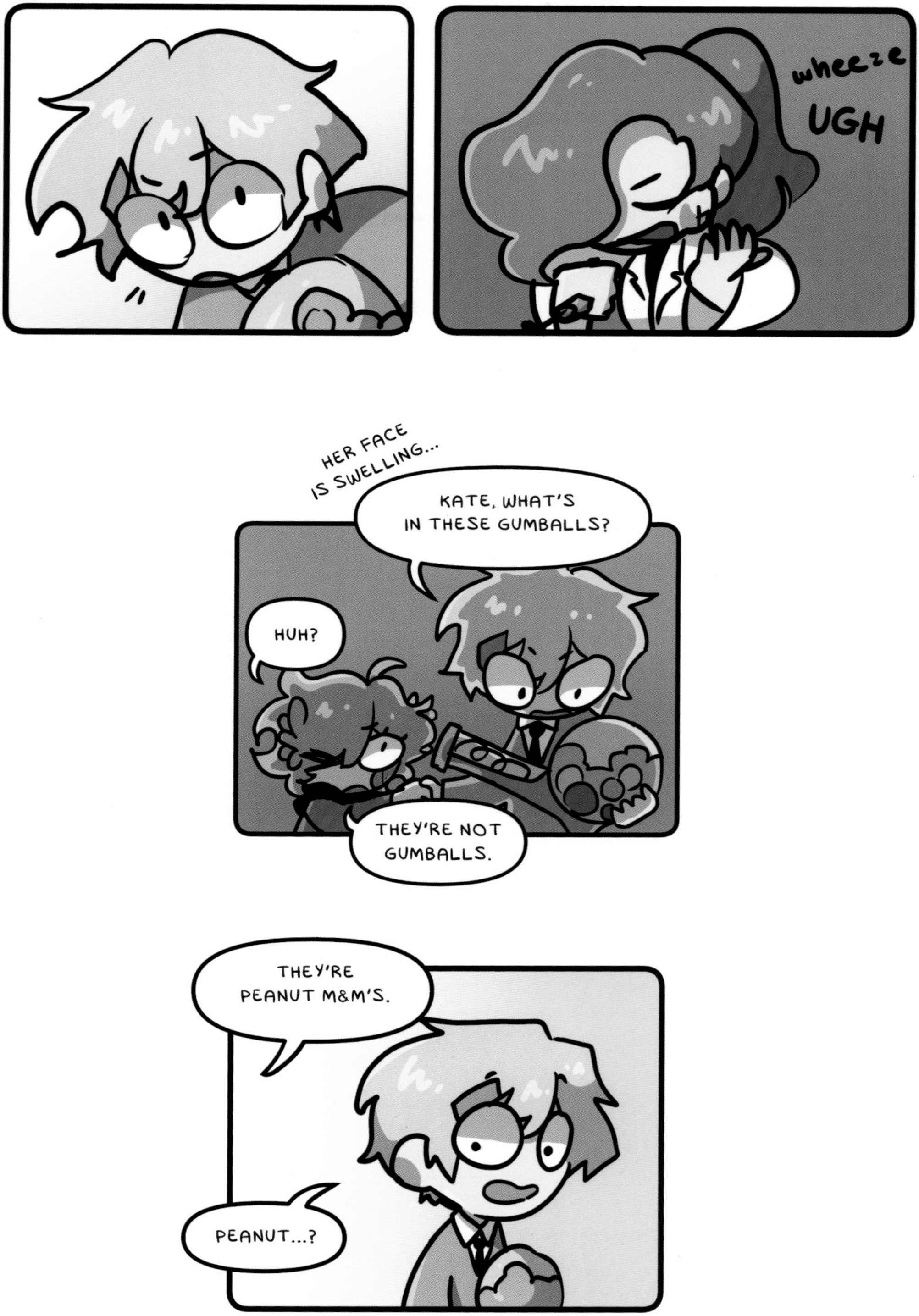
wheeze
UGH
HER FACE IS SWELLING...
KATE, WHAT'S IN THESE GUMBALLS?
HUH?
THEY'RE NOT GUMBALLS.
THEY'RE PEANUT M&M'S.
PEANUT...?

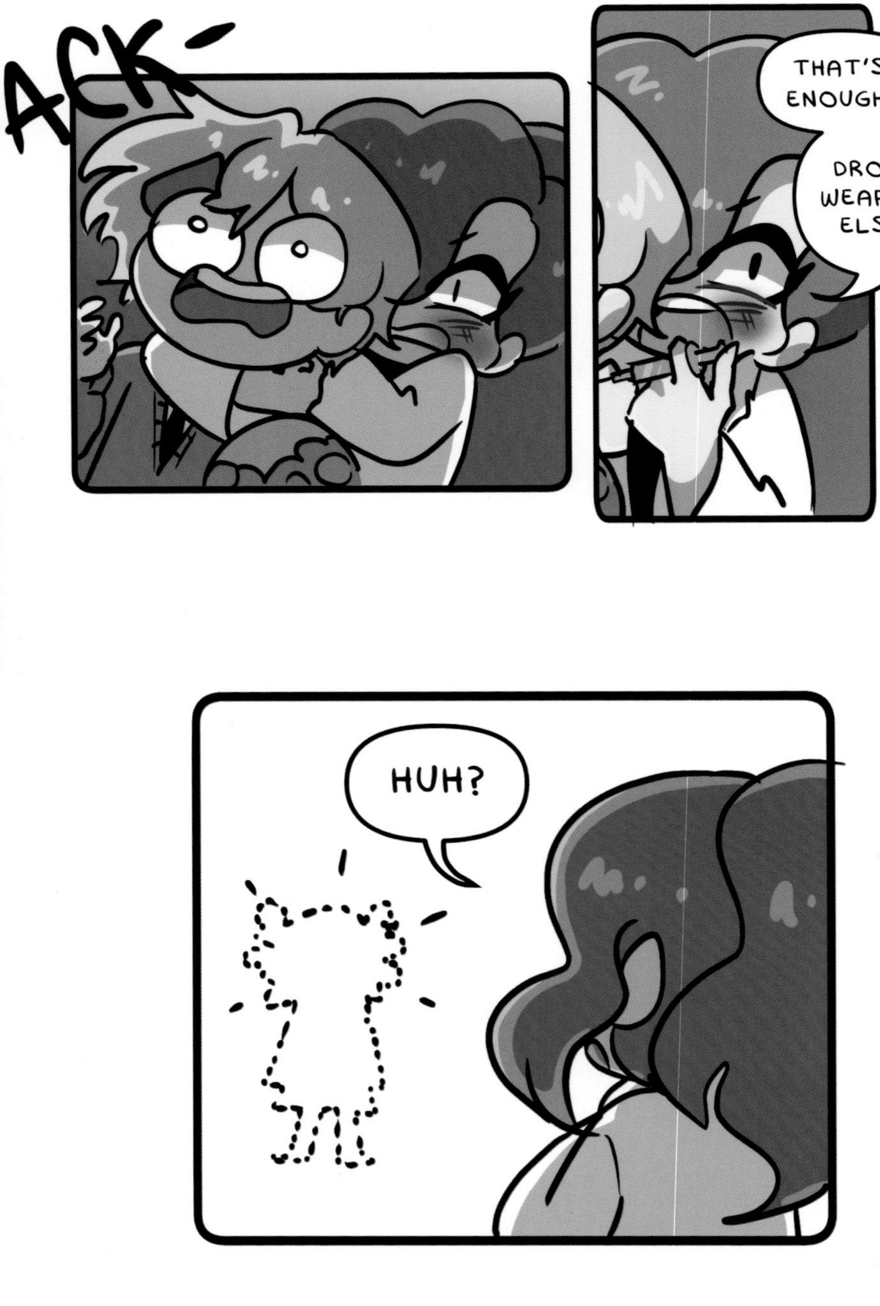
ACK-
THAT'S ENOUGH!
DROP YOUR WEAPONS OR ELSE I'LL-
HUH?

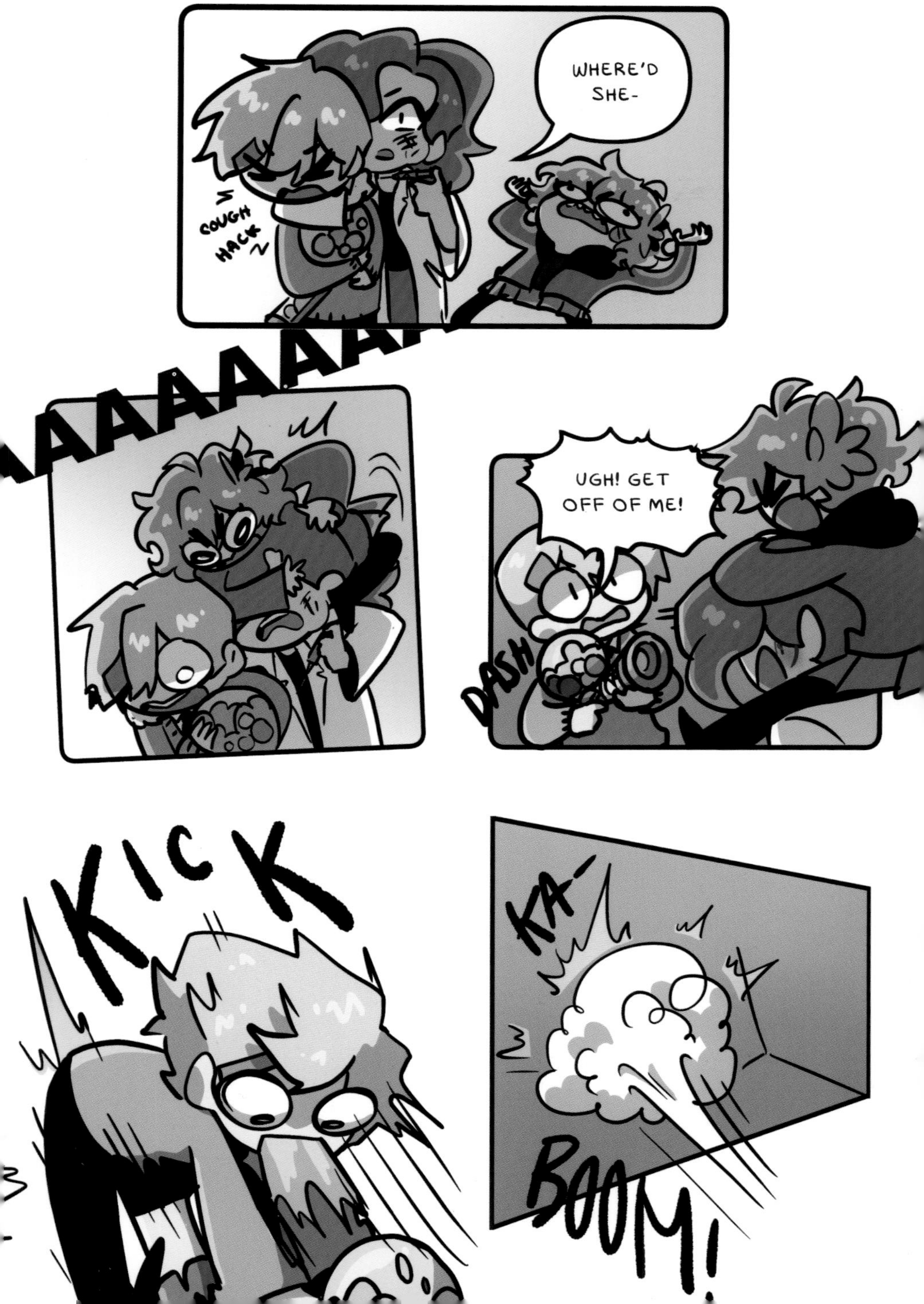

WHERE'D SHE-
COUGH HACK
AAAAAAA
UGH! GET OFF OF ME!
DASH
KICK
KA-
BOOM!

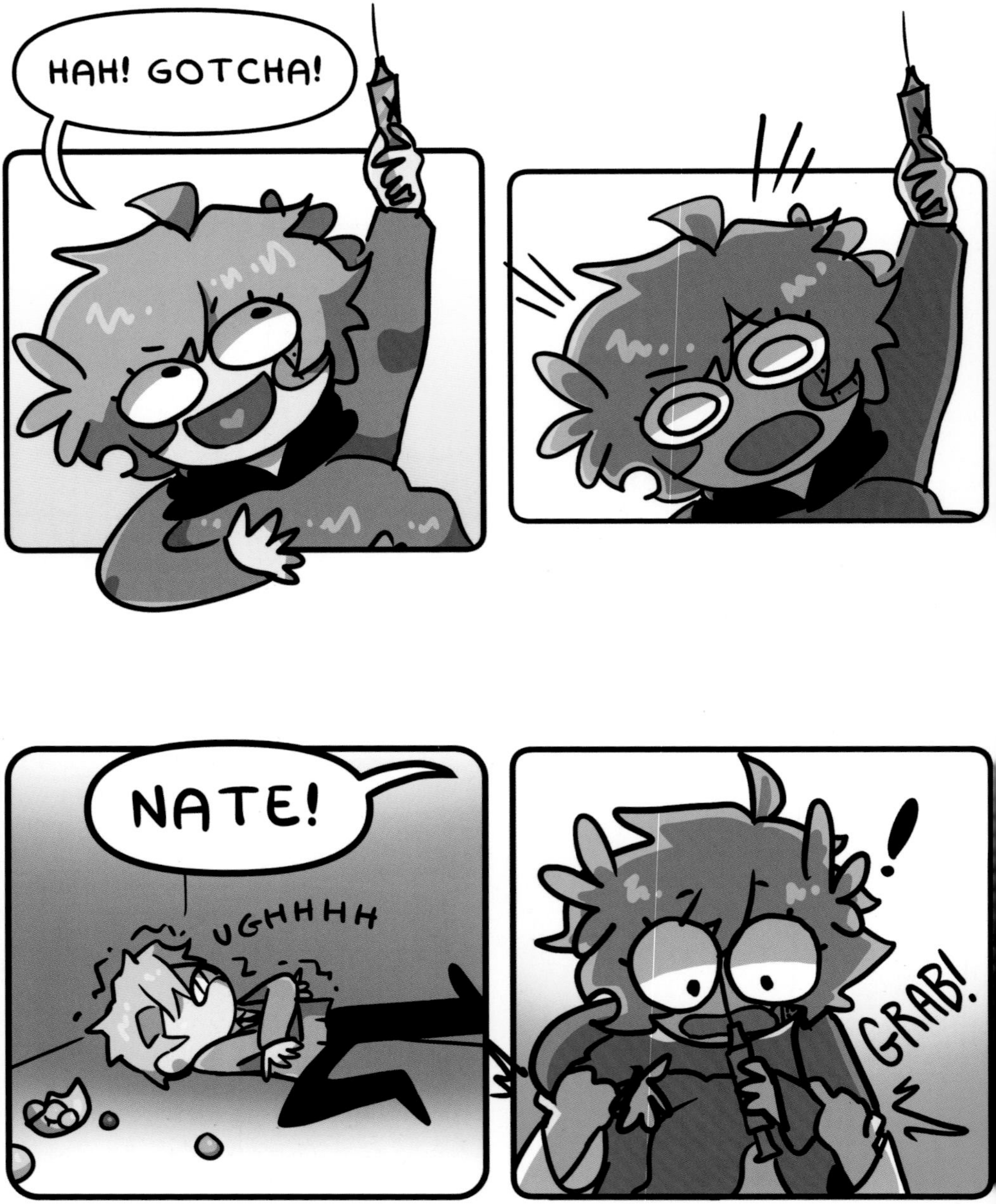
HAH! GOTCHA!
NATE!
UGHHHH
!
GRAB!

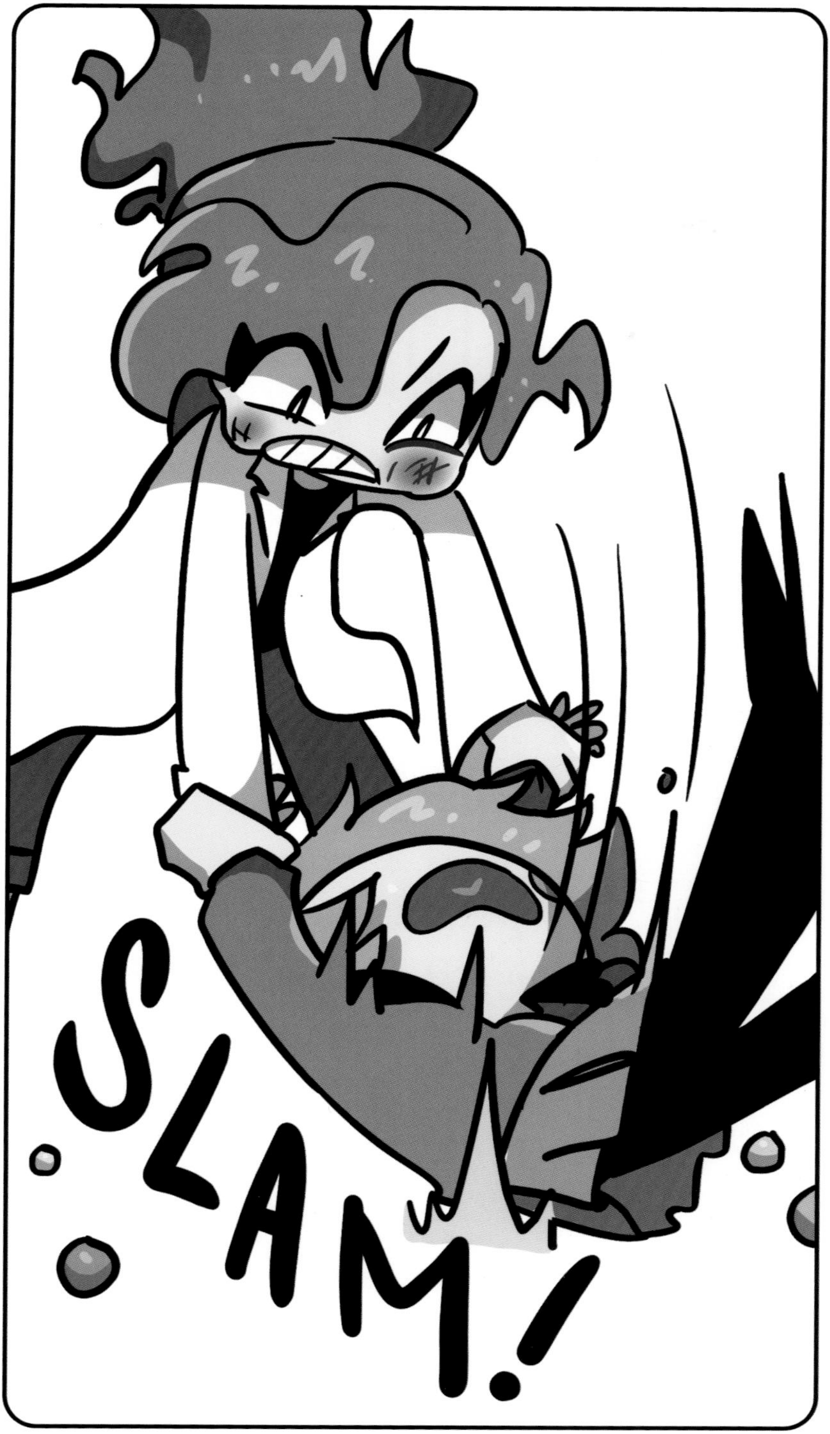
SLAM!

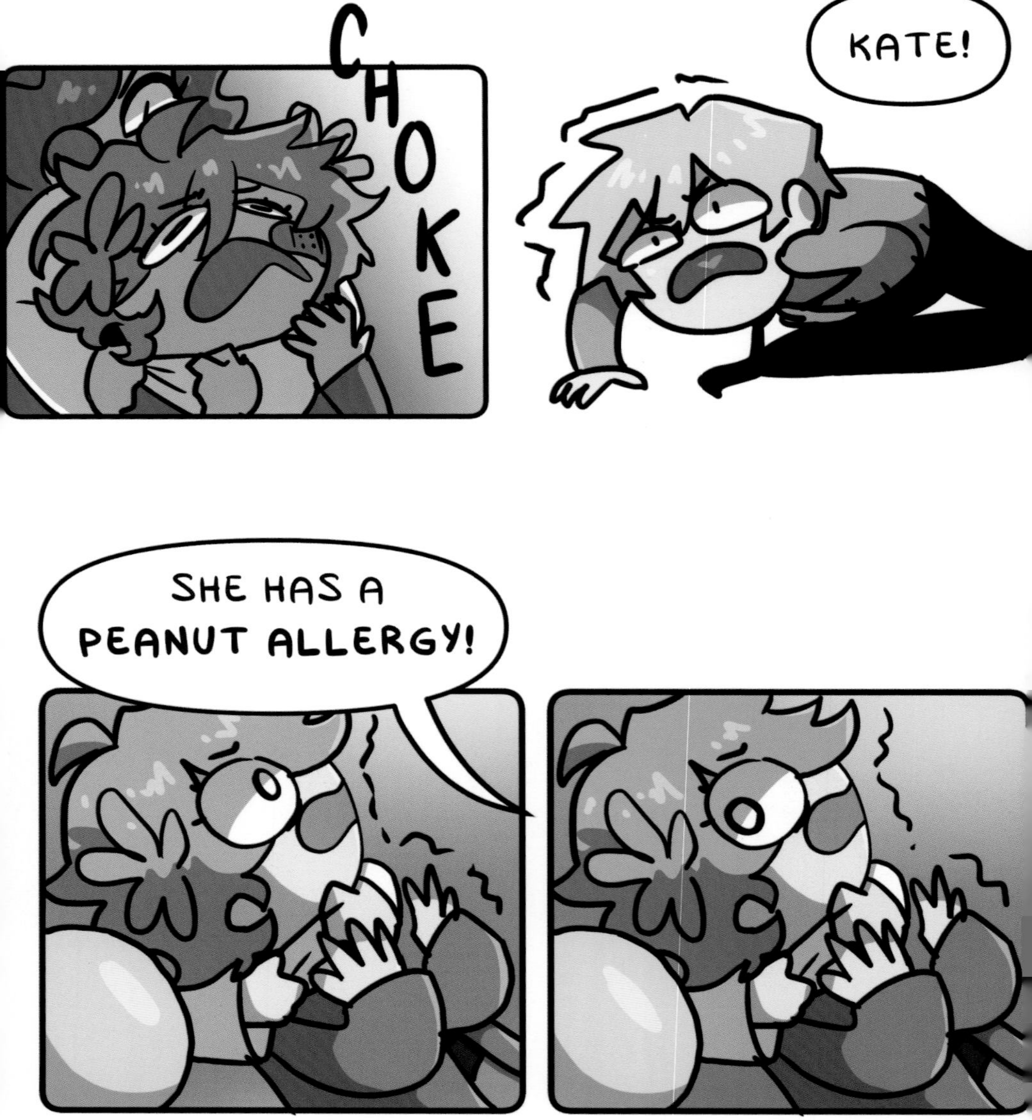
CHOKE
KATE!
SHE HAS A PEANUT ALLERGY!

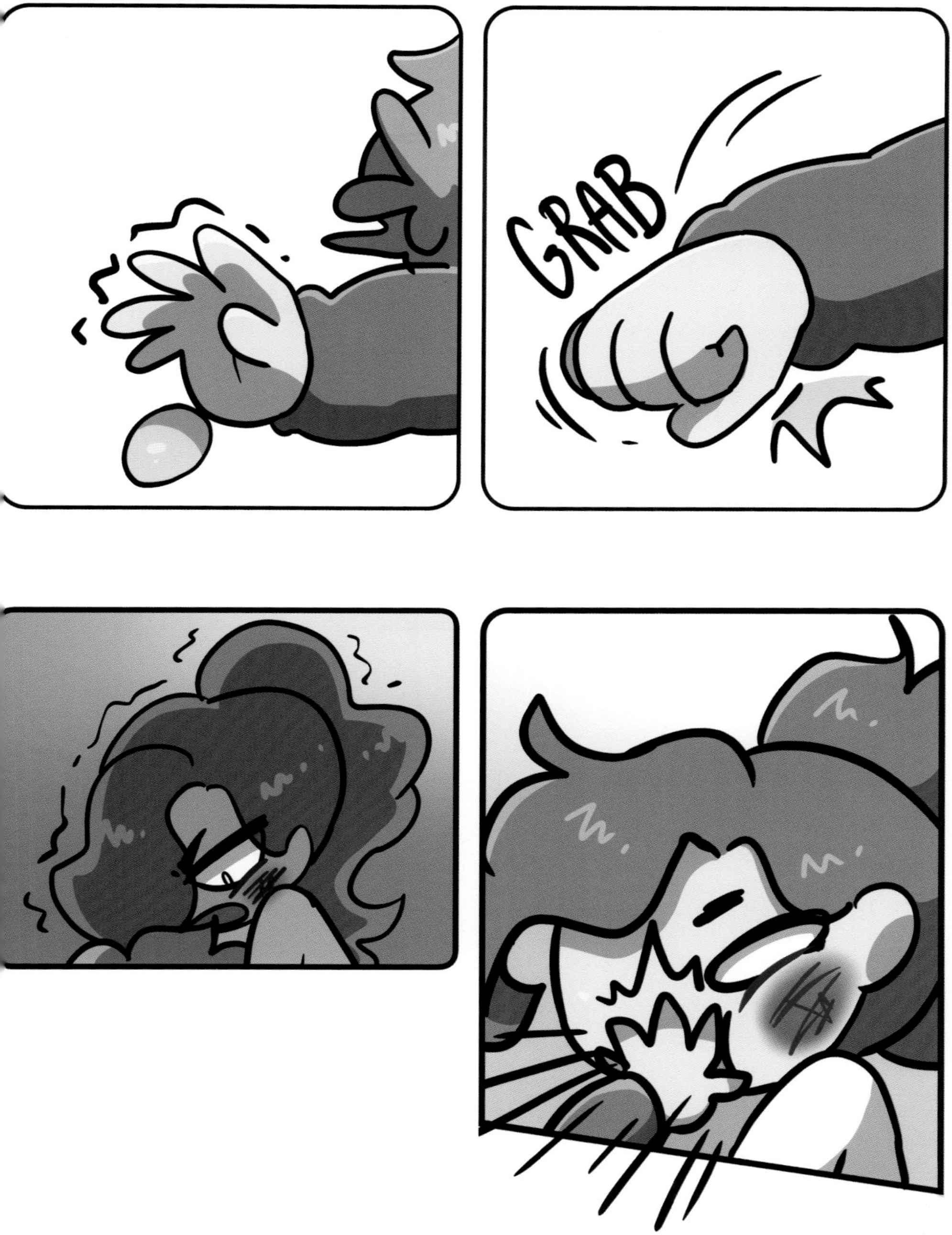
GRAB

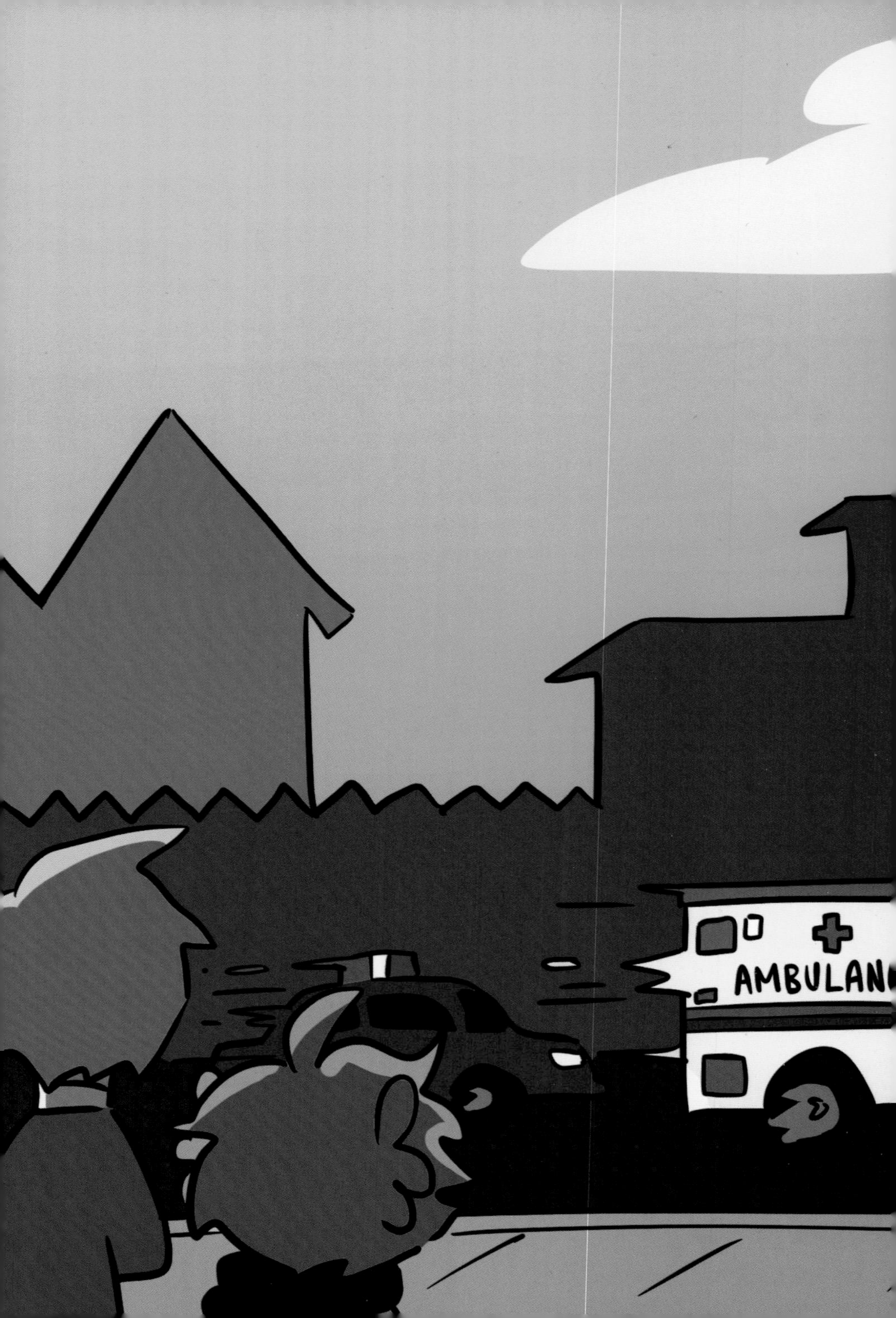
AMBULAN

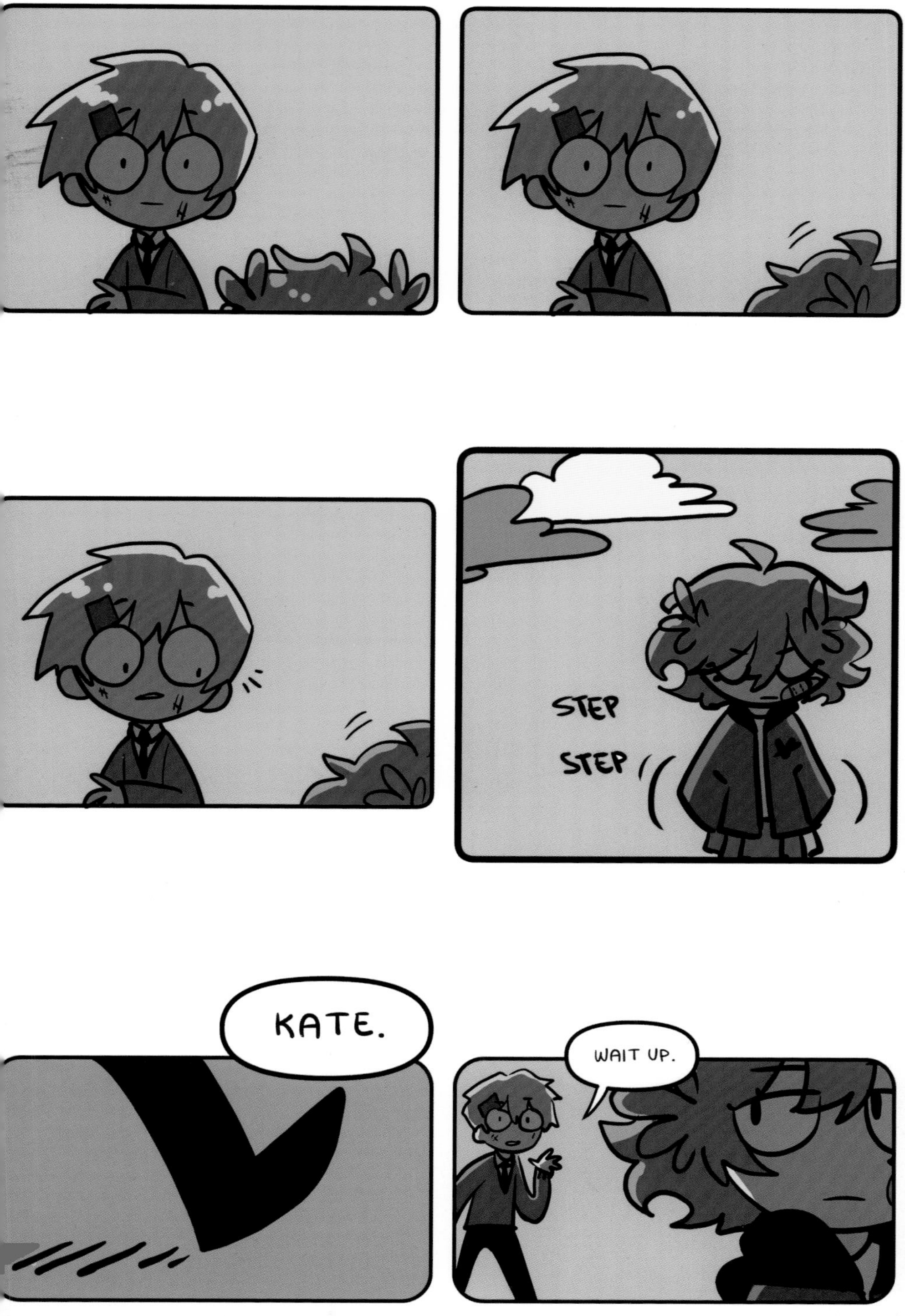
STEP
STEP
KATE.
WAIT UP.

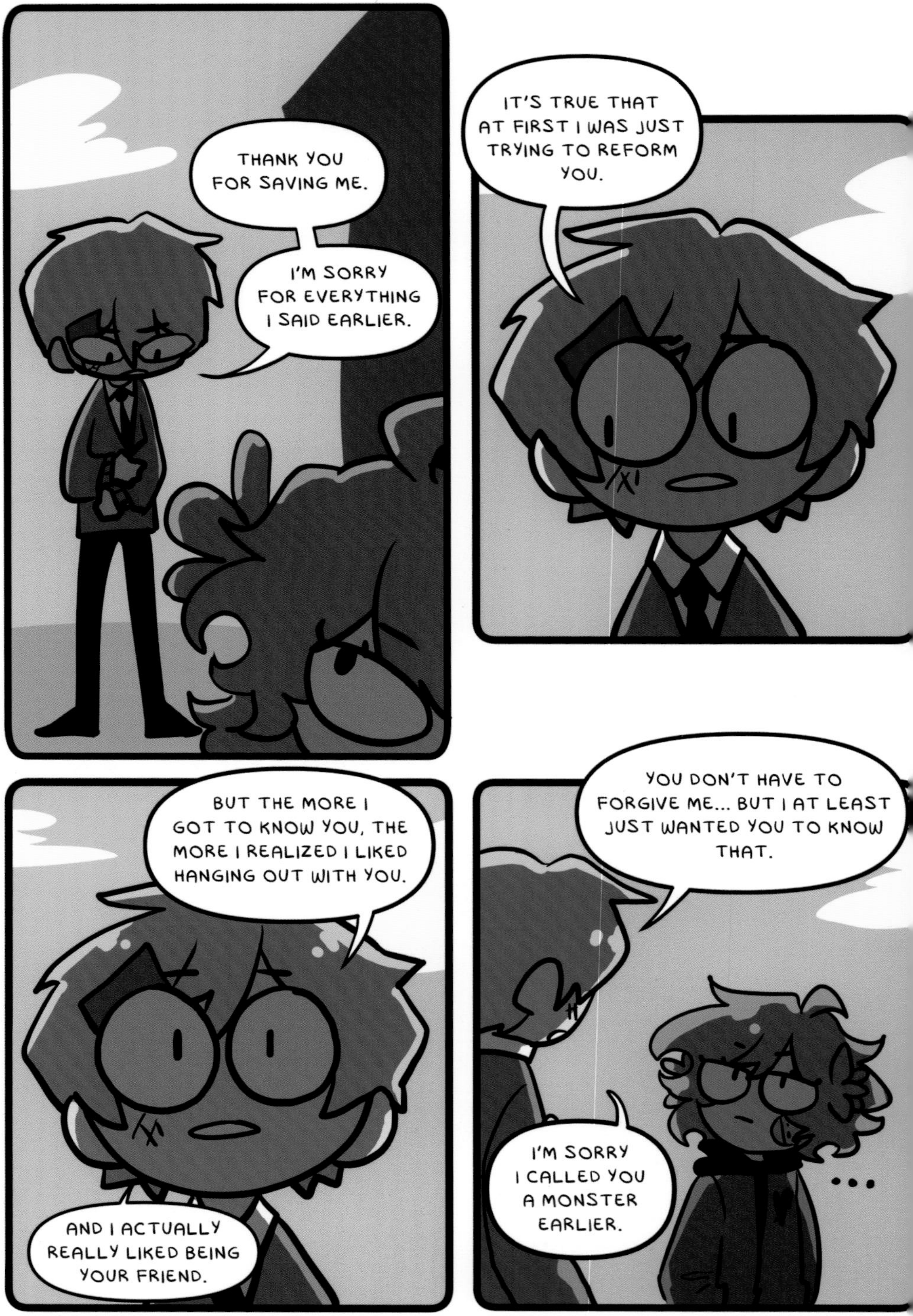
THANK YOU FOR SAVING ME.
I'M SORRY FOR EVERYTHING I SAID EARLIER.
IT'S TRUE THAT AT FIRST I WAS JUST TRYING TO REFORM YOU.
BUT THE MORE I GOT TO KNOW YOU, THE MORE I REALIZED I LIKED HANGING OUT WITH YOU.
AND I ACTUALLY REALLY LIKED BEING YOUR FRIEND.
YOU DON'T HAVE TO FORGIVE ME... BUT I AT LEAST JUST WANTED YOU TO KNOW THAT.
I'M SORRY I CALLED YOU A MONSTER EARLIER.
...

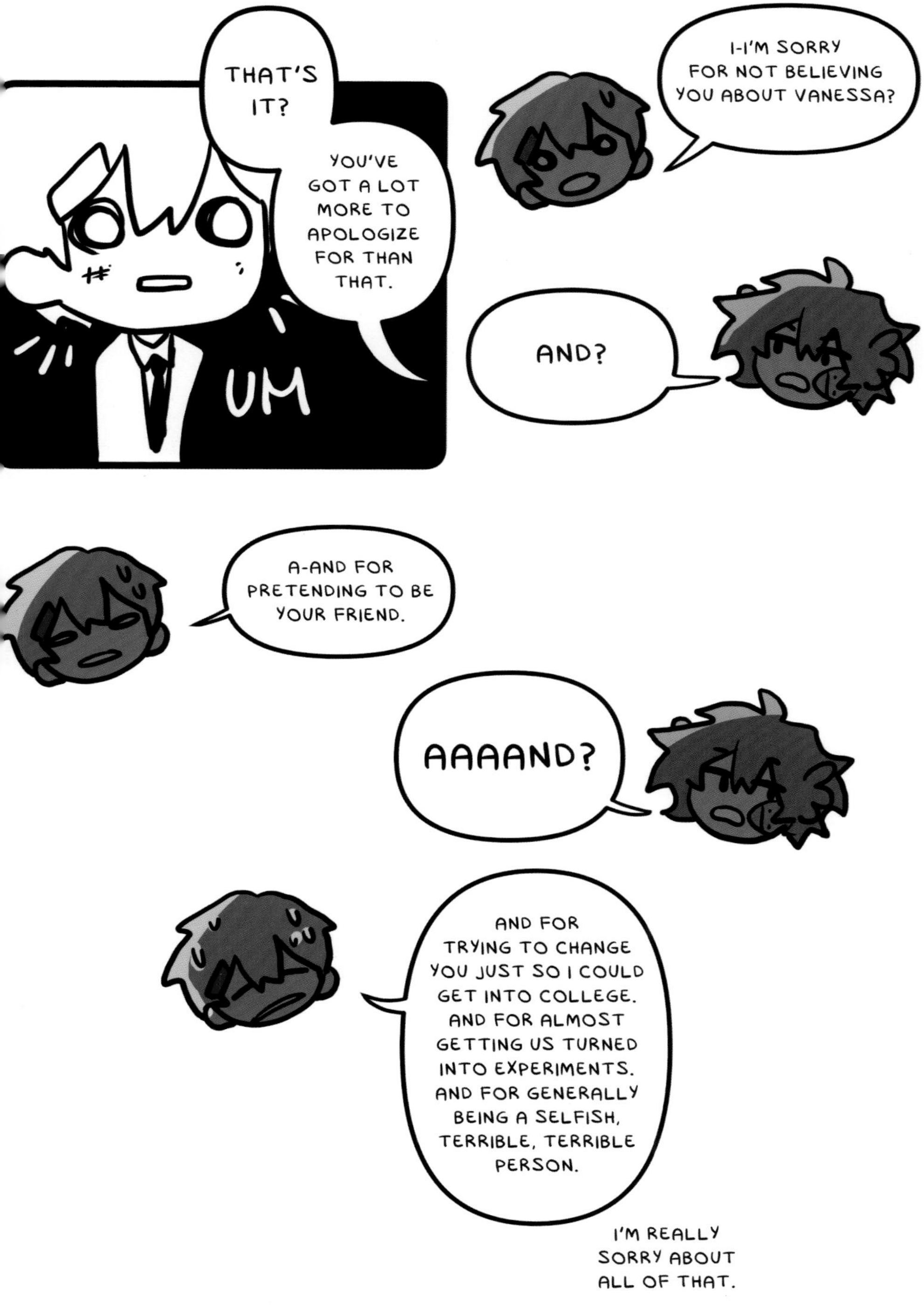
THAT'S IT?
YOU'VE GOT A LOT MORE TO APOLOGIZE FOR THAN THAT.
UM
I-I'M SORRY FOR NOT BELIEVING YOU ABOUT VANESSA?
AND?
A-AND FOR PRETENDING TO BE YOUR FRIEND.
AAAAND?
AND FOR TRYING TO CHANGE YOU JUST SO I COULD GET INTO COLLEGE. AND FOR ALMOST GETTING US TURNED INTO EXPERIMENTS. AND FOR GENERALLY BEING A SELFISH, TERRIBLE, TERRIBLE PERSON.
I'M REALLY SORRY ABOUT ALL OF THAT.

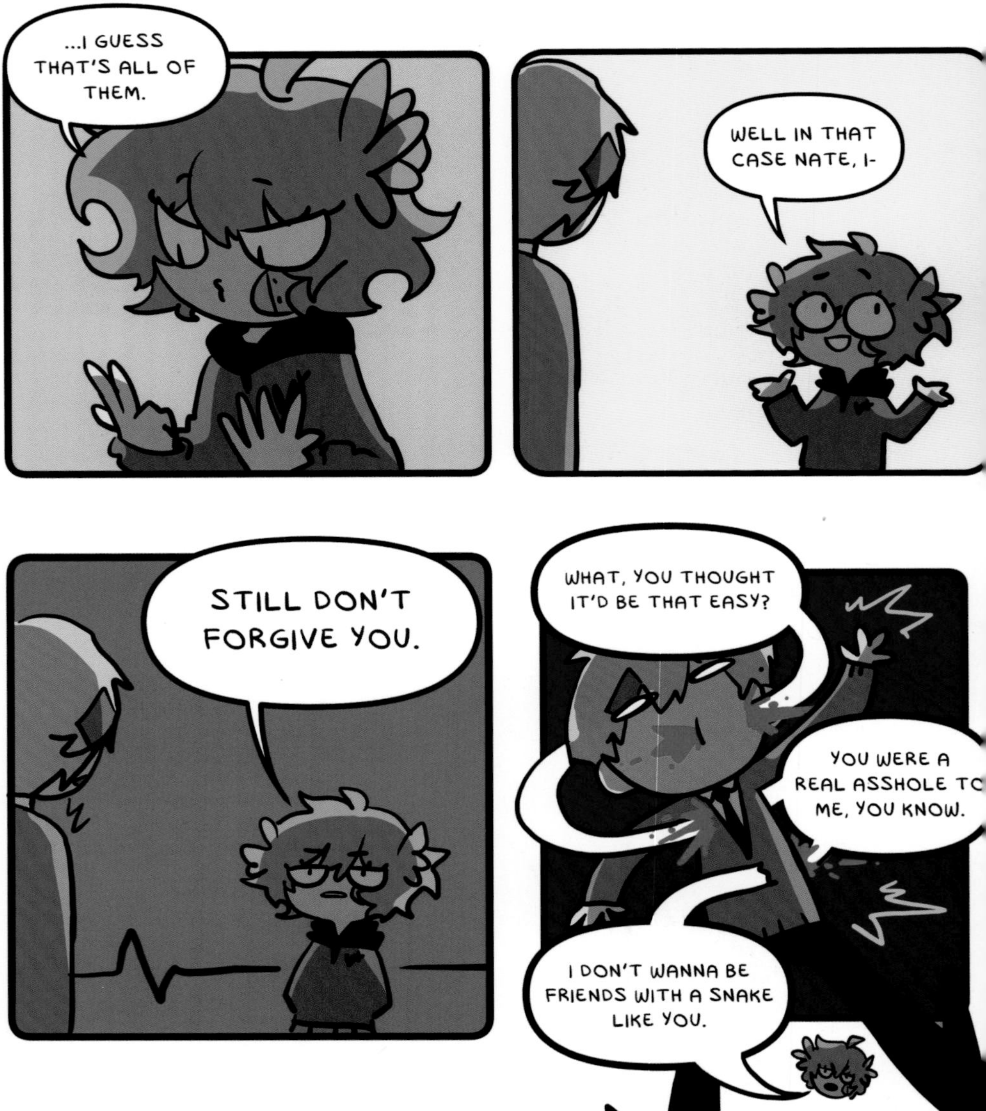
...I GUESS THAT'S ALL OF THEM.
WELL IN THAT CASE NATE, I-
STILL DON'T FORGIVE YOU.
WHAT, YOU THOUGHT IT'D BE THAT EASY?
YOU WERE A REAL ASSHOLE TO ME, YOU KNOW.
I DON'T WANNA BE FRIENDS WITH A SNAKE LIKE YOU.

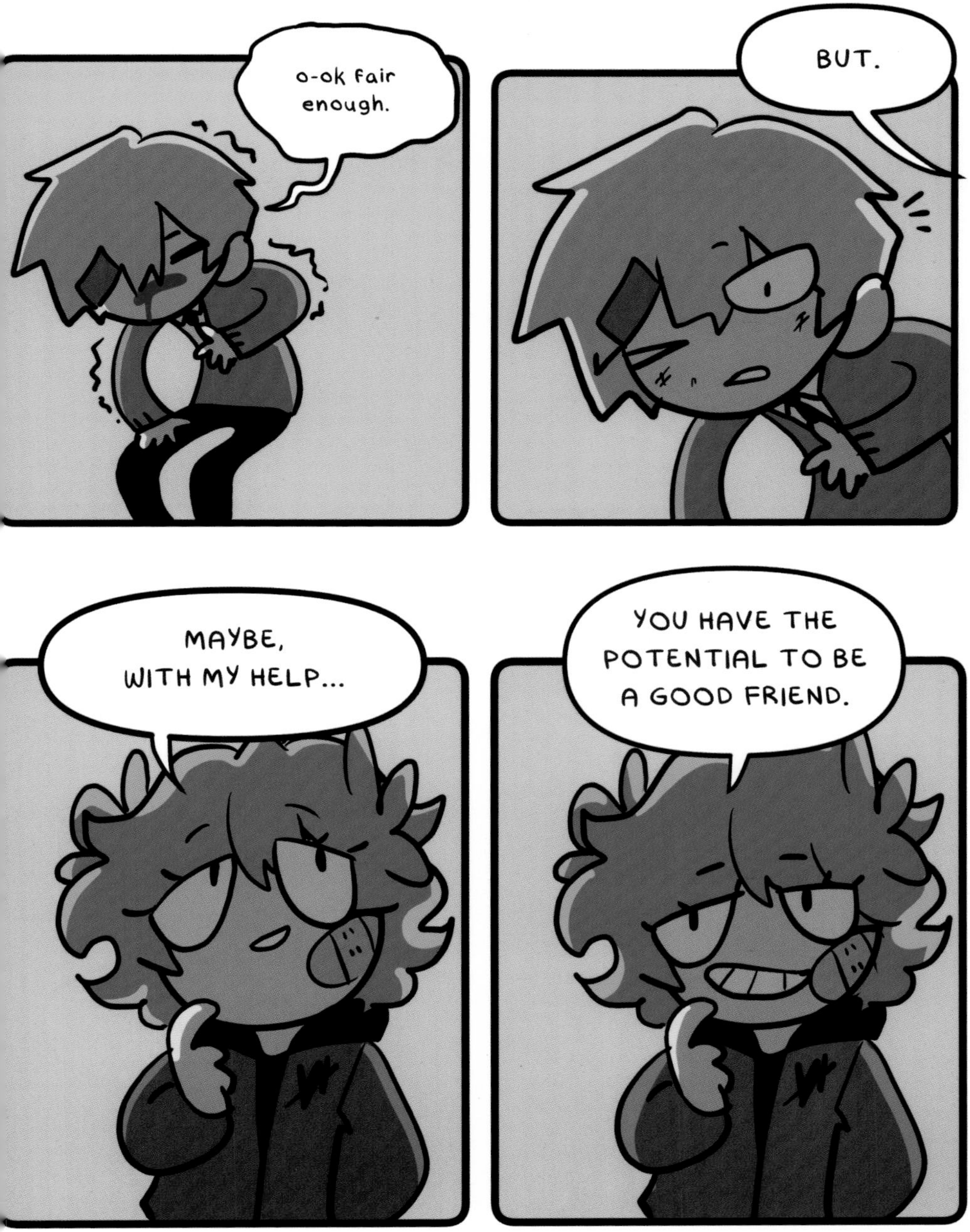
o-ok fair enough.
BUT.
MAYBE, WITH MY HELP...
YOU HAVE THE POTENTIAL TO BE A GOOD FRIEND.

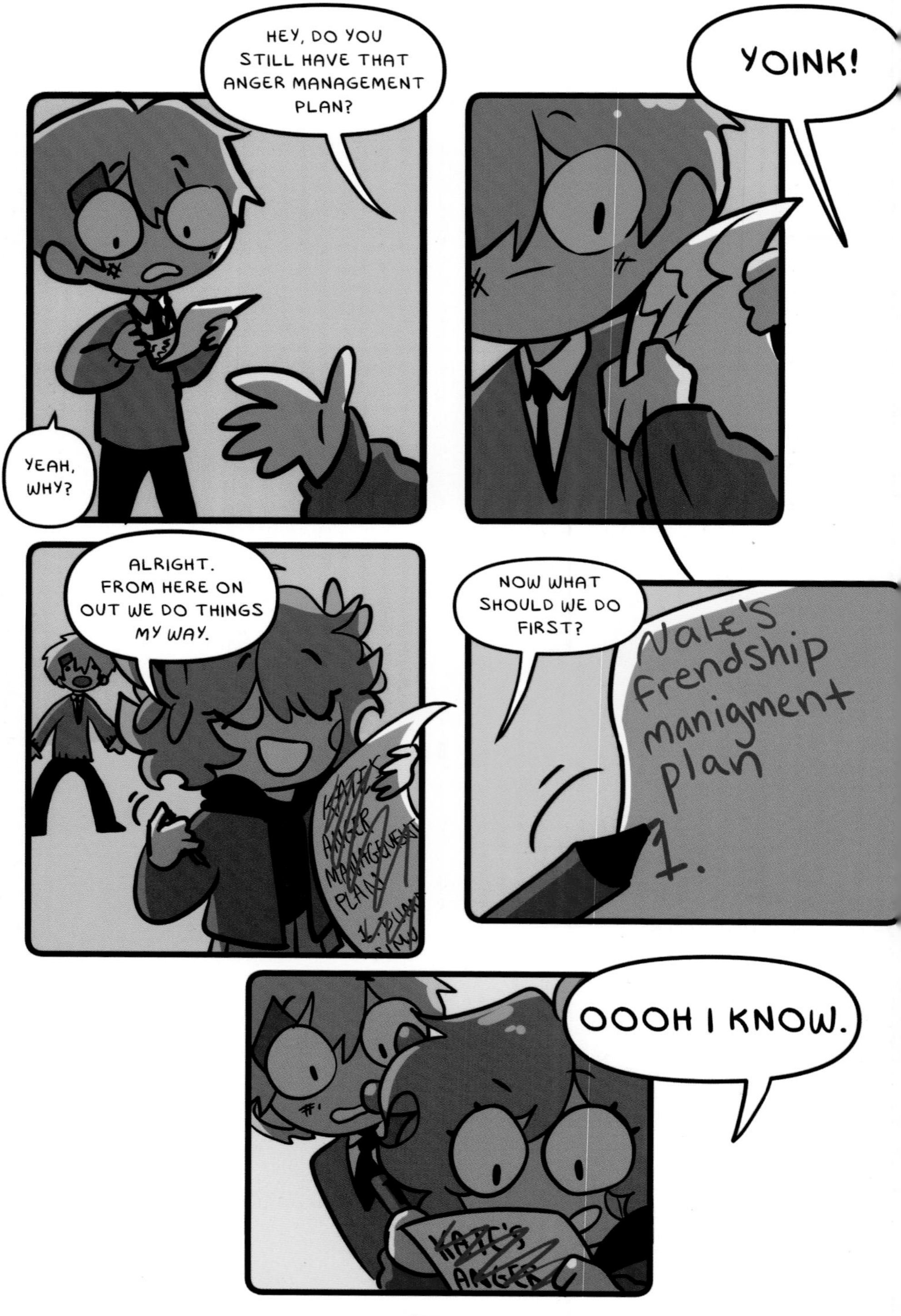
HEY, DO YOU STILL HAVE THAT ANGER MANAGEMENT PLAN?
YEAH, WHY?
YOINK!
ALRIGHT. FROM HERE ON OUT WE DO THINGS MY WAY.
NOW WHAT SHOULD WE DO FIRST?
Nate's frendship manigment plan
1.
OOOH I KNOW.

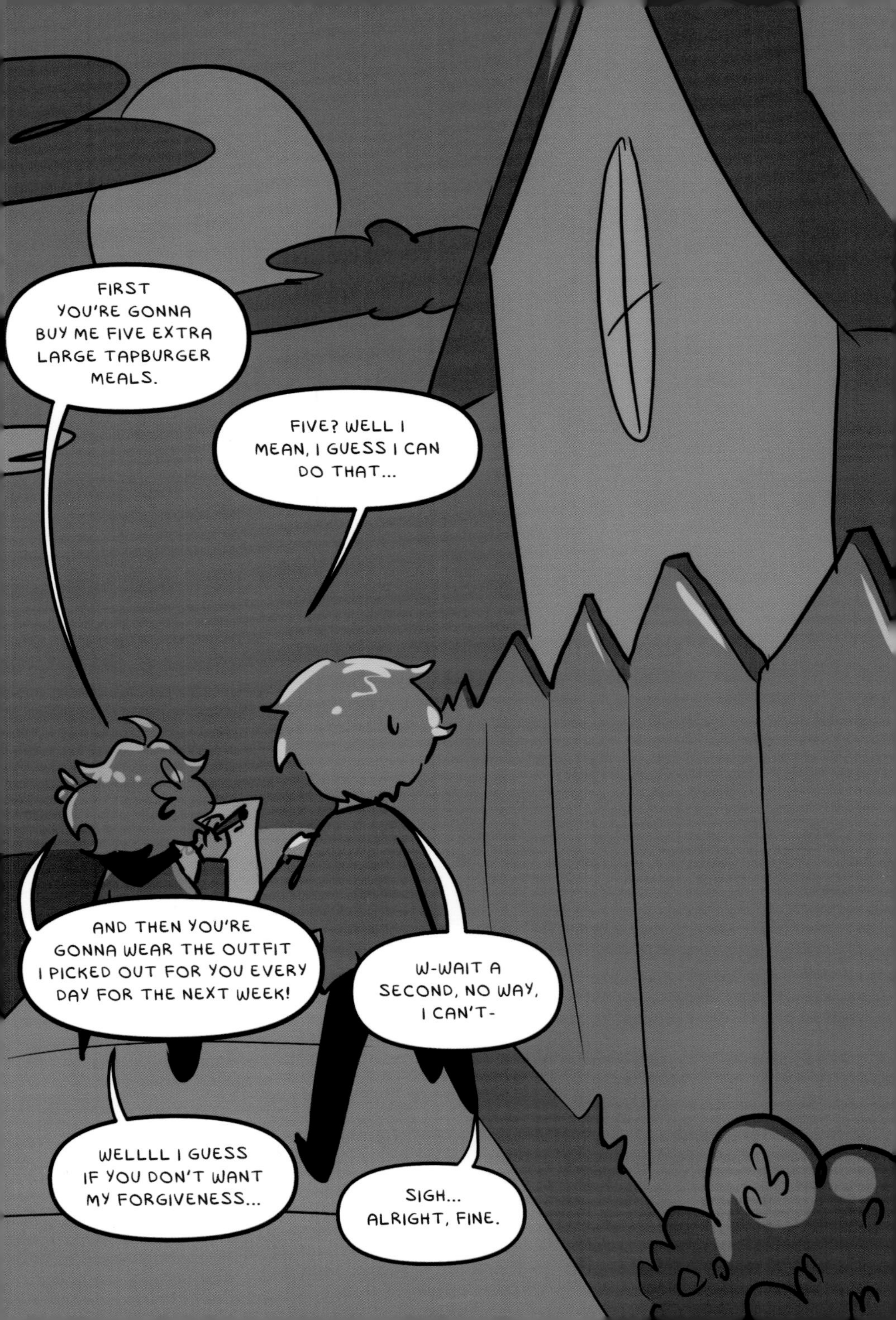
FIRST YOU'RE GONNA BUY ME FIVE EXTRA LARGE TAPBURGER MEALS.
FIVE? WELL I MEAN, I GUESS I CAN DO THAT...
AND THEN YOU'RE GONNA WEAR THE OUTFIT I PICKED OUT FOR YOU EVERY DAY FOR THE NEXT WEEK!
W-WAIT A SECOND, NO WAY, I CAN'T-
WELLLL I GUESS IF YOU DON'T WANT MY FORGIVENESS...
SIGH... ALRIGHT, FINE.

BAD
LOVE

@soaporsalad